Microsoft®

D0572345

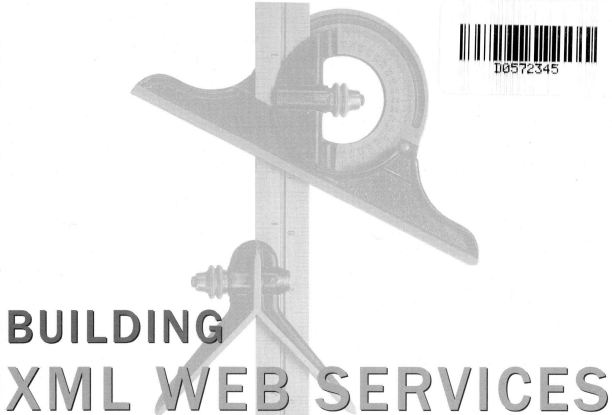

BUILDING
XML WEB SERVICES
FOR THE MICROSOFT®
.NET PLATFORM

Microsoft®
.net™

Scott Short

PUBLISHED BY
Microsoft Press
A Division of Microsoft Corporation
One Microsoft Way
Redmond, Washington 98052-6399

Library of Congress Cataloging-in-Publication Data
Short, Scott.
    Building XML Web Services for the Microsoft .NET Platform / Scott Short.
       p. cm.
    Includes index.
    ISBN 0-7356-1406-7
    1. Web site development.   2. Microsoft .net framework.   I. Title.

  TK5105.888 .S495   2002
  005.2'76--dc21   2001054638

Printed and bound in the United States of America.

1 2 3 4 5 6 7 8 9   QWT   7 6 5 4 3 2

Distributed in Canada by Penguin Books Canada Limited.

A CIP catalogue record for this book is available from the British Library.

Microsoft Press books are available through booksellers and distributors worldwide. For further information about international editions, contact your local Microsoft Corporation office or contact Microsoft Press International directly at fax (425) 936-7329. Visit our Web site at www.microsoft.com/mspress. Send comments to *mspinput@microsoft.com*.

Acquisitions Editor: David Clark
Project Editor: Kathleen Atkins
Technical Editor: Dail Magee, Jr.

Body Part No. X08-22435

Praise for
Building XML Web Services for the Microsoft .NET Platform

Great description of where Web services are today and how to get boot-strapped building your own.
Henrik Frystyk Nielsen
SOAP, HTTP, and GXA Specification Coauthor
Microsoft Corporation

Scott made me jealous—that's how good this book is.
Keith Ballinger
Program Manager, ASP.NET Web Services and GXA Specifications Coauthor
Microsoft Corporation

As programmers move from DCOM to the .NET platform, they are faced with the challenge of learning the details of Microsoft's architecture for both Web services and .NET Remoting. Scott provides programmers with a great jump start in building distributed applications by covering the essential details and explaining the difference between two different technologies.
Ted Pattison
Technologist and Author
DevelopMentor

This is a clear and concise book for developers who want to move beyond the hype and start building Web services for real.
James Utzschneider
Creator of UDDI
Microsoft Corporation

Scott hits the nail on the head with clear and concise coverage of topics that all Web service developers should know about. If you buy just one book on Web services, this should be the one.
Jeff Prosise
Cofounder and Author
Wintellect

This book provides developers with a practical guide for building Web services on the .NET platform. In it, Scott shares his knowledge and real-world expertise for building XML Web services.
Rob Howard
Program Manager, ASP.NET Team
Microsoft Corporation

Acknowledgments

As with any project of this magnitude, it took a considerable amount of effort from a lot of people to deliver a complete manuscript.

I couldn't ask for a more supportive and loving family. I would like to extend a very special thank you to my wife, Suzanne. Without your support, I never could have completed this book. You supported my decision to write this book even though you were pregnant with our first child when I signed the contracts and you gave birth to our son, Colin Patrick Short, toward the beginning of the project.

I would also like to thank my son Colin for being such a good little proofreader as he quietly sat in my lap as I typed, at least for the first 15 to 30 minutes. Now that the book is done, Daddy has much more time to play!

I have the unique opportunity to work for Microsoft but still enjoy the sunshine and the great skiing that Colorado has to offer. I would like to thank the Microsoft Rocky Mountain District management team for supporting my efforts. Specifically, I would like to thank Catharine Morris for your creativity in making this happen. Jim Sargent, Larry Shaw, Laura Neff, and Scott Johnson, without your support, this project would never have gotten off the ground. Catharine and Jim, good luck with your new positions at corporate. I miss you both!

I work with a very talented group of peers in Colorado and throughout Microsoft. Of those, I would like to thank Michel Barnett and Joe Hildebrand for your peer reviews of the first couple of chapters and Karsten Januszewski for reviewing the Discovery chapter.

I would also like to thank Mike Howard and Peter Roxburg. Your contributions to the manuscript directly affected getting this book in the hands of the readers in a timely fashion. Thank you both for reading my nagging e-mails about topics I wanted covered in your material.

I would also like to thank the Microsoft Press project team. You guys have been incredibly supportive throughout the entire project. David Clark and I met early on to discuss potential projects. David, thank you for thinking of me when the opportunity to write the Web services title presented itself. Kathleen Atkins was the enforcer. Kathleen, thank you for taking on the unenviable task of ensuring that I didn't slip the schedule too much. Dail Magee Jr. helped ensure the technical accuracy of the content. Dail, thank you for your colorful commentary in the edited text. I too believe that "the publishing industry went astray when it stopped using scrolls." Ina Chang had the responsibility of transforming my raw material into prose.

Through the course of the project, there were quite a few late nights in which I found myself staring at my computer screen completely exhausted and unmotivated. During these times, I would often fire up my Web browser and look at Jeff Prosise's *Book Blog* (*http://www.wintellect.com/about/instructors/prosise/blog/*), his online diary of the book-writing experience. Reading through a couple of entries always seemed to provide motivation to crank out a few more pages. Jeff, thank you for your inspiration as well as taking the time to give me advice now and then.

Finally I would also like to thank all of the folks in the product group for their support with this project. You all gave me the best material in the industry to write about. Specifically, I would like to thank Keith Ballinger, Rob Howard, Karsten Januszewski, Angela Mills, Jonathan Hawkins, Peter de Jong, Scott Guthrie, and Oliver Sharp.

Table of Contents

Introduction

You can hardly pick up a technical magazine, developer conference brochure, or corporate IT strategy document without seeing a reference to Web services. So what is all the hype about? Simply put, Web services allow developers to create unrestricted applications—applications that span different operating systems, hardware platforms, and geographic locations. In this book, I explain what Web services are and how you can leverage the Microsoft .NET platform to build and consume them.

Whom This Book Is For

To get the most out of this book, you should be an experienced programmer. The platform on which you have gained your experience is not important. However, you should have a reasonable handle on object-oriented concepts and basic programming constructs.

You should also have some familiarity with basic C# syntax. All examples in this book are written in C#. But even if your primary development language is not C#, the examples are simple enough that you should be able to easily port them to other .NET languages, such as Microsoft Visual Basic.

How This Book Is Organized

Developers generally fall into two groups: those who like to learn the underpinnings of a technology before they use it, and those who have little concern about what is going on under the hood and feel comfortable using a tool set that abstracts many of the details. I personally fall into the former category and, chances are, if you have purchased a 400-plus page book dedicated to Web services, so do you. Therefore, I've decided to take a bottom-up approach to presenting Web services and the support that the .NET platform provides for building and consuming them.

It is hard to make sense of the details unless you have a good grounding in how Web services fit into the overall solution, so the first two chapters of the book provide the necessary background. In Chapter 1, I explain the rationale behind Web services. I also present an overview of the underlying protocols and explain how they build on one another to provide an overall solution.

Chapter 2 offers a high-level overview of how to use Microsoft Visual Studio .NET to create and consume Web services hosted on the ASP.NET platform. My primary goals in this chapter are to give you an appreciation of how well the ASP.NET runtime abstracts the underlying protocols for the developer and to explain where the protocols come into play in the context of a functioning Web service.

In Chapters 3 through 5, I discuss the core underlying Web services protocols in detail—what some might consider too much detail. Frankly, much of the content in these chapters could have gone into the appendix, but unfortunately the limitations of the publishing process prevented me from making such a drastic change to the structure of the book. So you will have to wait until the second edition.

Meanwhile, I recommend that you skim those chapters the first time through. As you become more involved with Web services, you can give them a more thorough read. There is no better way to advance your understanding of Web services than to have a deep understanding of the underlying protocols, especially if you need to interoperate with a Web service that is hosted on another platform.

In Chapters 6 through 8, I get into the heart of the book and explain ASP.NET and Remoting, the core .NET technologies that enable developers to quickly build and consume Web services. These seemingly overlapping technologies have distinctly different goals. The primary focus of ASP.NET Web services is to maintain the fidelity of the instances of XML datatypes passed between the client and the server. This is in sharp contrast to Remoting, in which the primary focus is to maintain the fidelity of the instances of .NET types passed between the client and the server. In time, these two goals will be achieved by a unified technology set.

In the remaining chapters of the book, I cover specific topics relevant to most production-quality Web services. Chapter 9 explains how to leverage UDDI and DISCO to advertise your Web service and discover other Web services. In Chapter 10, I examine strategies for ensuring that your Web services are secure. In Chapter 11, I explain how to debug your Web service. Chapter 12 offers strategies for ensuring that your Web service meets your scalability and availability needs. Finally, in Chapter 13, I examine some of the problems involved in building Web services today and introduce emerging technologies that are aimed at addressing these problems.

If You Are in a Hurry

Sometimes I have been engaged in a project for which I need to use a technology that I know little or nothing about. In these cases, I try to learn just enough about the technology to solve the problem at hand. When you find yourself in such a situation, take advantage of the fact that I wrote each chapter of this book to be read individually, without requiring the previous chapters as background. For example, you can pick up the book and start reading Chapter 6, the ASP.NET chapter, without first reading the chapters on SOAP, XML Schema, or WSDL.

So, without further ado, here is what I recommend you do if you want to get up to speed as quickly as possible developing and consuming Web services:

Skim through Chapter 1 to get a sense of how the technologies and protocols that compose Web services fit together.

Read Chapter 2, and load Visual Studio .NET to follow the steps presented as I build two simple applications. This will help familiarize you with developing basic Web services using the Visual Studio .NET tool set.

Pick out the important pieces of Chapter 6 that apply to your project.

Read the "Interactive Debugging" section of Chapter 11, which is about debugging Web services using the Visual Studio .NET debugger.

Read Chapters 9 and 10 (on Discovery and Security, respectively) as needed.

Throughout the course of the project, thoroughly read Chapters 6 and 7 to get a concise but in-depth overview of how to use the ASP.NET platform to develop and consume Web services.

Finally read the other chapters as needed for your project. For example, if you plan to leverage UDDI, read Chapter 9 for relevant information about publishing your Web services and discovering other Web services.

System Requirements

To work through all the samples in this book, you need the hardware and software listed in Table I-1.

Table I-1   Hardware and Software Requirements

Component	Requirements
Visual Studio .NET	Enterprise Architect, Enterprise Developer, Professional, or Academic Edition
Processor	Pentium III class, 600 MHz or faster
RAM	128 MB or more for Windows 2000 or Windows XP Professional and 256 MB or more for Windows .NET Server
Hard disk	500 MB on the system drive and 3 GB on the installation drive
Operating system	Windows .NET Server, Windows XP, Windows 2000 or Windows NT 4.0
CD-ROM or DVD-ROM drive	Required
Video	800×600 high color (16-bit or higher)
Mouse	Microsoft mouse or compatible pointing device

The Companion CD

Many of the samples in this book were too long to print in their entirety without interruption by explanatory text. In reading reviews of other technical books, I have learned that some readers do not like this approach. If you prefer to see a sample application in its entirety, you can go to the companion CD, which contains most of the source code presented in the book.

You can view the contents of the CD by inserting it into your CD-ROM drive. If you have the Windows autorun feature enabled, a splash screen will appear and provide you with options for use.

If you don't feel like lugging around your laptop along with this book, then bag the book! The companion CD also contains an electronic version of the book (an eBook). One of the best features of the eBook is that it is fully searchable. For information about installing and using the eBook, see the Readme.txt file in the \eBook folder.

Support

I have made every effort to ensure the accuracy of the contents of this book and the accompanying code on the companion CD. Despite my efforts, some errors and omissions inevitably occur in this text. Therefore, monitor the list of updates and corrections that will be posted at *http://www.microsoft.com/mspress/support/*.

If you find what you believe is an error or have a suggestion as to how I could improve the book, please send correspondence to either of the following addresses:

Postal Mail:

    Microsoft Press
    Attn: Building XML Web Services for the Microsoft .NET Platform Editor
    One Microsoft Way
    Redmond, WA 98052-6399

E-mail:

    mspinput@microsoft.com
    Reference this book within the subject line or body of the e-mail.

Please note that product support is not available through the preceding addresses. For more information about product support, visit *http://www.microsoft.com/support* or call Standard Support at 425-635-7011 weekdays between 6 a.m. and 6 p.m. Pacific Time.

1

Why Web Services?

Component-based programming has become more popular than ever. Hardly an application is built today that does not involve leveraging components in some form, usually from different vendors. As applications have grown more sophisticated, the need to leverage components distributed on remote machines has also grown.

An example of a component-based application is an end-to-end e-commerce solution. An e-commerce application residing on a Web farm needs to submit orders to a back-end Enterprise Resource Planning (ERP) application. In many cases, the ERP application resides on different hardware and might run on a different operating system.

The Microsoft Distributed Component Object Model (DCOM), a distributed object infrastructure that allows an application to invoke Component Object Model (COM) components installed on another server, has been ported to a number of non-Windows platforms. But DCOM has never gained wide acceptance on these platforms, so it is rarely used to facilitate communication between Windows and non-Windows computers. ERP software vendors often create components for the Windows platform that communicate with the back-end system via a proprietary protocol.

Some services leveraged by an e-commerce application might not reside within the datacenter at all. For example, if the e-commerce application accepts credit card payment for goods purchased by the customer, it must elicit the services of the merchant bank to process the customer's credit card information. But for all practical purposes, DCOM and related technologies such as CORBA and Java RMI are limited to applications and components installed within the corporate datacenter. Two primary reasons for this are that by default these technologies leverage proprietary protocols and these protocols are inherently connection oriented.

Clients communicating with the server over the Internet face numerous potential barriers to communicating with the server. Security-conscious network administrators around the world have implemented corporate routers and firewalls to disallow practically every type of communication over the Internet. It often takes an act of God to get a network administrator to open ports beyond the bare minimum.

If you're lucky enough to get a network administrator to open up the appropriate ports to support your service, chances are your clients will not be as fortunate. As a result, proprietary protocols such those used by DCOM, CORBA, and Java RMI are not practical for Internet scenarios.

The other problem, as I said, with these technologies is that they are inherently connection oriented and therefore cannot handle network interruptions gracefully. Because the Internet is not under your direct control, you cannot make any assumptions about the quality or reliability of the connection. If a network interruption occurs, the next call the client makes to the server might fail.

The connection-oriented nature of these technologies also makes it challenging to build the load-balanced infrastructures necessary to achieve high scalability. Once the connection between the client and the server is severed, you cannot simply route the next request to another server.

Developers have tried to overcome these limitations by leveraging a model called *stateless programming*, but they have had limited success because the technologies are fairly heavy and make it expensive to reestablish a connection with a remote object.

Because the processing of a customer's credit card is accomplished by a remote server on the Internet, DCOM is not ideal for facilitating communication between the e-commerce client and the credit card processing server. As in an ERP solution, a third-party component is often installed within the client's datacenter (in this case, by the credit card processing solution provider). This component serves as little more than a proxy that facilitates communication between the e-commerce software and the merchant bank via a proprietary protocol.

Do you see a pattern here? Because of the limitations of existing technologies in facilitating communication between computer systems, software vendors have often resorted to building their own infrastructure. This means resources that could have been used to add improved functionality to the ERP system or the credit card processing system have instead been devoted to writing proprietary network protocols.

In an effort to better support such Internet scenarios, Microsoft initially adopted the strategy of augmenting its existing technologies, including COM Internet Services (CIS), which allows you to establish a DCOM connection between the client and the remote component over port 80. For various reasons, CIS was not widely accepted.

It became clear that a new approach was needed. So Microsoft decided to address the problem from the bottom up. Let's look at some of the requirements the solution had to meet in order to succeed.

- **Interoperability**   The remote service must be able to be consumed by clients on other platforms.

- **Internet friendliness**   The solution should work well for supporting clients that access the remote service from the Internet.

- **Strongly typed interfaces**   There should be no ambiguity about the type of data sent to and received from a remote service. Furthermore, datatypes defined by the remote service should map reasonably well to datatypes defined by most procedural programming languages.

- **Ability to leverage existing Internet standards**   The implementation of the remote service should leverage existing Internet standards as much as possible and avoid reinventing solutions to problems that have already been solved. A solution built on widely adopted Internet standards can leverage existing toolsets and products created for the technology.

- **Support for any language**   The solution should not be tightly coupled to a particular programming language. Java RMI, for example, is tightly coupled to the Java language. It would be difficult to invoke functionality on a remote Java object from Visual Basic or Perl. A client should be able to implement a new Web service or use an existing Web service regardless of the programming language in which the client was written.

- **Support for any distributed component infrastructure**   The solution should not be tightly coupled to a particular component infrastructure. In fact, you shouldn't be required to purchase, install, or maintain a distributed object infrastructure just to build a new remote service or consume an existing service. The underlying protocols should facilitate a base level of communication between existing distributed object infrastructures such as DCOM and CORBA.

Given the title of this book, it should come as no surprise that the solution Microsoft created is known as *Web services*. A Web service exposes an interface to invoke a particular activity on behalf of the client. A client can access the Web service through the use of Internet standards.

Web Services Building Blocks

The following graphic shows the core building blocks needed to facilitate remote communication between two applications.

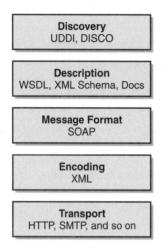

Let's discuss the purpose of each of these building blocks. Because many readers are familiar with DCOM, I will also mention the DCOM equivalent of each building block.

- **Discovery**   The client application that needs access to functionality exposed by a Web service needs a way to resolve the location of the remote service. This is accomplished through a process generally termed *discovery*. Discovery can be facilitated via a centralized directory as well as by more ad hoc methods. In DCOM, the Service Control Manager (SCM) provides discovery services.

- **Description**   Once the end point for a particular Web service has been resolved, the client needs sufficient information to properly interact with it. The description of a Web service encompasses structured metadata about the interface that is intended to be consumed by a client application as well as written documentation about the Web service including examples of use. A DCOM component exposes structured metadata about its interfaces via a type library (typelib). The metadata within a component's typelib is stored in a proprietary binary format and is accessed via a proprietary application programming interface (API).

- **Message format**   In order to exchange data, a client and a server have to agree on a common way to encode and format the messages.

A standard way of encoding data ensures that data encoded by the client will be properly interpreted by the server. In DCOM, messages sent between a client and a server are formatted as defined by the DCOM Object RPC (ORPC) protocol.

Without a standard way of formatting the messages, developing a toolset to abstract the developer from the underlying protocols is next to impossible. Creating an abstraction layer between the developer and the underlying protocols allows the developer to focus more on the business problem at hand and less on the infrastructure required to implement the solution.

- **Encoding**   The data transmitted between the client and the server needs to be encoded into the body of the message. DCOM uses a binary encoding scheme to serialize the data contained by the parameters exchanged between the client and the server.

- **Transport**   Once the message has been formatted and the data has been serialized into the body of the message, the message must be transferred between the client and the server over some transport protocol. DCOM supports a number of proprietary protocols bound to a number of network protocols such as TCP, SPX, NetBEUI, and NetBIOS over IPX.

Web Services Design Decisions

Let's discuss some of the design decisions behind these building blocks for Web services.

Choosing Transport Protocols

The first step was to determine how the client and the server would communicate with each other. The client and the server can reside on the same LAN, but the client might potentially communicate with the server over the Internet. Therefore, the transport protocol must be equally suited to LAN environments and the Internet.

As I mentioned earlier, technologies such as DCOM, CORBA, and Java RMI are ill suited for supporting communication between the client and the server over the Internet. Protocols such as Hypertext Transfer Protocol (HTTP) and Simple Mail Transfer Protocol (SMTP) are proven Internet protocols. HTTP defines a request/response messaging pattern for submitting a request and getting an associated response. SMTP defines a routable messaging protocol for asynchronous communication. Let's examine why HTTP and SMTP are well suited for the Internet.

HTTP-based Web applications are inherently stateless. They do not rely on a continuous connection between the client and the server. This makes HTTP an ideal protocol for high-availability configurations such as firewalls. If the server that handled the client's original request becomes unavailable, subsequent requests can be automatically routed to another server without the client knowing or caring.

Almost all companies have an infrastructure in place that supports SMTP. SMTP is well suited for asynchronous communication. If service is disrupted, the e-mail infrastructure automatically handles retries. Unlike with HTTP, you can pass SMTP messages to a local mail server that will attempt to deliver the mail message on your behalf.

The other significant advantage of both HTTP and SMTP is their pervasiveness. Employees have come to rely on both e-mail and their Web browsers, and network administrators have a high comfort level supporting these services. Technologies such as network address translation (NAT) and proxy servers provide a way to access the Internet via HTTP from within otherwise isolated corporate LANs. Administrators will often expose an SMTP server that resides inside the firewall. Messages posted to this server will then be routed to their final destination via the Internet.

In the case of credit card processing software, an immediate response is needed from the merchant bank to determine whether the order should be submitted to the ERP system. HTTP, with its request/response message pattern, is well suited to this task.

Most ERP software packages are not capable of handling large volumes of orders that can potentially be driven from the e-commerce application. In addition, it is not imperative that the orders be submitted to the ERP system in real time. Therefore, SMTP can be leveraged to queue orders so that they can be processed serially by the ERP system.

If the ERP system supports distributed transactions, another option is to leverage Microsoft Message Queue Server (MSMQ). As long as the e-commerce application and the ERP system reside within the same LAN, connectivity via non-Internet protocols is less of an issue. The advantage MSMQ has over SMTP is that messages can be placed and removed from the queue within the scope of a transaction. If an attempt to process a message that was pulled off the queue fails, the message will automatically be placed back in the queue when the transaction aborts.

Choosing an Encoding Scheme

HTTP and SMTP provide a means of sending data between the client and the server. However, neither specifies how the data within the body of the message should be encoded. Microsoft needed a standard, platform-neutral way to encode data exchanged between the client and the server.

Because the goal was to leverage Internet-based protocols, Extensible Markup Language (XML) was the natural choice. XML offers many advantages, including cross-platform support, a common type system, and support for industry-standard character sets.

Binary encoding schemes such as those used by DCOM, CORBA, and Java RMI must address compatibility issues between different hardware platforms. For example, different hardware platforms have different internal binary representation of multi-byte numbers. Intel platforms order the bytes of a multi-byte number using the little endian convention; many RISC processors order the bytes of a multi-byte number using the big endian convention.

XML avoids binary encoding issues because it uses a text-based encoding scheme that leverages standard character sets. Also, some transport protocols, such as SMTP, can contain only text-based messages.

Binary methods of encoding, such as those used by DCOM and CORBA, are cumbersome and require a supporting infrastructure to abstract the developer from the details. XML is much lighter weight and easier to handle because it can be created and consumed using standard text-parsing techniques.

In addition, a variety of XML parsers are available to further simplify the creation and consumption of XML documents on practically every modern platform. XML is lightweight and has excellent tool support, so XML encoding allows incredible reach because practically any client on any platform can communicate with your Web service.

Choosing a Formatting Convention

It is often necessary to include additional metadata with the body of the message. For example, you might want to include information about the type of services that a Web service needs to provide in order to fulfill your request, such as enlisting in a transaction or routing information. XML provides no mechanism for differentiating the body of the message from its associated data.

Transport protocols such as HTTP provide an extensible mechanism for header data, but some data associated with the message might not be specific to the transport protocol. For example, the client might send a message that needs to be routed to multiple destinations, potentially over different transport protocols. If the routing information were placed into an HTTP header, it would have to be translated before being sent to the next intermediary over another transport protocol, such as SMTP. Because the routing information is specific to the message and not the transport protocol, it should be a part of the message.

Simple Object Access Protocol (SOAP) provides a protocol-agnostic means of associating header information with the body of the message. Every SOAP message must define an envelope. The envelope has a body that contains the payload of the message and a header that can contain metadata associated with the message.

SOAP imposes no restrictions on how the message body can be formatted. This is a potential concern because without a consistent way of encoding the data, it is difficult to develop a toolset that abstracts you from the underlying protocols. You might have to spend a fair amount of time getting up to speed on the Web service's interface instead of solving the business problem at hand.

What was needed was a standard way of formatting a remote procedure call (RPC) message and encoding its list of parameters. This is exactly what Section 7 of the SOAP specification provides. It describes a standard naming convention and encoding style for procedure-oriented messages. I will discuss SOAP in more detail in Chapter 3.

Because SOAP provides a standard format for serializing data into an XML message, platforms such as ASP.NET and Remoting can abstract away the details for you. In the next chapter, I will show how to create and consume two Web services for which knowledge of SOAP is not required.

Choosing Description Mechanisms

SOAP provides a standard way of formatting messages exchanged between the Web service and the client. However, the client needs additional information in order to properly serialize the request and interpret the response. XML Schema provides a means of creating schemas that can be used to describe the contents of a message.

XML Schema provides a core set of built-in datatypes that can be used to describe the contents of a message. You can also create your own datatypes. For example, the merchant bank can create a complex datatype to describe the content and structure of the body of a message used to submit a credit card payment request.

A schema contains a set of datatype and element definitions. A Web service uses the schema not only to communicate the type of data that is expected to be within a message but also to validate incoming and outgoing messages.

A schema alone does not provide enough information to effectively describe a Web service, however. The schema does not describe the message patterns between the client and the server. For example, a client needs to know whether to expect a response when an order is posted to the ERP system. A client also needs to know over what transport protocol the Web service expects to receive requests. Finally, the client needs to know the address where the Web service can be reached.

This information is provided by a Web Services Description Language (WSDL) document. WSDL is an XML document that fully describes a particular Web service. Tools such as ASP.NET WSDL.exe and Remoting SOAPSUDS.exe can consume WSDL and automatically build proxies for the developer.

As with any component used to build software, a Web service should also be accompanied by written documentation for developers who program against the Web service. The documentation should describe what the Web service does, the interfaces it exposes, and some examples of how to use it. Good documentation is especially important if the Web service is exposed to clients over the Internet.

Choosing Discovery Mechanisms

Once you've developed and documented a Web service, how can potential clients locate it? If the Web service is designed to be consumed by a member of your development team, your approach can be pretty informal, such as sharing the URL of the WSDL document with your peer a couple of cubicles down. But when potential clients are on the Internet, advertising your Web service effectively is an entirely different story.

What's needed is a common way to advertise Web services. Universal Description, Discovery, and Integration (UDDI) provides just such a mechanism. UDDI is an industry-standard centralized directory service that can be used to advertise and locate Web services. UDDI allows users to search for Web services using a host of search criteria, including company name, category, and type of Web service.

Web services can also be advertised via DISCO, a proprietary XML document format defined by Microsoft that allows Web sites to advertise the services they expose. DISCO defines a simple protocol for facilitating a hyperlink style for locating resources. The primary consumer of DISCO is Microsoft Visual Studio .NET. A developer can target a particular Web server and navigate through the various Web services exposed by the server.

What's Missing from Web Services?

You might have noticed that some key items found within a distributed component infrastructure are not defined by Web services. Two of the more noticeable omissions are a well-defined API for creating and consuming Web services and a set of component services, such as support for distributed transactions. Let's discuss each of these missing pieces.

- **Web service–specific API** Most distributed component infrastructures define an API to perform such tasks as initializing the runtime, creating an instance of a component, and reflecting the metadata used to describe the component. Because most high-level programming languages provide some degree of interoperability with C, the API is usually exposed as a flat set of C method signatures. RMI goes so far as to tightly couple its API with a single high-level language, Java.

In an effort to ensure that Web services are programming language–agnostic, Microsoft has left it up to individual software vendors to bind support for Web services to a particular platform. I will discuss two Web service implementations for the .NET platform, ASP.NET and Remoting, later in the book.

■   **Component services**   The Web services platform does not provide many of the services commonly found in distributed component infrastructures, such as remote object lifetime management, object pooling, and support for distributed transactions. These services are left up to the distributed component infrastructure to implement.

Some services, such as support for distributed transactions, can be introduced later as the technology matures. Others, such as object pooling and possibly object lifetime management, can be considered an implementation detail of the platform. For example, Remoting defines extensions to provide support for object lifetime management, and Microsoft Component Services provides support for object pooling.

Summary

Component-based programming has proven to be a boon to developer productivity, but some services cannot be encapsulated by a component that resides within the client's datacenter. Legacy technologies such as DCOM, CORBA, and Java RMI are ill-suited to allowing clients to access services over the Internet, so Microsoft found it necessary to start from the bottom and build an industry-standard way of accessing remote services.

Web services is an umbrella term that describes a collection of industry-standard protocols and services used to facilitate a base-line level of interoperability between applications. The industry support that Web services has received is unprecedented. Never before have so many leading technology companies stepped up to support a standard that facilitates interoperability between applications, regardless of the platform on which they are run.

One of the contributing factors to the success of Web services is that they're built on existing Internet standards such as XML and HTTP. As a result, any system capable of parsing text and communicating via a standard Internet transport protocol can communicate with a Web service. Companies can also leverage the investment they have already made in these technologies.

2

Creating a Basic Web Service

In this chapter, I show you how to build a couple of Web services so that you can see how easy it is to do. In later chapters, when I discuss the underlying protocols, you will more fully appreciate how much complexity is abstracted for you by the .NET platform. In this chapter, I make high-level references to those underlying technologies to give you a basic understanding of where they fit into the larger picture.

In the first example, you create a simple commerce application in Microsoft ASP.NET—a Web Form for collecting payment information. Then you create a Web service that performs credit card validation business logic on behalf of the application. This example shows you how easy it is to refactor an existing .NET application to move business logic into a Web service so that it can be used by other applications.

In the second example, you create a Web service for sending and receiving binary files. As I mentioned in Chapter 1, messages between the Web service and the client are encoded in XML. Because XML is a text-based markup language, we can encode something into the message that might be surprising: the contents of a binary file. The binary file is contained within a complex type. The complex type also contains information about the file. This example demonstrates to you the robustness of the underlying .NET Framework.

These two scenarios should give you a good idea of what the .NET platform offers. I also show you in this chapter how the rapid application development capabilities of Microsoft Visual Studio .NET simplify development of applications that expose or consume Web services. Because the best way to learn is by doing, I encourage you to fire up Visual Studio .NET and step through the processes I describe to create the sample applications yourself.

A Simple Commerce Application

You will first create an ASP.NET Web Form that collects and validates credit card information. The Web Form allows users to enter their credit card information, and then it informs users whether the information they entered is valid. You then move the credit card validation logic into a Web service and modify the Web Form so that it calls the Web service to validate the credit card information.

Creating a Web Form

You can create a Web Form by opening Visual Studio .NET and creating a new Web Application project. Set the project type to your language of choice, and select the Web Application template. Name your project *Commerce*, and set the location to a URL that points to the targeted Web server, as shown here:

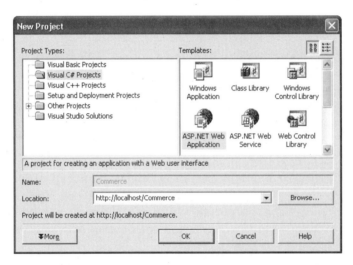

Visual Studio .NET creates a project on the specified Web server and places template Web application files into that directory. Included in these files is a Web Form page named WebForm1.aspx. Rename it *Order.aspx*, and then change the name of the class defined within Order.aspx from *WebForm1* to *Order* by following these steps:

1. Open the Order.aspx code-behind file by right-clicking on the filename in Solution Explorer and selecting View Code.

2. Change the name of the *WebForm1* class and its corresponding constructor to *Order*.

3. In the Properties pane, change the name of the label to *Status*, the text of the label to *Please enter your credit card information*, the name of the button to *PlaceOrder*, and the text of the button to *Place Order*. After you adjust the layout and add some additional text, the Web Form should look similar to the following:

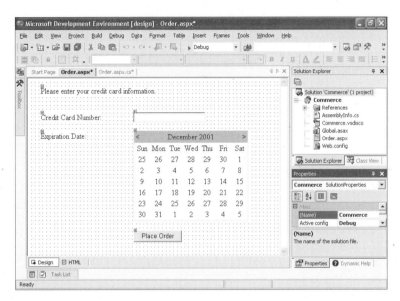

Next you provide the implementation for the Place Order button. To add an event handler for the order button, double-click it and write the following code so that when the user clicks the button, the *Validate* method is called to determine whether the credit card information the user entered is valid. The code will also adjust the label's text to display appropriate text to inform the user whether the credit card was valid.

```
public void PlaceOrder_Click(object sender. Syste.EventArgs e)
{
    if(Validate(TextBox1.Text, Calendar1.SelectedDate))
    {
        Status.Text = "Thank you for your order.";
    }
    else
    {
    Status.Text = "Credit card invalid.";
    }
}
```

Next you create the *Validate* method immediately following the *PlaceOrder_Click* method.

```
public bool Validate(string cardNumber, DateTime expDate)
{
    if(expDate >= DateTime.Today)
    {
        int total = 0;
        int temp = 0;
        char [] ccDigits = cardNumber.ToCharArray();

        for(int i = 0; i < cardNumber.Length; i++)
        {
            if(((i+1)%2) == 0)
            {
                total += int.Parse(ccDigits[i].ToString());
            }
            else
            {
                temp = int.Parse(ccDigits[i].ToString()) * 2;
                if(temp > 9)
                {
                    temp = (int)temp - 9;
                }
                total += temp;
            }
        }

        if((total%10) ==0)
        {
            return true;
        }
        else
        {
            return false;
        }
    }
    else
    {
        return false;
    }
}
```

The *Validate* method determines whether the expiration date has passed. If it has not, the *Validate* method uses a standard mod10 algorithm to validate the credit card number.

Now compile and test the Web application to ensure that it works as expected.

Creating a Payment Web Service

At this point, the validation functionality is embedded in the Web Form. Now I will show you how to leverage the validation functionality within other applications. For example, you might want to develop a WinForm application for running the cash registers. This application would probably need to call the same logic to validate credit cards. If you expose the validation logic as a Web service, any application that can send and receive XML over HTTP will be able to invoke the service to validate credit card information.

You have a couple of options for creating the new Web service. You can simply add the Web service to an existing application by choosing Add Web Service from the Project menu. Or you can create a new project to contain the Web service.

Recall that your intention is to have the credit card validation logic serve as a shared resource across multiple applications. It might have infrastructure and scalability requirements that differ from those of the commerce application. So, in this case you will create a separate application—a Visual Studio .NET Web service application.

First open Visual Studio .NET and select Create New Project. Set the project type to your language of choice, and select the Web Service template. Name the project *Payment*, and set the location to a URL that points to the targeted Web server, as shown here:

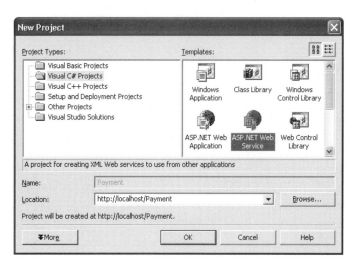

Change the name of the Service1.asmx file to CreditCard.asmx. Because it is good practice to have the class name match the name of the .asmx file, change the name of the *Service1* class to *CreditCard*. Visual Studio .NET creates a code-behind file for the .asmx file similar to those it creates for .aspx files, so you must open CreditCard.asmx.cs to modify the class declaration. To view the code-behind file, right-click on CreditCard.asmx and choose View Code. Change the name of the *Service1* class and its corresponding constructor to *CreditCard*.

Next cut the *Validate* method from the Order Web Form and paste it into the *CreditCard* class. Then decorate the class with the *WebMethod* attribute and compile the application. The *WebMethod* attribute is the only code required to expose the *Validate* method on the Web!

```
[WebMethod]
public bool Validate(string cardNumber, DateTime expDate)
{
    ⋮
}
```

The *WebMethod* attribute tells the ASP.NET runtime to provide all of the implementation required to expose a method of a class on the Web—including the ability to advertise the Web service's functionality in the form of Web Services Description Language (WSDL). Visual Studio .NET will use the automatically generated WSDL to create a reference to the Web service in your commerce application.

Another service that ASP.NET provides the Payment Web service is the automatic generation of documentation for the Web service and a test harness. To invoke this functionality, use a Web browser to navigate to the Credit-Card.asmx file, as shown here:

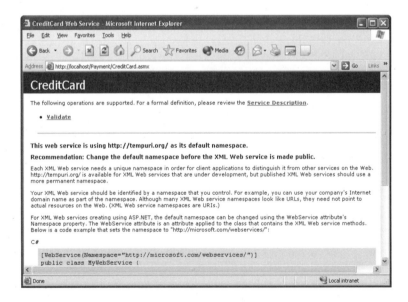

Next test the *Validate* method using the test harness supplied with the documentation. Entering a valid credit card number and a date of 1/1/2052 produces the following results (assuming you are not reading a 50-year-old book):

```
<?xml version="1.0" encoding="utf-8" ?>
<boolean xmlns="http://tempuri.org/">true</boolean>
```

As expected, the result is true. However, the XML response message is not a valid SOAP message. There are multiple ways in which an ASP.NET-hosted Web service can be called. The Web service will return a well-formed SOAP message only if the request was a SOAP message. I will discuss ASP.NET-hosted Web services in detail in Chapter 6.

Updating the Order Web Form

The next task is to switch back to the Commerce application and update the Order Web Form so that it calls the CreditCard Web service to validate the user's credit card. You first add a Web reference for the CreditCard Web service to the commerce application by using the Web Reference Wizard.

You start the wizard by choosing Add Web Reference from the Project menu. In the Address text box, enter the URL to the server that hosts your targeted Web service. Click on the link to the Payment Web service that is listed in the right pane, as shown here:

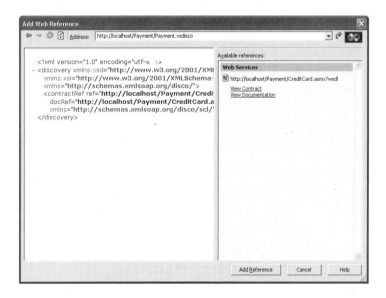

Click Add Reference. You should see the Web reference listed in Solution Explorer. Visual Studio .NET processes the WSDL metadata associated with the Payment Web service and automatically creates a proxy. You can think of WSDL as the Web services equivalent of a TypeLib. The resulting proxy allows the Web service to be treated like any other .NET class.

Next you alter the implementation of the *PlaceOrder_Click* method to call the Web service instead of the local *Validate* function. First create an instance of the *CreditCard* class by using the *new* keyword as you would with any other .NET type. Notice that the default namespace for the Web service is the name of the server on which it resides.

```
public void PlaceOrder_Click (object sender, System.EventArgs e)
{
    localhost.CreditCard cc = new localhost.CreditCard();
```

Finally you call the *Validate* method on the *cc* object to cause a communication exchange to occur between the client (the Order Web Form) and the CreditCard Web service.

```
    if(cc.Validate(TextBox1.Text, Calendar1.SelectedDate))
    {
        Status.Text = "Thank you for your order.";
    }
    else
    {
        Status.Text = "Credit card invalid.";
    }
}
```

If you are writing the code as you read this chapter, notice that you have full IntelliSense support for the *cc* object. After you type *cc.*, the list of methods supported by the object, including the *Validate* method, will be shown. As soon as you type the opening parenthesis for the method, the parameters for the method will be displayed—including the .NET equivalent of the Web service's parameter types.

As you have seen, it is easy to refactor a .NET application to expose its business logic via Web services. You simply copy the local method and place it into the .asmx code-behind file for the Web service. The only code required to expose the method via HTTP is the *WebMethod* attribute. Once the code is compiled and deployed, any client that supports HTTP and is capable of parsing strings can call the method.

The Web File Share Application

This example will create a Web service that allows binary files to be transferred over HTTP and SOAP. Because SOAP leverages an XML-based method of encoding, you must represent method parameters and return values in a way that is conducive to XML.

In the preceding example, it was rather straightforward to encode the credit card number and the expiration date. In this example, the Web service will encode complex types that contain, among other things, binary data. As you will see, the .NET platform will handle the encoding and decoding for you. It will ensure that byte arrays are encoded so that they do not introduce special characters into the SOAP message that would invalidate the XML.

Before I go any further, I want to throw in a little disclaimer: There are more efficient ways of sending the content of a file over the Web than encoding it into a SOAP message. The purpose of this example is not to create a replacement for FTP; it is to demonstrate the power and flexibility of Web services and the robustness of the .NET platform.

Creating the WebFileShare Web Service

The WebFileShare Web service will expose two methods, *ListFiles* and *GetFile*. *ListFiles* is used to obtain a list of files that are available from the Web service, and *GetFile* will allow the client to retrieve the specified file.

First you create a Visual Studio .NET Web Service project using steps similar to those shown in the previous example: Open Visual Studio .NET, and create a new project. Set the project type to your language of choice, and select the Web Service template. Name your project *WebFileShare*, and set the location to a URL that points to the targeted Web server.

Change the name of the Service1.asmx file to WebDirectory.asmx. Right-click on WebDirectory.asmx, and choose View Code. Change the name of the *Service1* class and its corresponding constructor to *WebDirectory*. Then modify the *Inherits* property in the ASMX header to point to the new class name.

Now that you have set up the Visual Studio .NET project, you will add the implementation to enable the client to request and retrieve files. First you need to create an alias for the *System.IO* namespace with the *using* keyword. Underneath the *using* statement that creates an alias for the *System.Web.Services* namespace, type the following statement:

```
using System.IO;
```

Next you define the *WebFile* structure, which encapsulates the contents of the file in addition to its metadata. The file structure contains the name of the file, the file's contents, and the file system attributes associated with the file.

Define the following structure immediately after the *WebFileShare* namespace is defined:

```
public struct WebFile
{
    public string    Name;
    public byte[]    Contents;
    public DateTime  CreationTime;
    public DateTime  LastAccessTime;
    public DateTime  LastWriteTime;
}
```

Next you need to create a number of methods within the *WebFileShare* class. These methods will be defined immediately before the example *HelloWorld* method.

The first method that must be defined returns a list of files available for download in the c:\Public directory. The list of files is returned as an array of strings. The .NET Framework will properly serialize the array for you.

```
[WebMethod]
public string[] ListFiles()
{
    return Directory.GetFiles("c:\\Public");
}
```

Next you create a *GetFile* method that allows the client to request a file. If the file is available, an instance of the *WebFile* structure should be sent back to the client. In this method, you use the *System.IO.File* object to obtain the necessary information about the file. You obtain a *Stream* object from the *File* object and write the contents of the stream into a byte array in the *WebFile* structure. You also set the *CreationTime*, *LastAccessTime*, and *LastWriteTime* fields to the values obtained from the associated static methods exposed by the *File* class.

```
[WebMethod]
public WebFile GetFile(string fileName)
{
    WebFile  webFile = new WebFile();
    string   filePath = "c:\\Public\\" + fileName;
```

```
        // Set the name of the file.
        webFile.Name = fileName;

        // Obtain the contents of the requested file.
        Stream s = File.Open(filePath, FileMode.Open);
        webFile.Contents = new byte[s.Length];
        s.Read(webFile.Contents, 0, (int)s.Length);
        s.Close
        // Retrieve the date/time stamps for the file.
        webFile.CreationTime = File.GetCreationTime(filePath);
        webFile.LastAccessTime = File.GetLastAccessTime(filePath);
        webFile.LastWriteTime = File.GetLastWriteTime(filePath);

        return webFile;
    }
```

After the *WebFile* structure is initialized, it is sent back to the client. Once again, the .NET Framework performs the appropriate serialization. In this case, the instance of the structure is serialized, including its data. The *Contents* byte array is encoded into its Base-64 representation. Base-64 encoding maps each byte of the array into an alphanumeric character that can be contained within the XML document without introducing any invalid characters. In addition, the values of the *Name*, *CreationTime*, *LastAccessTime*, and *LastWriteTime* fields are serialized into the SOAP message.

In future chapters, I will discuss in detail how the .NET Framework encodes more complex data types such as structures, byte arrays, and enumerations. The important thing to realize is that the resulting message is 100 percent compliant with the industry-standard SOAP specification. Therefore, clients on other platforms, operating systems, or hardware can interact with your WebDirectory Web service.

Now that you have built the Web service, let's create a client for retrieving files through the WebFileSystem Web service.

Creating the WebFileUtil Program

Next you will create a console application to retrieve files from the WebFile-Share Web service. This console application will accept at least two command-line arguments: a command specifying the action to take, and the name of the targeted file. You can optionally specify a third argument if you want to specify the name of the destination file. Otherwise, the default value is the original name of the file.

Start by opening Visual Studio .NET and selecting Create New Project. Set the project type to your language of choice, select the Console Application template, and name the project WebFileUtil, as shown here:

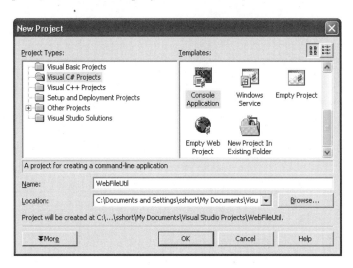

You can change the name of the Service1 file (with an extension based on the language you chose) to *WebFileUtil* and then delete the default implementation in WebFileUtil provided by Visual Studio .NET.

Next you add a Web reference to the WebDirectory Web service. Start the Web Reference Wizard by choosing Add Web Reference from the Project menu. In the Address text box, enter the URL of the server that hosts the Web service. Click on the link to the WebFileShare directory. The WebFileShare Web service will automatically be selected, as shown here:

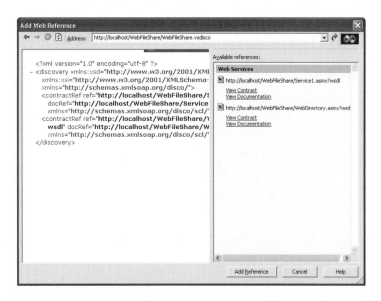

Click the Add Reference button. Change the name of the new Web reference listed in Solution Explorer to WebFileShare.

Now that you have created and configured a Web reference, let's step through a C# implementation of WebFileUtil.

First you import the *System.IO* namespace into the project. This will simplify your code when you use the *File* class in the code below. You must also import the namespace of your Web reference, *WebFileShare*.

```csharp
using System;
using System.IO;
using WebFileUtil.WebFileShare;

namespace WebFileUtil
{
```

You then change the name of the class from *Class1* to a more descriptive name, *WebFileUtil*.

```csharp
public class WebFileUtil
```

Ensure that the program was passed the correct number of command-line arguments, and then initialize the source and destination variables.

```csharp
{
    // Validate number of command-line arguments.
    if(args.Length < 1 || args.Length > 3)
    {
        DisplayUsage();
        return 1;
    }

    // Initialize variables.
    string source = args[1];
    string destination = source;

    if(args.Length == 3)
        destination = args[2];
```

Next process the commands that were passed. The appropriate helper function will be called for the *DIR* or *GET* command:

```csharp
    // Process command.
    switch(args[0].ToUpper())
    {
        case "DIR":
            ListFiles();
            break;
        case "GET":
            GetFile(source, destination);
            break;
```

(continued)

```
        default:
            DisplayUsage();
            break;
    }

    return 0;
}
```

Next create a *ListFiles* method to output to the console the list of files available from the Web service. To do this, create a *WebDirectory* object and a reference to an array of strings. Then set the reference to the array of strings equal to the return value from the *WebDirectory.ListFiles* method. Finally iterate through the array and write the name of each file out to the console.

```
private static void ListFiles()
{
    WebDirectory    webDir = new WebDirectory();
    string[]        files;

    files = webDir.ListFiles();
    foreach(string file in files)
    {
        Console.WriteLine(file);
    }

    Console.WriteLine("\n{0} file(s) in directory.", files.Length);
}
```

To create the *GetFile* method that will retrieve the requested file and save it to the file system, you first create a new instance of the *WebDirectory* class and a reference to *WebFile*. Then you call the *GetFile* method on the *WebDirectory* object to retrieve the *WebFile* object. You open the destination file and use the *stream* class to write the byte array to the file. Finally you set the date/time stamps for the file to the values contained within the *CreationTime*, *LastAccessTime*, and *LastWriteTime* fields.

```
private static void GetFile(string source, string destination)
{
    WebDirectory    webDir = new WebDirectory();
    WebFile         webFile = new WebFile();

    // Retrieve the requested file and then save it to disk.
    webFile = webDir.GetFile(source);
```

```
// Save the retrieved Web file to the file system.
FileStream fs = File.OpenWrite(destination);
fs.Write(webFile.Contents, 0, webFile.Contents.Length);
fs.Close();

// Set the date/time stamps for the file.
File.SetCreationTime(destination, webFile.CreationTime);
File.SetLastAccessTime(destination, webFile.LastAccessTime);
File.SetLastWriteTime(destination, webFile.LastWriteTime);
}
```

Finally you create a *DisplayUsage* method to write the proper syntax for WebFileUtil to the console.

```
private static void DisplayUsage()
{
    Console.WriteLine("WebFile is used to retrieve files from the
    WebDirectory Web service.");
    Console.WriteLine("\nUsage:  WebFile command source [destination]");
    Console.WriteLine("\tcommand     - Either DIR or GET.");
    Console.WriteLine("\tsource      - The name of the file to
    retrieve.");
    Console.WriteLine("\tdestination - Optionally the name of the
    destination file.");
    Console.WriteLine("\nExamples:");
    Console.WriteLine("\tWebFile GET somefile.exe");
    Console.WriteLine("\tWebFile GET somefile.exe c:\temp");
    Console.WriteLine("\tWebFile GET somefile.exe c:\temp\myfile.exe");
}
}
```

Note that this example uses .NET types throughout. The Web service declared classes that exposed methods with strongly typed parameters and return values. For example, the WebFileShare Web service declared a *WebFile* struct. The client code uses the *WebFile* struct as if it were a native .NET type even though the messages are passed between the WebFileUtil client and the WebDirectory Web service in XML.

As a result, many of the rich features of Visual Studio .NET are available to the developer, such as IntelliSense and the ability to catch type mismatch errors at compile time. For example, the *WebFile* structure was available to the client with no loss in fidelity. If the client attempts to set the *LastAccessTime* field to a string, an error would be generated at compile time. This was accomplished because the *WebFile* structure was exposed in the WSDL file that is automatically generated by the ASP.NET runtime. Visual Studio .NET uses the information in the WSDL file to create a strongly typed proxy for the Web service.

As you might assume, the byte array had to be encoded in some fashion before it could be included in an XML document. However, the .NET infrastructure handled all of the encoding for you. The byte array was transformed into a Base-64-encoded string, placed into the SOAP message, sent across the wire, and then decoded back into a byte array. (I will cover Base-64 and other XML data types in Chapter 4.)

Summary

This chapter demonstrates how easy it is to create and consume Web services using Visual Studio .NET. You create two Web services, one to validate a credit card and the other to send and retrieve files.

The first example demonstrates the ease with which you can factor Web services into your existing .NET applications. You are easily able to move the business logic for your Web application and place it into its own Web service. The second example, in which you create a Web service for receiving files, demonstrates the flexibility of Web services and the robustness of the .NET Framework.

Almost all of the code you write in this chapter is related to business logic instead of building infrastructure. The only code you write to expose methods as Web services is to decorate the method with the *WebMethod* attribute. The ASP.NET framework handled decoding the request message from the client and encoding the response message.

Microsoft .NET provides many services for the client as well. Visual Studio .NET automatically generates a proxy from the Web service's WSDL document. You can think of the WSDL document as the Web services equivalent to a COM TypeLib. It contains information about the properties, methods, and enumerations exposed by the Web service.

The Visual Studio .NET–generated proxy allows you to code against the Web service as if it were another strongly typed .NET object. One of the primary advantages of strong typing is that type mismatch errors can be caught at compile time instead of at run time. Another advantage is IntelliSense. As you code against the Visual Studio .NET–generated proxy object, IntelliSense displays the list of methods exposed by the Web service. Once a method is selected, IntelliSense displays the names and the types of each parameter within the method.

In subsequent chapters, you will learn about the protocols that Web services are built on, such as WSDL and SOAP, and about the .NET technologies such as ASP.NET that you can use to build and consume Web services.

3

SOAP

At the core of Web services is Simple Object Access Protocol (SOAP), which provides a standard way of packaging messages. SOAP has received a lot of attention because it facilitates RPC-style communication between a client and a remote server. But plenty of protocols have been created to facilitate communication between two applications—including Sun's RPC, Microsoft's DCE, JAVA's RMI, and CORBA's ORPC. So why is SOAP getting so much attention?

One of the primary reasons is that SOAP has incredible industry support. SOAP is the first protocol of its kind to be accepted by practically every major software company in the world. Companies that rarely cooperate with each other are rallying around this protocol. Some of the major companies that are supporting SOAP include Microsoft, IBM, Sun Microsystems, SAP, and Ariba.

Here are some of the advantages of SOAP:

- **It is not tightly coupled to one language.** Developers involved with new projects can choose to develop in today's latest and greatest programming language. But developers who are responsible for maintaining legacy applications might not have a choice about the programming language they use. SOAP does not specify an API, so the implementation of the API is left up to the programming language (such as Java) and the platform (such as Microsoft .NET).

- **It is not tightly coupled to a particular transport protocol.** The SOAP specification does describe how SOAP messages should be bound to HTTP. But a SOAP message is nothing more than an XML document, so it can be transported over any protocol that is capable of transmitting text.

- **It is not tied to any one distributed object infrastructure.** Most distributed object systems can be extended (and some of them are) to support SOAP. It is important to realize that even with SOAP, middleware such as COM+ still plays an important role in the enterprise. Component middleware is still responsible for some of the more advanced object management features such as object lifetime management, transactions, object pooling, and resource pooling. SOAP enables a degree of interoperability between different systems that are running component middleware from competing vendors.

■ **It leverages existing industry standards.** The primary contributors to the SOAP specification intentionally avoided reinventing anything. They opted to extend existing standards to meet their needs. For example, SOAP leverages XML for encoding messages. Instead of using its own type system, SOAP leverages the type definitions already defined within the XML Schema specification. And as I have mentioned, SOAP does not define a means of transporting the message; SOAP messages can be bound to existing transport protocols such as HTTP and SMTP.

■ **It enables interoperability across multiple environments.** SOAP was built on top of existing industry standards, so applications running on platforms that support these standards can effectively communicate via SOAP messages with applications running on other platforms. For example, a desktop application running on a PC can effectively communicate with a back-end application running on a mainframe that is capable of sending and receiving XML over HTTP.

This chapter covers the following key aspects of the SOAP specification:

■ **The SOAP envelope.** This is used to encode header information about the message and the body of the message itself.

■ **SOAP Encoding.** This is a standard way of serializing data into the body of a SOAP message.

■ **RPC-style messages.** I discuss the protocol you can use to facilitate procedure-oriented communication via request/response message patterns.

■ **The HTTP POST protocol binding.** This is the standard method of binding SOAP messages to HTTP.

Before I go any further, I want to discuss the status of SOAP. This chapter was written against version 1.1 of the SOAP specification (*http://www.w3.org/TR/SOAP*). The World Wide Web Consortium (W3C) is continuing to develop SOAP. On July 9, 2001, a working draft of SOAP 1.2 was published (*http://www.w3.org/TR/2001/WD-soap12-20010709*) by the XML Protocol Working Group.

As an acknowledgment of the phenomenal industry support that SOAP enjoys, the XML Protocol Working Group is committed to maintaining a smooth migration path from SOAP 1.1 to SOAP 1.2. Many of the proposed modifications are fit-and-finish and do not radically alter the use of SOAP. Much of what you have learned about SOAP 1.1 will directly translate to SOAP 1.2.

In addition, the majority of the Microsoft products that incorporate SOAP will likely not adopt SOAP 1.2 until it becomes an official W3C recommendation. Therefore, I recommend that you focus on learning the SOAP 1.1 protocol with an eye on the deltas in version 1.2.

Anatomy of a SOAP Message

SOAP provides a standard way of packaging a message. A SOAP message is composed of an envelope that contains the body of the message and any header information used to describe the message. Here is an example:

```xml
<?xml version="1.0"?>

<soap:Envelope xmlns:soap="http://schemas.xmlsoap.org/soap/envelope/">
    <soap:Header>
        <!--Optional header information goes here. -->
        <To>Scott</To>
        <From>Suzanne</From>
    </soap:Header>

    <soap:Body>
        <!--Message goes here. -->
        Please pick up some milk on your way home from work.
    </soap:Body>
</soap:Envelope>
```

The root element of the document is the *Envelope* element. The example contains two subelements, the *Body* and *Header* elements. A valid SOAP message can also contain other child elements within the envelope. You will see examples of this when I discuss serializing references using SOAP Encoding.

The envelope can contain an optional *Header* element, which contains information about the message. In the preceding example, the header contains two elements describing the individual who composed the message and the intended recipient of the message. (I describe the SOAP header in more detail later in the chapter.)

The envelope must contain one *Body* element. The body contains the message payload. In my example, the body contains a simple character string.

Notice that each SOAP-specific element has the *soap* namespace prefix. This prefix is defined within the *Envelope* element and points to the SOAP schema that describes the structure of a SOAP message. The prefix is appended to any elements defined within the SOAP namespace. These elements are fully qualified. The *soap* prefix indicates that the *Envelope* element is an instance of the SOAP *Envelope* type. I will drill deeper into XML namespaces in the next chapter.

SOAP Actors

Before I describe the individual parts of a SOAP message, I want to define a couple of terms I will be using. A *SOAP actor* is anything that acts on the content of the SOAP message. There are two types of SOAP actors, *default actors* and *intermediaries*.

The default actor is the intended final recipient of a SOAP message. An intermediary receives a SOAP message and might act on the message (including modifying it in some way) before forwarding it along the intended message path, as shown in the following diagram. Even though intermediaries might modify the data transferred from the client to the default actor, it is still considered the same message.

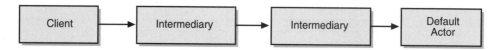

The *Header* Element

The optional *Header* element is used to pass data that might not be appropriate to encode in the body. For example, if the default actor receives a message in which the body is compressed, the default actor would need to know what type of compression algorithm was used in order to uncompress the message. Embedding information about the compression algorithm into the body does not make sense because the body itself will be compressed. Placing this type of information in the header of the message is more appropriate.

Other uses for the header include the following:

■ **Authentication.** The recipient might require the sender to authenticate himself before the message can be processed.

- **Security digest information.** If the recipient needs assurance that the contents of the message have not been tampered with, the sender can digitally sign the message body and place the resulting digest into the header.

- **Routing information.** If the message needs to be routed to many destinations, the destinations and their order can be included in the header.

- **Transactions.** The recipient might have to perform some action in the scope of the sender's transaction.

- **Payment information.** If the recipient of the message provides services to the client based on a per-usage fee, information necessary for collecting payment can be embedded in the header.

The *Header* element can be added as an immediate child element within the SOAP *Envelope*. The header entries appear as child nodes within the SOAP *Header* element. Here is an example:

```
<?xml version="1.0" encoding="utf-8"?>
<soap:Envelope xmlns:soap="http://schemas.xmlsoap.org/soap/envelope/">
  <soap:Header>
    <Digest>B839D234A3F87</Digest>
  </soap:Header>
  <soap:Body>
    <StockReport>
      <Symbol>MSFT</Symbol>
      <Price>74.56</Price>
    </StockReport>
  </soap:Body>
</soap:Envelope>
```

The SOAP message contains a *Digest* element in the header that the remote application can use to ensure that the message has not been tampered with. If the client is doing a routine check to see what her stock closed at, she might not be concerned about validating the message. But if the price of the stock triggers an event within the financial software package, she might be more interested in validating the message. For example, it would be unfortunate if the financial software package were to automatically liquidate her portfolio as the result of receiving a bogus message sent by some 14-year-old kid.

mustUnderstand Attribute

Because headers are optional, the recipient of the message can choose to ignore them. However, some information that can be embedded in the header should not be ignored by the intended recipient. If the header is not understood or cannot be handled properly, the application might not function properly. Therefore, you need a way to distinguish between header information that is informative and header information that is critical.

You can specify whether the message recipient must understand an element in the header by specifying the *mustUnderstand* attribute with a value of *1* in the root of the header element. For example, the SOAP message might request that a remote application perform an action on the client's behalf. The following example updates a user's account information within the scope of a transaction:

```xml
<?xml version="1.0" encoding="utf-8"?>
<soap:Envelope xmlns:soap="http://schemas.xmlsoap.org/soap/envelope/">
  <soap:Header>
    <TransactionId soap:mustUnderstand="1">123</TransactionId>
  </soap:Header>
  <soap:Body>
    <UpdateAccountInfo>
      <email>sshort@microsoft.com</email>
      <firstName>Scott</firstName>
      <lastName>Short</lastName>
    </UpdateAccountInfo>
  </soap:Body>
</soap:Envelope>
```

The recipient of the message must update the user's account information within the scope of the client's transaction. If the transaction is aborted, the remote application must roll back the requested changes to the user's account information. Therefore, I encoded the transaction ID within the header and set the *mustUnderstand* attribute to *1*. The remote application must either honor the transaction or not process the message.

actor Attribute

A SOAP message can be routed through many intermediaries before it reaches its final destination. For example, the previous document might be routed through an intermediary responsible for creating a transaction context. In this case, you might want to clearly specify that the *TransactionId* header is intended to be processed by the transaction intermediary rather than by the default actor.

The SOAP specification provides the *actor* attribute for annotating SOAP headers intended for certain intermediaries. The value of this attribute is the Uniform Resource Identifier (URI) of the intermediary for which the portion of the message is intended. If a header is intended to be processed by the next intermediary to receive the SOAP message, the *actor* attribute can be set to *http://schemas.xmlsoap.org/soap/actor/next*. Otherwise the *actor* attribute can be set to a URI that identifies a specific intermediary. Here is an example:

```
<?xml version="1.0" encoding="utf-8"?>
<soap:Envelope xmlns:soap="http://schemas.xmlsoap.org/soap/envelope/">
  <soap:Header>
    <TransactionId soap:mustUnderstand="1"
      actor="urn:TransactionCoordinator>123</TransactionId>
  </soap:Header>
  <soap:Body>
    <TransferFunds>
      <Source>804039836</Source>
      <Destination>804039836</Destination>
      <Amount>151.43</Amount>
    </GetWeather>
  </soap:Body>
</soap:Envelope>
```

Because the *TransactionId* header element is intended for the transaction coordinator intermediary, its *actor* attribute is set to the intermediary's URI. The *mustUnderstand* attribute has also been set so that if the transaction coordinator intermediary does not understand the *TransactionId* header element, it must raise an error.

If the message is passed to another recipient, any header elements designated for the intermediary must be removed before the message is forwarded. The intermediary can, however, add additional header elements before forwarding the message to the next recipient. In this example, the transaction coordinator intermediary must remove the router element before forwarding it to the billing application.

One important point to note is that routing the message directly to the default actor is not considered an error. Setting the *mustUnderstand* attribute to *1* in combination with setting the *actor* attribute to *urn:TransactionCoordinator* does not ensure that the message will be routed through the intermediary. It means only that if the message does reach the transaction coordinator intermediary, it must comprehend the *TransactionId* header entry or throw an error.

In the preceding example, the intermediary needs to perform a critical task before the message is routed to the default actor. Recall that if the message does reach the transaction coordinator intermediary, it must remove the *TransactionId* header before forwarding the message. Therefore, the default actor can check to see whether the *TransactionId* header exists, which would indicate that the message was not passed through its appropriate intermediaries. However, determining whether all of the headers were processed after the message reached the default actor is not always ideal. What if the SOAP request needs to be routed through the intermediaries shown here?

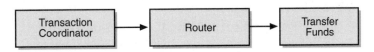

The request to transfer funds must pass through a router intermediary before the funds are transferred. Suppose the router charges the customer a processing fee for forwarding the request to the appropriate banking Web service. However, before funds are deducted, the message should be routed through the transaction coordinator to initiate a transaction before any data is modified. Therefore the router intermediary and the default actor should perform all work in the scope of the transaction. Because the banking Web service is the default actor, it can check the headers to see whether the message was routed through the necessary intermediaries.

But what if the banking Web service discovers that the message was never routed through the transaction manager intermediary? If an error occurred during the funds transfer, you might not be able to undo the work performed by the router intermediary. Worse yet, the SOAP message might have been routed through the router intermediary before being routed through the transaction coordinator. If this is the case, there might be no way to tell that the procurement application performed its work outside the scope of the transaction. Unfortunately, SOAP does not provide any mechanism to ensure that the message travels through all intended intermediaries in the proper order. In the "Futures" chapter, I will discuss one of the emerging protocols for addressing this problem.

The *Body* Element

A valid SOAP message must have one *Body* element. The body contains the payload of the message. There are no restrictions on how the body can be encoded. The message can be a simple string of characters, an encoded byte array, or XML. The only requirement is that the contents cannot have any characters that would invalidate the resulting XML document.

The SOAP specification describes a method of encoding that can be used to serialize the data into the message's body. It is a good idea to conform to an established encoding scheme such as this because it allows the sender to more easily interoperate with the recipient using a well-known set of serialization rules. (I describe this encoding method later in the chapter.)

SOAP messages can generally be placed into two categories: procedure-oriented messages and document-oriented messages. Procedure-oriented messages provide two-way communication and are commonly referred to as remote procedure call (RPC) messages. The body of an RPC message contains information about the requested action from the server and any input and output parameters. Document-oriented messages generally facilitate one-way communication. Business documents such as purchase orders are examples of document-oriented messages. Let's take a closer look at each of these document types.

Two SOAP messages are paired together to facilitate an RPC method call with SOAP: the request message and the corresponding response message. Information about the targeted method along with any input parameters is passed to the server via a request message. The server then invokes some behavior on behalf of the client and returns the results and any return parameters. Most of the examples in this chapter relate to RPC method invocations, and they all follow the SOAP specification's guidelines for encoding RPC messages.

A business document such as a purchase order or an invoice can be encoded within the body of a SOAP message and routed to its intended recipient. The recipient of the document might or might not send an acknowledgment message back to the sender. (The "SOAP Encoding" section later in this chapter describes how to use serialization rules to encode the data contained within these business documents.) Because business documents often span across multiple companies, organizations such as BizTalk.org and RosettaNet serve as facilitators and repositories for schemas that define common document exchanges.

Later in the book, I will describe how to leverage the .NET platform to create and consume both RPC and document-oriented messages.

Fault Element

Everything does not always go as planned. Sometimes the server will encounter an error while processing the client's message. SOAP provides a standard way of communicating error messages back to the client.

Regardless of which encoding style was used to create the message, the SOAP specification mandates the format for error reporting. The body of the message must contain a *Fault* element with the following structure:

```
<?xml version="1.0" encoding="utf-8"?>
<soap:Envelope xmlns:soap="http://schemas.xmlsoap.org/soap/envelope/">
  <soap:Body>
    <soap:Fault>
      <soap:faultcode>Client.Security</soap:faultcode>
      <soap:faultstring>Access denied.</soap:faultstring>
      <soap:faultactor>http://abc.com</soap:faultactor>
      <soap:detail>
        <MyError>
          <Originator>File System</Originator>
          <Resource>MySecureFile.txt</Resource>
        </MyError>
      </soap:detail>
    </soap:Fault>
  </soap:Body>
</soap:Envelope>
```

The fault code contains a value that is used to programmatically determine the nature of the error. The SOAP specification defines a set of fault codes that you can use to describe basic SOAP errors. The fault codes are listed in Table 3-1.

Table 3-1 **Base SOAP Fault Codes**

Fault Code	Description
VersionMismatch	An invalid namespace for the SOAP envelope element was specified.
MustUnderstand	An immediate child element within the SOAP header containing a *mustUnderstand* attribute set to *1* was either not understood or not obeyed by the server.
Client	The content of the message was found to be the root cause of the error. Possible root causes of errors resulting in a *Client* fault code include a malformed message or incomplete information in the message.
Server	The root cause of the error was not directly attributable to the content of the message. Examples of errors resulting in a *Server* fault code include the server not being able to obtain the appropriate resources (such as a database connection) to process the message or a logical error during the processing of the message.

You can append more specific fault codes to the core SOAP fault codes listed in the table by using the "dot" notation and ordering the individual fault codes from least specific to most specific. For example, if the server is unable to open a database connection that is required to process the client's message, the following fault code might be generated:

```
<faultcode>Server.Database.Connection</faultcode>
```

Because the error was not the direct result of the client's message, the base fault code is *Server*. A more descriptive fault code is appended to the end of the base fault code. In my example, I define a category of codes for the database and a fault code specific to connection-related errors.

The *faultstring* element should contain a human-readable string that describes the error encountered. Here is a *faultstring* value for the error connecting to the database:

```
<faultstring>Unable to open connection to the database.</faultstring>
```

You can use the optional *faultactor* element to indicate the exact source of the error. The only exception is if an intermediary generated the error. If the error was generated at any point other than the final recipient of the SOAP message, the *faultactor* element must contain a URI that identifies the source of the error. Otherwise, the URI can be omitted.

Using SOAP RPC Messages

One of the original design goals of SOAP was to provide an open and standard way to facilitate RPCs using Internet technologies such as XML and HTTP. In this section, I explain the method of encoding RPC-style messages described in version 1.1 of the SOAP specification.

As I stated earlier in the chapter, the SOAP specification does not dictate the way messages should be encoded, and encoding RPC-style messages is no exception. Section 7 of the SOAP 1.1 specification describes the recommended way to encode the request and response messages. The developer is free to create her own method of encoding RPC communication. In this section, however, I limit the discussion to the "standard" method of encoding RPC-style SOAP messages.

To facilitate the request/response behavior needed by RPC, you need two SOAP messages: one for the request and one for the response. Here is how the request message would be encoded for a simple C# function that adds two numbers:

```csharp
public int Add(int x, int y)
{
    return x + y;
}
```

The *Add* method accepts two integers as input parameters and passes the result back to the client as a return parameter. The input parameters must be packaged within the body of the request message so that they can be sent to the target application. This is accomplished by packaging the parameters in a struct-like format. Here is the resulting request message for *Add(1, 2)*:

```xml
<?xml version="1.0"?>
<soap:Envelope xmlns:soap="http://schemas.xmlsoap.org/soap/envelope/">
  <soap:Body>
    <Add>
      <x>1</x>
      <y>2</y>
    </Add>
  </soap:Body>
</soap:Envelope>
```

The *Body* element contains an *Add* element. Each of the input parameters is represented as a subelement within the *Add* element. The order of the *x* and *y* elements must match the order in which the parameters are specified in the method signature. In other words, placing *y* before *x* would be invalid. Furthermore, the names and the types of the *Add*, *x*, and *y* elements must be the same as the target method and its parameters. I will explain data typing in the next chapter. For now, suffice it to say that the body of the request message must be in a format expected by the remote application.

Now that I have created a properly formatted request message, take a look at the response generated by the remote application:

```
<?xml version="1.0"?>
<soap:Envelope xmlns:soap="http://schemas.xmlsoap.org/soap/envelope/">
  <soap:Body>
    <AddResult>
      <result>1</result>
    </AddResult>
  </soap:Body>
</soap:Envelope>
```

The response message returned by the remote application contains the result of the *Add* method. The return parameter is once again encoded in a struct-like format within the body of the SOAP message. The naming convention of the subelement within the body is the name of the method with *Result* appended to it. However, this naming convention is not dictated by the specification. The first (and in this case, only) parameter contains the return parameter of the method call. As with the *AddResult* element, the name of the element that contains the return parameter is not dictated by the specification.

What if more than one parameter is returned to the client? Let's take a look at a slight variation of the *Add* method. *Add2* returns the sum of the two numbers via an output parameter.

```
public int Add2(int x, int y, out int sum)
{
    sum = x + y;

    return sum;
}
```

Calling *Add2(1, 2)* produces the following SOAP message:

```
<?xml version="1.0" encoding="utf-8"?>
<soap:Envelope xmlns:soap="http://schemas.xmlsoap.org/soap/envelope/">
  <soap:Body>
    <Add2>
      <x>1</x>
      <y>2</y>
    </Add2>
  </soap:Body>
</soap:Envelope>
```

Notice that the third parameter, *sum*, does not get encoded. Because *sum* is declared as an output parameter, there is no reason to send its initial value to the remote application. Here is the response:

```
<?xml version="1.0" encoding="utf-8"?>
<soap:Envelope xmlns:soap="http://schemas.xmlsoap.org/soap/envelope/">
  <soap:Body>
    <Add2Response>
```

```
        <Add2Result>3</Add2Result>
        <sum>3</sum>
      </Add2Response>
    </soap:Body>
</soap:Envelope>
```

The response message contains the value of two parameters. As I mentioned earlier, the return parameter must always be listed first. I called the element containing the return parameter *Add2Result* to demonstrate that the name is not relevant. The value of the *sum* parameter is listed next.

SOAP Encoding

SOAP Encoding defines the way data can be serialized within a SOAP message. SOAP Encoding builds on the types defined in the XML specification, which defines a standard way of encoding data within an XML document. SOAP Encoding clarifies how data should be encoded and covers items not explicitly covered in the XML specification, such as arrays and how to properly encode references.

Simple Types

Simple types include strings, integers, date/time, Booleans, and so on. The SOAP specification defers to the "Built-in datatypes" section of the "XML Schema Part 2: Datatypes" specification. I will talk about the XML built-in data types in the next chapter.

An instance of a data type is encoded as an XML element. For example, an integer called *Age* would be encoded as follows:

```
<Age>31</Age>
```

Note that for RPC messages, the name of the element must correlate with the name of the parameter.

Compound Types

Often, it is not sufficient to pass simple types such as integers and strings as parameters; you need to pass compound types such as structures or arrays. In this section, I explain how SOAP Encoding handles compound types.

Structures

A structure is a collection of types that serve as a template for logically grouping data. For example, let's say you need to create a function that calculates the volume of a rectangular solid. Instead of passing the length, the width, and the height of the cube as separate parameters, you can logically group the dimensional data into a *RectSolid* structure. Then the method that calculates the volume of the solid can accept an instance of the *RectSolid* structure. Here is an example:

```
public struct RectSolid
{
    public int length;
    public int width;
    public int height;
}

public int CalcVolume(RectSolid r)
{
    return (r.length * r.width * r.height);
}
```

First I define a structure that contains the dimensions of a solid. Then I define the area. A request to calculate the volume of a rectangular solid that has a length of 2, a width of 3, and a height of 1 can be encoded as follows:

```
<?xml version="1.0" encoding="utf-8"?>
<soap:Envelope xmlns:soap="http://schemas.xmlsoap.org/soap/envelope/">
  <soap:Body>
    <CalcVolume>
      <r>
        <length>2</length>
        <width>3</width>
        <height>1</height>
      </r>
    </CalcVolume>
  </soap:Body>
</soap:Envelope>
```

As you can see, structures map nicely to XML. Each of the variables contained within the instance of the *RectSolid* structure is serialized as a child element of *r*. As you will see in the next chapter, this follows the method of encoding structures defined in Part 1 of the XML specification.

Arrays

Another common compound data type is the array. As of this writing, the XML specification does not specify how an array should be encoded. The SOAP 1.1 specification fills in the gaps. Here is an example:

```
public int AddArray(int[] numbers)
{
    int total = 0;

    foreach(int number in numbers)
```

```
    {
        total += number;
    }

    return total;
}
```

The *AddArray* method accepts an array of integers and returns the total. Here is how a client can call the *AddArray* function:

```
int[] a = {1, 2, 3};
int total;

total = AddArray(a);
```

The call to *AddArray* produces the following request message:

```
<?xml version="1.0" encoding="utf-8"?>
<soap:Envelope xmlns:soap="http://schemas.xmlsoap.org/soap/envelope/"
xmlns:soap-enc="http://schemas.xmlsoap.org/soap/encoding/" xmlns:xsi="http://
www.w3.org/2001/XMLSchema-instance">
  <soap:Body>
    <AddArray>
      <a soap-enc:arrayType="xsi:int[3]">
        <int>1</int>
        <int>2</int>
        <int>3</int>
      </a>
    </AddArray>
  </soap:Body>
</soap:Envelope>
```

The array is represented by a single element within the body tag. The element must contain the *soap-enc:arrayType* attribute. The value of the attribute describes the contents of the array and its dimensions. In the preceding example, *xsi:int[3]* specifies that the array contains three integers. In the next chapter, I will describe XML Schema and type definitions in more detail.

Each value in the array is listed as a subelement. The names of the subelements are not relevant, but often the names of the elements within the array will correlate with the type of data they contain.

SOAP-encoded arrays can contain different elements of different types. The following code returns an array containing an integer, a float, and a string:

```
object[] stuff = new object[3];

stuff[0] = (int)100;
stuff[1] = (float)2.456;
stuff[2] = (string)"Kitchen Sink";
```

(continued)

```
CollectThings(stuff);

public void CollectThings(object[] things)
{
    // ...
}
```

An array of objects called *stuff* is created, and then values of three different types are assigned to each of its three elements. The resulting response
SOAP message is encoded as follows:

```
<?xml version="1.0" encoding="utf-8"?>
<soap:Envelope xmlns:soap="http://schemas.xmlsoap.org/soap/envelope/"
xmlns:soap-enc="http://schemas.xmlsoap.org/soap/encoding/" xmlns:xsi="http://
www.w3.org/2001/XMLSchema-instance">
  <soap:Body>
    <CollectThings>
      <things soap-enc:arrayType="xsi:ur-type[3]">
        <object>100</object>
        <object>2.456</object>
        <object>Kitchen Sink</object>
      </things>
    </CollectThings>
  </soap:Body>
</soap:Envelope>
```

The *things* array is defined as type *xsi:ur-type*, which means that the elements can contain data of any type. In the next chapter, you will learn how to
declare the type of data in each element.

The final two array types I will cover are multidimensional and jagged
arrays. Multidimensional arrays are rectangular by nature. You can think of a
jagged array as an array contained within an array. SOAP defines a method for
encoding both types of arrays. This example creates a multidimensional array:

```
// Create a block of seats 3 rows deep and 4 seats wide.
string[,] seats = new string[3, 4];

for(int i = 0; i < 2; i++)
{
    for(int j = 0; i < 2; j++)
    {
        seats[i, j] = string.Format("row {0}, seat {1}");
    }
}

PrintSeatLabels(seats);

public void PrintSeatLabels(string[,] labels)
{
    // ...
}
```

A multidimensional array of labels is created, and then the array is passed to *PrintSeatLabels*. The resulting message is encoded as follows:.

```xml
<?xml version="1.0" encoding="utf-8"?>
<soap:Envelope xmlns:soap="http://schemas.xmlsoap.org/soap/envelope/"
xmlns:soap-enc="http://schemas.xmlsoap.org/soap/encoding/" xmlns:xsi="http://
www.w3.org/2001/XMLSchema-instance">
  <soap:Body>
    <PrintSeatLabels soap-enc:arrayType="xsi:string[3,4]">
      <seats>
        <string>row 1, seat 1</string>
        <string>row 1, seat 2</string>
        <string>row 1, seat 3</string>
        <string>row 1, seat 4</string>
        <string>row 2, seat 1</string>
        <string>row 2, seat 2</string>
        <string>row 2, seat 3</string>
        <string>row 2, seat 4</string>
        <string>row 3, seat 1</string>
        <string>row 3, seat 2</string>
        <string>row 3, seat 3</string>
        <string>row 3, seat 4</string>
      </seats>
    </PrintSeatLabels>
  </soap:Body>
</soap:Envelope>
```

As you can see, the values of the right-side element change more rapidly than those of the left-side element. Because the seat is the rightmost element, all of the seats for a particular row are encoded before the loop moves on to the next row.

In a jagged array, which you can think of as an array of arrays, each element can contain an array of varying lengths. Here is an example:

```
string[][] teams = new string[3][];

teams[0] = new string[3];
teams[0][0] = "Bob";
teams[0][1] = "Sue";
teams[0][2] = "Mike";

teams[1] = new string[2];
teams[1][0] = "Jane";
teams[1][1] = "Mark";

teams[2] = new String[4];
teams[2][0] = "Mary";
teams[2][1] = "Jill";
```

(continued)

```
teams[2][2] = "Jim";
teams[2][3] = "Tom";

RegisterTeams(teams);

public void RegisterTeams(string[][] teams)
{
    // ...
}
```

The *RegisterTeams* function accepts a list of teams. Because teams can vary in the number of players, a two-dimensional jagged array of strings is passed to the function. Each element of the array represents a team and contains an array of player names on that team. Here is how the jagged array is encoded:

```
<?xml version="1.0" encoding="utf-8"?>
<soap:Envelope xmlns:soap="http://schemas.xmlsoap.org/soap/envelope/"
xmlns:soap-enc="http://schemas.xmlsoap.org/soap/encoding/" xmlns:xsi="http://
www.w3.org/2001/XMLSchema-instance">
  <soap:Body>
    <RegisterTeams>
      <teams soap-enc:arrayType="xsi:string[3]">
        <team soap-enc:arrayType="xsi:string[3]">
          <player>Bob</player>
          <player>Sue</player>
          <player>Mike</player>
        </team>
        <team soap-enc:arrayType="xsi:string[2]">
          <player>Jane</player>
          <player>Mark</player>
        </team>
        <team soap-enc:arrayType="xsi:string[4]">
          <player>Mary</player>
          <player>Jill</player>
          <player>Jim</player>
          <player>Tom</player>
        </team>
      </teams>
    </RegisterTeams>
  </soap:Body>
</soap:Envelope>
```

Consistent with the array encoding rules I discussed earlier, the name of the individual elements is not important. For clarity, I named each element in the *teams* array *team* and named each element in the *team* array *player*. In jagged arrays, not only does the *teams* element contain a *soap-enc:arrayType* attribute, but each of the elements within the array of teams contains a *soap-enc:arrayType* attribute as well.

Optimization

In some cases, you might not want to encode the entire array in the body of the message. The SOAP 1.1 specification describes two ways to encode part of an array: partial arrays and sparse arrays. A partial array encodes a select range of elements in the array. A sparse array encodes select elements scattered throughout the array.

Let's say you create an array that can hold the names of up to 1000 registrants for an upcoming event. Periodically, the list of attendees needs to be sent to various interested parties. Soon after the event has been announced, there might be only 5 people registered. If you send the list of registrants, it is not very efficient to encode all 1000 elements because only the first 5 will contain values:

```
// Create an array of attendees, record the first five,
// and then pass the array to RegisteredAttendees.
string[] attendees[1000];

attendees[0] = "Bill Clinton";
attendees[1] = "Jimmy Carter";
attendees[2] = "Ronald Reagan";
attendees[3] = "George Bush";
attendees[4] = "Al Gore";

RegisteredAttendees(attendees);


public void RegisteredAttendees(string[] attendees)
{
    // ...
}
```

```
<?xml version="1.0" encoding="utf-8"?>
<soap:Envelope xmlns:soap="http://schemas.xmlsoap.org/soap/envelope/"
xmlns:soap-enc="http://schemas.xmlsoap.org/soap/encoding/" xmlns:xsi="http://
www.w3.org/2001/XMLSchema-instance">
  <soap:Body>
    <RegisteredAttendees>
      <attendees soap-enc:arrayType="xsi:string[1000]">
        <string>Bill Clinton</string>
        <string>Jimmy Carter</string>
        <string>Ronald Reagan</string>
        <string>George Bush</string>
        <string>Al Gore</string>
      </attendees>
    </RegisteredAttendees>
  </soap:Body>
</soap:Envelope>
```

As you can see in the resulting message, the *soap-enc:arrayType* attribute indicates that the array contains 1000 elements even though only the first 5 were encoded. If you want to encode a portion of the array that does not start with the first element, you can specify the starting element by using the *soap-enc:offset* attribute. For example, if you want to encode the next five attendees that registered for the event, the resulting message would be as follows:

```
<?xml version="1.0" encoding="utf-8"?>
<soap:Envelope xmlns:soap="http://schemas.xmlsoap.org/soap/envelope/"
xmlns:soap-enc="http://schemas.xmlsoap.org/soap/encoding/" xmlns:xsi="http://
www.w3.org/2001/XMLSchema-instance">
  <soap:Body>
    <RegisteredAttendees>
      <attendees soap-enc:arrayType="xsi:string[1000]"
      soap-enc:offset="[5]">
        <string>Gerald Ford</string>
        <string>George W. Bush</string>
        <string>Dick Cheney</string>
        <string>Walter Mondale</string>
        <string>Dan Quayle</string>
      </attendees>
    </RegisteredAttendees>
  </soap:Body>
</soap:Envelope>
```

As you can see, the *soap-enc:offset* element specifies that the array has been offset by five. Therefore, the contents of the array contain the sixth through the tenth elements.

What if the elements to be encoded within the array are not adjacent to each other? Another means of partially encoding arrays is to use the sparse array syntax. For example, say you want to create a message that contains the names of all the registered attendees that did not show up for the event. The ordinal of each attendee has significance, so you are once again creating 1000 elements in an array and populating only a subset of the elements with data.

This time, the data will not be located in a sequential set of elements. Instead, it will be contained in elements throughout the array. You can solve this problem by encoding an array of no-shows by using the sparse array syntax. Here is the resulting message:

```
<?xml version="1.0" encoding="utf-8"?>
<soap:Envelope xmlns:soap="http://schemas.xmlsoap.org/soap/envelope/"
xmlns:soap-enc="http://schemas.xmlsoap.org/soap/encoding/" xmlns:xsi="http://
www.w3.org/2001/XMLSchema-instance">
  <soap:Body>
    <NoShows>
      <registrants soap-enc:arrayType="xsi:string[1000]">
        <string soap-enc:position="[10]">Dan Quayle</string>
```

```
        <string soap-enc:position="[231]">Newt Gingrich</string>
        <string soap-enc:position="[357]">Trent Lott</string>
        <string soap-enc:position="[842]">Hillary Rodham Clinton
        </string>
      </registrants>
    </NoShows>
  </soap:Body>
</soap:Envelope>
```

Once again, the *soap-enc:arrayType* attribute is used to specify that the array contains a total of 1000 elements. However, the elements that contain data are the only ones encoded within the SOAP message. Because the position of the element within the array is relevant, the *soap-enc:position* attribute is used to indicate where the element resides within the array.

Passing Parameters by Reference

Up to this point, I have been explaining how to encode parameters that are passed by value to a Web service. But it is often necessary to pass parameters by reference. For example, a client might pass information about a customer to the server so that the server can update the information on behalf of the client. If the client structure were passed by value, changes made to the client's information would not be visible to the client.

Let's take a look at how parameters that are passed by reference are encoded in a SOAP message. In the first example, I create a series of Fibonacci numbers. A number in a Fibonacci series is determined by adding the two numbers directly preceding it. For example, if $n1 = 1$ and $n2 = 1$, then $n3 = 1 + 1 = 2$ and $n4 = 1 + 2 = 3$. Here is the method I use to output a series of Fibonacci numbers:

```
public void FibonacciIncrement(ref int n1, ref int n2)
{
    int temp = n2;

    // Set n1 and n2 to the next two Fibonacci numbers.
    n1 += n2;
    n2 = temp + n1;
}


// The following code prints the following output:
// 1, 1, 2, 3, 5, 8, 13, 21, 34, 55,
int x = 1;
int y = 1;

for(int i = 1, i < 11, i += 2)
{
    Console.Write("{0}, {1}", x, y);
    FibonacciIncrement(x, y);
}
```

FibonacciIncrement accepts the last two numbers and then returns the next two numbers in the series. Here are the request and response messages for the first call to *FibonacciIncrement*:

```
<!-- Request Message -->
<?xml version="1.0" encoding="utf-8"?>
<soap:Envelope xmlns:soap="http://schemas.xmlsoap.org/soap/envelope/">
  <soap:Body>
    <FibonacciIncrement>
      <n1>1</n1>
      <n2>1</n2>
    </FibonacciIncrement>
  </soap:Body>
</soap:Envelope>


<!-- Request Message -->
<?xml version="1.0" encoding="utf-8"?>
<soap:Envelope xmlns:soap="http://schemas.xmlsoap.org/soap/envelope/">
  <soap:Body>
    <FibonacciIncrementResponse>
      <n1>2</n1>
      <n2>3</n2>
    </FibonacciIncrementResponse>
  </soap:Body>
</soap:Envelope>
```

There is nothing surprising about the first message. The two parameters are encoded as usual. What distinguishes a parameter passed by reference from one that is passed by value is that the client needs to be notified of any changes to the value. Therefore, the new values of *n1* and *n2* are encoded in the response message. Notice that I also follow the convention of appending *Response* to the method element within the body.

Another reason for passing parameters by reference is to maintain the identity of the variable being passed. Consider the following example:

```
// Server Code:
public struct Person
{
    public double    Height;
    public int       Weight;
    public int       Age;
    public string    Hobby;
}

public string Introduce(ref Person p1, ref Person p2)
{
    string result = "";
```

```
    // Do p1 and p2 reference the same variable?
    if(p1.ReferenceEquals(p2))
    {
        throw new Exception("Can't introduce to self.");
    }

    // Are p1 and p2 equal in value?
    if(p1.Equals(p2))
    {
        result = "We have a lot in common!";
    }
    else
    {
        result = "Nice to meet you.";
    }

    return result;
}


// Client Code:
Person p = new Person();
p.Height = 5.7;
p.Weight = 150;
p.Age = 31;
p.Hobby = "Skiing";

// Attempt to introduce a person to himself.
Introduce(ref p, ref p);
```

The *Introduce* method accepts two references to variables of type *Person*. This is similar to passing two integers by reference to *FibonacciIncrement*. However, unlike *FibonacciIncrement*, the *Introduce* method behaves differently depending on whether the two parameters are equal or identical (point to the same instance of *Person*).

The way I encode the parameters passed by reference in the Fibonacci example is not sufficient for the *Introduce* method because it does not maintain the identity of the parameters. SOAP provides the *id/href* pattern for maintaining the identity of the parameters. Here is how the call to *Introduce* would be encoded:

```
<?xml version="1.0" encoding="utf-8"?>
<soap:Envelope xmlns:soap="http://schemas.xmlsoap.org/soap/envelope/"
xmlns:soap-enc="http://schemas.xmlsoap.org/soap/encoding/">
  <soap:Body>

    <Introduce>
      <p1 soap-enc:href="#ref1"/>
```

(continued)

```
    <p2 soap-enc:href="#ref1"/>
  </Introduce>

  <Person soap-enc:id="ref1">
    <Height>5.7</Height>
    <Weight>150</Weight>
    <Age>31</Age>
    <Hobby>Skiing</Hobby>
  </Person>

  </soap:Body>
</soap:Envelope>
```

The encoded parameters do not contain any data. Instead, because both parameters reference the same instance of the *Person* type, the data is encoded once within the body of the message. The root element of the parameter's data is given a unique ID via the *id* attribute.

Instead of containing data themselves, the parameters each refer to the element containing the actual data. This is done by setting the parameter element's *href* attribute equal to the ID of the element containing the data.

As you will see in later chapters, different .NET technologies have varying degrees of support in the way they encode reference parameters. Hopefully, this section has shown why you need to understand the degree to which encoding references are supported by the technology underlying your application. This understanding can help you avoid unexpected behavior within your application.

root Attribute

Sometimes, the root of a serialized object graph is not readily apparent within the resulting SOAP message. Suppose you want to serialize the following object graph that shows the relationships between Kevin Bacon and other actors:

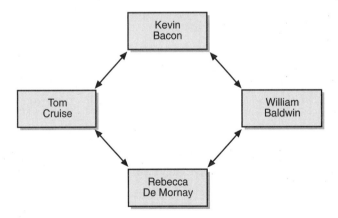

The graph represents two paths from Kevin Bacon to Rebecca De Mornay. Rebecca De Mornay was in the motion picture *Risky Business* (1983) with Tom Cruise, and Tom Cruise was in *A Few Good Men* (1992) with Kevin Bacon. Rebecca De Mornay was also in *Backdraft* (1991) with William Baldwin, and William Baldwin was in *Flatliners* (1990) with Kevin Bacon. The next step is to serialize this data into the body of a SOAP message.

Once this object graph is serialized, you will no longer be able to distinguish which element is the root element. For such cases, SOAP Encoding defines the *root* attribute. You can use this attribute to distinguish serialization roots from other elements that are present in a serialization but are not roots of a serialized value graph. The preceding object graph would be serialized as you see here:

```
<?xml version="1.0" encoding="utf-8"?>
<soap:Envelope xmlns:soap="http://schemas.xmlsoap.org/soap/envelope/"
xmlns:soap-enc="http://schemas.xmlsoap.org/soap/encoding/"
xmlns:hw="urn:hollywood>
  <soap:Body>

    <RelationsToKevinBaconResult>
      <objectGraph soap-enc:href="#actor1"/>
    </RelationsToKevinBaconResult>

    <Actor soap-enc:id="actor1" soap-enc:root="1">
      <Name>Kevin Bacon</Name>
      <Relationships soap-enc:arrayType="hw:Actor[2]">
        <Actor soap-enc:href="actor2"/>
        <Actor soap-enc:href="actor3"/>
      </Relationships>
    </Actor>

    <Actor soap-enc:id="actor2">
      <Name>Tom Cruise</Name>
      <Relationships soap-enc:arrayType="hw:Actor[2]">
        <Actor soap-enc:href="actor1"/>
        <Actor soap-enc:href="actor4"/>
      </Relationships>
    </Actor>

    <Actor soap-enc:id="actor3">
      <Name>William Baldwin</Name>
      <Relationships soap-enc:arrayType="hw:Actor[2]">
        <Actor soap-enc:href="actor1"/>
        <Actor soap-enc:href="actor4"/>
      </Relationships>
    </Actor>
```

(continued)

```
    <Actor soap-enc:id="actor4">
      <Name>Rebecca De Mornay</Name>
      <Relationships soap-enc:arrayType="hw:Actor[2]">
        <Actor soap-enc:href="actor2"/>
        <Actor soap-enc:href="actor3"/>
      </Relationships>
    </Actor>

  </soap:Body>
</soap:Envelope>
```

The *root* attribute identifies Kevin Bacon as the root in the object graph of actors. I could also have optionally decorated nonroot objects with the *root* attribute and set it to *0*.

Protocol Binding

You have learned how to properly encode a SOAP message, but you still need a way to send the message to the remote application. One advantage of SOAP is that it is not tied to a particular transport protocol. SOAP messages can be sent over any transport protocol that is capable of carrying XML.

Arguably the most popular transport protocol used to send SOAP messages is HTTP. However, SOAP messages can also be sent via SMTP, via fax, to a ship at sea via a shortwave radio, or whatever else can be dreamed up.

How a SOAP message is carried by a particular transport protocol is known as the *protocol binding*. A protocol binding can be defined to exploit any unique characteristics of the transport protocol. As you will soon learn, the HTTP POST binding extends the protocol so that HTTP-aware firewalls have the ability to filter SOAP messages.

The SOAP specification describes only one protocol binding: sending SOAP messages via HTTP POST. Therefore, the only protocol binding I will discuss is HTTP POST.

Most SOAP implementations, including .NET, support the HTTP protocol. Because most systems support HTTP, it has arguably become the protocol of choice for ensuring that a Web service has a high degree of interoperability between different platforms. The advantages of the HTTP protocol include the following:

- **It is firewall friendly.** Older protocols such as Distributed Component Object Model (DCOM) are not. Most firewalls have port 80, at the very least, open for HTTP traffic.

- **It has a robust supporting infrastructure.** Many technologies have been introduced in the effort to increase the scalability and availability of HTTP-based applications. I will discuss this further in Chapter 12.

■   **It is inherently stateless.** The stateless nature of HTTP helps ensure that communication between the client and the server is reliable, especially across the Internet. Intermittent dropped connections pose problems for protocols such as DCOM and CORBA.

■   **It is simple.** The HTTP protocol is composed of a header section and a body section.

■   **It maps nicely to RPC-style message exchanges.** HTTP is a natural protocol for RPC-style communication because a request is always accompanied by a response.

■   **It is open.** Practically every network-aware system supports HTTP.

An HTTP request is composed of two parts, a header and a body. The header contains information about the request and about the client that sent the request. The body follows the header and is delimited by two carriage-return/linefeed pairs. The body contains the payload, which in this case would be the SOAP message. Here is an example of an HTTP request that contains a SOAP message:

```
POST /SomeWebService HTTP/1.1
Content-Type: text/xml
SOAPAction: "http://somedomain.com/SomeWebService.wsdl"
Content-Length: 243
Host: sshort3


<?xml version="1.0" encoding="utf-8"?>
<soap:Envelope xmlns:soap="http://schemas.xmlsoap.org/soap/envelope/"
xmlns:soap-enc="http://schemas.xmlsoap.org/soap/encoding/">
  <soap:Body>
    <Add>
      <x>2</x>
      <y>2</y>
    </Add>
  </soap:Body>
</soap:Envelope>
```

The HTTP header for a SOAP message is similar to that for an HTML request, with a couple of differences: The *Content-Type* header entry is always set to *text/xml*, and the body of the message contains the SOAP message. The other difference is that every SOAP HTTP POST request must contain a *SOAPAction* header entry.

The *SOAPAction* header entry is used to communicate the intent of the SOAP message. The URI can be represented in any format and is not required to be resolvable. In my example, the URI resolves to the Web Services Description Language (WSDL) document for the Web service. I will cover WSDL in Chapter 5.

The value of the *SOAPAction* header can be blank if the intent of the SOAP message is conveyed in the HTTP request header entry. The HTTP request is the first entry in the header and contains the action (in this case, always POST) and the targeted URI. If the URI in the HTTP request header entry adequately communicates the intent of the SOAP message, either of the following entries would be valid:

```
SOAPAction: ""
SOAPAction:
```

The HTTP response is used to communicate the results of the SOAP request.

```
HTTP/1.1 200 OK
Server: Microsoft-IIS/5.0
Date: Sun, 25 Mar 2001 19:44:55 GMT
Content-Type: text/xml
Content-Length: 243
```

```
<?xml version="1.0" encoding="utf-8"?>
<soap:Envelope xmlns:soap="http://schemas.xmlsoap.org/soap/envelope/">
  <soap:Body>
    <AddResponse>
      <result>4</result>
    </AddResponse>
  </soap:Body>
</soap:Envelope>
```

Once again, the MIME type is set to *text/xml*. For RPC-style messages, the HTTP body contains the SOAP response message. Otherwise, the HTTP body would be empty. Because the example request message results in a response message being generated from the server, the HTTP body contains the results.

In either case, the status reported in the first line of the HTTP header must contain a value between 200 and 299. In the event of an error while processing the SOAP message, the HTTP status must be 500, indicating that an internal server error occurred.

Summary

In this chapter, you learned about the underlying messaging protocol of Web services, SOAP. Specifically, you learned about the following:

- **The SOAP envelope.** How it is used to encode header information about the message and the body of the message itself

- **SOAP Encoding.** How data can be serialized into a SOAP message

- **RPC messages.** How RPC messages facilitate procedure-oriented communication via request/response message patterns

- **The HTTP POST protocol binding.** How SOAP messages can be transported via HTTP

You learned that, at a bare minimum, a SOAP message must be contained within a well-formed SOAP envelope. An envelope is composed of a single *Envelope* element. The envelope can contain a *Header* element and must contain a *Body* element. If present, the header must be the immediate child element within the envelope, with the body immediately following the header. The body contains the payload of the message, and the header contains additional data that does not necessarily belong in the body of the message.

In addition to defining a SOAP envelope, the SOAP specification defines a way of encoding the data contained within a message. SOAP Encoding provides a standard means of serializing data types that are not defined within part 1 of the XML Schema specification. This includes arrays and references to instances of data types.

The SOAP specification also provides a standard message pattern for facilitating RPC-style behavior. Two SOAP messages are paired together to facilitate a request message and an associated response.

The method call and its parameters are serialized in the body of the request message in the form of a structure. The root element carries the same name as the targeted method, with each inbound parameter encoded as a subelement.

The response message will either contain the results of the method call or a well-defined fault structure. The results of the method call are serialized in the body of the request as a structure. By convention, the root element carries the same name as the original method call with *Result* appended to it. The return parameters are serialized as child elements, with the return parameter appearing first. If an error is encountered, the body of the response message will contain a well-defined fault structure.

4

XML Schema

SOAP provides a standard method of encoding data into an XML document. This technology is also extremely flexible. Anything can be encoded into the body of a SOAP message as long as it does not invalidate the XML. The body of a message can contain a request for the latest weather information, a purchase order, part of an instant message thread, a satellite image, or whatever else the implementer of a Web service can dream up.

With the variety of content and types of data that can be contained within a SOAP message, you need a way of expressing the structure of a message. You also need a way to determine the type of data that should appear within a message.

One potential solution could be for the developer to provide a sample of what a valid SOAP message should look like. For example, say you need to interface with a Web service to place an order with a vendor, and the vendor has provided the following sample message:

```
<?xml version="1.0" encoding="utf-8"?>
<soap:Envelope xmlns:soap="http://schemas.xmlsoap.org/soap/envelope/">
  <soap:Body>
    <PurchaseItem>
      <Item>Apple</Item>
      <Quantity>12</Quantity>
    </PurchaseItem>
  </soap:Body>
</soap:Envelope>
```

The XML document is pretty straightforward. From the sample message, you can see that the Web service accepts two parameters, *Item* and *Quantity*. Both of these parameters are child elements of the *PurchaseItem* element.

The problem is that the sample message leaves a lot of ambiguity remaining. For example, you know you need to pass an *Item* parameter, but should it contain a short description of the item? Should it contain one of a select number of enumerations? Is the value limited to a maximum number of characters?

There are just as many questions regarding the *Quantity* parameter. Can you specify partial quantities such as 1.5 cases? Is there a minimum number that must be purchased? Is there a maximum number that can be purchased?

One way to clear up the ambiguity would be to have the sample message be accompanied by a document that describes all of the nuances of the message because at the very least, the Web service needs to validate the received message. Also, you would probably want to validate the message before you sent it to the Web service. But with this approach, both you and the developer of the Web service would probably be stuck hand-writing validation code. This doesn't sound very pleasant or productive.

What's needed is a standard way of describing the structure and the type of information that should be contained within an XML message sent to the Web service. In other words, you need a way of representing the schema an XML message must conform to in order to be processed by the Web service. Furthermore, the schema needs to be standardized and accompanied by a set of APIs that can be used to programmatically validate an XML document against the schema.

By the end of this chapter, you will be armed with more than enough information to create schemas for your Web services. In this chapter, I will create a schema for the Commerce Web service. This schema will describe the expected format of the request and response message of the *PurchaseItem* method.

Describing XML Documents

You can use a schema to describe the structure of an XML document and its type information. The two dominant technologies for defining an XML schema are document type definitions (DTDs) and XML Schema. You can use DTDs to define the structure of an XML document but not to describe the contents of a document. Here is an example:

```
<!-- Request Message -->
<!ELEMENT PurchaseItem      (Quantity, Item)>
    <!ELEMENT Quantity      (#PCDATA)>
    <!ELEMENT Item          (#PCDATA)>

<!-- Response Message -->
<!Element PurchaseItemResult    (Amount)>
    <!ELEMENT Amount            (#PCDATA)>
```

At first glance, it should be apparent that the DTD syntax is not XML-based. DTDs cannot be parsed using XML parsers and cannot be easily embedded into other XML documents. You will see why this is important for Web services when WSDL is discussed in the next chapter.

DTDs do describe the structure of the document, but they cannot express the type of data it contains. There is no notion of fundamental types within DTDs such as integers and strings, nor is there support for defining your own types.

In the preceding example, both the *Quantity* and the *Item* elements are declared as *#PCDATA*. This doesn't give you any insight into the type of data they can contain. For example, the DTD doesn't indicate whether it is valid to list partial quantities such as 1.5 cases. It also doesn't indicate whether the *Item* element should contain a numeric product ID or just a string containing a description of the item.

A proposed standard submitted to the W3C called Datatypes for DTDs (DT4DTD) 1.0 (*http://www.w3.org/TR/dt4dtd*) provides a means of grafting type information into DTD schemas. As of this writing, the proposal has been listed as a note for more than a year and a half and does not appear to be gaining much traction. DTDs should be considered legacy technology for defining XML schemas because of their limitations and lack of industry support.

The recommended way to express schemas for XML-based Web services is via XML Schema. XML Schema comprises two specifications managed by the W3C, XML Schema Part 1: Structures (*http://www.w3.org/TR/xmlschema-1/*) and XML Schema Part 2: Datatypes (*http://www.w3.org/TR/xmlschema-2/*). As of May 2, 2001, both specifications are recommendations of the W3C.

XML Schema provides a rich syntax for defining schemas used to validate XML instance documents. It not only allows you to define the structure of an XML document, but it also allows you to define the type of data the document contains and any constraints on that data. Also, it lets you specify foreign key and referential integrity constraints. Here is a simple example:

```
<?xml version='1.0'?>
<schema xmlns='http://www.w3.org/2001/XMLSchema'>

  <!-- Response Message (work-in-progress) -->
  <element name='Amount'/>

</schema>
```

As you can see, the sample schema is a valid XML document that is capable of being consumed by any standard XML parser. A schema definition is contained within a root *schema* element. The example schema defines one element named *Amount*.

XML documents that can be validated against a schema are called *instance documents*. The following is an instance document for the schema described previously:

```
<?xml version='1.0'?>
<Amount>351.43</Amount>
```

Built-In Datatypes

One of the more useful features of XML Schema is that it defines a core set of datatypes. These include basic programming types such as *string, int, float,* and *double*; mathematical types such as *integer* and *decimal*; and XML types such as *NMTOKEN* and *IDREF*.

One of the most significant advantages of the XML Schema type system is that it is completely platform independent. Values of types are consistently represented no matter what hardware, operating system, or XML processing software is used. The XML Schema type system allows XML-based protocols such as SOAP to achieve strong interoperability in heterogeneous computing environments.

Datatypes are useful for defining schemas that describe the type of data that must be contained within a document. I will heavily leverage datatypes when I describe how to create schemas later in this chapter. Another way that you can leverage the XML Schema type system is by annotating an XML document with the type of data it contains. This helps remove ambiguity about the intentions of the document's creator.

In the previous section, I created a SOAP message to submit a *PurchaseItem* request. Here, I will use the built-in datatypes to indicate the types of the parameters being passed:

```
<?xml version="1.0" encoding="utf-8"?>
<soap:Envelope xmlns:soap="http://schemas.xmlsoap.org/soap/envelope/"
xmlns:xsi="http://www.w3.org/2001/XMLSchema-instance">
  <soap:Body>
    <PurchaseItem>
      <item xsi:type="xsi:string">Apple</item>
      <quantity xsi:type="xsi:int">1</quantity>
    </PurchaseItem>
  </soap:Body>
</soap:Envelope>
```

I added an *xsi:type* attribute to each parameter element. The value of the attribute represents the datatype of the encoded parameter. Decorating elements within an XML document with type information removes all ambiguity regarding the type of data the sender encoded into the message. The recipient of the preceding message will know that *quantity* is represented as an *int* and *item* is represented as a *string*.

The SOAP specification defines a *polymorphic accessor* as an element whose type is determined at run time. The polymorphic accessor is conceptually similar to the *Object* type in Visual Basic .NET. If a polymorphic accessor appears within a SOAP message, it must contain a *type* attribute indicating the type of data the element contains.

The Appendix provides a full list of XML Schema built-in datatypes. Note that SOAP 1.1 was defined against a working draft of the XML Schema specification published in 1999. Some of the built-in types have undergone name changes through the course of becoming a recommendation. Even though the SOAP 1.1 specification and its related schemas reference a previous version of the XML Schema, most SOAP implementations including ASP.NET and Remoting reference the built-in datatypes defined by the current XML Schema specification.

In the remainder of this section, I cover a few of the more interesting datatypes.

Integers

The XML Schema language defines a number of types that are used to describe integers. The two types that often get confused are *integer* and *int*. The *int* type is actually a derivative of the *integer* type with additional restrictions.

Even though both *int* and *integer* represent an integer value, they serve different purposes. Elements and attributes of type *integer* contain a value that meets the mathematical definition of an integer. Numbers of type *integer* are boundless and therefore might contain values that cause an overflow condition if copied into a CPU's register. Because elements and attributes of type *int* are restricted to containing a 32-bit integer, they are better suited for computer science applications.

The same distinction holds true for decimal numbers. Instances of the *float* type conform to the Institute of Electrical and Electronics Engineers (IEEE) single-precision floating point type. On the other hand, the *decimal* type represents an arbitrary precision decimal number.

Strings

XML Schema defines a *string* datatype, but it is not identical to the *string* type in many database or programming languages. In particular, *string* types in many database and programming languages allow characters that are forbidden to appear in the XML Schema *string* datatype.

Characters that might invalidate or alter the meaning of the XML document cannot be contained within an element or attribute of type *string*. For example, reserved characters such as the less than and ampersand signs carry special meaning and cannot appear within an XML document. Other characters such as quotation marks and apostrophes cannot appear within the value of an attribute. These characters must be escaped or encoded in some fashion before they can be serialized into an XML document.

XML defines a means of encoding individual characters within an XML document by using character references. A character reference consists of an ampersand followed by a character identifier and then a semicolon. The character identifier can be either the numeric identifier of a Unicode character or a character entity reference.

A numeric character reference is used to identify a specific character in the Unicode (ISO/IEC 10646) character set. The character identifier is either the decimal or hexadecimal value of the character, prefixed by a pound sign. For example, the character *A* can be encoded as *A* or *A*.

The XML specification provides character entity references, which are more readable character identifiers for a small subset of Unicode characters. Even though the HTML 4 specification defines hundreds of character entity references, the XML specification defines only five, for characters that interfere with well-formed XML, as shown in Table 4-1.

Table 4-1 XML Character Entity References

Character	Numeric Character Reference	Character Entity Reference
"	*"* or *"*	*"*
'	*'* or *'*	*'*
&	*&* or *&*	*&*
<	*<* or *<*	*<*
>	*>* or *>*	*>*

Double quotes and apostrophes have character entity references defined for them because under certain conditions they are not allowed within the value of an attribute. If the value of an attribute is surrounded by double quotes, a double quote cannot appear within the value of the attribute. The same holds true for apostrophes. For example, the following elements contain illegal characters:

```
<e a="Scott says, "This is illegal."">
<e a='Don't do this, either.'>
```

The following elements are valid:

```
<e a='Scott says, "This is perfectly fine."'>
<e a="This isn't a problem, either.">
```

Yet another way to embed strings with reserved characters within an XML document is within CDATA sections. XML defines the sequence of characters *<![CDATA[* to tell the XML processor to ignore special characters until *]]>* is encountered. Here is an example:

```
<myString><![CDATA[I can now use all five reserved characters. (", ', &, <,
and >)]]></myString>
```

When you serialize string variables into an XML document, be sure to encode special characters using character references or escape the string within a CDATA section.

Binary Data

Binary data must be encoded before being inserted into an XML document to ensure that it does not introduce any characters that might invalidate the XML. The XML Schema specification defines two built-in datatypes for binary data, *base64Binary* and *hexBinary*.

Type *hexBinary* encodes each binary octet into its two-character hexadecimal equivalent. For example, the binary value of *11111111* would be encoded as *FF*, *ff*, *Ff*, or *fF*.

The .NET platform provides support for encoding and decoding binhex. You can use the *XmlTextReader.ReadBinHex* method to decode binhex to binary data and the *XmlTextWriter.WriteBinHex* method to encode binary data to binhex.

It is far more common to see binary data of type *base64Binary*. This is especially true with Web services because the SOAP 1.1 specification recommends that all binary data embedded in a message be encoded using the base64 algorithm defined by RFC 2045.

Elements and attributes of type *base64Binary* contain data that are encoded using the Base64 encoding algorithm described in RFC 2045. As Table 4-2 shows, each 6-bit chunk of an array of binary octets is encoded into an XML-compatible character.

Table 4-2 The Base64 Alphabet

Binary	Base64	Binary	Base64	Binary	Base64	Binary	Base64
000000	A	010000	Q	100000	g	110000	w
000001	B	010001	R	100001	h	110001	x
000010	C	010010	S	100010	i	110010	y
000011	D	010011	T	100011	j	110011	z
000100	E	010100	U	100100	k	110100	0
000101	F	010101	V	100101	l	110101	1
000110	G	010110	W	100110	m	110110	2
000111	H	010111	X	100111	n	110111	3
001000	I	011000	Y	101000	o	111000	4
001001	J	011001	Z	101001	p	111001	5
001010	K	011010	a	101010	q	111010	6
001011	L	011011	b	101011	r	111011	7
001100	M	011100	c	101100	s	111100	8
001101	N	011101	d	101101	t	111101	9
001110	O	011110	e	101110	u	111110	+
001111	P	011111	f	101111	v	111111	/

Base64 also defines a 65th character for padding purposes. One or more = signs can appear at the end of the encoded string. If the binary object fits neatly into 6-bit chunks, no padding characters are applied to the end of the Base64 string. All other conditions require zeros added to the end of the binary object. An = character is appended to the end of the encoded string for every two zeros added to the binary object. Because a binary object is composed of a series of bytes (8 bits), there are three possible scenarios, including the one just mentioned:

- **A single byte remains to be encoded.** In this case, four zeros are appended, the two resulting 6-bit chunks are encoded, and two = characters are appended to the end of the encoded string.

- **Two bytes remain to be encoded.** In this case, two zeros are appended, the three resulting 6-bit chunks are encoded, and a single = character is appended to the end of the encoded string.

- **Three bytes remain to be encoded.** In this case, the remaining bytes can be evenly divided into four 6-bit chunks, so no = character is appended to the end of the encoded string.

Much like binhex, *XmlTextWriter* and *XmlTextReader* provide the *WriteBase64* and *ReadBase64* methods for encoding and decoding Base64-encoded data. In addition, the .NET platform take cares of properly encoding and decoding binary data for Web services built on top of the ASP.NET and Remoting frameworks. You saw an example of this in Chapter 2, where I created an ASP.NET Web service that sent and received binary files.

Namespaces

Namespaces are leveraged heavily in XML schemas, so I can't go much further without first discussing what namespaces are and how they are defined.

Namespaces provide logical boundaries for entities defined within a schema. For example, in the previous section I created a schema that defines the *Amount* element. What if someone else defines an *Amount* element? If an *Amount* element appears in an instance document, how do I know whether it is an instance of the one defined by my schema or theirs? If each *Amount* element were defined within a separate namespace, the *Amount* element would be fully qualified to a particular namespace and therefore would be unambiguous.

targetNamespace Attribute

The *targetNamespace* attribute is used to set the identifier of the namespace. The value of this attribute is a URI that serves as an opaque pointer to reference the namespace. The following are examples of valid identifiers for namespaces:

```
http://somedomain.com/
http://somedomain.com/Commerce
urn:Commerce-SomeDomain-Com
urn:Com:SomeDomain:Commerce
urn:WebService:SoapBased:Commerce
```

The first two URIs are URLs that specify a registered domain name. The last three URIs are location-independent Uniform Resource Names (URNs). One of the benefits of defining a namespace within the context of a registered domain name is that you avoid potential naming collisions with namespaces defined by others.

A namespace identified by a URI is defined within a schema document. Entities that can be scoped to namespaces include datatypes, elements, and attributes. Within an XML Schema document, the *schema* element can contain a *targetNamespace* parameter that contains a URI for the schema.

The following code defines a namespace of the schema for the Commerce Web service. For now, it contains the definition for the *Amount* element. I will enhance it later.

```
<?xml version='1.0'?>
<schema xmlns='http://www.w3.org/2001/XMLSchema' targetNamespace='urn:Commerce'>

  <!-- Response Message (work-in-progress) -->
  <element name='Amount'/>

</schema>
```

I added the *targetNamespace* attribute to the *schema* element and then set its value to the *Commerce* URN. All entities defined by the schema are scoped within the *Commerce* namespace. In this case, the only entity defined is the *Amount* element.

xmlns Attribute

To fully qualify the entities referenced within an XML document, you need to reference one or more schemas. XML documents that reference schemas are instance documents and schemas themselves. Instance documents must refer to the namespace URI in order to fully qualify the entities referenced. You can accomplish this by adding an *xmlns* attribute to any element within the document. Here is an example:

```
<?xml version='1.0'?>
<Amount xmlns='urn:Commerce'>123.45<Amount/>
```

In the instance document, I set the default namespace to *Commerce*. As a result, *Amount* and its subelements, if it had any, are fully qualified within the *Commerce* namespace.

When you reference a namespace, you can assign the reference a moniker. The assignment of a moniker to a referenced namespace takes the form of *xmlns:moniker='SomeURI'*. You can then use the moniker to fully qualify entities appearing within the XML document that are defined within the referenced namespace.

To fully qualify an entity such as a type definition or an element declaration, you prefix the entity with the moniker followed by a colon. You saw this type of use of namespace monikers in the previous chapter. All of the example SOAP messages defined the *soap:* namespace moniker within the reference to the SOAP schema, as shown here:

```
<?xml version="1.0" encoding="utf-8"?>
<soap:Envelope xmlns:soap="http://schemas.xmlsoap.org/soap/envelope/">
  <soap:Body>

    <!-- SOAP message -->

  </soap:Body>
</soap:Envelope>
```

It is often necessary to reference multiple schemas. You can do this by adding multiple *xmlns* attributes. These are often added to the root element of the document for better readability and developer convenience. However, schema references can be made in any element within the instance document. Here is a SOAP message that contains two *Amount* elements in the message body:

```
<?xml version="1.0" encoding="utf-8"?>
<soap:Envelope xmlns:soap="http://schemas.xmlsoap.org/soap/envelope/">
  <soap:Body>
    <Amount xmlns='urn:Commerce'>123.45</Amount>
    <soap:Amount xmlns:soap='urn:Commerce'>123.45</soap:Amount>
  </soap:Body>
</soap:Envelope>
```

Even though I used different syntax, both *Amount* elements in the preceding document are equivalent. Let's look at how I used the individual namespace references.

Three namespace references were made. The first reference was made in the root element and defines the *soap:* moniker that is used to fully qualify entities referenced in the SOAP Envelope schema. The second reference sets *Commerce* as the default namespace for the first *Amount* element and its child elements (if any existed). The final reference overrides the *soap:* moniker defined earlier to instead reference the Commerce schema for the second *Amount* element and its children (if any existed).

Namespace references apply to the element that contains the *xmlns* attribute and all of its child elements. Therefore, if a namespace declaration is made within the SOAP *Header* element, the declaration applies to all elements within the header. Because references are scoped to the element in which they are declared, the reference made in the SOAP *Header* element does not apply to the SOAP *Body* element or any of its child elements.

Namespace references are also used heavily in schema documents. Within schema documents, it is often necessary to reference entities defined within the document. You can do this by creating a reference within the schema document to itself. By convention, this reference is usually associated with the *tns:* moniker, which is short for "this namespace." Here is a portion of the SOAP Envelope schema that shows the use of the *tns:* moniker:

```
<?xml version='1.0'?>
<!-- XML Schema for SOAP v 1.1 Envelope -->

<!-- Copyright 2000 DevelopMentor, International Business Machines Corporation,
     Lotus Development Corporation, Microsoft, UserLand Software -->

<schema xmlns='http://www.w3.org/1999/XMLSchema'
```

(continued)

```
              xmlns:tns='http://schemas.xmlsoap.org/soap/envelope/'
              targetNamespace='http://schemas.xmlsoap.org/soap/envelope/'>

  <!-- Definition for the Envelope element -->
  <element name="Envelope" type="tns:Envelope"/>

  <!-- Definition for the Envelope type -->
  <complexType name='Envelope'>
    <element ref='tns:Header' minOccurs='0'/>
    <element ref='tns:Body' minOccurs='1'/>
    <any minOccurs='0' maxOccurs='*'/>
    <anyAttribute/>
  </complexType>

  <!-- The rest of the SOAP Envelope schema... -->

</schema>
```

The *schema* element sets the target namespace to *http://schemas.xml-soap.org/soap/envelope/*. It also contains a reference to itself that is given the moniker *tns:*. The schema defines the *Envelope* element. The *Envelope* element is declared as type *Envelope*. Because the type definition is contained within the schema, it is prefixed by *tns:*.

schemaLocation Attribute

The URI of a namespace reference is an opaque pointer. So even if the URI is specified in the form of a URL, you cannot count on it to resolve to the actual schema document. However, you can use the *schemaLocation* attribute to give the parser hints on where the schema documents that define the referenced namespaces are located.

The value of the *schemaLocation* attribute is a whitespace-delimited string. It contains the URI of the schema followed by the URL that resolves to the schema document that is used to define the namespace. Multiple hints can be given within a single *schemaLocation* attribute. Here is an example:

```
<?xml version='1.0'?>
<Amount xmlns='urn:Commerce'
xmlns:xsi='http://www.w3.org/2001/XMLSchema-instance'
xsi:schemaLocation='urn:Commerce http://somedomain/Commerce.xsd
http://www.w3.org/2001/XMLSchema-instance
http://www.w3.org/2001/XMLSchema.xsd'>

   123.45

</Amount>
```

For illustrative purposes, the instance document references two namespaces, the *Commerce* namespace and the *XML Schema Instance* namespace. Because the

URI for the Commerce schema is in the form of a URN, it is not resolvable. However, even though the URI for the XML Schema Instance schema is in the form of a URL, it is not directly resolvable either. Therefore, I use the *schemaLocation* attribute to provide a hint about where the schema documents for the associated namespace URIs can be located.

I will cover a couple more points regarding the *schemaLocation* attribute before moving on to the next topic. The *schemaLocation* attribute can be applied to any element within the instance document. However, unlike most other XML Schema attributes, the *schemaLocation* attribute stays in effect for the remainder of the document, not just for its child elements. Finally, because the *schemaLocation* attribute serves as a hint, the parser might choose to locate the schema document for a particular namespace using some other method.

noNamespaceSchemaLocation Attribute

Schemas are not required to define namespaces. You can use the *noNamespace-SchemaLocation* attribute to reference schemas with no namespace. Here is an example:

```
<?xml version='1.0'?>
<!-- File named Commerce.xsd -->

<schema>
  <!-- Response Message (work-in-progress) -->
  <element name='Amount' type=/>
</schema>
```

I defined a schema without a namespace definition that is contained within the file Commerce.xsd. Next I will create an instance document that references the schema:

```
<?xml version='1.0'?>
<Amount xmlns:xsi='http://www.w3.org/2001/XMLSchema-instance'
xsi:noNamespaceSchemaLocation='file:Commerce.xsd'>
  123.45
</Amount>
```

Because the *Amount* element is not defined within a namespace, I used the *noNamespaceSchemaLocation* attribute to reference the schema. The *Amount* element is then fully qualified with respect to the Commerce.xsd schema.

Even though entities not defined within a namespace can be referenced, this syntax is awkward and fragile. Therefore, you should avoid defining schemas without namespaces. If you do have to reference a schema that does not contain a namespace definition, consider importing the schema into a namespace definition. I discuss importing schemas later in this chapter.

XML Schema and *XML Schema Instance* Namespaces

The XML specification defines two fundamental namespaces, the *XML Schema* namespace and the *XML Schema Instance* namespace. Even though they share a common subset of entities such as type, element, and attribute definitions, each namespace serves a specific purpose. The *XML Schema* namespace should be referenced within schema documents, and the *XML Schema Instance* namespace should be referenced within instance documents.

The *XML Schema* namespace contains the entities used to define schemas. For example, the *element* and *schema* elements used in the *Commerce* schema are defined in the *XML Schema* namespace. The URI for the *XML Schema* namespace is *http://www.w3.org/2001/XMLSchema,* and by convention the namespace is often referenced by the *xsd:* moniker.

The *XML Schema Instance* namespace should be referenced by instance documents that use entities defined within the namespace. For example, the *schemaLocation* attribute used in instance documents is defined within the *XML Schema Instance* namespace. The URI for the XML Schema Instance namespace is *http://www.w3.org/2001/XMLSchema-instance*, and by convention the namespace is often referenced by the *xsi:* moniker.

Element Definitions

As you have seen, elements are defined using the *element* element. The *name* attribute is used to specify the name of the element that will appear in the instance document. You can also use the *type* attribute to indicate what type of data the element can contain. I will enhance the definition of the *Amount* element to indicate that it can contain only data of the built-in type *double*:

```
<?xml version='1.0'?>
<schema xmlns='http://www.w3.org/2001/XMLSchema'
targetNamespace='urn:Commerce'>
  <element name='Amount' type='double'/>
</schema>
```

Element definitions can also specify whether an element can contain a *nil* value. You can optionally set the element's *nillable* attribute to *true* or *false*. If the *nillable* attribute is not specified, the default value is *false*. For example, when a client calls the *PurchaseItem* method on my Commerce Web service, I might or might not have access to the pricing information to return the cost of the purchase. If the pricing information is unavailable, I do not want to give away products for free. Therefore, I should return a *null* value to indicate that pricing was unavailable instead of zero. The following is a modified version of the previous schema that allows the *Amount* element to contain a *null* value:

```
<?xml version='1.0'?>
<schema xmlns='http://www.w3.org/2001/XMLSchema'
targetNamespace='urn:Commerce'>
  <!-- Response Message (work-in-progress) -->
  <element name='Amount' type='double' nillable='true'/>
</schema>
```

To specify that the element within an instance document contains a *nil* value, you use the *xsi:nil* attribute:

```
<?xml version='1.0'?>
<Amount xmlns:xsi='http://www.w3.org/2001/XMLSchema-instance'
xmlns='urn:Commerce' xsi:nil='true'/>
```

Because the *Amount* element is set to *nil*, the instance document is valid even though the *Amount* element does not contain a value of type *double*. It is also worth noting that the *xsi:nil* attribute applies only to the value of the element and does not apply to its attributes, if any are defined.

Custom Datatypes

The XML Schema type system is highly extensible. It provides a mechanism for defining new datatypes that inherit from either built-in datatypes or custom datatypes. Datatypes fall into two categories, simple types and complex types. Simple types cannot contain subelements or attributes; custom types can.

Simple Types

Simple types are datatypes that can be used to describe the type of data contained within an element or an attribute. Instances of simple types cannot contain attributes or other elements. Examples of simple types include *int*, *long*, *string*, and *dateTime*. A simple type can also define an enumeration or a union.

A simple type definition always derives from another simple type. The three types of derivations allowed by XML Schema are by restriction, by list, and by union.

A simple type derived from its base type by restriction can define additional restrictions imposed on the values that instances of the simple type can contain. Therefore, instances of a simple type derived by restriction can contain only a subset of the values that can be contained by its base type.

For example, the built-in *double* type is a restricted version of the *decimal* type. Instances of the *decimal* type are unbounded, and instances of the *double* type are restricted to values that meet the IEEE single-precision 64-bit floating type. Following are a couple of simple type definitions that derive by restriction.

```xml
<?xml version='1.0'?>
<schema xmlns="http://www.w3.org/2001/XMLSchema.xsd">

  <simpleType name="MyInt">
    <restriction base="int"/>
  </simpleType>

  <simpleType name="GenericProductId">
    <restriction base="string">
      <minLength value="1"/>
      <maxLength value="20"/>
    </restriction>
  </simpleType>

  <simpleType name="Percent">
    <restriction base="integer">
      <minInclusive value="0"/>
      <maxInclusive value="100"/>
    </restriction>
  </simpleType>

</schema>
```

The first simple type definition, *MyInt,* defines a datatype to which no additional restrictions were applied. A value of type *MyInt* can contain any value defined by its base type, *int*.

The second simple type definition, *GenericProductId*, defines a restricted version of the *string* datatype. Values of the type can contain a string from 1 to 20 characters. The *Percent* definition is similar; it restricts values of the type to integers between 0 and 100.

The XML Schema describes a whole host of constraints (shown in Table 4-3) that can be applied to simple type definitions.

Table 4-3   XML Schema Datatype Constraints

Constraints	Definition
length	Instances of the type must contain a fixed-length number of units.
minLength	Instances of the type must contain a minimum number of units.
maxLength	Instances of the type can contain only a maximum number of units.
pattern	Instances of the type can contain only data that matches a specific pattern defined by a regular expression. For example, a regular expression that can be used to define a Social Security Number would be *[0-9]{3}-[0-9]{2}-[0-9]{4}*.
enumeration	Instances of the type can contain only a specified set of values.

Table 4-3   XML Schema Datatype Constraints   *(continued)*

Constraints	Definition
whiteSpace	Instances of the type derived from *string* are processed by the XML parser one of three ways depending on the attribute's value. The default value *preserve* states that the value is left unchanged. The value *replace* states that all occurrences of tabs, line feeds, and carriage returns will be replaced with spaces. The value *collapse* states that any sequence of spaces will be collapsed to a single space.
minInclusive	Instances of the type cannot contain a value less than the value specified. The value of *minInclusive* must be at least as restrictive as its base type.
minExclusive	Instances of the type cannot contain a value less than or equal to the value specified. The value of *minExclusive* must be at least as restrictive as its base type.
maxInclusive	Instances of the type cannot contain a value less than the value specified. The value of *maxInclusive* must be at least as restrictive as its base type.
maxExclusive	Instances of the type cannot contain a value less than or equal to the value specified. The value of *maxExclusive* must be at least as restrictive as its base type.
totalDigits	Specifies the maximum number of digits an instance of the type can contain. The type must derive from *decimal*.
fractionDigits	Specifies the maximum number of digits to the right of the decimal point an instance of the type can contain. The type must derive from *decimal*.

One of the more interesting constraints is *pattern*. The *pattern* constraint allows you to define a regular expression that will be used to limit to potential values of a particular type. By leveraging *pattern* constraints within your simple type definition, you can significantly reduce the amount of validation code you need to write for your Web service.

Let's take a look at an example of where a pattern restriction can be helpful. Recall that the *OrderItem* method exposed by the Commerce Web service accepts a parameter called *Item*. In the previous example, I defined a type called *ProductId* for defining the type of data that can be contained within the *Item* element.

In addition to length restrictions, suppose that an instance of a *ProductId* cannot contain the following characters: / \ [ ] : ; | = , + * < >. If I were to use the *ProductId* type as defined previously, I would have to write code to ensure that no illegal characters were included within the *Item* element. Instead, I will add a *pattern* constraint to the *ProductId* definition that restricts the type of characters that values of that type can contain.

```
<?xml version='1.0'?>
<schema xmlns="http://www.w3.org/2001/XMLSchema.xsd"
xmlns:tns="urn:Commerce" targetNamespace="urn:Commerce">

  <simpleType name="ProductId">
    <restriction base="string">
      <minLength value="1"/>
      <maxLength value="20"/>
      <pattern value='[^/\&#x5B;&#x5D;:;|=,+*?&gt;&lt;]+'/>
    </restriction>
  </simpleType>

  <!-- Request Message (work-in-progress) -->
  <element name='Item' type='tns:ProductId'/>

  <!-- Response Message (work-in-progress) -->
  <element name='Amount' type='double' nillable='true'/>

</schema>
```

Another useful constraint is the enumeration. The value of an enumeration can contain one of a fixed set of possible values. For example, suppose I want to restrict the value of the *Item* attribute to one of a set of possible values. The following example creates a datatype called *Items* that can contain the possible values of the *Item* element:

```
<?xml version='1.0'?>
<schema xmlns="http://www.w3.org/2001/XMLSchema.xsd"
xmlns:tns="urn:Commerce" targetNamespace="urn:Commerce">

  <!-- Removed the ProductId type definition for clarity -->

  <simpleType name="Items">
    <restriction base="ProductId">
      <enumeration value="Apple"/>
      <enumeration value="Banana"/>
      <enumeration value="Orange"/>
    </restriction>
  </simpleType>

  <!-- Request Message (work-in-progress) -->
  <element name='Item' type='tns:Items'/>

  <!-- Response Message (work-in-progress) -->
  <element name='Amount' type='double' nillable='true'/>

</schema>
```

The *Items* type definition creates an enumeration of type *ProductId* with three possible values. The *Item* element is defined as type *Items*, so it can contain only the value *Apple*, *Banana*, or *Orange*.

Simple types can also derive by list. Deriving by list indicates that the value of the type can contain one or more values of the base type, where each value is delimited by whitespace. An example is the SOAP *encodingStyle* attribute. Recall that this attribute can accept a whitespace-delimited list of URIs. The following example defines the SOAP *encodingStyle* attribute:

```
<simpleType name='encodingStyle'>
  <list base='uri-reference'/>
</simpleType>
```

List types are not a substitute for SOAP encoded arrays. SOAP arrays provide a standard method of encoding for instances of simple types as well as complex types. SOAP Encoding also defines syntax for the partial serialization of arrays.

Simple types can also be derived by union. An instance of a type derived by union can contain a value of one of the types contained within the union. The following example defines two unions, *MyUnion* and *PhoneNumber*:

```
<?xml version='1.0'?>
<schema xmlns="http://www.w3.org/2001/XMLSchema.xsd">

  <simpleType name="MyUnion">
    <union memberTypes="string int"/>
  </simpleType>

  <simpleType name="PhoneNumber">
    <union>
      <simpleType name="UsPhoneNumber"/>
        <restriction base="string"/>
          <pattern value="([0-9]{3}) [0-9]{3}-[0-9]{4}"/>
        </restriction>
      </simpleType>

      <simpleType name="UkPhoneNumber">
        <restriction base="string">
          <pattern value="+[0-9]{2} ([0-9])[0-9]{3} [0-9]{3} [0-9]{4}"/>
        </restriction>
      </simpleType>
    </union>
  </simpleType>

</schema>
```

The preceding schema shows two ways of defining union simple types. The first type definition uses the *memberTypes* attribute to list the types contained within the union. The *MyElement* element can contain *string* or *int* values. The second type definition defines a union composed of embedded simple type definitions. The two embedded types define a U.S. phone number and a U.K. phone number. The *PhoneNumber union* can contain values such as (303) 555-1212 or +44 (0)121 643 2345.

Type definitions can be either named or anonymous. If a type definition is embedded within another definition (an element definition, for example), you do not have to provide the type with a name. Here is a modified version of the Commerce Web service schema that defines the enumeration as an anonymous type:

```
<?xml version='1.0'?>
<schema xmlns="http://www.w3.org/2001/XMLSchema.xsd"
xmlns:tns="urn:Commerce" targetNamespace="urn:Commerce">

  <!-- Portions of the schema have been removed for clarity. -->

  <!-- Request Message (work-in-progress) -->
  <element name='Item'>
    <simpleType>
      <restriction base="ProductId">
        <enumeration value="Apple"/>
        <enumeration value="Banana"/>
        <enumeration value="Orange"/>
      </restriction>
    </simpleType>
  </element>

</schema>
```

The enumeration containing possible values for the *Item* element is defined as an anonymous type. Because the enumeration is defined within the scope of the element definition, the *type* attribute does not need to be specified because it is implied. Because the enumeration type can be referenced only by the element itself, it is not necessary to specify a name for the type.

You should define anonymous types with caution. Types that are used only once are good candidates for anonymous type definitions. However, if the datatype might be reused in other contexts, you should avoid declaring anonymous type definitions.

You should also be cautious about using simple types, including built-in types, within RPC-style Web services. Parameters that are passed by value can be defined using simple types. But parameters passed by reference should not. Recall that SOAP Encoding specifies a means of encoding parameters passed by reference using the *id* and *href* attributes. Because elements defined using simple types cannot contain attributes, they cannot be properly encoded within the SOAP message. For this reason, the SOAP Encoding schema defines wrapper types for the built-in types defined by XML Schema.

Complex Types

A complex type is a logical grouping of element and/or attribute declarations. One can argue that XML instance documents aren't very interesting or useful without complex types. For example, the SOAP Envelope schema defines numerous complex types. The *Envelope* itself is a complex type because it must contain other elements such as the *Body* element and possibly a *Header* element. I will use complex types to define the body of the response and request SOAP messages for the Commerce Web service.

A complex type is defined using the *complexType* element. The *complexType* element contains declarations for all elements and attributes that can be contained within the element. For example, the body of the *PurchaseItem* request and response messages can be described by creating a complex type. Here is the schema definition for the Commerce Web service:

```xml
<?xml version='1.0'?>
<schema xmlns="http://www.w3.org/2001/XMLSchema.xsd"
xmlns:tns="urn:Commerce" targetNamespace="urn:Commerce">

  <!-- Type Definitions -->
  <simpleType name="ProductId">
    <restriction base="string">
      <minLength value="1"/>
      <maxLength value="20"/>
      <pattern value='[^/\&#x5B;&#x5D;:;|=,+*?&gt;&lt;]+'/>
    </restriction>
  </simpleType>

  <simpleType name="Items">
    <restriction base="ProductId">
      <enumeration value="Apple"/>
      <enumeration value="Banana"/>
      <enumeration value="Orange"/>
    </restriction>
  </simpleType>

  <!-- Request Message (work-in-progress) -->
  <element name='PurchaseItem'>
    <complexType>
      <element name='Item' type='tns:ProductId'/>
      <element name='Quantity' type='int'/>
    </complexType>
  </element>

  <!-- Response Message (work-in-progress) -->
  <element name='PurchaseItemResponse'>
    <complexType>
      <element name='Amount' type='double' nillable='true'/>
    </complexType>
  </element>

</schema>
```

The schema defines two complex types that define the body of the SOAP request and response message. In accordance with the SOAP specification, I defined a *PurchaseItem* element to contain all of the parameters passed to the *PurchaseItem* method of the Commerce Web service. The body of the response message will contain an element named *PurchaseItemResponse* and will contain one subelement for the return type.

Complex types can be divided into two categories: types that contain other elements and types that do not. Within a complex type definition, you can specify either a *complexContent* or a *simpleContent* element. The previous datatype definitions did not contain either of these elements. If neither element is used in the complex type definition, *complexContent* is assumed. Therefore, the following more verbose definition of the *PurchaseItem* element is equivalent to the previous definition:

```
<?xml version='1.0'?>
<schema xmlns="http://www.w3.org/2001/XMLSchema.xsd"
xmlns:tns="urn:Commerce" targetNamespace="urn:Commerce">

  <!-- Portions of the schema have been removed for clarity. -->

  <!-- Request Message (work-in-progress) -->
  <element name='PurchaseItem'>
    <complexType>
      <complexContent>
        <extension>
          <element name='Item' type='tns:ProductId'/>
          <element name='Quantity' type='int'/>
        </extension>
      </complexContent>
    </complexType>
  </element>

</schema>
```

Notice that the schema also includes the *extension* element. If either *simpleContent* or *complexContent* is specified, its immediate child element must be either the *restriction* or *extension* element. By default, a complex type will define an extended version of its base type. If the base type is not specified, the type definition will extend *anyType*. In other words, a complex type definition that does not explicitly state whether it contains complex or simple content will default to containing complex content and deriving from *anyType* by extension.

As with simple type definitions, you can create complex types that are more restrictive than the base type. Unlike simple types, which restrict the string value of an instance of a type, complex types have restrictions related to the element and attribute definitions contained within the type. The following example defines the *Family* complex type and then defines some types that derive by restriction:

```xml
<?xml version='1.0'?>
<schema xmlns='http://www.w3.org/2001/XMLSchema'>

  <!-- Base type -->
  <complexType name='Family'>
    <element name='Parent' minOccurs='1' maxOccurs='2'/>
    <element name='Child' type='string' minOccurs='0'/>
  <complexType name='Children'>

  <!-- The number of parents is restricted to one. -->
  <complexType name='SingleParentFamily'>
    <complexContent>
      <restriction base='Family'>
        <element name='Parent' type='string' minOccurs='1' maxOccurs='1'/>
        <element name='Child' type='string' minOccurs='0'/>
      </restriction>
    </complexContent>
  </complexType>

  <!-- No Child elements are allowed. -->
  <complexType name='ChildlessFamily'>
    <complexContent>
      <restriction base='Family'>
        <element name='Parent' type='string' minOccurs='1' maxOccurs='1'/>
        <element name='Child' type='string' minOccurs='0' maxOccurs='0'/>
      </restriction>
    </complexContent>
  </complexType>

  <!-- The name of the children can only be George. -->
  <complexType name='ForemanFamily'>
    <complexContent>
      <restriction base='Family'>
        <element name='Parent' type='string' minOccurs='0' maxOccurs='2'/>
        <element name='Child' type='string' minOccurs='0' fixed='George'/>
      </restriction>
    </complexContent>
  </complexType>

  <!-- Not a legal type declaration -->
  <complexType name='OrphanedFamily'>
    <complexContent>
      <restriction base='Family'>
        <element name='Parent' type='string' minOccurs='0' maxOccurs='0'/>
        <element name='Child' type='string' minOccurs='0'/>
      </restriction>
    </complexContent>
  </complexType>

</schema>
```

I defined three valid restricted derivatives of the *Family* type. The *SingleParentFamily* datatype restricts the number of *Parent* elements that can appear within an instance. The *ChildlessFamily* datatype disallows the optional *Child* element from appearing within an instance. Then, in true George Foreman fashion, the *ForemanFamily* datatype allows *Child* elements as long as the name of each is George.

One caveat with restricted types—and with extended types, for that matter—is that the derived types must be able to be substituted for their base type without any issue. The two derived types in the example, *SingleParentFamily* and *ForemanFamily*, meet this requirement. The *OrphanedFamily* type definition does not meet this requirement. Because the base type *Family* states that you must have at least one *Parent* element, an instance of *OrphanedFamily* cannot serve as a substitute.

Recall that SOAP Encoding provides a means of maintaining the identity of parameters passed by reference. This is accomplished with the *id* and *href* attributes. These attributes allow an element to reference data that is encoded at another location within or even outside of the SOAP message. (See Chapter 3 for more information.) The following example illustrates the need for such a mechanism:

```
// Server Code:
public void TestReference(ref int x, ref int y)
{
    x += 3;
    y += 10;
}


// Client Code:
int z = 2;
TestReference(ref z, ref z);
// z should now equal 20 (2 + 3 + 10).
```

For the *TestReference* method to run correctly, the identity of *z* must be maintained. Therefore, the elements for parameters *x* and *y* cannot be of type *int* defined by XML Schema because the elements will not be able to contain the *href* and *id* attributes to be defined. So, the SOAP Encoding schema extends the built-in types. The following example performs the same redefinition:

```
<?xml version='1.0'?>
<schema xmlns="http://www.w3.org/2001/XMLSchema.xsd"
targetNamespace='urn:ExtendedBuiltinTypes'>

  <complexType name='int'>
    <simpleContent>
      <extension base='int'>
```

```
        <attribute name='id' type='ID'/>
        <attribute name='href' type='uriReference'/>
      </extension>
    <simpleContent>
  </complexType>

</schema>
```

SOAP Encoding specifies that the order in which parameters of an RPC-style message appear is significant. Therefore, I use the *sequence* element in the schema to indicate that the *Item* element must appear first, followed by the *Quantity* element. You can also specify any combination of the *minOccurs* and *maxOccurs* attributes. In this case, neither attribute was specified, so the default value of *1* will be assumed. The following is the complete schema for the Commerce Web service:

```
<?xml version='1.0'?>
<schema xmlns="http://www.w3.org/2001/XMLSchema.xsd"
xmlns:tns="urn:Commerce" targetNamespace="urn:Commerce">

  <!-- Type Definitions -->
  <simpleType name="ProductId">
    <restriction base="string">
      <minLength value="1"/>
      <maxLength value="20"/>
      <pattern value='[^/\&#x5B;&#x5D;:;|=,+*?&gt;&lt;]+'/>
    </restriction>
  </simpleType>

  <simpleType name="Items">
    <restriction base="ProductId">
      <enumeration value="Apple"/>
      <enumeration value="Banana"/>
      <enumeration value="Orange"/>
    </restriction>
  </simpleType>

  <!-- Request Message (work-in-progress) -->
  <element name='PurchaseItem'>
    <complexType>
      <sequence>
        <element name='Item' type='tns:ProductId'/>
        <element name='Quantity' type='int'/>
      </sequence>
    </complexType>
  </element>

  <!-- Response Message (work-in-progress) -->
  <element name='PurchaseItemResponse'>
```

(continued)

```
<complexType>
  <element name='Amount' type='double' nillable='true'/>
</complexType>
</element>

</schema>
```

Other elements that can be used to achieve specific behavior related to the elements defined within a type include the *choice* and *all* elements. The *choice* element allows only one of the elements defined within the complex type to appear within an instance of the type. The *all* element allows any subset of the elements defined within the type to appear in any order.

There is one more difference between the *all* element and the *sequence* and *choice* elements. Complex type declarations made within the latter elements can contain *maxOccurs* and *minOccurs* attributes. However, elements defined within the *all* element can specify only a *maxOccurs* and a *minOccurs* attribute with a value of *0* or *1*.

By default, datatypes defined using the *complexContent* element do not allow mixed content. Mixed content means values that contain text as well as child elements. You can override this behavior by adding a *mixed* attribute and setting its value to *true*. In most cases, including this one, disallowing mixed content is preferred.

Sometimes it is necessary to specify that any element or attribute can appear within an instance of a complex type. For example, the *anyType* type indicates that any element or attribute can appear within an element of type *anyType*. You can do this by using the *any* and *anyAttribute* elements within the complex type definition. Here is the definition of the *anyType* type:

```
<?xml version='1.0'?>
<schema xmlns='http://www.w3.org/2001/XMLSchema'
xmlns:tns='http://schemas.xmlsoap.org/soap/envelope/'
targetNamespace='http://schemas.xmlsoap.org/soap/envelope/'>

  <xs:complexType name="anyType" mixed="true">
    <xs:annotation>
      <xs:documentation>
      Not the real urType, but as close an approximation as we can
      get in the XML representation</xs:documentation>
    </xs:annotation>
    <xs:sequence>
      <xs:any minOccurs="0" maxOccurs="unbounded"/>
    </xs:sequence>
    <xs:anyAttribute/>
  </xs:complexType>

</schema>
```

The preceding portion of the schema for XML Schema itself defines the *anyType* complex type. The *any* element states that any element can appear within an element of type *anyType*. The *minOccurs* and *maxOccurs* attributes are also used to indicate that zero or more elements can appear.

You can also impose additional constraints on the attributes and elements that can appear within an instance document by using the *namespace* attribute. This attribute allows you to declare what namespace-scoped attributes and elements can and cannot be contained within an instance document. Table 4-4 lists the possible values of the *namespace* attribute.

Table 4-4   Values of the *namespace* Attribute

namespace Attribute	Description
##any (default)	The parent element can contain any well-formed XML element/attribute from any namespace.
##local	The parent element can contain any well-formed XML element/attribute that does not belong to a namespace.
##targetNamespace	The parent element can contain any well-formed element/attribute that is defined within the schema's target namespace where the type is being defined.
##other	The parent element can contain any well-formed element/attribute not defined within the schema's target namespace where the type is being defined.
Space-delimited list of URIs	The parent element can contain any well-formed element/attribute from the specified namespaces.

The other attribute that can be specified in either the *any* or *anyAttribute* element is *processContents*. The *processContents* attribute indicates how the instance document should be processed by the system. Table 4-5 lists the possible values of the *processContents* attribute.

Table 4-5   Values of the *processContents* Attribute

processContents Attribute	Description
strict (default)	The system must validate all elements/attributes against their respective namespaces.
skip	The system must attempt to validate all elements/attributes against their respective namespaces. If the attempt fails, no errors will be generated.
lax	The system will not attempt to validate elements/attributes against their respective namespaces.

Element and Attribute Groups

You might often find yourself adding the same set of attributes or elements to multiple complex type definitions. The XML Schema provides the *group* and *attributeGroup* elements for logically grouping elements and attributes together. Attribute and element groups provide a convenient way to define a set of attributes or elements once and then reference them multiple times in complex type definitions.

One example in which an attribute group is used is within the SOAP Encoding schema. The schema contains complex type definitions that extend the XML Schema built-in types so they can be passed by reference within the body of a SOAP message. Here is an attribute group definition defined by the SOAP Encoding schema:

```
<attributeGroup name='commonAttributes'>
  <attribute name='id' type='ID'/>
  <attribute name='href' type='uriReference'/>
  <anyAttribute namespace='##other'/>
</attributeGroup>
```

The preceding fragment defines the *commonAttributes* attribute group. It contains the attribute definition for the *id* and *href* attributes, which are necessary for encoding parameters passed by reference. Here is a type definition that derives from the built-in *string* data type that references the attribute group:

```
<element name='string' type='tns:string'/>
<complexType name='string'>
  <complexContent>
    <extension base='string'>
      <attributeGroup ref='tns:commonAttributes'/>
    </extension>
  </complexContent>
</complexType>
```

The above type definition is actually an updated version of the one that appears in the SOAP Encoding schema. The original schema was written against a previous version of the XML Schema specification. The complex type definition references the attribute group using the *ref* attribute, which contains the value of the targeted attribute group definition. Elements can be grouped together using the *group* element and can be referenced using the *ref* attribute as well.

Namespace Scoping

Element and attribute declarations that are locally scoped within a complex type definition can be either qualified or unqualified. The default value is unqualified, which means that the element or attribute is not affiliated with any namespace. Here is an example:

```
<?xml version='1.0'?>
<schema xmlns='http://www.w3.org/2001/XMLSchema'
xmlns:tns='urn:Example:Scoping' targetNamespace='urn:Example:Scoping'>

  <element name='GloballyScoped'/>

  <element name='MyElement'>
    <complexType>
      <element name='LocallyScoped'/>
      <element ref='tns:GloballyScoped'/>
    </complexType>
  </element>

</schema>
```

The schema defines two globally scoped elements, *GloballyScoped* and *MyElement*. The *MyElement* element declaration defines an anonymous complex type that contains two element declarations: a locally scoped element named *LocallyScoped* and a reference to a globally scoped element named— what else—*GloballyScoped*. Next I'll create an instance document:

```
<?xml version='1.0'?>
<ex:MyElement xmlns:ex='urn:Example:Scoping'>
  <LocallyScoped/>
  <ex:GloballyScoped/>
</ex:MyElement>
```

The instance document contains a single *MyElement* element. Notice that the child elements of the *MyElement* element are qualified differently. The *LocallyScoped* element does not have a prefix because it is not affiliated with any namespace. The *GloballyScoped* element is fully qualified within the *ex:* prefix. Because the *GloballyScoped* element was defined as a global element, it is affiliated with the *urn:Example:Scoping* namespace.

Be aware that, if you set the default namespace within an instance document, locally scoped elements and attributes do *not* belong to the default namespace. For example, the following instance document is not valid because the *LocallyScoped* element is not a part of the *urn:Example:Scoping* namespace:

```
<?xml version='1.0'?>
<MyElement xmlns='urn:Example:Scoping'>
  <!-- Invalid because LocallyScoped is not affiliated
  with the default namespace -->
  <LocallyScoped/>
  <GloballyScoped/>
</MyElement>
```

There are two ways to avoid this problem. The first solution is to assign a prefix to the namespace reference instead of assigning a default namespace. In the first example, I associated the *ex:* prefix with the *urn:Example:Scoping* namespace. The second solution is to override the default namespace declaration in each local element or attribute, as in this example:

```
<?xml version='1.0'?>
<MyElement xmlns='urn:Example:Scoping'>
  <!-- Valid because LocallyScoped overrides the default namespace -->
  <LocallyScoped xmlns=''/>
  <GloballyScoped/>
</MyElement>
```

You can avoid problems with locally scoped elements and attributes by affiliating them with the namespace in which they are defined. You can do this by setting the *form* attribute within the element or attribute declaration to *qualified*. This requires the locally scoped element or attribute to be qualified with respect to its namespace. Here is an updated version of the schema:

```
<?xml version='1.0'?>
<schema xmlns='http://www.w3.org/2001/XMLSchema'
xmlns:tns='urn:Example:Scoping2' targetNamespace='urn:Example:Scoping2'>

  <element name='GloballyScoped'/>

  <element name='MyElement'>
    <complexType>
      <element name='LocallyScoped' form='qualified'/>
      <element ref='tns:GloballyScoped'/>
    </complexType>
  </element>

</schema>
```

This time, I indicated that the *LocallyScoped* element must be fully qualified within the instance document. Here is the instance document updated to reflect the changes made to the schema:

```
<?xml version='1.0'?>
<MyElement xmlns='urn:Example:Scoping2'>
  <!-- Valid since LocallyScoped element must be fully qualified -->
  <LocallyScoped/>
  <GloballyScoped/>
</MyElement>
```

You can also override the default value for the *form* attribute. You can do this by setting two attributes in the *schema* element: *elementFormDefault* and *attributeFormDefault*. Schemas automatically generated by the .NET platform for Web services will generally set *elementFormDefault* and *attributeFormDefault* to *qualify*.

Polymorphism

Polymorphism is when instances of different types can be treated similarly. The XML Schema provides two mechanisms for enabling polymorphic behavior: inheritance and substitution groups.

As I demonstrated in the previous sections, XML Schema provides a rich inheritance model. You can create new simple types that derive by restriction, and you can create new complex types that derive by extension as well as restriction.

One of the rules of a derived type is that it must be able to be substituted for its base type. As a result, an instance of a derived type can be substituted in an instance document for its base type. The system is informed that the instance document contains an instance of a derived type via the *xsi:type* attribute.

For example, suppose you want to create a common type system for describing tires. You want any tire dealer or manufacturer to be able to use this type system to create a Web service for obtaining price quotes for the tires they sell. Here are the common datatypes used to describe tires:

```xml
<?xml version='1.0'?>
<schema xmlns='http://www.w3.org/2001/XMLSchema'
targetNamespace='urn:TireTypes'>

  <complexType name='Tire' abstract='true'>
    <element name='WheelDiameter' type='int'/>
    <element name='Width' type='int'/>
  </complexType>

  <complexType name='AutoTire'>
    <complexContent>
      <extension base='Tire'>
        <element name='WheelDiameter' type='int'/>
        <element name='Width' type='int'/>
        <element name='AspectRatio' type='int'/>
      </extension>
    </complexContent>
  </complexType>

  <element name='MountainBikeTire'>
    <complexContent>
      <extension base='Tire'>
        <element name='WheelDiameter' type='int'/>
        <element name='Width' type='int'/>
        <element name='Position'/>
          <simpleType>
            <restriction base='string'>
              <enumeration value='Front'/>
              <enumeration value='Rear'/>
```

(continued)

```
            </restriction>
          </simpleType>
        </element>
      </extension>
    </complexContent>
  </element>

</schema>
```

This schema defines the *Tire* base type. It contains two child elements for the rim size and the width of the tire. It then derives two separate types from the *Tire* base type called *AutoTire* and *MountainBikeTire*. In both instances, the *Tire* type is extended to add additional elements needed to describe the specific type of tire.

Instances of the *Tire* base type include insufficient information to describe a specific tire. Therefore, the *abstract* property within the type declaration is set to *true*. Setting the *abstract* property of the *Tire* complex type definition to *true* indicates that the *Tire* type is not intended to be directly creatable.

A fictitious company, The Round Rubber Tire Company, sells all types of tires and wants to expose a Web service for getting price quotes on tires. Here is a schema for the NewTires Web service that leverages the tire types:

```xml
<?xml version='1.0'?>
<schema xmlns='http://www.w3.org/2001/XMLSchema' xmlns:vt='urn:TireTypes'
targetNamespace='http://roundrubbertire.com/NewTires'
elementFormDefault='qualified'>

  <element name='GetQuote'>
    <complexType>
      <element name='Tire' type='vt:Tire'/>
      <element name='Quantity' type='int'/>
    </complexType>
  </element>

  <element name='GetQuoteResults'>
    <complexType>
      <element name='Result' type='double'/>
    </complexType>
  </element>

</schema>
```

The *GetQuote* method accepts information about the requested tire and the quantity. The price of the new tires is then returned as a *double*. However, because the *Tire* datatype is abstract, the Web service needs to receive a derivative of the *Tire* type. The following SOAP message requests a quote for new tires of type *AutoTire*:

```
<?xml version="1.0" encoding="utf-8"?>
<soap:Envelope xmlns:soap="http://schemas.xmlsoap.org/soap/envelope/"
xmlns:xsi="http://www.w3.org/2001/XMLSchema-instance"
xmlns:tires="http://bigrubbertire.com/NewTires" xmlns:vt="urn:TireTypes">
  <soap:Body>
    <tires:GetQuote>
      <tires:Tire xsi:type="vt:AutoTire"/>
        <tires:WheelDiameter>16</tires:WheelDiameter>
        <tires:Width>225</tires:Tires>
        <tires:AspectRatio>50</tires:AspectRatio>
      </tires:Tire>
      </tires:Quantity>4</tires:Quantity>
    </tires:GetQuote>
  </soap:Body>
</soap:Envelope>
```

The body of the SOAP message contains the *GetQuote* element that contains the *Tire* parameter. The *Tire* parameter contains an instance of the *AutoTire* type, as indicated by the *xsi:type* attribute. The parameter is a legal substitution because *AutoTire* is a derivative of *Tire*.

XML Schema also supports polymorphic behavior at the element level via the concept of substitution groups. A substitution group is a group of elements that can serve as substitutes for a given element within an instance document. You can add element definitions to a substitution group by using the *substitutionGroup* attribute.

The *substitutionGroup* attribute contains a reference to the element for which it can serve as a substitute. All element definitions within a substitution group must be the same type or a derivative of the type of the target element. In the following example, the schema for the NewTires Web service is rewritten to use group substitution instead of type substitution:

```
<?xml version='1.0'?>
<schema xmlns='http://www.w3.org/2001/XMLSchema' xmlns:vt='urn:TireTypes'
targetNamespace='http://rubbertire.com/NewTires'
xmlns:tns='http://rubbertire.com/NewTires' elementFormDefault='qualified'>

  <element name='GetQuote'>
    <complexType>
      <element ref='tns:Tire'/>
      <element name='Quantity' type='int'/>
    </complexType>
  </element>

  <element name='GetQuoteResults'>
    <complexType>
      <element name='Result' type='double'/>
```

(continued)

```
        </complexType>
    </element>

    <!-- Declare the Tire element and its substitutes. -->
    <element name='Tire' type='vt:Tire' abstract='true'/>
    <element name='AutoTire' type='vt:AutoTire' substitutionGroup='tns:Tire'/>
    <element name='MountainBikeTire type='vt:MountainBikeTire'
    substitutionGroup='tns:Tire'/>

</schema>
```

In the new schema, the definition of the *Tire* element was moved from within the *GetQuote* complex type (locally scoped) to directly under the *schema* element (globally scoped). Because I did not want the tire element to appear within the instance document, I set the *abstract* property to *true* within the element definition. I then defined two other elements to serve as substitutions for the *Tire* element. Here is the resulting SOAP message for ordering a set of automobile tires:

```
<?xml version="1.0" encoding="utf-8"?>
<soap:Envelope xmlns:soap="http://schemas.xmlsoap.org/soap/envelope/"
xmlns:tires="http://bigrubbertire.com/NewTires">
  <soap:Body>
    <tires:GetQuote>
      <tires:AutoTire/>
        <tires:WheelDiameter>16</tires:WheelDiameter>
        <tires:Width>225</tires:Tires>
        <tires:AspectRatio>50</tires:AspectRatio>
      </tires:AutoTire>
      <tires:Quantity>4</tires:Quantity>
    </tires:GetQuote>
  </soap:Body>
</soap:Envelope>
```

The *Tire* element was replaced by the *AutoTire* element within the document. There was no need to decorate the element with the *xsi:type* attribute because the element is strongly typed by the schema itself.

Restricting Inheritance

Because any derived type can be substituted for its base type, you might sometimes want to state how a base class can be inherited. For example, the *urn:TireTypes* namespace defined earlier defines the *Tire* datatype. The *Tire* datatype is defined as abstract because an instance of that type would not contain enough information to adequately describe a tire. However, setting the type to abstract does not provide a full solution.

A client can easily circumvent using a more rich type by deriving a new type from *Tire* by restriction. The client can then invoke the *GetQuote* method and pass it an instance of the new type. Here is an example:

```
<?xml version='1.0'?>
<schema xmlns='http://www.w3.org/2001/XMLSchema' xmlns:tire='urn:TireTypes'
targetNamespace='urn:DerivedTireTypes'>

  <complexType name='SkinnyTire' abstract='true'/>
    <complexContent base='tire:Tire'>
      <restriction >
        <element name='WheelDiameter' type='int'/>
        <element name='Width' type='int' fixed='1'/>
      </restriction>
    </complexContent>
  </complexType>

</schema>
```

I first derived a more restricted version of the *Tire* type. I'll then pass an instance of this new type to the *GetQuote* method:

```
<?xml version="1.0" encoding="utf-8"?>
<soap:Envelope xmlns:soap="http://schemas.xmlsoap.org/soap/envelope/"
xmlns:tires="http://bigrubbertire.com/NewTires"
xmlns:vt="urn:DerivedTireTypes"
xmlns:xsi="http://www.w3.org/2001/XMLSchema-instance">
  <soap:Body>
    <tires:GetQuote>
      <tires:Tire xsi:type="dt:SkinnyTire"/>
        <tires:WheelDiameter>16</tires:WheelDiameter>
        <tires:Width>1</tires:Tires>
      </tires:Tire>
      <tires:Quantity>2</tires:Quantity>
    </tires:GetQuote>
  </soap:Body>
</soap:Envelope>
```

As I stated earlier, the Web service cannot quote the price of a tire based on only the wheel diameter and width. Therefore, if the Web service receives an instance of *SkinnyTire*, a restricted derivation of the *Tire* datatype, it will be unable to provide a price quote. One solution is to disallow inheritance by restriction.

An example of where you might want to disallow inheritance by extension is if you use a type that represents the long version of the U.S. Federal income tax form. It might not be necessary for all filers to complete the entire long form, so the government issues the EZ form. The EZ form is a derivative of the long form with restrictions on the amount of data it can contain.

You can dictate how a datatype can be inherited by setting the *final* attribute in the *complexType* element. Table 4-6 describes the possible values.

Table 4-6 Values of the *final* Attribute

final Attribute	Description
#all	The type cannot serve as a base type for types that are derived by extension and restriction.
restriction	The type can be a base type only for types that derive by extension.
extension	The type can be a base type only for types that derive by restriction.

If the *final* attribute is not set, the default value is *#all*. You can override the default value by setting the *finalDefault* attribute within the *schema* element.

Sometimes it makes sense to allow others to inherit from datatypes but limit instances of derived types from appearing in instance documents. For example, tax preparation services often collect information beyond what is called for on the long income tax form. The tax preparation service might therefore want to derive from the *long form* datatype by extension for use within its own internal system.

When it comes time to electronically file the tax form, the schema for the Web service needs a means of disallowing instances of the extended versions of the *long form* datatype. This is accomplished by setting the *block* attribute on the tax form element declaration to *extension*. The other possible values of the *block* attribute are listed in Table 4-7.

Table 4-7 Values of the *block* Attribute

block Attribute	Description
restriction	The element cannot contain an instance of a type derived by restriction.
extension	The element cannot contain an instance of a type derived by extension.
substitution	The element cannot be substituted for another element within its substitution group.
#all	The element cannot contain an instance of a derived type and cannot be substituted for another element within its substitution group.

If the *block* attribute is not specified, the default behavior is to allow the element to contain an instance of a derived type or be substituted with another element within its substitution group. You can override the default value by setting the *finalDefault* attribute within the *schema* element to the desired value.

Summary

XML Schema provides a comprehensive and flexible means of describing the structure as well as the type of data that should appear within an instance document. It is superior to the DTD schema language first introduced with XML 1.0.

XML Schema provides a standard type system. The type system is used to define a platform-independent way of describing the type of data that can be contained within an element or attribute. The type system also provides a set of built-in types that specify the data that can be contained by instances of types such as *string*, *int*, and *float*. Because SOAP is an XML-based protocol, messages can be created and consumed regardless of the hardware, operating system, or XML processing software used.

The type system is also extensible. XML Schema provides the means to define new simple types and complex types. A simple type cannot contain any child elements. Complex types provide a logical way to group related elements and attributes.

A custom type always inherits from another custom type or a built-in type. Simple types can be derived by restriction using a rich syntax for defining additional constraints. They can also be derived by list and by union.

Complex types can be derived by restriction or by extension. They can also contain attributes only (simple content) or attributes and elements (complex content). These attributes and elements can be locally defined or can be references of globally defined entities. If the entities within a complex type are locally defined, they should be associated with the namespace by having their *form* attribute set to *qualified*. This makes it easier to author instance documents that reference a default namespace.

XML Schema enables polymorphic behavior by allowing elements to contain instances of derived types to appear within the document. XML Schema also allows elements to be substituted with elements of a compatible type via substitution groups. In order to facilitate polymorphic behavior, instances of derived types must be able to be substituted in place of an instance of its base type.

XML Schema also provides mechanisms for restricting inheritance and polymorphic behavior. Complex type definitions can restrict how the type can be inherited by setting the *final* attribute. Element definitions can also restrict the type of substitutions that are allowed by setting the *block* attribute.

A schema document can contain element, attribute, and type definitions. These definitions can be scoped within a particular namespace by setting the *targetNamespace* attribute within the *schema* element. The schema can then be referenced by its namespace within an instance document. You can reference a namespace by adding the *xmlns* attribute to an element within the document. The reference will be scoped to the element that contains the *xmlns* attribute and any elements or attributes contained within the element.

A reference to a schema namespace can be assigned a moniker. Any entities referenced within the schema must then be prefixed by the moniker. By convention, the *XML Schema* namespace is assigned the *xsd* moniker and the *XML Schema Instance* namespace is assigned the *xsi* moniker. Also, if the schema contains references to its own definitions, a reference to its own namespace is usually assigned the *tns* moniker.

A reference to a namespace that is not assigned a moniker is used to define the default namespace. Attributes and elements that are not fully qualified with a prefix that is within the scope of the default namespace declaration are qualified with respect to the default namespace.

XML Schema provides a means of creating a schema that is composed of more than one schema document. The *include* element is used to include other schema definitions into its namespace. Schemas that do not define a namespace can be included into any schema. If the included schema defines a namespace, it must match the target namespace of the schema that includes it.

XML Schema is the preferred way of describing the schema of messages exchanged between the client and the server. It provides a robust and flexible way to describe the structure and the type of data that can appear within an instance document. As you will see in later chapters, the .NET platform provides a rich framework for creating and consuming XML Schema schemas for Web services.

5

Using WSDL to Document Web Services

In the previous chapter, you learned how to create a schema to describe the format of a SOAP message. You can use XML Schema to describe the layout of a message and the type of data the message contains, and the resulting schema can be used to validate the message received by the Web server. However, XML Schema alone cannot fully describe a Web service.

Let's say I have created a Calculator Web service. The Web service exposes two methods, *Add* and *Subtract*. Both methods accept two integers and return a single integer containing the result—*Add* returns the sum of the two integers, and *Subtract* returns the difference of the two numbers.

In an effort to describe how a client will interact with my Web service, I define a schema for the messages that will be exchanged between the client and the server. My schema contains a complex type definition for the request and response messages for both the *Add* and *Subtract* methods. Remember that the ultimate goal is not to have developers pore through schema definitions trying to decipher how to interact with a Web service. Instead, I want to describe my Web service in such a way that a tool can decipher it and create a proxy on the client's behalf.

In addition to the information provided by the schema, what else does a client need to know in order to invoke methods exposed by the Calculator Web service? Because the body of a SOAP message can contain anything that does not invalidate the XML, individual SOAP messages can be combined to support a wide variety of message exchange patterns. The message exchange patterns for the Calculator Web service are pretty straightforward, but a formal association between the Add and Subtract request messages and their associated response messages would remove any possible ambiguity.

A formal description of the message patterns is even more important for more complex Web services. Some Web services might accept a request but not send a corresponding response back to the client. Others might only send messages to the client.

The schema also does not contain information about how to access the Web service. Because SOAP is protocol independent, messages can be exchanged between the client and the server any number of ways. How do you know whether you should send a message over HTTP, SMTP, or some other transport protocol? Furthermore, how do you know the address to which the message should be sent?

Web Service Description Language (WSDL) is an XML-based dialect layered on top of the schema that describes a Web service. A WSDL document provides the information necessary for a client to interact with the Web service. WSDL is extensible and can be used to describe practically any network service, including SOAP over HTTP and even protocols that are not XML-based, such as DCOM over UDP.

In this chapter, I build the WSDL document that describes the Calculator Web service. Along the way, I describe the various parts of a WSDL document and the roles they play in describing the Web service.

WSDL Document Syntax

WSDL documents can be intimidating at first glance. But the syntax of a WSDL document is not nearly as complex as that of an XML Schema document. A WSDL document is composed of a series of associations layered on top of an XML Schema document that describes a Web service. These associations add to the size and the perceived complexity of a WSDL document. But once you look underneath the covers, WSDL documents are rather straightforward.

The root of a WSDL document is the *definitions* element. Within this element are five types of child elements:

- **types**   Contains the schema definitions of the messages that can be sent and received by the service. The most common way of representing the schema is using XML Schema.

- **message**   Serves as a cross-reference that associates the message with its definition within the schema.

- **portType**   Defines a set of interfaces that the Web service can expose. An interface is associated with one or more messages.

- **binding**   Associates the *portType* definition with a particular protocol.

- **service**   Defines a collection of related endpoints (ports) exposed by the Web service.

The following diagram illustrates how these five elements are layered on top of the schema definition to describe the Web service:

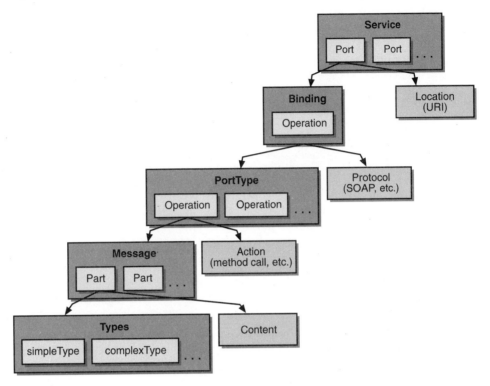

As you can see, a WSDL document is composed of a series of associations. For example, message parts are used to associate a datatype definition with a portion of the content of a message.

definitions Element

The root element in a WSDL document, the *definitions* element, serves much the same role as the *schema* element in an XML Schema document. It contains child elements that define a particular service.

Much like an XML Schema document, a WSDL document can define its own namespace by adding a *targetNamespace* attribute to the *definitions* element. The only restriction is that the value of the *targetNamespace* attribute cannot contain a relative URI.

The WSDL namespace allows you to fully qualify references to entities defined within a WSDL document. For example, a message definition is referenced by a *portType* definition. Later in the chapter, I reference entities defined within another WSDL namespace to facilitate interface inheritance.

The following WSDL fragment defines the *definitions* element for the Calculator Web service:

```
<?xml version="1.0" encoding="utf-8"?>
<definition targetNamespace="http://somedomain/Calculator/wsdl"
xmlns:tns="http://somedomain/Calculator/wsdl"
xmlns="http://schemas.xmlsoap.org/wsdl/">

<!--Definitions will go here.-->

</definitions>
```

The preceding WSDL document contains a *definitions* element. Within the target namespace, the target namespace is set to *http://somedomain/Calculator*. Then a reference is made to the target namespace, assigning it a prefix of *tns:*. This prefix will be used within the document to fully qualify references to entities defined within the document. Finally, the WSDL namespace is set to the default namespace.

The *definitions* element defines the boundaries of a particular *name scope*. Elements declared within a WSDL document are used to define entities such as ports and messages. These entities are assigned a name using the *name* attribute. All name attributes within a name scope must be unique. For example, if a WSDL document contains a port named *Foo*, it cannot contain another port or message named *Foo*.

It might not always be practical to define a unique fully qualified URI for a namespace—for example, early in the development cycle or when you want to create a couple of experimental Web services. In these cases, you can use *http://tempuri.org*, a special URI that is used by convention to define namespaces that do not need to be uniquely identified.

types Element

The *types* element contains schema information referenced within the WSDL document. The default type system supported by WSDL is XML Schema. If XML Schema is used to define the types contained within the *types* element, the *schema* element will appear as an immediate child element.

You can use other type systems by extension. If you use another type system, an extensibility element can appear under the *types* element. The name of the element should identify the type system used. In this chapter, I limit my discussion to XML Schema because it is the dominant type system used in WSDL documents, including those for Web services developed on the .NET platform.

The Calculator Web service will expose two RPC-style methods, an *Add* method and a *Subtract* method. The messages will be encoded in much the same way that I showed you in Chapter 4. The only difference is that the schema will be embedded within a WSDL document, as shown here:

```
<?xml version="1.0" encoding="utf-8"?>
<definitions targetNamespace="http://somedomain/Calculator/wsdl"
xmlns:tns="http://somedomain/Calculator/wsdl"
xmlns:xsd="http://www.w3.org/2001/XMLSchema"
xmlns:s="http://somedomain/Calculator/schema"
xmlns="http://schemas.xmlsoap.org/wsdl/">

    <types>
    <schema attributeFormDefault="qualified"
    elementFormDefault="qualified"
    xmlns="http://www.w3.org/2001/XMLSchema"
    targetNamespace="http://somedomain/Calculator/schema">
      <!-- Definitions for both the Add and Subtract SOAP messages -->
      <element name="Add">
        <complexType>
          <all>
            <element name="x" type="int"/>
            <element name="y" type="int"/>
          </all>
        </complexType>
      </element>
      <element name="AddResult">
        <complexType>
          <all>
            <element name="result" type="int"/>
          </all>
        </complexType>
      </element>

      <element name="Subtract">
        <complexType>
          <all>
            <element name="x" type="int"/>
            <element name="y" type="int"/>
          </all>
        </complexType>
      </element>
      <element name="SubtractResult">
        <complexType>
          <all>
            <element name="result" type="int"/>
          </all>
        </complexType>
      </element>

      <!-- Common SOAP fault detail element used by Add and Subtract -->
      <element name="CalculateFault">
```

(continued)

```
      <complexType>
        <all>
          <element name="x" type="int"/>
          <element name="y" type="int"/>
          <element name="Description" type="string"/>
        </all>
      </complexType>
    </element>

  </schema>
</types>

<!-- More definitions will go here. -->

</definitions>
```

Within the *types* element are schema definitions for the *Add* and *Subtract* methods, which use the reference to the schema's namespace that appears within the *definitions* element earlier in the document.

WSDL is not limited to describing XML-based serialization formats. You can use it to describe services that use other formats, including binary. For example, you can use WSDL to describe a service exposed via DCOM. In this case, you can still use XML Schema to describe the data being sent across the wire. The WSDL specification provides the following recommendations for doing so:

- Describe the data using elements, not attributes. For example, each parameter should be encoded within its own element, much like in SOAP Encoding.

- Describe only data that is related to the message and is not particular to the wire encoding. For example, the parameters passed to a remote COM object should be described in the schema. However, the DCOM object identifier (OID) is wire-protocol-specific data that identifies the object and should not be described in the schema.

- Array types should be derived from the *Array* complex type defined in the SOAP Encoding schema. By convention, the name of the type should be the type of items within the array, prefixed by *ArrayOf*.

- Parameters that can contain data of any type should be defined by an element of type *xsd:anyType*.

message Element

The *message* element provides a common abstraction for messages passed between the client and the server. Because you can use multiple schema-definition formats within a WSDL document, it is necessary to have a common way of identifying the messages. The *message* element provides this common level of abstraction that will be referenced in other parts of the WSDL document.

Multiple *message* elements can and often do appear in a WSDL document, one for each message being communicated between the client and the server. Each message contains one or more *part* elements that describe pieces of content within the message. An example of a part is the body of a SOAP message or a parameter contained within the query string, a parameter encoded in the body of a SOAP message, or the entire body of a SOAP message.

Each *part* element contains attributes that associate *type* and *element* definitions found in the *types* element. Because parts are abstract definitions of content, the binding information must be examined in order to determine the meaning of the parts.

Two attributes that can appear within the *part* element are the *element* and *type* attributes. The *element* attribute refers to an element definition in a schema. The *type* attribute refers to a type definition in a schema.

Because the Calculator Web service contains two methods, each with a request and response message, and a fault message was defined, the WSDL document will contain five *message* elements:

```xml
<?xml version="1.0" encoding="utf-8"?>
<definitions targetNamespace="http://somedomain/Calculator/wsdl"
xmlns:tns="http://somedomain/Calculator/wsdl"
xmlns:s="http://somedomain/Calculator/schema"
xmlns:xsd="http://www.w3.org/2001/XMLSchema"
xmlns="http://schemas.xmlsoap.org/wsdl/">

  <!-- Type definitions removed for clarity -->

  <message name="AddMsgIn">
    <part name="parameters" element="s:Add"/>
  </message>
  <message name="AddMsgOut">
    <part name="parameters" element="s:SubtractResult"/>
  </message>
  <message name="SubtractMsgIn">
    <part name="parameters" element="s:Add"/>
  </message>
  <message name="SubtractMsgOut">
    <part name="parameters" element="s:SubtractResult"/>
  </message>
  <message name="CalculateFaultMsg">
    <part name="fault" element="s:CalculateFault"/>
  </message>

  <!-- More definitions will go here. -->

</definitions>
```

I created a *message* element for the request and response message of the *Add* and *Subtract* methods. I could have instead specified a *part* element for each parameter. For example, the *AddMsgIn* message could have been written as follows:

```
<message name="AddMsgIn">
  <part name="x" type="xsd:int"/>
  <part name="y" type="xsd:int"/>
</message>
```

Parameters *x* and *y* are contained within their own part of the message. The protocol binding will have a lot of influence over how messages are represented. When I discuss binding later in the chapter, I will represent each parameter contained within an HTTP query string as its own message part.

Because each part can serve as an abstract definition of a piece of data, a message can be composed of multiple pieces of data from multiple sources. Although it is not recommended, you could describe a message in which some of the parameters were encoded within a SOAP body and some of the parameters were encoded within the query string.

portType Element

The *portType* element contains a set of abstract operations representing the types of correspondences that can occur between the client and the server. For RPC-style Web services, a *portType* can be thought of as an interface definition in which each method can be defined as an operation.

A port type is composed of a set of *operation* elements that define a particular action. The *operation* elements are composed of the messages defined within the WSDL document. WSDL defines four types of operations, known as *operation types*:

- **Request-response**   RPC-style communication in which the client makes a request and the server issues a corresponding response.

- **One-way**   Document-style communication in which the client sends a message but does not receive a response from the server indicating the result of the processed message.

- **Solicit-response**   The opposite of the request-response operation. The server sends a request, and the client sends back a response.

- **Notification**   The opposite of the one-way operation. The server sends a document-style communication to the client.

An operation is composed of a subset of *input, output,* and *fault* elements. The type of elements and the ordering of the elements within the operation determine the type of operation. For example, one-way defines an input message, and request-response defines an input and an output message. The solicit-response and the notification operation types are the opposite of request-response and one-way, respectively. The solicit-response operation lists the output message and then the input message, and the notification operation contains an output message instead of an input message.

Table 5-1 lists the type and ordering of messages for each operation type.

Table 5-1   Message Ordering for Operation Types

Operation Type	*input*	*output*	*fault*
Request-response	1	2	3*
One-way	1		
Solicit-response	2	1	3*
Notification		1	

* The fault message is optional. Any number of fault messages can appear in an operation.

Operations involving two-way communication can optionally specify one or more fault messages. Like Java method definitions, fault messages allow you to declare the type of exceptions that can be thrown by the server application. However, the list of possible faults should not include errors that are specified by the underlying transport protocol. For example, you would not need to represent the HTTP 500 error in the WSDL document.

The names of the *input, output,* and *fault* elements have a default value if one was not specified. For one-way and notification operation types, the default name is the name of the *operation* element in which they are contained. For request-response operation types, the name of the *input* and *output* elements default to the name of the operation with *Request* or *Response* appended to the end. For solicit-response, the name of the *output* element defaults to the name of the operation with *Solicit* or *Response* appended to the end.

Because multiple *fault* elements can be defined within an operation, there is no default name for the *fault* element. Therefore, each *fault* element must be uniquely named within its parent *operation* element.

Here is the *portType* definition for the Calculator Web service:

```
<?xml version="1.0" encoding="utf-8"?>
<definitions targetNamespace="http://somedomain/Calculator/wsdl"
xmlns:tns="http://somedomain/Calculator/wsdl"
xmlns:xsd="http://www.w3.org/2001/XMLSchema"
xmlns="http://schemas.xmlsoap.org/wsdl/">
```

(continued)

```
<!-- Type and message definitions removed for clarity -->

<portType name="CalculatorPortType">
  <operation name="Add">
    <input message="tns:AddMsgIn"/>
    <output message="tns:AddMsgOut"/>
    <fault message="tns:CalculateFaultMsg" name="CalculateFault"/>
  </operation>
  <operation name="Subtract">
    <input message="tns:SubtractMsgIn"/>
    <output message="tns:SubtractMsgOut"/>
    <fault message="tns:CalculateFaultMsg" name="CalculateFault"/>
  </operation>
</portType>

<!-- More definitions will go here. -->

</definitions>
```

The preceding snippet of the Calculator WSDL document defines the *port-Type* named *CalculatorPortType*. It contains two request-response operations, *Add* and *Subtract*. Because the operations are of type request-response, they both define an input and an output message. Both operations also contain a *fault* element named *CalculateFault*.

RPC-style operations can optionally use the *parameterOrder* attribute to specify the order of the expected parameters. This attribute is of type *nmTokens* and contains a list of names of the parameters. Because SOAP specifies a clear way to serialize parameters and the name and ordering of the parameters can be described using XML Schema, this attribute is not often used.

Some services described using WSDL can support overloaded methods—methods that have the same name but accept a different set of parameters. Therefore, within a *portType* definition, more than one *operation* element can have the same name but specify different messages. In this case, the different *operation* elements must be identified by the combination of the operation name plus the name of the *input*, *output*, and *fault* elements. As a result, the default name for the *input*, *output*, and *fault* elements might not ensure that *operation* elements with the same name can be uniquely identified.

binding Element

The *binding* element contains binding definitions for binding a protocol such as SOAP to a particular *bindingType*. The *binding* definitions specify message formatting and protocol details. For example, the binding information specifies whether you can access an instance of a *portType* in an RPC-like manner.

The *binding* definitions also indicate the number of network communications required to perform a particular action. For example, a SOAP RPC call over HTTP might involve one HTTP communication exchange, but that same call over SMTP would involve two discrete SMTP communication exchanges.

Binding is accomplished through the use of extension elements. Each protocol has its own set of extension elements for specifying the details of the protocol and the formatting of the messages. For a particular protocol, extension elements are often used to decorate the individual actions within an operation and the operation itself with protocol binding information. Sometimes, extension elements are used at the *portType* level itself.

The following simplified WSDL document shows the binding for the Calculator Web service. It also contains placeholders for extensibility elements to show where they can be placed in relation to the containing *binding* element. (I discuss extensibility elements defined by the WSDL specification later in the chapter.)

```
<?xml version="1.0" encoding="utf-8"?>
<definitions xmlns:ext="http://somedomain/MyBindingExt"
xmlns="http://schemas.xmlsoap.org/wsdl/">

  <!-- Type, message, and port type definitions removed for clarity -->
  <!-- All attributes also removed for clarity -->

  <binding name="CalculatorBinding" type="tns:CalculatorPortType">
    <ext:SomeExtElement/>
    <operation name="Add">
      <ext:SomeExtElement/>
      <input>
        <ext:SomeExtElement/>
      </input>
      <output>
        <ext:SomeExtElement/>
      </output>
      <fault>
        <ext:SomeExtElement/>
      </fault>
    </operation>
    <operation name="Subtract">
      <ext:SomeExtElement/>
      <input>
        <ext:SomeExtElement/>
      </input>
      <output>
        <ext:SomeExtElement/>
      </output>
```

(continued)

```
      <fault>
        <ext:SomeExtElement/>
      </fault>
    </operation>
  </binding>

  <!-- More definitions will go here. -->

</definitions>
```

The *binding* element is associated with a particular *portType* element via the *type* attribute. In the preceding WSDL document, I associated the binding named *CalculatorBinding* with the *CalculatorPortType* port type. Within the *binding* element, I created two *operation* elements to correlate to those defined in the *portType* element.

Each *operation* element must have corresponding *input*, *output*, and *fault* elements defined in the *portType* element. In addition, the names of the *operation* element and its child *input*, *output,* and *fault* elements must exactly match the names of their counterparts defined in the corresponding *portType* element.

service Element

A service is a group of related ports and is defined by the *service* element. A port is a particular endpoint for the Web service that is referenced by a single address. Ports defined within a particular service are orthogonal. For example, the output of one port cannot serve as the input of another.

Here is a simplified service definition for the Calculator Web service. The document contains placeholders for extensibility elements to show where they can be placed in relation to the containing *service* element:

```
<?xml version="1.0" encoding="utf-8"?>
<definitions xmlns:ext="http://somedomain/MyBindingExt"
xmlns="http://schemas.xmlsoap.org/wsdl/">

  <!-- Type, message, port type, and binding definitions removed for clarity -->
  <!-- All attributes also removed for clarity -->

  <service name="CalculatorService">
    <ext:SomeExtElement/>
    <port name="CalculatorPort" binding="tns:CalculatorBinding">
      <ext:SomeExtElement/>
    </port>
  </service>

  <!-- More definitions will go here. -->

</definitions>
```

The *service* element is used to group a set of related ports. The preceding WSDL document defines a service called *CalculatorService*. It contains one port called *CalculatorPort*. *CalculatorPort* is associated with the binding element *CalculatorBinding*.

A port contains an extension element that provides the address where it is located. If you need to specify more than one address, you must create one port for each address. If you define multiple ports of the same port type (and possibly different addresses) within the same Web service, they should be considered alternatives.

They should provide the same behavior, but over different transport protocols. The client can iterate through the ports to find a compatible binding with an appropriate *portType* and protocol.

Extensibility Elements

Extensibility elements are used to represent particular technologies. For example, you can use extensibility elements to specify the schema language used within the *types* element.

The schema for a particular set of extensibility elements must be defined within a different namespace than WSDL. The definition of the elements themselves can contain a *wsdl:required* attribute that specifies a Boolean value. If the *required* attribute is set to *true* within an element definition, a binding that references the particular set of extensibility elements must include that element.

Most often, extensibility elements are used to specify binding information. The WSDL specification defines sets of extension elements for binding to SOAP, HTTP GET, HTTP POST, and MIME. However, the specification defines the bindings for only two of the four operation types, one-way and request-response. Let's look at the three bindings supported by the .NET platform: SOAP, HTTP GET, and HTTP POST.

SOAP Extensions

The SOAP extensions provide a set of elements for binding a port type to a SOAP message sent over a particular transport protocol. For example, SOAP extension elements are used to indicate where the individual parts are located within the SOAP message. They are also used to indicate the transport protocol used to send the SOAP message.

SOAP extension elements are contained within the *http://schemas. xmlsoap.org/wsdl/soap/* namespace. The convention I use in the rest of this chapter is to associate references to the namespace with the *soap:* moniker.

binding Element Binding

Extensibility elements added to the *binding* element provide information about how the parameters are encoded within the SOAP message. Extensibility elements are added to the *bind, operation, input, output,* and *fault* messages. They provide information about the transport protocol used to send the SOAP message and how the data is encoded within the SOAP envelope.

The *soap:binding* element's primary purpose is to signal that SOAP binding is applied to a particular binding definition. Therefore, all *binding* elements containing SOAP specific binding must contain the *soap:binding* element. The *soap:binding* element can also be used to specify the style of the message and the transport protocol that will be used to send the SOAP message. The following portion of the Calculator Web service WSDL document demonstrates the use of the *soap:binding* element:

```xml
<?xml version="1.0" encoding="utf-8"?>
<definitions targetNamespace="http://somedomain/Calculator/wsdl"
xmlns:tns="http://somedomain/Calculator/wsdl"
xmlns:soap="http://schemas.xmlsoap.org/wsdl/soap/"
xmlns="http://schemas.xmlsoap.org/wsdl/">

  <!-- Type, message, and port type definitions removed for clarity -->

  <binding name="CalculatorBinding" type="tns:CalculatorPortType">
    <soap:binding style="document"
    transport="http://schemas.xmlsoap.org/soap/http"/>
    <!-- Operation elements removed for clarity -->
  </binding>

  <!-- More definitions will go here. -->

</definitions>
```

The *soap:binding* element can contain a *transport* attribute to specify a transport. The *transport* attribute must contain a URI that uniquely identifies the transport. The only URI defined in the specification is for the HTTP transport: *http://schemas.xmlsoap.org/soap/http.* Because the *soap:binding* element is applied to the entire binding definition, it will apply to all operations referenced by the binding definition.

The style of the message is indicated by the *style* attribute. The value is either *rpc* or *document.* If the style is set to *rpc,* each part within the operation will represent a parameter. The parameters must be encoded in the body of the SOAP message in a struct-like fashion as dictated by the SOAP specification. The name of the *operation* element must match the name of the element that contains the parameters in the SOAP message. If the style is set to *document,* the message parts will appear directly within the body of the SOAP message.

As you will see shortly, the message style can also be set at the operation level. Because the *style* attribute defined at the operation level takes precedence, setting the *style* attribute within the *soap:binding* element does not determine the message style; it merely sets the default value. If the *style* attribute is not set, the default value is *document*.

The *soap:operation* element provides binding information for the operation as a whole. You can use it to specify the document style as well as the *SOAP-Action* HTTP header value for HTTP bindings. The following portion of the Calculator Web service WSDL document demonstrates the use of the *soap:binding* element:

```
<?xml version="1.0" encoding="utf-8"?>
<definitions targetNamespace="http://somedomain/Calculator/wsdl"
xmlns:tns="http://somedomain/Calculator/wsdl"
xmlns:soap="http://schemas.xmlsoap.org/wsdl/soap/"
xmlns="http://schemas.xmlsoap.org/wsdl/">

  <!-- Type, message, and port type definitions removed for clarity -->

  <binding name="CalculatorBinding" type="tns:CalculatorPortType">
    <soap:binding style="document"
    transport="http://schemas.xmlsoap.org/soap/http"/>
    <operation name="Add">
      <soap:operation soapAction=http://somedomain/Calculator/Add"/>
      <input>
        <soap:body use="literal"/>
      </input>
      <output>
        <soap:body use="literal"/>
      </output>
      <fault>
        <soap:fault name="CalculateFault" use="literal"/>
      </fault>
    </operation>
    <operation name="Subtract">
      <soap:operation soapAction=http://somedomain/Calculator/Subtract"/>
      <input>
        <soap:body use="literal"/>
      </input>
      <output>
        <soap:body use="literal"/>
      </output>
      <fault>
        <soap:fault name="CalculateFault" use="literal"/>
      </fault>
    </operation>
  </binding>

  <!-- More definitions will go here. -->

</definitions>
```

As I mentioned earlier, the *style* attribute can be set to either *rpc* or *document* to indicate the style of the message.

The *soapAction* attribute specifies the value of the *SOAPAction* header. The *soapAction* attribute is required if HTTP is the transport protocol. The value can be blank if the HTTP request URL adequately describes the intent of the message. The client should pass the value of the *soapAction* attribute unchanged when sending a message to the Web service. If the protocol is not HTTP, the *soapAction* attribute can be omitted.

The *soap:body* element specifies how parts of the message are encoded inside the SOAP message body. This element is used to specify which parts of a message appear within the SOAP message body. It can also be used to declare the type of encoding used to serialize the parts within the message body.

You can optionally specify the list of parts that can be found within the body of the SOAP message. The *parts* attribute can contain a list of named tokens, where each token is the name of a part contained within the SOAP body. If the *parts* attribute is not specified, all parts defined by the message are assumed to be included in the SOAP body. An example of where the *parts* attribute would be used is if an HTTP message contained a multipart message that included a SOAP message in addition to a MIME attachment. One part of the message not included in the SOAP body would be the attachment itself.

Sometimes a schema alone cannot adequately represent the way in which data can be serialized. For example, SOAP Encoding defines multiple ways that an array can be serialized: the entire array, a partial array, or a sparse array. (See Chapter 3 for more information.)

The *use* attribute is required and must be either *literal* or *encoded*. The *literal* value means that parts within the SOAP body must comply with the schema. The part within the message definition must reference the schema using either the *type* or *element* attribute.

If parts within the body should be serialized using a particular method of encoding, the value of the *use* attribute should be *encoded*. Each part of the message encoded within the SOAP body must reference an abstract type using the *type* attribute. For example, a part containing a SOAP array would reference the SOAP *Array* type. If the encoding style supports variations in the way data can be encoded (such as the SOAP *Array* type), the service must support all of these variations.

If parts of a message are based on abstract type definitions rather than a concrete format specified by a schema definition, the encoding style should be referenced. The encoding style is specified by the *wsdl:encodingStyle* attribute and can contain a white-space-delimited list of URIs (similar to the *encodingStyle* attribute defined by SOAP).

If an *encodingStyle* attribute is specified for a message part and the *use* attribute is set to *literal*, the *encodingStyle* will serve as a hint about how the data is encoded. This is handy if you want to accept only one variation of a particular SOAP encoded datatype. For example, a Web service might accept only SOAP arrays that are fully serialized.

service Element Binding

The only SOAP extension element specified within the *service* element is *soap:address*. It is contained within the port definition and is used to specify the ` re the Web service can be reached.

```
.f-8"?>
:tp://somedomain/Calculator/wsdl"
lculator/wsdl"
oap.org/wsdl/soap/"
rg/wsdl/">

э, and binding definitions removed for clarity -->

vice">
:" binding="tns:CalculatorBinding">
"http://somedomain/Calculator"/>
```

n states that the Calculator Web service can be *in/Calculator*. If the address cannot be specified by ement can be replaced with a custom *address* ele- ecify the location.

to invoke a Web service by passing the parameters as he same mechanism as a standard HTML form post. d via the query string or a form POST. This sometimes nt to invoke a Web service without having to create a age.

OST extensions provide a set of elements for binding protocol. For example, SOAP extension elements are the individual parts are located within the SOAP mes- ed to indicate the transport protocol used to send the

In this section, I create two additional bindings for the Calculator Web service, one for HTTP GET and one for HTTP POST. I have a lot of freedom in how I specify the binding, so I will create bindings that closely parallel how Web services developed on the .NET platform behave. In particular, Web services developed using the .NET platform accept standard name/value pairs that are URL encoded and either appended on the query string or POSTed within the body of the HTTP request message. If results are returned, they are passed as a simple XML document in the body of the HTTP response message.

Before I specify the binding information, I need to create an additional element declaration to hold the value of the return parameters. Because individual parameters must be represented as individual parts of a message, I also need to create a couple of new message definitions for the *Add* and *Subtract* methods, where each parameter is contained within its own message part. Here are the additions:

```
<?xml version="1.0" encoding="utf-8"?>
<definitions targetNamespace="http://somedomain/Calculator/wsdl"
xmlns:tns="http://somedomain/Calculator/wsdl"
xmlns:s="http://somedomain/Calculator/schema"
xmlns:xsd="http://www.w3.org/2001/XMLSchema"
xmlns:http="http://schemas.xmlsoap.org/wsdl/http/"
xmlns:mime="http://schemas.xmlsoap.org/wsdl/mime/"
xmlns="http://schemas.xmlsoap.org/wsdl/">

  <!-- Note: Previously defined type definitions omitted for clarity -->
  <types>
    <schema attributeFormDefault="qualified" elementFormDefault="qualified"
    xmlns="http://www.w3.org/2001/XMLSchema"
    targetNamespace="http://somedomain/Calculator/schema">
      <!-- Common result element for HTTP GET/POST binding -->
      <element name="Result" type="int"/>

    </schema>
  </types>


  <!-- Messages for HTTP GET/POST-based Web service -->
  <!-- Note: Previously defined messages omitted for clarity -->
  <message name="AddHttpMsgIn">
    <part name="x" type="xsd:string"/>
    <part name="y" type="xsd:string"/>
  </message>
  <message name="AddHttpMsgOut">
    <part name="result" element="s:Result"/>
  </message>
  <message name="SubtractHttpMsgIn">
    <part name="x" element="xsd:string"/>
    <part name="y" element="xsd:string"/>
  </message>
  <message name="SubtractHttpMsgOut">
    <part name="result" element="s:Result"/>
  </message>

  <!-- More definitions will go here. -->

</definitions>
```

The preceding WSDL document defines a new element of type *int* called *Result* that will be used to contain the result of the *Add* and *Subtract* methods returned to the client. This element is referenced by two new outbound messages, one for each method. The document also defines new inbound messages for the *Add* and *Subtract* methods. The outbound messages define individual parts for each parameter. Since the name/value pairs containing the parameters are not strongly typed, the type of each part is defined as *string*.

HTTP GET/POST extension elements are contained within the *http:// schemas.xmlsoap.org/wsdl/http/* namespace. The convention I follow throughout the remainder of this chapter is to associate references to the namespace using the *http:* moniker. In a few scenarios, HTTP GET/POST bindings leverage the MIME extension elements. They are defined within the *http://schemas.xmlsoap.org/wsdl/mime/* namespace and referenced using the *mime:* moniker.

binding Element Binding

Extensibility elements added to the *binding* element provide information about how the parameters are encoded within the HTTP message. Extensibility elements are added to the *bind*, *operation*, *input*, *output*, and *fault* messages.

The *http:binding* element specifies whether the parameters are passed within the URL or within the body of the HTTP request: The "verb" of the *http:binding* attribute is set to either *GET* or *POST*. The following WSDL document demonstrates the use of the *http:binding* element within the definition of the Calculator Web service:

```
<?xml version="1.0" encoding="utf-8"?>
<definitions targetNamespace="http://somedomain/Calculator/wsdl"
xmlns:tns="http://somedomain/Calculator/wsdl"
xmlns:http="http://schemas.xmlsoap.org/wsdl/http/"
xmlns="http://schemas.xmlsoap.org/wsdl/">

  <!-- Type, message, and port type definitions removed for clarity -->

  <binding name="CalculatorHttpGetBinding" type="tns:CalculatorPortType"/>
    <http:binding verb="GET"/>
    <!-- Operation elements removed for clarity -->
  </binding>

  <!-- More definitions will go here. -->

</definitions>
```

The *http:operation* element specifies the relative address for each operation. Each *input* and *output* message is decorated with an extension element that indicates the method used to encode the parameters passed to the Web service. The three upcoming scenarios for encoding the parameters show the URL encoding of parameters on the query string, nonstandard encoding within the URL, and URL encoding of the parameters in the body of the post.

Parameters can be passed to a Web service via a URL encoded within the query string. URL encoding specifies appending a *?* to the end of the URL and then appending a name/value pair separated with an *=*. If multiple name/value pairs are appended to the URL, they are separated from each other by an *&*. For example, the *Add* method can be called as follows:

```
http://somedomain/Calculator/Add?x=2&y=3
```

In this case, the *input* element within the binding for a particular operation would be decorated with an *http:urlEncoded* element. Here is the resulting HTTP GET binding definition for the Calculator Web service:

```
<?xml version="1.0" encoding="utf-8"?>
<definitions targetNamespace="http://somedomain/Calculator/wsdl"
xmlns:tns="http://somedomain/Calculator/wsdl"
xmlns:http="http://schemas.xmlsoap.org/wsdl/http/"
xmlns="http://schemas.xmlsoap.org/wsdl/">

  <!-- Type, message, and port type definitions removed for clarity -->

  <binding name="CalculatorHttpGetBinding" type="tns:CalculatorPortType"/>
    <http:binding verb="GET"/>
    <operation name="Add">
      <http:operation location="/Add"/>
      <input>
        <http:urlEncoded/>
      </input>
      <output>
        <mime:mimeXml part="Body"/>
      </output>
      <fault>
        <mime:mimeXml part="Fault"/>
      </fault>
    </operation>
    <operation name="Subtract">
      <http:operation location="/Subtract"/>
      <input>
        <http:urlEncoded/>
      </input>
      <output>
        <mime:mimeXml part="Body"/>
      </output>
      <fault>
        <mime:mimeXml part="Fault"/>
      </fault>
    </operation>
  </binding>
```

```
<!-- More definitions will go here. -->
```

```
</definitions>
```

Parameters can also be encoded within the URL in a nonstandard way. In this case, the *location* attribute of the *http:operation* element will contain information about how the parameters are encoded. For example, the parameters for the *Add* method could be encoded within the URL as follows:

```
http://somedomain/Calculator/Add/2plus3
```

The parameters *2* and *3* were encoded within the path info of the URL where the parameters were delimited by *plus*. The resulting *http:operation* element would appear as follows within the binding definitions:

```
<http:operation location="Add/(x)plus(y)"/>
```

The individual message parts enclosed in parentheses are shown in their respective position within the relative URL. In this case, the *input* element within the binding for a particular operation would be decorated with an *http:urlReplacement* element.

The third and final way of encoding the parameters that I will discuss is embedding the URL encoded parameters within the body of the HTTP request message (HTTP POST). For example, the parameters would be encoded within the body of the HTTP request as follows:

```
Add="x=2&y=3"
```

In this case, the *input* element can be described using the MIME type *application/x-www-form-urlencoded*. Therefore, the *operation* element would be decorated with a *mime:content* element. Here is the resulting HTTP POST binding definition for the Calculator Web service:

```
<?xml version="1.0" encoding="utf-8"?>
<definitions targetNamespace="http://somedomain/Calculator/wsdl"
xmlns:tns="http://somedomain/Calculator/wsdl"
xmlns:http="http://schemas.xmlsoap.org/wsdl/http/"
xmlns="http://schemas.xmlsoap.org/wsdl/">

  <!-- Type, message, and port type definitions removed for clarity -->

<binding name="CalculatorHttpPostBinding" type="tns:CalculatorPortType"/>
  <http:binding verb="POST"/>
  <operation name="Add">
    <http:operation location="/Add"/>
    <input>
      <mime:content type="application/x-www-form-urlencoded"/>
    </input>
```

(continued)

```
    <output>
      <mime:mimeXml part="Body"/>
    </output>
    <fault>
      <soap:fault name="CalculateFault" use="literal"/>
    </fault>
  </operation>
  <operation name="Subtract">
    <http:operation location="/Subtract"/>
    <input>
      <mime:content type="application/x-www-form-urlencoded"/>
    </input>
    <output>
      <mime:mimeXml part="Body"/>
    </output>
    <fault>
      <soap:fault name="CalculateFault" use="literal"/>
    </fault>
  </operation>
</binding>

<!-- More definitions will go here. -->

</definitions>
```

The *type* attribute contains a valid MIME type used to indicate the type of content contained within the body of the HTTP message. The content of the HTTP message can also be labeled as being a member of a family of MIME types by using a wildcard. Here are a couple of examples:

```
<!-- The content belongs to the MIME family of text types. -->
<mime:content type="text/*"/>

<!-- Either declaration specifies all MIME types. -->
<mime:content type="text/*"/>
<mime:content/>
```

The *mime:content* element can also contain a *part* attribute, which is used to specify which part is contained within the body of the HTTP message.

If the message has a MIME type of *multipart/related*, the message can contain a collection of MIME-formatted parts. For example, a multipart message can contain a SOAP message (*text/xml*) along with a JPEG image (*image/jpeg*).

A multipart message can be represented within the binding definition using the *mime:multipartRelated* element. The *mime:multipartRelated* element contains a collection of *mime:part* elements. Each *mime:part* element represents a particular MIME-formatted part where its type is declared using the *mime:content* element.

The following example demonstrates how a multipart message containing a SOAP message and a JPEG image is represented within a WSDL document:

```
<mime:multipartRelated>
  <mime:part>
    <soap:body use="literal" part="xyCoordinates"/>
  </mime:part>
  <mime:part>
    <mime:content type="image/jpeg" part="graph"/>
  </mime:part>
</mime:multipartRelated>
```

Notice that you can use the *soap:body* element to indicate that a particular MIME part contains a SOAP message. The message part is assumed to have a MIME type of *text/xml* and be contained within a valid SOAP envelope.

If the MIME message part contains XML but is not SOAP compliant, you can use the *mime:mimeXml* element. The associated *part* element defines the root XML element instead of the body of a SOAP message. This element is used extensively in ASP.NET because the HTTP GET/POST version of a Web service returns the results using non-SOAP-compliant XML.

service Element Binding

The only HTTP extension element specified within the *service* element is *http:address*. Like its SOAP counterpart, it is contained within the port definition and is used to specify the URI where the Web service can be reached. Here is the service definition for the Calculator Web service:

```
<?xml version="1.0" encoding="utf-8"?>
<definitions targetNamespace="http://somedomain/Calculator/wsdl"
xmlns:tns="http://somedomain/Calculator/wsdl"
xmlns:soap="http://schemas.xmlsoap.org/wsdl/soap/"
xmlns="http://schemas.xmlsoap.org/wsdl/">

  <!-- Type, message, port type, and binding definitions removed for clarity -->

  <service name="CalculatorService">
    <port name="CalculatorHttpGetPort" binding="tns:CalculatorHttpGetBinding">
      <http:address location="http://somedomain/Calculator"/>
    </port>
    <port name="CalculatorHttpPostPort" binding="tns:CalculatorHttpPostBinding">
      <http::address location="http://somedomain/Calculator"/>
    </port>
  </service>

</definitions>
```

The preceding WSDL document defines two ports, one for HTTP GET and the other for HTTP POST. Both ports can be reached at *http://somedomain/Calculator*.

import Element

Like XML Schema documents, WSDL documents can import other documents. You can thus achieve the same level of modularity that you can with XML Schema documents. Because a WSDL document can get rather large rather quickly, breaking it up into a number of smaller documents can help make the document easier to understand and possibly easier to maintain.

A common way to divide a single service definition into multiple WSDL documents is to place protocol binding information in a separate document. This allows you to write the interface definitions once and then import them into a WSDL document that defines the specific protocols supported by a particular instance of the Web service.

Unlike its XML Schema counterpart, the *import* element must contain both a *namespace* and a *location* attribute. Imagine that I took the WSDL document for the Calculator Web service and separated it into three parts. I placed the schema definitions into Calculator.xsd, the interface definitions into i_Calculator.wsdl, and the protocol into Calculator.wsdl. Calculator.wsdl serves as the WSDL document for the Web service by importing the other two documents. Here is Calculator.wsdl:

```
<definitions xmlns="http://schemas.xmlsoap.org/wsdl/">

    <!-- First import the schema definitions. -->
    <import namespace="http://somedomain/myschema/"
    location="http://somedomain/Calculator.xsd">

    <!-- Next import the port types and message definitions. -->
    <import namespace="http://somedomain/Calculator/"
    location="http://somedomain/i_Calculator.wsdl">

    <!-- Finally provide the protocol-specific binding definitions. -->

</definitions>
```

Documentation

You can include documentation within a WSDL document by using the *definitions* element's *name* attribute or the *document* element. The *name* attribute can contain a short description of the WSDL document, and the *document* element can contain text as well as other elements. For example, I could use the *document* element to record metadata about the document.

```
<definitions xmlns="http://schemas.xmlsoap.org/wsdl/"
name="The Calculator Web service provides the results of adding and
subtracting two numbers.">
  <document>
    <author>Scott Short</author>
    <version>1.0</version>
  </document>

  <types>
    <document>The following are defined using XML Schema.</document>
    <!-- Type definitions removed for clarity -->
  </types>

  <!-- Additional definitions removed for clarity -->

</definitions>
```

As you can see, the *document* element can be used inside any WSDL language element.

The Calculator Web Service WSDL Document

Here is the WSDL document that I built over the course of this chapter:

```
<?xml version="1.0" encoding="utf-8"?>
<definitions targetNamespace="http://somedomain/Calculator/wsdl"
xmlns:tns="http://somedomain/Calculator/wsdl"
xmlns:xsd="http://www.w3.org/2001/XMLSchema"
xmlns:s="http://somedomain/Calculator/schema"
xmlns:soap="http://schemas.xmlsoap.org/wsdl/soap/"
xmlns:http="http://schemas.xmlsoap.org/wsdl/http/"
xmlns:mime="http://schemas.xmlsoap.org/wsdl/mime/"
xmlns="http://schemas.xmlsoap.org/wsdl/">

  <types>
    <schema attributeFormDefault="qualified" elementFormDefault="qualified"
    xmlns="http://www.w3.org/2001/XMLSchema"
    targetNamespace="http://somedomain/Calculator/schema">
      <!-- Definitions for both the Add and Subtract SOAP messages -->
      <element name="Add">
        <complexType>
          <all>
            <element name="x" type="int"/>
            <element name="y" type="int"/>
          </all>
        </complexType>
      </element>
      <element name="AddResult">
        <complexType>
          <all>
```

(continued)

```xml
            <element name="result" type="int"/>
          </all>
        </complexType>
      </element>

      <element name="Subtract">
        <complexType>
          <all>
            <element name="x" type="int"/> ·
            <element name="y" type="int"/>
          </all>
        </complexType>
      </element>
      <element name="SubtractResult">
        <complexType>
          <all>
            <element name="result" type="int"/>
          </all>
        </complexType>
      </element>

      <!-- Common SOAP fault detail element used by Add and Subtract -->
      <element name="CalculateFault">
        <complexType>
          <all>
            <element name="x" type="int"/>
            <element name="y" type="int"/>
            <element name="Description" type="string"/>
          </all>
        </complexType>
      </element>

      <!-- Common result element for HTTP GET/POST binding -->
      <element name="Result" type="int"/>

    </schema>
  </types>


  <!-- Messages for SOAP-based Web service -->
  <message name="AddMsgIn">
    <part name="parameters" element="s:Add"/>
  </message>
  <message name="AddMsgOut">
    <part name="parameters" element="s:SubtractResult"/>
  </message>
  <message name="SubtractMsgIn">
    <part name="parameters" element="s:Add"/>
  </message>
```

```xml
<message name="SubtractMsgOut">
  <part name="parameters" element="s:SubtractResult"/>
</message>
<message name="CalculateFaultMsg">
  <part name="fault" element="s:CalculateFault"/>
</message>

<!-- Messages for HTTP GET/POST-based Web service -->
<message name="AddHttpMsgIn">
  <part name="x" type="xsd:string"/>
  <part name="y" type="xsd:string"/>
</message>
<message name="AddHttpMsgOut">
  <part name="result" element="s:Result"/>
</message>
<message name="SubtractHttpMsgIn">
  <part name="x" element="xsd:string"/>
  <part name="y" element="xsd:string"/>
</message>
<message name="SubtractHttpMsgOut">
  <part name="result" element="s:Result"/>
</message>


<portType name="CalculatorPortType">
  <operation name="Add">
    <input message="tns:AddMsgIn"/>
    <output message="tns:AddMsgOut"/>
    <fault message="tns:CalculateFaultMsg" name="CalculateFault"/>
  </operation>
  <operation name="Subtract">
    <input message="tns:SubtractMsgIn"/>
    <output message="tns:SubtractMsgOut"/>
    <fault message="tns:CalculateFaultMsg" name="CalculateFault"/>
  </operation>
</portType>


<!-- SOAP Binding -->
<binding name="CalculatorBinding" type="tns:CalculatorPortType">
  <soap:binding style="document"
  transport="http://schemas.xmlsoap.org/soap/http"/>
  <operation name="Add">
    <soap:operation soapAction="http://somedomain/Calculator/Add"/>
    <input>
      <soap:body use="literal"/>
    </input>
    <output>
      <soap:body use="literal"/>
    </output>
```

(continued)

```
        <fault>
          <soap:fault name="CalculateFault" use="literal"/>
        </fault>
      </operation>
      <operation name="Subtract">
        <soap:operation soapAction="http://somedomain/Calculator/Subtract"/>
        <input>
          <soap:body use="literal"/>
        </input>
        <output>
          <soap:body use="literal"/>
        </output>
        <fault>
          <soap:fault name="CalculateFault" use="literal"/>
        </fault>
      </operation>
    </binding>

    <!-- HTTP GET Binding -->
    <binding name="CalculatorHttpGetBinding" type="tns:CalculatorPortType">
      <http:binding verb="GET"/>
      <operation name="Add">
        <http:operation location="/Add"/>
        <input>
          <http:urlEncoded/>
        </input>
        <output>
          <mime:mimeXml part="Body"/>
        </output>
        <fault>
          <mime:mimeXml part="Fault"/>
        </fault>
      </operation>
      <operation name="Subtract">
        <http:operation location="/Subtract"/>
        <input>
          <http:urlEncoded/>
        </input>
        <output>
          <mime:mimeXml part="Body"/>
        </output>
        <fault>
          <mime:mimeXml part="Fault"/>
        </fault>
      </operation>
    </binding>

    <!-- HTTP POST Binding -->
    <binding name="CalculatorHttpPostBinding" type="tns:CalculatorPortType">
      <http:binding verb="POST"/>
      <operation name="Add">
```

```
        <http:operation location="/Add"/>
        <input>
          <mime:content type="application/x-www-form-urlencoded"/>
        </input>
        <output>
          <mime:mimeXml part="Body"/>
        </output>
        <fault>
          <soap:fault name="CalculateFault" use="literal"/>
        </fault>
      </operation>
      <operation name="Subtract">
        <http:operation location="/Subtract"/>
        <input>
          <mime:content type="application/x-www-form-urlencoded"/>
        </input>
        <output>
          <mime:mimeXml part="Body"/>
        </output>
        <fault>
          <soap:fault name="CalculateFault" use="literal"/>
        </fault>
      </operation>
    </binding>

    <service name="CalculatorService">
      <port name="CalculatorPort" binding="tns:CalculatorBinding">
        <soap:address location="http://somedomain/Calculator"/>
      </port>
      <port name="CalculatorHttpGetPort" binding="tns:CalculatorHttpGetBinding">
        <http:address location="http://somedomain/Calculator"/>
      </port>
      <port name="CalculatorHttpPostPort" binding="tns:CalculatorHttpPostBinding">
        <http:address location="http://somedomain/Calculator"/>
      </port>
    </service>

</definitions>
```

Summary

WSDL provides a flexible and extensible means of documenting network services. A WSDL document is composed of five elements under the root *definitions* element: *types*, *message*, *portType*, *binding*, and *service*. These elements
are used to define Web services through a series of associations.

The *types* element contains schema definitions for the data exchanged between the client and the server. The default schema language is XML Schema. However, you can specify another schema language through the use of extensibility elements.

The *message* element identifies a particular message that is exchanged between the client and the server. A message is composed of one or more parts. Each part is represented by the *part* element and can refer to an element or type definition defined within the *types* element.

The *portTypes* element contains one or more *operation* elements. You can think of an operation as an interface—a contract about how the client and the server will interact with each other to perform an action. An operation can be one of four types: request-response, solicit-response, one-way, or notification.

The *binding* element is used to associate a port type with a particular protocol. This is accomplished via extensibility elements. Extensibility elements are elements defined outside the WSDL namespace. The WSDL specification defines three sets of extensibility elements for specifying binding information: SOAP, HTTP GET/POST, and MIME. Because specific technologies such as SOAP and HTTP are represented by extensibility elements, WSDL can be used to describe practically any service.

The *service* element contains one or more *port* elements. A *port* element is used to define an address where a Web service that supports a particular binding can be reached.

6

ASP.NET

ASP.NET, the next generation of the Microsoft Active Server Pages (ASP) platform, is known for the ease with which it allows you to develop Web applications. It provides a layer of abstraction that lets you focus on solving business problems instead of developing the underlying plumbing, which can greatly increase your productivity. This model has been extended beyond Web Forms to include Web services.

ASP.NET is also popular because it offers a rich set of services that you can leverage when you build applications. With the introduction of ASP.NET, the platform facilitates the rapid creation and consumption of Web services. ASP.NET abstracts the underlying Web services protocols such as SOAP, WSDL, and HTTP away from the developer. As I demonstrated in Chapter 1, Web services that expose simple interfaces require little, if any, knowledge of the underlying protocols.

Sometimes you need to exercise a high degree of control over the serialization of the SOAP messages and the format of the WSDL document used to describe the Web service. Fortunately, ASP.NET provides the necessary hooks that allow you to control practically every aspect of the implementation of a Web service. In this chapter, I discuss the hooks ASP.NET provides as well as examples of when to use them.

Web application developers have come to rely on services provided by the ASP platform, such as state management and security. These services have been significantly improved in ASP.NET and can be leveraged to create robust Web services. Additional services such as automatic generation of documentation have also been introduced specifically for Web services.

For a version 1 product, ASP.NET is a remarkably feature-rich and solid development platform. However, as with any V1 product, ASP.NET has some quirks. In this chapter, I talk about many of them and show you how to work through them.

Creating an ASP.NET Web Service

Let's say that an online brokerage firm wants to provide a Web service to its customers. It could accomplish this by writing an ASP.NET Web application. However, the firm wants to extend the reach of its services so that they can be leveraged from other applications. For example, a portal site such as MSN or Yahoo! might want to provide these services but might lack the expertise or the desire to take on the burden of building the services themselves.

Instead, the portal site can provide a UI to the customer and use the brokerage firm's Web service as the back end. At worst, the portal will retain the customer within its site and potentially increase its ad revenue. At best, the portal can charge an incremental amount on top of the fees provided by the brokerage firm. Either way, it is potentially a win-win situation for the portal company and the brokerage firm.

In this chapter, I build the Securities Web service, which allows the client to perform actions such as obtaining a quote for a particular stock, bond, or mutual fund. The individual methods will contain skeleton implementations that let you focus on the mechanics of building Web services using ASP.NET.

The first thing I need to do is define the endpoint for the Securities Web service. A Web service is defined by an .asmx file, which serves as the endpoint for the Web service. Calls made to .asmx files are intercepted and processed by the ASP.NET runtime.

The implementation of the Web service is encapsulated within a class. The class definition can either appear inline within the .asmx file or be contained in a separate dynamic link library (DLL). The .asmx page needs to contain information that the runtime can use to locate the class.

Each .asmx page contains a directive at the top of the page that specifies where and in what form the implementation of the Web service can be found. This directive is used by the ASP.NET runtime to bind the Web service to a class that contains the implementation.

Here is an example in which the implementation of the Web service is contained within the .asmx file:

```
<%@ WebService Language="c#" Class="BrokerageFirm.Securities" %>

namespace BrokerageFirm
{
    // Inline definition of the Securities class
    public class Securities
    {
        Implementation...
    }
}
```

The *Class* attribute contains the fully qualified name of the class that implements the Web service. If the code resides within the .asmx file, you must set the *Language* attribute, which specifies the language in which the code was written.

The first time the Web service is accessed, the ASP.NET runtime will use the *Language* attribute to compile the code with the appropriate compiler. Thus, even if the code implementing the Web service is contained within the .asmx file, it will always be executed as compiled machine code.

Out of the box, ASP.NET is configured to dynamically compile code written in C#, Visual Basic, Visual Basic .NET, and JScript .NET. You can configure additional languages within the web.config file or the machine.config file. The following is the compilation section of the machine.config file found in the C:\WINNT\Microsoft.NET\Framework*version*\CONFIG directory:

```
<!-- compilation Attributes:
  tempDirectory="directory"
  debug="[true|false]"
  strict="[true|false]"
  explicit="[true|false]"
  batch="[true|false]"
  batchTimeout="timeout in seconds"
  maxBatchSize="max number of pages per batched compilation"
  numRecompilesBeforeAppRestart="max number of recompilations
  before appdomain is cycled"
  defaultLanguage="name of a language as specified
  in a <compiler/> tag below"
-->
<compilation debug="false" explicit="true" defaultLanguage="vb">

  <compilers>
    <compiler language="c#;cs;csharp" extension=".cs"
    type="Microsoft.CSharp.CSharpCodeProvider, System,
    Version=1.0.xxxx.0, Culture=neutral,
    PublicKeyToken=1234567890abcde1" />
    <compiler language="vb;visualbasic;vbscript" extension=".vb"
    type="Microsoft.VisualBasic.VBCodeProvider, System,
    Version=1.0.xxxx.0, Culture=neutral,
    PublicKeyToken=1234567890abcde1" />
    <compiler language="js;jscript;javascript" extension=".js"
    type="Microsoft.JScript.JScriptCodeProvider, Microsoft.JScript" />
  </compilers>

  <assemblies>
    <add assembly="mscorlib"/>
    <add assembly="System, Version=1.0.xxxx.0,
    Culture=neutral, PublicKeyToken=1234567890abcde1"/>
```

(continued)

```
    <add assembly="System.Web, Version=1.0.xxxx.0,
    Culture=neutral, PublicKeyToken=1234567890abcde1"/>
    <add assembly="System.Data, Version=1.0.xxxx.0,
    Culture=neutral, PublicKeyToken=1234567890abcde1"/>
    <add assembly="System.Web.Services, Version=1.0.xxxx.0,
    Culture=neutral, PublicKeyToken=1234567890abcde1"/>
    <add assembly="System.Xml, Version=1.0.xxxx.0,
    Culture=neutral, PublicKeyToken=1234567890abcde1"/>
    <add assembly="System.Drawing, Version=1.0.xxxx.0,
    Culture=neutral, PublicKeyToken=1234567890abcde1"/>
    <add assembly="*"/>
  </assemblies>

</compilation>
```

As you can see, the default language is Visual Basic .NET (*vb*), so my C#
example must set the *Language* attribute to *c#*, *cs*, or *csharp*.

The compilation section also includes a list of assemblies that are referenced by code within the .asmx file. If the Securities Web service were to reference entities from an assembly other than those listed in the preceding code, I
could add a new machine-wide reference to my machine.config file or an appli-
cation-wide reference to my web.config file.

The last *add* element specifies a wildcard for the assembly name. If an
assembly is referenced within an .asmx file that was not previously listed, the
ASP.NET runtime will search for the assembly. (See the product documentation
for the exact search order.)

The class implementing the Web service can also reside within a compiled
assembly. By convention, the assembly is placed in the Web application's *bin*
directory because this directory is always included in the search path of the
runtime. This is the default configuration for Web services created using Visual
Studio .NET. The following is the *WebService* directive that Visual Studio .NET
creates automatically:

```
<%@ WebService Language="c#" Codebehind="Service1.asmx.cs" Class="BrokerageFirm
.Service1" %>
```

As is typical in the Visual Studio product line, most of the attributes
defined in the *WebService* directive are used by the editor and are ignored by
the runtime. As I mentioned, you must specify the *Language* attribute only if
the implementation of the Web service resides within the .asmx file. In addition,
the code-behind file is always ignored by the ASP.NET runtime and is used by
Visual Studio .NET to bring up the appropriate source code file when you select
View Code within the IDE.

One other potential gotcha is that Visual Studio .NET will only partially
maintain this file. When you rename the .asmx file to something more meaningful, Visual Studio .NET will automatically rename the associated code-behind

file and update the *WebService* directive accordingly. As a common practice, I also rename the class that implements the Web service to match the name of the .asmx file.

Unfortunately, Visual Studio .NET will not automatically update the *Class* attribute. If you rename the class, you have to manually update this attribute yourself. Furthermore, double-clicking the .asmx file to update this attribute will display the design surface, not the file text. Visual Studio .NET does not provide the same buttons shown on an .aspx file's design surface that allow you to switch between the design view and the underlying text of the file. You have to right-click the file, choose Open With, and then select Source Code (Text) Editor.

Now that I have discussed the two options—placing the implementation for your Web service within the .asmx file or within its own assembly—I am sure you are wondering which one you should use. Well, as with most design decisions, it depends. Placing the code within the .asmx file provides the simplest means of deployment because ASP.NET will compile the code dynamically for you. However, deploying the implementation within an assembly ensures that your code will not contain compilation errors. Also, if you are deploying the Web service outside the confines of your data center, others will not have access to the source code.

Another potential advantage of having the implementation of your Web service reside within an assembly is that it can be directly referenced by other applications hosted on the same machine. For example, suppose I provide an HTML-based UI that allows my customers access to the functionality of the Securities Web service. If the class containing the implementation of the Web service is in its own assembly, the Web application can reference the assembly and directly access the Web service class. This avoids the unnecessary overhead of accessing the functionality remotely.

You should take this approach with caution, however. Some Web services rely on services provided by the ASP.NET runtime to function correctly. For example, a Web method might set an attribute stating that the ASP.NET runtime must create a new transaction on its behalf. Because ASP.NET is responsible for ensuring that a transaction is created, no transaction will be created if the class implementing the Web service is accessed directly.

Regardless of which option you choose, the code for implementing the Web service will be the same. For starters, I will implement one method within my Securities Web service, *InstantQuote*. Plenty of services on the Web give quotes on the price of a company's stock. However, these quotes are often time delayed and can be more than 20 minutes old. *InstantQuote* will use an extremely complex algorithm to obtain the price a security is trading at on the floor. Following is the implementation.

```csharp
using System;
using System.Web.Services;

namespace BrokerageFirm
{
    public class Securities : WebService
    {
        [WebMethod]
        public double InstantQuote(string symbol)
        {
            double price = 0;

            switch(symbol)
            {
                case "MSFT":
                    price = 197.75;
                    break;

                case "SUNW":
                    price = 2.50;
                    break;

                case "ORCL":
                    price = 2.25;
                    break;
            }

            return price;
        }
    }
}
```

All right, so the algorithm is not that complex. What do you expect with an example? The important thing to note is that the implementation of the Web service is a standard public class declaration with a *WebMethod* attribute decorating the *InstantQuote* method. This class declaration can be either compiled into an assembly or placed as is within the .asmx file, and it is the same whether it is contained within the .asmx file or compiled into a separate DLL.

Each method that is intended to be exposed by the Web service must be public and must be decorated with the *WebMethod* attribute. This tells the ASP.NET runtime to expose the method as publicly accessible. From this point on, I will refer to a method of a class decorated with the *WebMethod* attribute as a Web method.

When you decorate a method with the *WebMethod* attribute, you can also set various properties that modify the behavior of the ASP.NET runtime. Table 6-1 lists the properties exposed by the *WebMethod* attribute.

Table 6-1   **Properties of the *WebMethod* Attribute**

Property	Description
BufferResponse	Specifies whether the response to the client should be buffered.
CacheDuration	Specifies the amount of time, in seconds, that a response will be cached in memory by the Web server for a given response. The default is 0.
Description	Specifies the value of the *description* element under each *operation* element within each type definition within the ASP.NET-generated WSDL document.
EnableSession	Specifies whether the ASP.NET session state services will be available for the implementation of the method.
MessageName	Specifies the name of the method exposed by the Web service. Specifically, it sets the name of the element within the body of the SOAP message that contains the parameters as well as the suffix of the SOAP action. It also specifies the prefix of the names of the *message*, *input*, and *output* elements within the ASP.NET-generated WSDL document.
TransactionOption	Specifies the transactional support that should be provided for the implementation of the method. The method can serve only as the root of a transaction and cannot participate in the caller's transaction.

The ASP.NET page framework also provides the *WebService* attribute. This attribute is set at the class level and is used to modify properties of the Web service as a whole. Changes made via the *WebService* attribute will be reflected in the Web service's WSDL document. Table 6-2 lists the properties exposed by the *WebService* attribute.

Table 6-2   **Properties of the *WebService* Attribute**

Property	Description
Description	Specifies the *description* element under the *service* element within the ASP.NET-generated WSDL document.
Name	Specifies the name of the *service* element within the ASP.NET-generated WSDL document. It also specifies the prefix for the names of the *portType*, *binding*, and *port* elements.
Namespace	Specifies the target namespace for the WSDL document as well as the schema document that defines the structures for encoding the parameters within the body of a SOAP message. It also specifies the prefix of the namespace for the schema that contains any custom types defined by the Web service and the value of the SOAP action.

Now that I have defined the Securities Web service, let's talk about how clients can access it.

Transport Protocols and Bindings

The Securities Web service can be accessed by the client only over HTTP because HTTP is the only transport protocol supported by ASP.NET. However, by default the Securities Web service supports three styles of binding to the HTTP protocol: SOAP, HTTP GET, and HTTP POST.

All ASP.NET Web services support the SOAP binding. Of the three binding styles, SOAP is most often preferred because data contained within the messages is strongly typed using XML Schema. In addition, XML datatypes can be mapped fairly well to .NET datatypes.

Support for the HTTP GET/POST bindings is more limited than for SOAP. Some factors that limit the ability of the ASP.NET runtime to support the HTTP GET/POST bindings are the following:

- **Required SOAP headers** The HTTP GET/POST bindings do not provide a means of sending and receiving header information. If a Web service's WSDL document states that a header must always be included in a message exchanged between the client and the server, the message must be encoded using SOAP.

- **Complex input parameters** ASP.NET does not support encoding complex types encoded within the name/value pair on the query string or in the body of the HTTP request.

- **Multiple parameters returned to the client** Only the return parameter can be passed back to the client. ASP.NET does not support encoding *in/out* or *out* parameters within the message returned to the client as a result of an HTTP GET/POST request.

If the Web service exposes relatively simple interfaces, it can also be exposed via HTTP GET and HTTP POST. These bindings are simpler than SOAP, so they might make it easier for developers using less-sophisticated toolsets to interface with the Web service.

For example, it would be relatively straightforward to interface with the Securities Web service using the XML Document Object Model (DOM). To get the current price for Microsoft stock, you load the DOM with the results of the Web method call by passing *http://localhost/Calculator.asmx/InstantQuote?symbol=MSFT* to the *load* method. The DOM will be initialized with the following XML returned from the Web service:

```
<?xml version="1.0" encoding="utf-8" ?>
<double xmlns="http://tempuri.org/">197.75</double>
```

Once the XML DOM has been initialized, you can navigate the DOM to obtain the value of the *double* element.

You can easily specify which protocol bindings your Web service will support. ASP.NET provides a flexible means of configuring Web applications via a hierarchical structure of XML configuration files. The machine-wide configuration file is located at C:\WINNT\Microsoft.NET\Framework*version*\CONFIG\machine.config. The machine.config file contains the default configuration for all Web applications on the machine.

A web.config file, which you can optionally create within the root directory of the Web application, extends or overrides the configuration settings within machine.config. You can also place a web.config file within a subdirectory of the Web application to extend or override the configuration settings within the Web application's web.config file.

By default, the machine.config file is configured to support all three protocols. You can modify the machine.config or web.config file for the particular application to disable any one of the three bindings. For example, you can add the following *webServices* section to your web.config file to disable HTTP POST and HTTP GET:

```
<configuration>

  <!-- Portions of the configuration file removed for clarity -->
  <system.web>
    <webServices>
      <protocols>
        <remove name="HttpPost"/>
        <remove name="HttpGet"/>
      </protocols>
    </webServices>
  </system.web>

</configuration>
```

The protocols added to the machine.config file by default are *HttpSoap*, *HttpPost*, *HttpGet*, and *Documentation*. I discuss *Documentation* in the next section. Unfortunately, in this version of ASP.NET the supported protocols are not extensible.

Valid child elements for the *protocols* element are *add*, *remove*, and *clear*. The *add* and *remove* elements add and remove a particular protocol specified by the *name* attribute, respectively. The *clear* element clears all settings that are inherited from parent configuration files. For example, the following configuration file ensures that only *HttpSoap* and *Documentation* are supported, regardless of what was set in parent configuration files:

```
<configuration>

  <!-- Portions of the configuration file removed for clarity -->
  <system.web>
    <webServices>
      <protocols>
        <clear/>
        <add name="HttpSoap"/>
        <add name="Documentation"/>
      </protocols>
    </webServices>
  </system.web>

</configuration>
```

First I clear any configuration settings that might have been set by a parent configuration file. Then I explicitly add *HttpSoap* and *Documentation* to the list of protocols supported by the Web service.

Web Service Documentation

The ASP.NET runtime includes a set of services that provide documentation for your Web service. The ASP.NET runtime uses reflection to generate two types of documentation: human-readable documentation, and documentation used by client applications to interact with the Web service.

You can reach HTML-based documentation by entering the URL of the Web service into a Web browser. Both the *WebService* and *WebMethod* attributes expose a *Description* property. The following example is a modified version of the Securities Web service I created earlier:

```
using System;
using System.Web.Services;

namespace BrokerageFirm
{
    [WebService(Description="This Web service provides services
    related to securities.")]
    public class Securities : WebService
    {
        [WebMethod(Description="Used to obtain a real-time quote
        for a given security.")]
        public double InstantQuote(string symbol)
        {
```

```
        double price = 0;

        switch(symbol)
        {
            case "MSFT":
                price = 197.75;
                break;

            case "SUNW":
                price = 2.50;
                break;

            case "ORCL":
                price = 2.25;
                break;
        }

        return price;
    }
  }
}
```

The HTML-based documentation that is automatically generated for the Securities Web service is shown here:

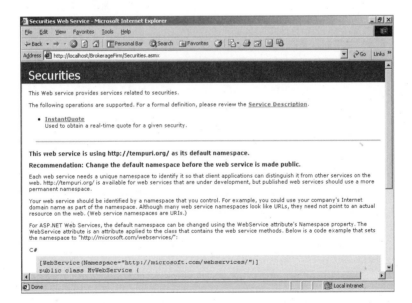

The Web page lists the method exposed by the Web service, *InstantQuote*. The Web page also provides a recommendation to set the default namespace of the

Web service and provides code examples for C# and Visual Basic .NET. I cover how to set the default namespace later in the chapter.

If you click on a particular method, you see documentation for that particular method, as shown here:

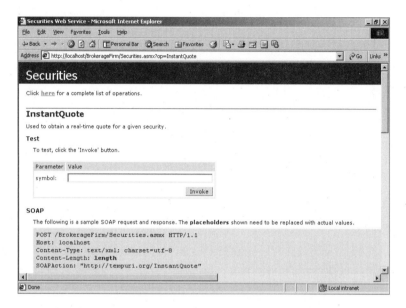

The documentation for the *InstantQuote* method shows the parameter that is expected to be passed. The text set by the *WebMethod* attribute's *Description* property is also displayed. The Web page also provides an example template for how the parameters should be encoded within SOAP, HTTP GET, and HTTP POST messages.

If the parameters are simple, as in the case of the *InstantQuote* method, the generated documentation for the method also includes a test harness for posting data via HTTP GET to the Web service. This simple test harness can come in handy for testing the logic within the Web service. It also serves as the default client when you debug your Web service in Visual Studio .NET.

The documentation automatically generated by ASP.NET serves as a good starting point. However, you should consider expanding it to include more descriptive information about the Web service. You should also consider showing a few examples, including the contents of the request and response messages—especially for Web services that will be publicly exposed via the Internet.

You can configure ASP.NET to display your custom documentation when a user navigates to the .asmx file by setting the *wsdlHelpGenerator* element within the configuration file. The HTML documentation for the Securities Web service displayed in the preceding graphic is generated by DefaultWsdlHelp-

Generator.aspx, which is located in the C:\WINNT\Microsoft.NET\Framework*version*\CONFIG directory. The entry within the machine.config file for the default HTML documentation is as follows:

```
<configuration>

  <!-- Portions of the configuration file removed for clarity -->
  <system.web>
    <webServices>
      <wsdlHelpGenerator href="DefaultWsdlHelpGenerator.aspx" />
    </webServices>
  </system.web>


</configuration>
```

Despite the *wsdl* prefix, the *wsdlHelpGenerator* element is used to set the file that will display the HTML-based documentation, not the WSDL documentation. The *href* attribute specifies the name of the file that will be used to display the documentation. If the filename is fully qualified, it should contain the file path to the document, not the document's URL.

The ASP.NET runtime also generates documentation about a Web service in a format that can be programmatically consumed by clients. The ASP.NET runtime automatically generates a WSDL document that describes the Web service. You can access this by passing the value *wsdl* to the .asmx file within the query string. The following is a portion of the WSDL generated for the Securities Web service:

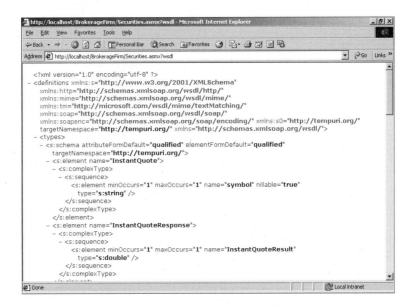

The WSDL document describes the Web service and can be used by the ASP.NET platform to create proxies for calling Web methods. I discuss how to create and use Web service proxies in the section titled "Using the WSDL Utility to Generate Proxy Code" later in this chapter. I discussed WSDL in more detail back in Chapter 5.

The autogeneration of both the HTML and the WSDL documentation is enabled by default within the machine.config file. You can disable autogeneration of documentation for the entire machine by modifying the machine.config file, or you can disable it for an individual Web directory by modifying the web.config file. The following example disables the documentation support:

```
<configuration>

  <!-- Portions of the configuration file removed for clarity -->
  <system.web>
    <webServices>
      <protocols>
        <remove name="Documentation"/>
      </protocols>
    </webServices>
  </system.web>

</configuration>
```

Unfortunately, there is no way to disable the HTML and WSDL documentation separately.

Raising Errors

Recall that the *InstantQuote* Web method exposed by the Securities Web service returns the price of a particular security. However, there is one problem with its current implementation. If the Web method does not recognize a symbol, a price of zero will be returned to the client. This is obviously a problem, especially because the current implementation supports only three symbols. To avoid striking panic in the hearts of investors, we need a way to raise an error stating that an invalid symbol was passed.

An error of type *SoapException* can be thrown when an error is encountered within the Securities Web service. If a *SoapException* error is thrown by a Web method, the ASP.NET runtime will serialize the information into a SOAP *Fault* message that will be sent back to the client.

As you learned in Chapter 3, a well-formed *Fault* element must contain at least two child elements, *faultstring* and *faultcode*. The constructor for the

SoapException class takes a minimum of two parameters to set the value of these elements. Once an instance of the *SoapException* object has been created, the values can be accessed by the *Message* and *Code* properties.

The *Code* property is of type *XmlQualifiedName*. For convenience, the *SoapException* class defines static fields for each of the base fault codes defined by the SOAP specification. The following extended version of the Securities Web service throws an exception resulting from an error on the server:

```csharp
using System;
using System.Web.Services;
using System.Web.Services.Protocols;

namespace BrokerageFirm
{
    [WebService(Description="This Web service provides services
    related to securities.")]
    public class Securities : WebService
    {
        [WebMethod(Description="Used to obtain a real-time quote
        for a given security.")]
        public double InstantQuote(string symbol)
        {
            double price = 0;

            switch(symbol.ToUpper())
            {
                case "MSFT":
                    price = 197.75;
                    break;

                case "SUNW":
                    price = 2.50;
                    break;

                case "ORCL":
                    price = 2.25;
                    break;
                default:
                    throw new SoapException("Invalid symbol.",
                    SoapException.ClientFaultCode);
            }

            return price;
        }
    }
}
```

As I explained in Chapter 3, you can define more-specific fault codes. These developer-defined codes can be appended to the base fault code delimited by a period. The following throws an exception that contains a more-specific fault code:

```
XmlQualifiedName invalidSymbolsFaultCode =
    new XmlQualifiedName("Client.InvalidSymbol",
    "http://schemas.xmlsoap.org/soap/envelope/");
throw new SoapException("Invalid symbol.", invalidSymbolsFaultCode);
```

Recall that additional elements can also appear within the *Fault* element. The *SoapException* class exposes a number of read-only properties to access this information. Because the properties are read-only, the *SoapException* class has numerous overloaded constructors that enable the properties to be set. Table 6-3 lists the properties that can be set via an overloaded constructor.

Table 6-3 **Properties of the *SoapException* Class**

Property	Description
Actor	Specifies the value of the *faultactor* element
Code	Specifies the value of the *faultcode* element
Detail	Specifies the contents of the *faultdetail* element
Message	Specifies the value of the *faultstring* element
InnerException	Specifies the value of the inner exception
OtherElements	Used to access any other child elements that might be present within the *Fault* element

Both the *Detail* and the *OtherElements* properties can contain an arbitrary hierarchy of data. The *Detail* property is of type *XmlNode* and can contain more-detailed information about the *Fault* element. The *OtherElements* property contains an array of type *XmlNode* and is used to contain other child elements that might reside within the *Fault* elements.

If an exception is thrown by the Web method that is not of type *SoapException*, the ASP.NET runtime will serialize it into the body of the SOAP *Fault* element. The *faultcode* element will be set to *Server*, and the *faultstring* element will be set to the output of the *ToString* method of the exception object. The output usually contains the call stack and other information that would be useful for the Web service developer but not the client. Therefore, ensuring that a client-friendly *SoapException* class will be thrown from the Web method is recommended.

SOAP Encoding Styles

I mentioned in Chapter 5 that the WSDL SOAP extensibility elements define two different encoding styles, Document and RPC. The RPC style of encoding formats the message as described in the section titled "SOAP Encoding" in Chapter 3 and is intended to support procedure-oriented interaction between the client and the server. The Document style of encoding is intended to support document-oriented messages that will be exchanged between the client and the server. See the section titled "Extensibility Elements" in Chapter 4 for more information.

The encoding style affects the format in which the Web service expects SOAP requests to be encoded by the client and how the response received from the Web service will be encoded. ASP.NET Web services have overwhelmingly been showcased as an easy way to facilitate procedure-based communication between the client and the server. But ironically, Document is the default encoding style.

Recall that the default encoding style is set in the WSDL document via the *style* attribute of the *binding* extensibility element. You can set the default encoding style value by decorating the class with the *SoapDocumentService* or *SoapRpcService* element. Because the *InstantQuote* Web method is intended to support procedure-oriented communication between the client and the server, the following example uses the *SoapRpcService* attribute to set the style to RPC:

```
using System;
using System.Web.Services;
using System.Web.Services.Protocols;

namespace BrokerageFirm
{
    [WebService(Description="This Web service provides services
    related to securities.")]
    [SoapRpcService]
    public class Securities : WebService
    {
        [WebMethod(Description="Used to obtain a real-time quote
        for a given security.")]
        public double InstantQuote(string symbol)
        {
            double price = 0;

            // Implementation...

            return price;
        }
    }
}
```

All methods defined by the *Securities* class, including *InstantQuote*, will default to RPC-style encoding. You can override this default by decorating a method with the *SoapDocumentMethod* attribute. On the other hand, if you want to formally state that the default is Document, you can do so using the *SoapDocumentService* attribute.

The *SoapDocumentService* attribute exposes three properties that you can set to control how the SOAP documents are formatted. Of the three, the *SoapRpcService* attribute supports only the *RoutingStyle* property. Table 6-4 describes these properties.

Table 6-4   Properties of the *SoapDocumentService* Attribute

Property	Description
ParameterStyle	Specifies whether the parameters are wrapped in a single element within the body of the SOAP message
RoutingStyle	Specifies whether the HTTP *SOAPAction* header should be populated or left blank
Use	Specifies whether the default for the encoding style of the messages is *Literal* or *Encoded*

Recall from Chapter 4 that the SOAP extension elements also allow you to specify whether the individual messages within an operation are literal or encoded. Literal means that the message must be formatted exactly as dictated by the schema. Encoded means that the message can be encoded as specified. For RPC-style documents, the *use* attribute is always set to *Encoded*.

The WSDL SOAP extension elements do not provide a means of specifying a default for the *use* attribute. Conveniently, the *SoapDocumentService* attribute does so via the *Use* property. The ASP.NET runtime will propagate the value of this property to every WSDL message definition. The *Use* property can be set to one of three values defined in the *SoapBindingUse* enumeration: *Literal*, *Encoded*, or *Default*. The default is *Literal*.

The value of the *use* attribute for RPC-style documents is *encoded*. The *SoapRpcService* attribute does not expose a *Use* property, so the value cannot be changed.

In Chapter 3, I also mentioned that the *SOAPAction* HTTP header can be empty if the intent of the SOAP message is conveyed in the HTTP request header entry. As you will see in Chapter 9, Universal Description, Discovery, and Integration (UDDI) messages require the *HTTPAction* header to be empty because each action is posted to a unique URL that conveys the intent of the request.

You can specify whether the *SOAPAction* header should be populated by setting the *RoutingStyle* parameter of the *SoapDocumentService* or *SoapRpcService* attribute. The *RoutingStyle* parameter is of type *SoapServiceRoutingStyle* and can be set to *SoapAction* or *RequestElement*. The default is *SoapAction*.

You can also use the *SoapDocumentService* attribute to indicate how parameters should be encoded within the body of the message. The *ParameterStyle* property can be set to one of three values defined in the *SoapParameterStyle* enumeration: *Bare*, *Wrapped*, or *Default*.

Wrapped means that the parameters will be wrapped within a parent element. The parent element will have the same name as the Web method. *Bare* means that the parameter elements will appear as direct children of the SOAP body element. The default is *Wrapped*. Because RPC-style documents follow the encoding style specified by Section 7 of the SOAP specification, parameters are always wrapped.

The *SoapDocumentMethod* and the *SoapRpcMethod* attributes are associated with a particular Web method and can be used to override the defaults set by their Web service counterparts. You can also use them to further define how messages sent and received by a Web method should be encoded. Table 6-5 lists the properties exposed by the *SoapDocumentMethod* attribute. The *SoapRpcMethod* attribute supports the same set of properties minus the *ParameterStyle* and *Use* properties.

Table 6-5   Properties of the *SoapDocumentMethod* Attribute

Property	Description
Action	Specifies the URI placed in the HTTP *SOAPAction* header
Binding	Associates a Web method with a particular binding specified by the *WebServiceBinding* attribute
OneWay	Specifies whether the client will receive a response in association with the request
ParameterStyle	Specifies whether the parameters are wrapped in a single element within the body of the SOAP message
RequestElementName	Specifies the name of the request element within the body of the SOAP message
RequestNamespace	Specifies the namespace URI that contains request element definition
ResponseElementName	Specifies the name of the response element within the body of the SOAP message
ResponseNamespace	Specifies the namespace URI that contains response element definition
Use	Specifies whether the encoding style of the messages is *Literal* or *Encoded*

ASP.NET supports two of the four message exchange patterns defined by WSDL, request-response and one-way. So far in this chapter, the examples have all been based on the default message pattern, request-response. Both the *SoapDocumentMethod* and the *SoapRpcMethod* attributes expose the *OneWay* property. When set to *true*, this property states that no response will be returned to the client when that particular Web method is invoked.

The *SoapDocumentMethod* and the *SoapRpcMethod* attributes also allow you to specify the name of the element used to wrap the parameters within the request and response messages. You can set the *ResponseElementName* and *RequestElementName* properties to the name assigned to their respective elements.

You can also set the namespace in which the datatype of the request or response element is defined by setting the *RequestNamespace* or *Response-Namespace* property. If this property is not set, the namespace defaults to */encodedTypes* relative to the Web service's namespace.

If the *ParameterStyle* property is set to *Wrapped*, the properties used to set the element name and the namespace of the response and request messages will be ignored.

Encoding References

When you pass parameters to a remote service, you need to take into account whether the identity of the parameters will be maintained. In some cases, maintaining the identity of the parameters is extremely important. Consider the following Web service, which registers rock climbers for a competition:

```
public struct Person
{
    public string Name;
    public int Age;
}


public class ClimbingCompetition
{
    [WebMethod]
    public void Register(Person contestant, Person belay)
    {
        // Implementation...
    }
}
```

The *contestant* is the individual who will be climbing. The climber will be attached to a rope in case she falls. The *belay* is the individual who will be holding the other end of the rope on behalf of the climber. With that information in mind, consider the following example:

```
ClimbingCompetition competition = new ClimbingCompetition();
Person climber = new Person();

competition.Register(climber, climber);
```

The preceding code contains an error: it registers a climber as both the contestant and the belay. Needless to say, the climber better be darn sure she is not going to fall! Unfortunately, the *Register* method has no way to capture this runtime error because structures are, by default, passed by value. Therefore, two independent copies of *climber* will be passed to the *Register* Web method.

I am fairly certain that the sponsors of the competition would want to ensure that every climber is being belayed. However, unless identity is maintained, the *Register* method will have no idea whether the contestant and the belay are one and the same. I will explain two potential ways of solving this problem.

The first way is to pass a unique identifier with each of the entities. For example, in addition to passing the person's name and age, you might also want to pass the person's driver's license number (assuming that the driver's license number is guaranteed to be unique). The implementation of the *Register* method could then check to ensure that the license number of the contestant does not match the license number of the belay.

The second way to solve this problem is to pass the instance of the *Person* structure by reference. In Chapter 3 you learned how SOAP Encoding specifies the use of the *href* and *id* attributes to maintain the identity of a parameter passed by reference. ASP.NET leverages this mechanism to maintain the identities of instances of structures that are passed by reference. Let's take a look at a modified version of the *Register* method:

```
public struct Person
{
    public string Name;
    public int Age;
}

public class ClimbingCompetition
{
    [WebMethod]
    [SoapRpcMethod]
    public void Register(ref Person contestant, ref Person belay)
    {
        // Verify that the contestant and the belay
        // are not the same person.
        if(Object.ReferenceEquals(contestant, belay))
        {
            throw new SoapException(
                "The contestant and the belay cannot be the same person.",
                SoapException.ClientFaultCode);
        }

        // Implementation...
    }
}
```

In the preceding example, the *Register* Web method is decorated with the *SoapRpcMethod* attribute. This instructs the ASP.NET runtime to serialize the parameters using SOAP Encoding as specified in Section 5 of the SOAP 1.1 specification. In addition, each parameter is decorated with the *ref* keyword, which indicates that the parameter will be passed by reference. This instructs the ASP.NET runtime to maintain the identity of the instance of the structure passed to the *Register* method. Note that ASP.NET will maintain identity only for Web methods decorated with the *SoapRpcMethod* attribute or contained within a class decorated with the *SoapRpcService* attribute.

Unfortunately, ASP.NET is somewhat inconsistent when handling parameters passed by reference. There is one case in which ASP.NET will not maintain the identity of parameters passed by reference. There is another case in which the identity is maintained, but modifications to the parameters passed by reference are not passed back to the caller. Let's examine each of these situations separately.

With the first issue, the ASP.NET runtime does not properly maintain the identity of parameters when core value types such as *Int32* and *String* are passed by reference. Consider the following example:

```
public class Issues
{
    [WebMethod]
    [SoapRpcMethod]
    public void Issue1(ref int x, ref int y)
    {
        x += 10;
        y += 30;
    }
}
```

Since both *x* and *y* are decorated with the *ref* keyword, their values will be round-tripped to the caller. Therefore, any modifications made to the values of *x* and *y* by the *Issue1* Web method will be reflected on the client. However, because the identities of the parameters are not maintained, your application could be left in an inconsistent state. Consider the following client code:

```
Issues issues = new Issues();
int z = 10;
issues.Issue1(ref z, ref z);
```

This code leverages a proxy class generated by the ASP.NET WSDL.exe command line utility and generates the following SOAP request message:

```
<?xml version="1.0" encoding="utf-8"?>
<soap:Envelope xmlns:soap="http://schemas.xmlsoap.org/soap/envelope/"
xmlns:soapenc="http://schemas.xmlsoap.org/soap/encoding/"
xmlns:tns="http://tempuri.org/"
xmlns:types="http://tempuri.org/encodedTypes"
xmlns:xsi="http://www.w3.org/2001/XMLSchema-instance"
xmlns:xsd="http://www.w3.org/2001/XMLSchema">
```

```
<soap:Body
  soap:encodingStyle="http://schemas.xmlsoap.org/soap/encoding/">
   <tns:Issue1>
     <x xsi:type="xsd:int">10</x>
     <y xsi:type="xsd:int">10</y>
   </tns:Issue1>
 </soap:Body>
</soap:Envelope>
```

Notice that two distinct copies of the value of *z* were encoded into the request message. Unfortunately, the *Issue1* Web method has no way of knowing that the parameters *x* and *y* actually point to the same variable *z* on the client and therefore will act on *x* and *y* independently. If identity was maintained, *z* would equal 50 as a result of calling *Issue1*. However, because identity wasn't maintained, *x* is set equal to 20 and *y* is set equal to 40, as shown in the resulting SOAP response message:

```
<?xml version="1.0" encoding="utf-8"?>
<soap:Envelope xmlns:soap="http://schemas.xmlsoap.org/soap/envelope/"
xmlns:soapenc="http://schemas.xmlsoap.org/soap/encoding/"
xmlns:tns="http://tempuri.org/"
xmlns:types="http://tempuri.org/encodedTypes"
xmlns:xsi="http://www.w3.org/2001/XMLSchema-instance"
xmlns:xsd="http://www.w3.org/2001/XMLSchema">
  <soap:Body
    soap:encodingStyle="http://schemas.xmlsoap.org/soap/encoding/">
     <tns:Issue1Response>
       <x xsi:type="xsd:int">20</x>
       <y xsi:type="xsd:int">40</y>
     </tns:Issue1Response>
   </soap:Body>
</soap:Envelope>
```

The ASP.NET-generated proxy will first set *z* equal to 20 and then set *z* equal to 40. Therefore the final state of *z* will be 40 instead of the correct value of 50. One potential—albeit clumsy—workaround is to wrap the common value type within a structure. The following example demonstrates this technique:

```
public class Issues
{
    public struct Parameter
    {
        public int Value;
    }

    [WebMethod]
    [SoapRpcMethod]
    public void Issue1(ref Parameter x, ref Parameter y)
    {
        x.Value += 10;
        y.Value += 30;
    }
}
```

Unlike core value types, the ASP.NET runtime will maintain the identity of an instance of a structure that is passed by reference. Unfortunately the ASP.NET runtime will also maintain the identity of an instance of a structure that is passed by value. Therefore, the preceding example will exhibit the same behavior even if the *ref* keyword is specified. If you do not want the identities of the parameters to be maintained, you can decorate the Web method with the *SoapDocumentMethod* parameter instead of the *SoapRpcMethod* parameter.

The final issue is that the ASP.NET runtime will serialize .NET reference types in only the SOAP request message and not the response message. By default, reference types are passed by reference to a method. To achieve this behavior, the client must receive the state of the reference type after the message has returned. However, because the ASP.NET runtime will not serialize parameters containing instances of reference types in the return SOAP response message, the client does not have sufficient information to update its variables accordingly.

If you want parameters containing instances of reference types to be passed by reference, you need to decorate the parameter with the *ref* keyword. Parameters containing instances of reference types that are decorated with the *ref* keyword will be serialized in both the SOAP request message and the response message.

Granted, it is helpful to have a means by which to pass data contained in reference types one way across the wire in an effort to reduce the amount of data sent. However, this should be accomplished without overloading the meaning of existing keywords. The meanings of keywords should remain the same whether the code is executed locally or remotely. The companion CD contains sample code for the three issues I describe in this section.

Interface Inheritance

As I mentioned at the beginning of the chapter, the Securities Web service is intended to be consumed by portals such as MSN and Yahoo! Come to find out that other brokerage companies have approached MSN as well. In an effort to accommodate the numerous requests, MSN has defined a standard interface in which it will communicate with the various online brokerage firms.

Interface-based programming has been popularized by technologies such as COM, CORBA, and Java. Within the .NET platform, interfaces continue to play an important role. They facilitate treating different objects in a polymorphic fashion without the overhead and complexity of implementation inheritance.

An interface defines a contract by which classes that inherit a particular interface must support all the methods defined by the interface. Code that can interact with a particular interface can consume any object that exposes that interface. For example, the *IClonable* interface can be exposed by an object that knows how to clone itself. Code written against the *IClonable* interface will be able to clone any object that exposes the interface.

In the case of MSN, it would not be ideal to write custom client code to interface with every single securities-related Web service. Instead, MSN can define a standard interface that all the securities-related Web services must comply with.

The first task for MSN is to create an abstract interface for the Securities Web service. As you learned in the previous chapter, a Web service interface is defined within a WSDL document. A transport-specific interface definition is represented by a binding definition, while a transport-agnostic interface definition is represented by a port type definition.

The easiest way to generate a WSDL document that describes the interface is to have ASP.NET automatically generate the WSDL for you. The following example creates a Web service that defines an abstract class:

```
<%@ WebService Language="c#" Class="MSN.Securities" %>

using System;
using System.Web.Services;
using System.Web.Services.Protocols;

namespace MSN
{
    [WebService(Namespace="http://msn.com/Securities")]
    [SoapRpcService]
    public abstract class Securities : WebService
    {
        [WebMethod]
        public abstract double InstantQuote(string symbol);
    }
}
```

The preceding code defines an interface for the Securities Web service. Unfortunately, the *abstract* keyword is not recognized by the ASP.NET platform, so the code will define a full WSDL document, not just the interfaces.

One way to overcome this problem is to save the WSDL that is generated by the ASP.NET runtime with its service definitions removed. Without the service definitions, a client will have no way of locating the endpoints, which makes the interface definitions abstract. Here is the WSDL document with its service definitions removed:

```
<?xml version="1.0" encoding="utf-8"?>
<definitions xmlns:s="http://www.w3.org/2001/XMLSchema"
 xmlns:http="http://schemas.xmlsoap.org/wsdl/http/"
 xmlns:mime="http://schemas.xmlsoap.org/wsdl/mime/"
 xmlns:tm="http://microsoft.com/wsdl/mime/textMatching/"
```

(continued)

```
xmlns:soap="http://schemas.xmlsoap.org/wsdl/soap/"
xmlns:soapenc="http://schemas.xmlsoap.org/soap/encoding/"
xmlns:tns="http://msn.com/Securities"
targetNamespace="http://msn.com/Securities"
xmlns="http://schemas.xmlsoap.org/wsdl/">
  <types />
  <message name="InstantQuoteSoapIn">
    <part name="symbol" type="s:string" />
    <part name="count" type="s:int" />
  </message>
  <message name="InstantQuoteSoapOut">
    <part name="InstantQuoteResult" type="s:double" />
  </message>
  <portType name="SecuritiesSoap">
    <operation name="InstantQuote">
      <input message="tns:InstantQuoteSoapIn" />
      <output message="tns:InstantQuoteSoapOut" />
    </operation>
  </portType>
  <binding name="SecuritiesSoap" type="tns:SecuritiesSoap">
    <soap:binding
    transport="http://schemas.xmlsoap.org/soap/http" style="rpc" />
    <operation name="InstantQuote">
      <soap:operation
      soapAction="http://msn.com/Securities/InstantQuote" style="rpc" />
      <input>
        <soap:body use="encoded" namespace="http://msn.com/Securities"
        encodingStyle="http://schemas.xmlsoap.org/soap/encoding/" />
      </input>
      <output>
        <soap:body use="encoded" namespace="http://msn.com/Securities"
        encodingStyle="http://schemas.xmlsoap.org/soap/encoding/" />
      </output>
    </operation>
  </binding>
</definitions>
```

In addition to removing the service definitions, I also remove any definitions not directly related to the SOAP binding. I will readdress this issue in a moment when I discuss some of the limitations of the ASP.NET support for interface inheritance.

A Web service can inherit an interface by referencing a port type or a binding that is defined by another Web service. ASP.NET does not provide a mechanism for providing protocol-agnostic interface inheritance. For example, you cannot inherit an interface from a Web service that is exposed only via SMTP. To do this, you would have to hand-roll the WSDL used to describe the service so that it references the port type defined within another namespace. You would also need to disable the WSDL document that is automatically generated by ASP.NET. (See the "Web Service Documentation" section earlier in the chapter.)

ASP.NET does provide a mechanism for facilitating transport-specific interface inheritance. You use the *WebServiceBinding* attribute to reference a binding defined within another namespace. You use the *Binding* property of the *SoapDocumentMethod* or *SoapRpcMethod* attribute to reference the binding definition referenced by the *WebServiceBinding* attribute.

Next I modify the definition of the Securities Web service to inherit the interface defined within the MSN namespace. I do so by referencing the *SecuritiesSoap* binding definition. Suppose the preceding WSDL document is located at *http://msn.com/Securities.wsdl*. The following code defines the Securities Web service provided by *www.woodgrovebank.com*:

```
using System;
using System.Web.Services;
using System.Web.Services.Protocols;

namespace BrokerageFirm
{
    [SoapRpcService]
    [WebServiceBinding("SecuritiesSoap",
    "http://msn.com/Securities", "http://msn.com/Securities.wsdl")]
    public class Securities : WebService
    {
```

I reference the *SecuritiesSoap* binding definition using the *WebServiceBinding* attribute. The three parameters I pass to the attribute's constructor are the name of the referenced binding definition, the namespace containing the definition, and the location of the WSDL document containing the definition.

If the binding definition is referenced within the Web method, the ASP.NET runtime will add a reference to the WSDL namespace that contains the binding. The ASP.NET runtime will also add an *import* element to the autogenerated WSDL document. Finally, the ASP.NET runtime will add a port within the service definition that is associated with the referenced binding definition, as shown here:

```
        [WebMethod]
        [SoapRpcMethod(Binding="SecuritiesSoap")]
        public double InstantQuote(string symbol)
        {
            double price = 0;

            // Implementation...

            return price;
        }
    }
}
```

I use the *Binding* property of *SoapRpcMethod* to associate the Web method with the binding definition. The value of the binding property must match the name assigned to a *WebServiceBinding* attribute defined at the class level; otherwise, a run-time exception will occur.

Using the *WebServiceBinding* attribute to facilitate interface inheritance has some limitations. First, you can reference only SOAP binding definitions. There is also no tool support for referencing external binding definitions. Developers must take it upon themselves to create Web methods that match the referenced binding definition. Finally, there is no validation either at compile time or at run time to ensure that the Web service implements all the methods exposed by the inherited interface.

To ensure that the Web service supports all the methods of the inherited interface, you can use the WSDL.exe tool to generate an abstract class representing the Web service. You can then add the resulting code to your project and derive from the abstract class instead of the *WebService* class. The following example creates the BaseSecurities.cs file that contains an abstract class definition for the base Web service:

```
wsdl /server /out:BaseSecurities.cs http://msn.com/Securities.wsdl
```

Once BaseSecurities.cs has been created and added to my project, I can derive the Web service as follows:

```
using System;
using System.Web.Services;
using System.Web.Services.Protocols;

namespace BrokerageFirm
{
    [WebService(Description="This Web service provides services related to
    securities.")]
    [SoapRpcService]
    [WebServiceBinding("SecuritiesSoap", "http://msn.com/Securities",
    "http://msn.com/Securities.wsdl")]
    public class Securities : MSN.Securities
    {

        // Implementation...

    }
}
```

If the *Securities* class does not implement all the abstract methods defined within the *MSN.Securities* class, I will receive a compiler error.

Managing State

HTTP is by nature a stateless protocol. Even with the introduction of the *connection keep-alive* protocol in HTTP 1.1, you cannot assume that all requests from a given client will be sent over a single connection. If the Web application needs to maintain state on behalf of the user, you often have to roll your own solutions.

Furthermore, state is usually scoped to the application. Application configuration parameters such as database connection strings are an example. Defining a Web application and providing a mechanism to store state that is scoped to the application is an implementation detail of the Web development platform.

The ASP development platform defines a Web application and provides a service for maintaining both session and application state. However, the ASP state management services have some serious limitations. ASP.NET provides a much-improved state management service. The service can be leveraged by Web Forms as well as Web services.

Session State

It is considered good practice to avoid having to maintain state between requests, when practical. For that reason, session state is disabled by default. You have to explicitly enable it for a particular Web method.

Maintaining state on behalf of a user involves associating multiple HTTP requests with one user session. ASP.NET uses a unique identifier that is passed by the client to identify the session. This identifier can be saved in a cookie maintained by the client or embedded within the URL of the request. Even though Web Forms supports both, Web services support only cookies.

If the proxy used by the client to access the Web service supports cookies, the session ID will automatically be sent with every request. ASP.NET uses a transient cookie to store the session ID. By definition, the cookie is intended to be maintained only for the life of the proxy used to access the Web service.

Because cookies are HTTP-specific, the session state mechanism is bound to the HTTP protocol. A transport protocol–agnostic way of passing the session ID would be to place the session ID within the header of the SOAP message. But this is not supported by ASP.NET, so you would have to roll your own state management system to support this scenario.

Once the session is identified, you need a repository to store the data associated with the session. The following three scenarios are supported, each with its advantages and disadvantages:

- **In Process** This is the fastest scenario because calls to read/write session state will be handled in process. However, this is also the least robust configuration. If the ASP.NET worker process (aspnet_wp.exe) is terminated for any reason, all session state being maintained for the application will be lost. This configuration is ideal for Web services hosted on a single machine that need the most performant way of accessing state.

- **Out of Process** In this configuration, session state is maintained in a separate process that can even reside on another machine. One advantage of this configuration is that if the ASP.NET worker process is terminated, the session state for the application will still be preserved. Because session state is maintained in memory, if the session state server (aspnet_state.exe) is terminated, all session state will be lost. Another advantage of this configuration is that state can be shared across multiple Web servers. All Web servers within the Web farm can be configured to point to the same state management process. This configuration is ideal for Web services hosted in a Web farm where the loss of state information should be avoided but is not critical.

- **SQL Server** This is the most robust and scalable of the three configurations. Session state is maintained within a SQL Server database. The session state service maintains a set of tables in which the session state data is serialized into a binary blob. This is the ideal configuration for Web services hosted in a Web farm if you can afford to purchase and maintain SQL Server. This configuration is mandatory if you need to ensure that session state is never lost.

Of the three configurations, In Process is the only one available via the .NET Framework. You must purchase either the Professional or Enterprise Edition of ASP.NET to obtain the Out of Process and SQL Server configuration options.

To use the ASP.NET session state service, you must add the module named SessionStateModule to the application. The default machine-wide configuration file (C:\WINNT\Microsoft.NET\Framework*version*\CONFIG\machine.config) adds this module.

Once you add SessionStateModule, you can configure the session state service within the *sessionState* element of the machine.config or web.config configuration file. Table 6-6 lists the attributes that you can set within the *sessionState* element.

Table 6-6   Attributes of the *sessionState* Element

Attribute	Description
mode	Specifies where ASP.NET will save session state. The possible values are
	Off Session state is disabled.
	InProc Session state is stored within the ASP.NET worker process.
	StateServer Session state is stored by the out-of-process session state server.
	SqlServer Session state is stored within SQL Server.
	The default is *InProc*.
cookieless	Specifies whether cookieless sessions should be enabled. The default is *false*.
timeout	Specifies the number of minutes the session can be idle before the session is abandoned. The default is 20 minutes.
stateConnectionString	Specifies the location of the session state server. The default value is *tcpip=127.0.0.1:42424*.
sqlConnectionString	Specifies the location of the SQL server. The default value is *data source=127.0.0.1;user id=sa;password=*.

Once you have the session state service properly configured, session state is enabled on a per-Web-method basis. You can enable session state for a particular Web method by setting the *EnableSession* property of the *WebMethod* attribute to *true*.

Regardless of which configuration you choose, the API for reading/writing session state is exactly the same. The class that contains the Web method should inherit from the *WebService* class. The *WebService* class exposes the *Session* property, which returns an instance of the *HttpSessionState* class, otherwise known as the session object.

The session object is used to maintain a collection of information related to the user's session. Items can be added to and retrieved from the collection via an *int* or *string* indexer.

The following example expands the Securities Web service to use session state. The *SetCurrency* Web method allows the client to select a particular currency. Future calls to *InstantQuote* will return the price of the security using the selected currency.

```csharp
using System;
using System.Web.Services;

namespace BrokerageFirm
{
    [SoapRpcService]
    public class Securities : WebService
    {
        public Securities()
        {
            // Set the default value of the target currency.
            if(this.Session["TargetCurrency"] == null)
            {
                this.Session["TargetCurrency"] = CurrencyType.US_DOLLAR;
            }
        }

        public enum CurrencyType
        {
            US_DOLLAR,
            UK_POUND,
            GE_DEUTSCHMARK
        }

        [WebMethod(true)]
        public void SetCurrency(CurrencyType targetCurrency)
        {
            this.Session["TargetCurrency"] = targetCurrency;
        }

        [WebMethod(true)]
        public double InstantQuote(string symbol)
        {

            // Implementation...

            return Convert(price,
            (CurrencyType)this.Session["TargetCurrency"]);
        }

        private double Convert(double usPrice, CurrencyType targetCurrency)
        {
            double targetCurrencyPrice = usPrice;

            // Implementation ...

            return targetCurrencyPrice;
        }
    }
}
```

The *SetCurrency* method persists the client's currency preference within the session. The *InstantQuote* method then retrieves the currency preference from the client's session and converts the price of the security appropriately.

As shown in the preceding example, you can use the *string* indexer to both set and retrieve values from the session object. However, you can use the *int* indexer only to retrieve values contained within the session object. You can also use the *Add* method to add items to the collection managed by the session object.

Because the client might not have selected a target currency, a default value is set within the *Securities* object constructor. Even with session state enabled, ASP.NET will still create a new instance of the *Securities* object for every request. The constructor will initialize the value of the target currency only if the value is *null*.

A potential issue can arise in the preceding example if the client does not support cookies. By default, ASP.NET clients do not support cookies. In the example, a client that does not support cookies will always have the price of a stock returned in U.S. dollars. A better design would be to extend the method signature of *InstantQuote* to accept the symbol of the security as well as the targeted currency. This would also eliminate a network round-trip because the client would no longer need to call the *SetCurrency* Web method.

The session object also supports the *ICollection* and *IEnumerable* interfaces, which allow polymorphic enumeration through the items within the collection. The following example uses the *IEnumerable* interface to iterate through the collection:

```
[WebMethod(true)]
public override string ToString()
{
    StringBuilder sb = new StringBuilder();
    foreach(string index in this.Session)
    {
        sb.AppendFormat("{0} = {1}\n", index, this.Session[index].ToString());
    }

    return sb.ToString();
}
```

This method declaration overrides the *Object.ToString* method and exposes it as a Web method. The implementation of the Web method enumerates through the session object via the *IEnumerable* interface by using the *foreach* keyword. Each name/value pair stored within the session object is appended to an instance of the *StringBuilder* class. Finally the resulting string is returned from the Web method.

Application State

State that is global to the application can be stored within the application object. An example of this is a database connection string. Unlike session state, application state is always handled in process and cannot be shared between servers in a Web farm. Also unlike session state, application state is not dependent on the client supporting cookies.

Classes that derive from the *WebService* class expose the *Application* property. This property retrieves an instance of the *HttpApplicationState* object containing state that is global to the Web application. The *HttpApplicationState* class derives from the *NameObjectCollectionBase* class. Because the implementation of the *NameObjectCollectionBase* class creates a hash table, retrieving a particular value from the application object is very efficient.

Let's say I want to implement a counter to record the number of times the Web service has been accessed because the application has been started. I could add the following code to the *InstantQuote* method just before I return the price to the customer:

```
// Record the access to the Web service.
this.Application["HitCounter"] = (int)this.Application["HitCounter"] + 1;
```

Unfortunately, the code has two problems. First, the *HitCounter* application variable is never initialized. Every time the above code is executed, it will generate an exception. Second, because multiple clients can potentially increment the *HitCounter* application variable simultaneously, a potential race condition might occur. Let's address these issues one at a time.

ASP.NET provides a framework for handling application startup code within a Web service. Every Web application can contain a global.asax file. Within the file, you can implement code that is executed when certain predefined events occur, such as application startup/shutdown and session startup/shutdown. Application startup is an ideal point to initialize application variables. The following code initializes the *HitCounter* application variable during the application start event within the Global.asax page:

```
using System;
using System.Web;

namespace BrokerageFirm
{
    public class Global : HttpApplication
    {
        protected void Application_Start(Object sender, EventArgs e)
        {
            // Initialize the hit counter to 0.
            this.Application["HitCounter"] = (int)0;
        }
    }
}
```

In the *Application_Start* method, I initialize the *HitCounter* application variable to zero. I also explicitly cast it to an *int* to avoid any ambiguity. Because the ASP.NET runtime executes the *Application_Start* method once during the life of the application, you do not have to worry about concurrency issues.

However, the *InstantQuote* method can be called by multiple clients simultaneously. Therefore, you must avoid potential race conditions when you update the data. Even though incrementing the *HitCounter* application variable is represented by a single line of C# code, the single line will be translated into multiple machine instructions when it is compiled. Here is the resulting IL code:

```
IL_0074:   ldarg.0
IL_0075:   call        instance class
                       [System.Web]System.Web.HttpApplicationState
                       [System.Web.Services]System.
                       Web.Services.WebService::get_Application()
IL_007a:   ldstr       "HitCounter"
IL_007f:   ldarg.0
IL_0080:   call        instance class
                       [System.Web]System.Web.HttpApplicationState
                       [System.Web.Services]System.Web.Services.
                       WebService::get_Application()
IL_0085:   ldstr       "HitCounter"
IL_008a:   callvirt    instance object
                       [System.Web]System.Web.HttpApplicationState::
                       get_Item(string)
IL_008f:   unbox       [mscorlib]System.Int32
IL_0094:   ldind.i4
IL_0095:   ldc.i4.1
IL_0096:   add
IL_0097:   box         [mscorlib]System.Int32
IL_009c:   callvirt    instance void
                       [System.Web]System.Web.HttpApplicationState::
                       set_Item(string,object)
IL_00a1:   ldarg.0
IL_00a2:   call        instance class
                       [System.Web]System.Web.HttpApplicationState
                       [System.Web.Services]System.Web.Services.
                       WebService::get_Application()
```

The single line of C# code translates to 15 lines of IL, and then the IL is compiled to numerous machine codes before it is executed. Because the code can be executed simultaneously by two or more clients, this will lead to unpredictable results.

As an example of the problems that can occur if two clients (A and B) attempt to run the same code simultaneously, suppose that the *HitCounter* application variable was initially set to 1 and client A executes the above IL to increment the value to 2. *IL_008a* obtains the initial value of 1 for *HitCounter*. *IL_009c* sets *HitCounter* to a new value of 2. Suppose also that client B updates the value of *HitCounter* to 2 somewhere between *IL_008a* and *IL_009c*. Because client A will be incrementing the previously retrieved value of 1, *Hit-Counter* will be incorrectly set to 2 instead of the correct value of 3.

The application object provides a locking mechanism to ensure that writes made to the data are performed serially, thereby avoiding race conditions such as the one described in the preceding paragraph. Operations that require serialized access to the data can be performed between the *Lock* and *Unlock* methods provided by the application object. The following example properly updates the *HitCounter* application variable each time the *InstantQuote* Web method is invoked:

```
using System;
using System.Web.Services;

namespace BrokerageFirm
{
    [SoapRpcService]
    public class Securities : WebService
    {
        public enum CurrencyType
        {
            US_DOLLARS,
            UK_POUNDS,
            GE_DEUTSCHMARKS
        }

        [WebMethod]
        public double InstantQuote(string symbol,
        CurrencyType targetCurrency)
        {
            double price = 0;

            // Implementation...

            // Record the access to the Web service.
            this.Application.Lock();
            this.Application["HitCounter"] =
            (int)this.Application["HitCounter"] + 1;
            this.Application["LastSymbol"] = symbol;

            return Convert(price, targetCurrency);
        }

        private double Convert(double usPrice,
        CurrencyType targetCurrency)
        {
            double targetCurrencyPrice = usPrice;

            // Implementation...

            return targetCurrencyPrice;
```

```
        }
    }
}
```

By locking the application object before attempting to increment it, you ensure that you will have exclusive access to the lock on the application object. Because all calls to *Unlock* will be blocked, you should call the *Unlock* method as quickly as possible to avoid hindering throughput. Note, however, that even when you have locked the application object, you do not have exclusive access to the data. Therefore, to avoid race conditions from being introduced into your application, you must ensure that a common locking scheme is used throughout your application.

You should also look for opportunities where application scoped data can be updated without locking the application object. Notice that I also updated the *LastSymbol* application variable with the last symbol that was successfully processed by the Web method. In this case, I was not concerned about race conditions because by definition the last security quoted would have been processed by the Web method that last updated the *LastSymbol* application variable.

If both the *LastSymbol* and the *LastPrice* application variables needed to be set, I would have updated both of them before unlocking the application object. This would avoid a situation in which client A was the last one to update *LastPrice* and client B was the last one to update *LastSymbol*.

Before moving to the next topic, I want to offer a word of caution about the use of the *Lock* and *Unlock* methods. You should ensure that every time a Web method calls *Lock*, *Unlock* is called as soon as possible; otherwise, you run the risk of blocking other requests that are currently being processed by the Web service. A good design pattern is to call the *Unlock* method within the *finally* section of a *try/catch* block. Here is an updated example of the *Purchase* method:

```
// Record the access to the Web service.
try
{
    this.Application.Lock();
    this.Application["HitCounter"] = (int)this.Application["HitCounter"] + 1;
}
catch(Exception e)
{
    // Handle exception ...
}
finally
{
    this.Application.UnLock();
}

// Significant processing to quote the price...

this.Application["LastSymbol"] = symbol;
```

Because the *Unlock* method call was placed within the *finally* section of the *try/catch* block, *Unlock* will be called even if the code to update the *HitCounter* application variable fails (for example, when an *OverflowException* is thrown as a result of the addition). This ensures that other ASP.NET worker threads will not be needlessly blocking on a call to *Lock*.

What if you forget to unlock the application object before your Web method returns? A mistake such as this could have a detrimental effect on your application. The next time you try to obtain the lock for the application object, the call to *Unlock* will deadlock. Fortunately, the ASP.NET runtime prevents this from happening. When a Web method returns, the ASP.NET runtime ensures that the lock obtained on the application object is freed.

One of the biggest problems with using the application object to implement a hit counter is that it is the developer's responsibility to ensure that the application object is locked before the counter is incremented. A better alternative would be to leverage static properties. As with the application object, static properties are scoped to the application. Unlike the application object, you can associate behavior with static properties. For example, consider the following *HitCounter* class.

```
public class HitCounter
{
    private static int count = 0;
    private static object countLock = new object();

    private HitCounter() {}

    public static int Count
    {
        get { return count; }
    }

    public static void Increment()
    {
        lock(countLock)
        {
            count++;
        }
    }
}
```

Instead of storing the hit counter within the application object, I define a class that implements a property and a method for accessing and manipulating the hit counter. Because the field containing the current count is declared as private, developers that use the class cannot increment it directly. Instead, the *HitCounter* class exposes a public read-only static property to access the current count and a public static method to increment the hit counter. The *Incre-ment* method uses the *lock* keyword to ensure that there is no potential for a race condition while incrementing the counter.

Defining and Processing SOAP Headers

Recall that SOAP headers are used to contain metadata related to the body of the message. ASP.NET provides a mechanism for defining and processing SOAP headers. In this section, I explain how to formally define SOAP headers that are exposed by an ASP.NET Web service. I also explain how to process SOAP headers that are received from the client.

You can define a new header by deriving from the *SoapHeader* class. You can associate the new header with a particular endpoint within the Web service by using the *SoapHeader* attribute. Table 6-7 lists the properties exposed by the *SoapHeader* class.

Table 6-7   Properties of the *SoapHeader* Class

Property	Description
Actor	Indicates the intended recipient of the header
DidUnderstand	Indicates whether a header whose *mustUnderstand* attribute is *true* was understood and processed by the recipient
EncodedMustUnderstand	Indicates whether a header whose *mustUnderstand* attribute is *true* and whose value is encoded was understood and processed by the recipient
MustUnderstand	Indicates whether the header must be understood and processed by the recipient

By default, the name of the class derived from *SoapHeader* will become the name of the root header element, and any public fields or properties exposed by the class will define elements within the header.

As I mentioned earlier in the chapter, price quotes from other services on the Web are often time-delayed and can be more than 20 minutes old. Price quotes obtained using the *InstantQuote* Web method are not subject to these delays. Because the *InstantQuote* Web method obtains the price that a particular stock is currently trading at on the exchange's floor, I feel that I can charge the client $1.50 for each quote. I will therefore require every SOAP request made to the *InstantQuote* Web method to be accompanied by the *Payment* SOAP header, which will contain the client's credit card information. This information will be used to pay the $1.50 transaction fee.

SOAP headers are defined by classes derived from the *SoapHeader* class. Elements within the header are defined by public fields or read/writable properties. Here is the definition of the *Payment* header:

```
[XmlRoot("Payment")]
public class SoapPaymentHeader : SoapHeader
{
    private string nameOnCard;
    private string creditCardNumber;
    private CardType creditCardType;
    private DateTime expirationDate;

    public enum CardType
    {
        VISA,
        MC,
        AMX,
        DISCOVER
    }

    public string NameOnCard
    {
        get { return nameOnCard; }
        set { nameOnCard = value; }
    }

    public string CreditCardNumber
    {
        get { return creditCardNumber; }
        set { creditCardNumber = value; }
    }

    public CardType CreditCardType
    {
        get { return creditCardType; }
        set { creditCardType = value; }
    }

    public DateTime ExpirationDate
    {
        get { return expirationDate; }
        set { expirationDate = value; }
    }
}
```

The preceding class definition defines a SOAP header named *Payment* with four child elements: *nameOnCard*, *creditCardNumber*, *creditCardType*, and *expirationDate*. The *XmlRoot* attribute is used to instruct the XML Serializer to name the header element *Payment* instead of the class name. I will cover the XML Serializer in Chapter 7.

Once the payment has been received and the Web method has been processed, I want to send a header containing a confirmation of the purchase back to the client. SOAP headers sent from the server to the client are defined in the same manner. The following code defines a header containing the amount that was charged as well as the reference number of the credit card transaction:

```
[XmlRoot("Receipt")]
public class SoapReceiptHeader : SoapHeader
{
    private double amount;
    private int referenceNumber;

    public double Amount
    {
        get { return amount; }
        set { amount = value; }
    }

    public int ReferenceNumber
    {
        get { return referenceNumber; }
        set { referenceNumber = value; }
    }
}
```

Once you define the headers, the next step is to associate them with the *InstantQuote* Web method. The *SoapHeader* attribute is used to associate a SOAP header with a Web method.

A public member variable is added to the *WebService* class to hold an instance of the class derived from the *SoapHeader* class. The name of the member variable is then communicated to the ASP.NET runtime via the *SoapHeader* attribute. Here is the *Securities* class definition:

```
public class Securities : WebService
{

    public PaymentHeader paymentHeader;
    public ReceiptHeader receiptHeader = new ReceiptHeader();

    public enum CurrencyType
    {
        US_DOLLARS,
        UK_POUNDS,
        GE_DEUTSCHMARKS
    }

    [WebMethod]
```

(continued)

```
[SoapHeader("paymentHeader",
Direction=SoapHeaderDirection.In, Required=true)]
[SoapHeader("receiptHeader",
Direction=SoapHeaderDirection.Out, Required=true)]
public double InstantQuote(string symbol, CurrencyType targetCurrency)
{
    double price = 0;

    // Implementation ...

    return Convert(price, targetCurrency);
}

private double Convert(double usPrice, CurrencyType targetCurrency)
{
    double targetCurrencyPrice = usPrice;

    // Implementation...

    return targetCurrencyPrice;
}
}
```

I create two member variables to hold the data contained in the *Payment* and the *Receipt* SOAP headers. I create an instance of the *SoapReceiptHeader* class because the *Receipt* header will be passed to the client. I do not create an instance of the *SoapPaymentHeader* class because the ASP.NET runtime is responsible for creating this object and populating its properties with the data contained within the *Payment* header received from the client.

Next I add two *SoapHeader* attributes to declare that the headers should formally be described as part of the Web method. The constructor of the *Soap-Header* attribute takes a string that contains the name of the public member variable that should be associated with the SOAP header.

I also set two optional properties, *Direction* and *Required*. The *Direction* property indicates whether the client or the server is supposed to send the header. The *Required* property indicates whether the property must appear within the SOAP message. Let's discuss each property in detail.

The *Direction* property indicates whether the header is received from the client, sent to the client, or both. The *Payment* header is received from the client, and the *Receipt* header is sent to the client, so I set the *Direction* property to *SoapHeaderDirection.In* and *SoapHeaderDirection.Out*, respectively. If a SOAP header is received from the client and then sent back to the client, the value of the *Direction* property should be set to *SoapHeaderDirection.InOut*.

The *Required* property indicates whether the header must appear within the SOAP message to be considered valid by the Web service. If the *Required* property is not set within the *attribute* tag, the default value is *true*. Inbound headers marked as required must be included in the request message; otherwise, a *SoapException* will be thrown by the ASP.NET runtime.

Because a *Payment* header must be included in every request and a matching *Receipt* header must be included in every response, I set the *Required* property to *true* for both SOAP headers. The *Required* property has no bearing on whether the header will be processed or even understood by the recipient of the message. For example, the *Receipt* header must always be passed back to the client, but the client is not required to process the header.

Now that I have associated the *Payment* and *Receipt* headers with the Web method, the next task is to process the *Payment* headers. The following code uses the information within the *Payment* header to bill the client's credit card using an arbitrary credit card processing component:

```
public class Securities : WebService
{

    public SoapPaymentHeader paymentHeader;
    public SoapReceiptHeader receiptHeader = new SoapReceiptHeader();

    public enum CurrencyType
    {
        US_DOLLARS,
        UK_POUNDS,
        GE_DEUTSCHMARKS
    }

    [WebMethod]
    [SoapHeader("payment", Direction=SoapHeaderDirection.In, Required=true)]
    [SoapHeader("receipt", Direction=SoapHeaderDirection.Out, Required=true)]
    public double InstantQuote(string symbol, CurrencyType targetCurrency)
    {
        // Declare and initialize variables.
        double    price = 0;
        int       merchantNumber = 123456789;
        double    fee = 1.50;
        int       referenceNumber = 0;

        // Apply the fee to the client's credit card.
        CreditCardProcessor creditCardProcessor =
        new CreditCardProcessor(merchantNumber);
        referenceNumber =
        creditCardProcessor.Bill(fee, paymentHeader);

        // Verify that the credit card was processed.
        if(referenceNumber > 0)
```

(continued)

```
    {
        // Set the return header information.
        receiptHeader.ReferenceNumber = referenceNumber;
        receiptHeader.Amount = fee;
    }
    else
    {
        throw new SoapException("The Payment header was either
        missing or contained invalid information.",
        SoapException.ClientFaultCode);
    }

    // Implementation...

    return Convert(price, targetCurrency);
    }
}
```

The preceding code uses the information within the *Payment* header to charge the required fee to the client's credit card. If the credit card is successfully processed, the *Receipt* header will be populated with the reference number of the transaction as well as the amount that was charged to the card. If the credit card is not successfully processed, a *SoapException* will be raised. Because the exception is a result of insufficient information sent from the client, the fault code is set to *Client*.

The current implementation has one problem related to processing headers. In Chapter 3, I said that the client has the ability to send additional headers other than what was expected. The client can also set the *mustUnderstand* attribute to *true* on these additional headers. I will discuss how to process headers you were not expecting shortly. But let's first discuss setting and analyzing the *mustUnderstand* attribute for a particular SOAP header.

The *MustUnderstand* property exposed by the *SoapHeader* class is fundamentally different from the *Required* property set by the *SoapHeader* attribute (which I discussed earlier). The *Required* property specifies whether a header must be included within a message. If the header resides within a message, the *MustUnderstand* property is used to specify whether the recipient of the message must understand and process the header. Let's discuss these two properties in detail.

The *Required* property specifies whether the header must be included within the message exchanged between the client and the server for a particular Web method. Because this property is specific to the interface of a Web service, changes to it are reflected in the WSDL document. If the *Required* property is set to *true*, the *required* attribute within the *header* element defined by the SOAP binding extensibility elements will be set to *true*. Finally, if a Web method defines a SOAP header as required, ASP.NET cannot support the HTTP GET/POST bindings.

The *MustUnderstand* property specifies whether a specific header within a message must be understood and processed by the client. Because this property is specific to a particular exchange between the client and the server, changes to it are reflected in the SOAP message itself. If the *MustUnderstand* property is set to *true*, the *mustUnderstand* attribute within an instance of the header will be set to *true*.

The *DidUnderstand* property of an object derived from *SoapHeader* notifies the ASP.NET runtime to tell the client which headers were processed by the Web method.

The default value of the *DidUnderstand* property is *true* for headers formally defined by the Web method, so make sure that there cannot be a code path in which the method returns without processing a header. The client might have set the *mustUnderstand* attribute to *true*. If so, this is considered an error if the Web method does not throw a *SoapException*.

In the case in which a header might not be processed, you might want to set the *DidUnderstand* property to *false* at the beginning of the Web method. Once the header is processed, set the *DidUnderstand* property back to *true*.

Another option is to include the value of the *MustUnderstand* property in the decision about whether to process the header. For example, the *Instant-Quote* method sets the *Required* property of the *Payment* header to *true*. However, the *InstantQuote* method is responsible for processing the header only if the *MustUnderstand* property is *true*. Let's say that if the administrator invokes the *InstantQuote* Web method, the *Payment* header should not be processed unless the *MustUnderstand* property is *true*, as shown here:

```
// Apply the fee to the client's credit card only if the user is not
// the administrator or if the header must be processed.
if(User.Identity != "Administrator" || paymentHeader.MustUnderstand)
{
    CreditCardProcessor creditCardProcessor =
    new CreditCardProcessor(merchantNumber);
    referenceNumber = creditCardProcessor.Bill(fee, payment);
}
```

I want to discuss one final point about the *MustUnderstand* and *DidUnderstand* properties. After the Web method returns, the ASP.NET runtime will determine whether any headers passed by the client containing a *mustUnderstand* attribute set to *true* also have their associated *DidUnderstand* property set to *false*. If this is the case, the ASP.NET runtime will automatically throw a *SoapException*. The Web method might have code that attempts to undo actions done on a client's behalf before throwing the exception. Because this exception is thrown after the Web method has returned, this code will never execute.

Let's say a client calls the *InstantQuote* Web method within the context of a transaction. The client passes a *Transaction* header along with the *Payment* header and sets its *mustUnderstand* attribute to *true*. Because the previous implementation does not check for the presence of a *Transaction* header, the Web service processes the request, including billing the client's credit card. After the method returns, the ASP.NET runtime notices that the *Transaction* header's *DidUnderstand* property is set to *false* and throws an exception. In this case, the client does not receive the quote but will still be billed the $1.50 transaction fee. This scenario would result in one unhappy customer.

There are at least two ways to avoid this adverse side effect. If the affected resources are all managed by a DTC Resource Manager, you can set the *TransactionOption* property of the *WebMethod* attribute to *Required*. Once the ASP.NET runtime throws an exception, the transaction will be aborted and all changes rolled back. If the *CreditCardProcessor* component can participate in a DTC-controlled distributed transaction, the fee charged to the card will automatically be rolled back.

Another option is to verify that all headers received by the Web service with a *mustUnderstand* attribute set to *true* have been processed before the Web method returns. Catching headers that must be understood but cannot be processed by the Web service early on within the Web method can potentially save unnecessary processing cycles. If the Web method does not know how to process one of the headers passed to it, it can take appropriate action before throwing an exception. In the next section, I discuss how to examine the *MustUnderstand* property of unknown headers.

Processing Unknown Headers

The ASP.NET page framework provides a mechanism for inspecting and processing headers that are not formally defined by the Web method. You can, for example, determine up front whether there are any unknown headers that have their *mustUnderstand* attribute set to *true*. If there are any headers that must be understood, but that the Web method does not know how to process, you can throw an appropriate *SoapException* up front.

The *SoapUnknownHeader* class is derived from *SoapHeader* and can be used to inspect or process headers not formally defined by the Web method. Because the *SoapUnknownHeader* class is derived from *SoapHeader*, it exposes properties such as *MustUnderstand* and *DidUnderstand*.

An object of type *SoapUnknownHeader* is loosely typed because the only additional property defined is *Element*, which is of type *XmlElement*. The *Element* property serves as an entry point to the root element of the header. You can use the XML DOM to interrogate the contents of the header.

You can associate the *SoapUnknownHeader* class with a Web method using the *SoapHeader* attribute (just as you can with any other class that derives from *SoapHeader*). If more than one header can be received by the Web method, as is the case with unknown headers, the property associated with the Web method can be an array.

Recall that the previous implementation of the *InstantQuote* Web method had a flaw. If an unknown header that must be understood by the Web service is received by the client, credit card users will be charged the fee but will receive a SOAP fault automatically generated by the ASP.NET runtime. To solve this problem, the following example obtains a list of unknown headers, iterates through the list, and then throws a *SoapException* once the first *SoapUnknown-Header* is encountered that has its *MustUnderstand* property set to *true*:

```
[WebMethod]
[SoapHeader("paymentHeader", Direction=SoapHeaderDirection.In, Required=true)]
[SoapHeader("receiptHeader", Direction=SoapHeaderDirection.Out, Required=true)]
[SoapHeader("unknownHeaders", Required=false)]
public double InstantQuote(string symbol, CurrencyType targetCurrency)
{
    // Declare and initialize variables.
    double  price = 0;
    int     merchantNumber = 123456789;
    double  fee = 1.50;
    int     referenceNumber = 0;

    // Check to see whether any unknown headers must be processed.
    foreach(SoapUnknownHeader header in unknownHeaders)
    {
        if(header.MustUnderstand)
        {
            string message = "The " + header.Element.Name +
            " header could not be processed.";
            throw new SoapException(message,
            SoapException.MustUnderstandFaultCode);
        }
    }

    // The rest of the implementation...

}
```

The Web method checks for unknown headers that must be understood by the client before the credit card is processed. If a header that must be understood cannot be processed, the client will not be charged the fee for using the Web service.

Using SOAP Extensions

In the preceding section, I wrote a fair amount of code to process the SOAP *Payment* header. A Web service might potentially expose many Web methods that require the *Payment* header to be processed, so it is not ideal to have every method contain code to process the payment information. The code within the method should be responsible for the business logic, not handling tasks that can be pushed to the infrastructure. In this section, I show you how to provide extended services, such as processing the *Payment* SOAP header, that can be applied to any Web method.

SOAP extensions provide a way of creating encapsulated reusable functionality that you can apply declaratively to your Web service. The SOAP extensions framework allows you to intercept SOAP messages exchanged between the client and the Web service. You can inspect or modify a message at various points during the processing of the message. You can apply a SOAP extension to either the server or the client.

A SOAP extension is composed of a class derived from the *SoapExtension* class. It contains the implementation details that are generally used to examine or modify the contents of a SOAP message. You can then define an attribute derived from *SoapExtensionAttribute* that associates the SOAP extension with a particular Web method or a class.

SOAP Extension Attributes

You use a SOAP extension attribute to indicate that a particular SOAP extension should be called by the ASP.NET runtime for a particular Web method. You can also use the SOAP extension attribute to collect information that will be used by the SOAP extension.

My first SOAP extension example will automatically process the *Payment* and *Receipt* headers I created in the last section. Instead of including code within the implementation of the *InstantQuote* Web method, I will create an attribute called *ProcessPayment* that can be used to decorate Web methods that require the *Payment* header to be processed. Later I will create the *ProcessPaymentExtension* class, which will contain the actual implementation. Here is the implementation of the *ProcessPayment* attribute:

```
[AttributeUsage(AttributeTargets.Method)]
public class ProcessPaymentAttribute : SoapExtensionAttribute
{
    int        merchantNumber = 0;
    double     fee = 0;
    int        priority = 9;

    public ProcessPaymentAttribute(int merchantNumber, double fee)
    {
        this.merchantNumber = merchantNumber;
        this.fee = fee;
    }

    public int MerchantNumber
```

```
    {
        get { return merchantNumber; }
        set { merchantNumber = value; }
    }

    public double Fee
    {
        get { return fee; }
        set { fee = value; }
    }

    public override Type ExtensionType
    {
        get { return typeof(ProcessPaymentExtension); }
    }

    public override int Priority
    {
        get { return priority; }
        set { priority = value; }
    }
}
```

The *ProcessPayment* attribute is responsible for gathering the information needed by the SOAP extension. The SOAP extension will require the merchant account number and the fee the client should be charged to process the payment. Thus, both the merchant number and the fee must be passed as part of the *ProcessPayment* attribute's constructor. I also create associated *Merchant-Number* and *Fee* properties because the only mechanism for passing information from the SOAP extension attribute to the SOAP extension is by exposing the information as a public field or a public property.

Attributes that derive from *SoapExtensionAttribute* must override the *ExtensionType* property. This property returns an instance of the *Type* object of the SOAP extension class. The ASP.NET runtime will access this property to locate its associated SOAP extension.

All SOAP extension attributes must override the *Priority* property. This property specifies the priority in which the SOAP extension will be executed with respect to other SOAP extensions. I gave the *Priority* property a default value of 9 so that it can be optionally set by the user of the attribute.

The priority of the SOAP extension is used by ASP.NET to determine when it should be called in relation to other SOAP extensions. The higher the priority, the closer the SOAP extension is to the actual message being sent by the client and the response sent by the server. For example, a SOAP extension that compresses the body and the header of a SOAP message should have a high priority. On the other hand, the *ProcessPayment* SOAP extension does not need to have a high priority because it can function properly after other SOAP extensions have processed.

SOAP Extension Class

The SOAP extension class contains the implementation of the SOAP extension. In the case of the *ProcessPaymentExtension* class, it will process the *Payment* header on behalf of the Web method. A SOAP extension derives from the *SoapExtension* class. The ASP.NET runtime invokes methods exposed by the class at various points during the processing of the request. These methods can be overridden by the SOAP extension to provide custom implementation. Table 6-8 describes the methods that can be overridden by a custom SOAP extension.

Table 6-8 *SoapExtension* **Class Methods**

Method	Description
ChainStream	Provides a means of accessing the memory buffer containing the SOAP request or response message.
GetInitializer	Used to perform initialization that is specific to the Web service method. This method is overloaded to provide a separate initializer for a single method or for all methods exposed by a type.
Initialize	Used to receive the data that was returned from *GetInitializer*.
ProcessMessage	Provides a means of allowing the SOAP extension to inspect and modify the SOAP messages at each stage of processing the request and response messages.

The SOAP extension framework provides two methods of accessing the contents of the message. One way is through a stream object received by the *ChainStream* method that contains the raw contents of the message. The other way is through the properties and methods exposed by the instance of the *SoapMessage* object passed to the *ProcessMessage* method. For the *ProcessPaymentExtension* class, I will use the *SoapMessage* class.

The SOAP extension framework also provides a two-step initialization process through the *GetInitializer* and *Initialize* methods. The initialization process is designed to reduce the overall initialization cost associated with the extension. I discuss this in more detail later in this section.

The following diagram shows the order of the individual calls the ASP.NET runtime makes to the SOAP extension:

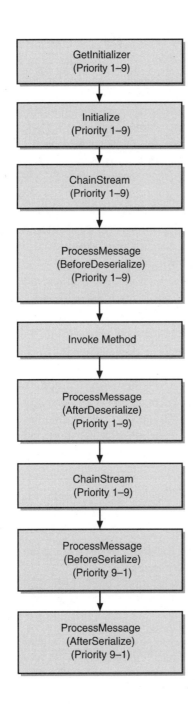

If multiple extensions are associated with a Web method, every extension will be called during each stage in the order of priority. For example, the *GetInitializer* method will be called on each SOAP extension before the *ChainStream* method is called. Except for the *BeforeSerialize* and *AfterSerialize* modes of the *ProcessMessage* method, each method will first call SOAP extensions that have a priority of 1 and then call the remaining extensions in ascending order of priority. When you invoke the *ProcessMessage* method during the *BeforeSerialize* and *AfterSerialize* modes, *ProcessMessage* will call the extensions in reverse order of priority.

Initialization

A new SOAP extension object is created each time the Web method associated with it is invoked. The SOAP extension often performs initialization that is generic across all invocations of the Web method. The SOAP extension framework provides a means of executing initialization code that should occur once.

The SOAP extension framework supports a two-phase initialization sequence. The *GetInitializer* method performs the initialization for a particular Web method, in this case the *InstantQuote* method. *GetInitializer* will be called only once per Web method for the life of the Web application. The *Initialize* method will be called each time the Web method is invoked.

To process the *Payment* header, I need to initialize a credit card processor object. Once it is initialized, it can be used to process any number of *Payment* headers. Let's assume that there is a nontrivial cost associated with initializing the object. I can initialize it once within the *GetInitializer* method and then use it each time the *InstantQuote* Web method is invoked. Here is the implementation of the *GetInitializer* method:

```
public override object GetInitializer(LogicalMethodInfo methodInfo, SoapExtensi
onAttribute attribute)
{
    ProcessPaymentAttribute processPaymentAttribute = (ProcessPaymentAttribute)
attribute;

    // Set up connection to credit card authorization service.
    creditCardProcessor = new CreditCardProcessor(processPaymentAttribute.Merch
antNumber);

    // Return the initialized credit card processor object and the fee.
    return new object [] {creditCardProcessor, processPaymentAttribute.Fee};
}
```

Notice that when ASP.NET invokes the *GetInitializer* method, the extension's associated attribute is passed as a parameter. The attribute is used to obtain the *MerchantNumber* as well as the *Fee* properties. The method initializes the credit card processor.

This same credit card processor will then be used each time the *InstantQuote* Web method is invoked. However, recall that a new instance of the *ProcessPaymentExtension* object is created each time the Web method is invoked. So how can I use the same instance of the credit card processor object across all invocations of the Web method? The following diagram illustrates the problem.

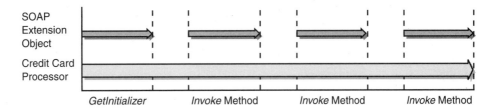

You might have noticed that *GetInitializer* has a return parameter of type *object*. The implementation of the *GetInitializer* method for the *ProcessPaymentExtension* object returns a two-element array containing the initialized credit card processor object as well as the fee that should be charged to the customer. The ASP.NET runtime retains a reference to this array and passes it to the *Initialize* method each time a new object is created as a result of invoking the *InstantQuote* Web method.

One of the responsibilities of the *Initialize* method is to obtain the data returned to the ASP.NET runtime by the *GetInitializer* method. The *Initialize* method can also be used to perform any additional initialization that needs to occur for a particular Web method invocation. The following code shows the implementation of the *GetInitializer* and *Initialize* methods:

```
public class ProcessPaymentExtension : SoapExtension
{
    CreditCardProcessor   creditCardProcessor;
    double                fee = 0;
    int                   referenceNumber = 0;
    SoapPaymentHeader     payment = null;
    SoapReceiptHeader     receipt = new SoapReceiptHeader();

    public override object GetInitializer(Type type)
```

(continued)

```
    {
        return typeof(ProcessPaymentExtension);
    }

    public override object GetInitializer(LogicalMethodInfo
    methodInfo, SoapExtensionAttribute attribute)
    {
        ProcessPaymentAttribute processPaymentAttribute =
        (ProcessPaymentAttribute)attribute;

        // Set up connection to credit card authorization service.
        creditCardProcessor =
        new CreditCardProcessor(processPaymentAttribute.MerchantNumber);

        // Return the initialized credit card processor object and the fee.
        return new object [] {creditCardProcessor,
        processPaymentAttribute.Fee};
    }

    public override void Initialize(object initializer)
    {
        // Retrieve the credit card processor and the fee
        // from the initializer parameter.
        creditCardProcessor = (CreditCardProcessor)((object[])initializer)[0];
        fee = (double)((object[])initializer)[1];
    }

    // The rest of the implementation...

}
```

The *Initialize* method performs any initialization that is specific to the method invocation. In the case of the *ProcessPaymentExtension* extension, no initialization needs to be accomplished. The only action is assigning the credit card processor object and the fee to a member variable within the class.

Processing the Message

The *ProcessMessage* method contains the implementation for processing the request message received from the client and the response message sent by the Web service. *ProcessMessage* is called by the ASP.NET runtime at four points. It is called twice during the process of deserializing the request message, once before the message is deserialized and once after. The *ProcessMessage* method is also called twice during the process of serializing the response message, once before serialization and once after.

Each time the *ProcessMessage* method is called, it is passed an instance of the *SoapMessage* class. During the *BeforeSerialize* and *AfterSerialize* stages, the object is initialized with the data contained within the SOAP message. Here is the implementation of the *ProcessMessage* method:

```
public override void ProcessMessage(SoapMessage message)
{
    switch (message.Stage)
    {
        case SoapMessageStage.BeforeDeserialize:
            Trace.WriteLine("ProcessMessage(BeforeDeserialize) called.");
            break;

        case SoapMessageStage.AfterDeserialize:
            Trace.WriteLine("ProcessMessage(AfterDeserialize) called.");

            // Set the return header information.
            foreach(SoapUnknownHeader h in message.Headers)
            {
                Trace.WriteLine(h.Element.Name);
            }
            if(message.Headers.Contains(payment))
            {
                referenceNumber = this.creditCardProcessor.Bill(fee, payment);
            }
            else
            {
                // Throw exception.
                throw new SoapException
                ("The required Payment header was not found.",
                    SoapException.ClientFaultCode);
            }

            // Verify that the credit card was processed.
            if(referenceNumber > 0)
            {
                // Set the return header information.
                receipt.ReferenceNumber = referenceNumber;
                receipt.Amount = fee;
            }
            else
            {
                throw new SoapException
                ("The credit card number could not be confirmed.",
                    SoapException.ClientFaultCode);
            }
```

(continued)

```
            break;

        case SoapMessageStage.BeforeSerialize:
            Trace.WriteLine("ProcessMessage(BeforeSerialize) called.");
            message.Headers.Add(receipt);
            break;

        case SoapMessageStage.AfterSerialize:
            Trace.WriteLine("ProcessMessage(AfterSerialize) called.");
            break;

        default:
            throw new SoapException("An invalid stage enumeration was passed.",
                SoapException.ServerFaultCode);
    }
}
```

The *SoapMessageStage* property determines at which of the four stages the message is called. I use a *switch case* statement to identify the stage at which *ProcessMessage* is called.

The code to process the *Payment* header accesses the header information via the *message* parameter. The *message* object is populated with the data contained within the SOAP request message only after the message has been deserialized. Therefore, the code to process the payment information is placed within the *SoapMessageStage.AfterDeserialize* case block.

Likewise, the code to add the *Receipt* header to the SOAP response message does so via the *message* object's *Header* property. The *message* object is populated with the data contained within the SOAP request message only before the request message has been deserialized. Therefore, the code to process the payment information is placed within the *SoapMessageStage.BeforeSerialize* case block.

The code to process the payment information differs only slightly from the code I implemented in the SOAP Header section. One difference is that I use the preinitialized instance of the *ProcessCreditCard* object instead of creating a new one. The other difference is that the *Payment* header is obtained from the message object. The message object exposes the *Headers* property, which is of type *SoapHeaderCollection*. I obtain the *Payment* header by calling the *Contains* method on the instance of the *SoapHeaderCollection* object exposed by the *Headers* property.

The *SoapMessage* class contains other methods and properties that can be used within the *ProcessMessage* method. Table 6-9 describes some of them.

Table 6-9   Selected Properties and Methods of the *SoapMessage* Class

Property	Description
Action	Contains the value of the *SOAPAction* HTTP header
ContentType	Gets/sets the value of the *Content-Type* HTTP header
Exception	Gets the *SoapException* thrown from the method
Headers	Gets a collection of SOAP headers (*SoapHeaderCollection*) within the message
MethodInfo	Gets an object of type *LogicalMethodInfo* that can be used to reflect on the method signature
OneWay	Indicates whether the request message is accompanied by a response
Stage	Indicates the stage of processing during which the call was made to *ProcessMessage*
Stream	Obtains an object of type *Stream* containing the SOAP message
Url	Gets the base URL of the Web service

Method	Description
GetInParameterValue	Obtains a parameter at a particular index that was passed to the Web service
GetOutParameterValue	Obtains an *out* parameter at a particular index that was passed to the Web service
GetReturnValue	Obtains the return parameter intended for the client

ChainStream Method

Another way to access the data contained within a SOAP message is using the *ChainStream* method. This method is used by the extension to receive a raw stream containing the contents of the message and to pass the modified version of the stream back to the ASP.NET runtime.

The next example uses a SOAP extension that logs the messages being exchanged between the client and the server. The *SoapTrace* attribute can be applied to any method. Its associated *SoapTrace* extension accesses the stream to write the contents of the message to a file.

```
[AttributeUsage(AttributeTargets.Method)]
public class SoapTraceAttribute : SoapExtensionAttribute
{
    private string fileName = "c:\\temp\\SoapTrace.log";
```

(continued)

```
private int priority;

public SoapTraceAttribute() {}

public SoapTraceAttribute(string fileName)
{
    this.fileName = fileName;
}

public override Type ExtensionType
{
    get { return typeof(SoapTraceExtension); }
}

public override int Priority
{
    get {return priority;}
    set {priority = value;}
}

public string FileName
{
    get {return fileName;}
    set {fileName = value;}
}
}
```

First I declare the *SoapTrace* attribute. It contains an optional constructor that can be used to set the name of the trace log. If the filename is not set, it defaults to *c:\temp\SoapTrace.log*.

```
public class SoapTraceExtension : SoapExtension
{
    string fileName;
    Stream inboundStream;
    Stream outboundStream;
    bool postSerializeHandlers = false;
```

I declare a few private member variables. The *fileName* variable holds the filename of the log file obtained by the *SoapTrace* attribute. The *inbound-Stream* and *outboundStream* variables hold references to the inbound and outbound streams, respectively. Finally *postSerializeHandlers* indicates whether the *BeforeSerialize* and *AfterSerialize* methods have been called. This variable will be used by the *ChainStream* method.

```
public override object GetInitializer(Type type)
{
    return typeof(SoapTraceExtension);
}
```

```
public override object GetInitializer(LogicalMethodInfo methodInfo,
SoapExtensionAttribute attribute)
{
    return ((SoapTraceAttribute) attribute).FileName;
}


public override void Initialize(object initializer)
{
    fileName = (string) initializer;
}
```

During *GetInitializer*, I retrieve the *FileName* property from the *SoapExtension* attribute. As with the previous extension, this value will be passed to the *Initialize* method.

```
public override Stream ChainStream( Stream stream )
{
    // Set the streams based on whether we are about to call
    // the deserialize or serialize handlers.
    if(! postSerializeHandlers)
    {
        inboundStream = stream;
        outboundStream = new MemoryStream();

        return outboundStream;
    }
    else
    {
        outboundStream = stream;
        inboundStream = new MemoryStream();

        return inboundStream;
    }
}
```

Recall that *ChainStream* is called twice by the ASP.NET runtime: before the message received from the client is deserialized, and again before the message that will be sent from the server is serialized.

Each time *ChainStream* is called, two stream references are passed between the ASP.NET runtime and the SOAP extension. The *ChainStream* method receives a reference to an inbound stream that contains the original contents of the message. It also returns a reference to an outbound stream that will contain the contents of the new message. This effectively creates a chain of streams between the SOAP extensions associated with the method. The following diagram illustrates the chain that is created:

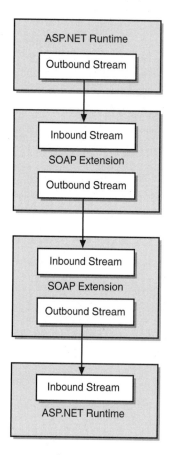

At least two aspects of *ChainStream* can easily trip you up. First, the parameters of the *ChainStream* method have a different meaning depending on whether the method is being called for the first time or the second time. Second, each time *ChainStream* is called, you need to create a new stream. The new stream is created for the outbound stream the first time it is called and for the inbound stream the second time it is called. Let's talk about each issue in detail.

ChainStream accepts a single parameter of type *Stream* and returns a parameter of type *Stream*. The first time *ChainStream* is called, the inbound stream is passed by the ASP.NET runtime and *ChainStream* is responsible for returning the outbound stream. The second time *ChainStream* is called, the outbound stream is passed by the ASP.NET runtime and *ChainStream* is responsible for returning the inbound stream.

To keep my code as straightforward as possible, I use the *postSerialize-Handlers* member variable to signal whether *ChainStream* is being called for the first time or the second time. I use an *if/else* statement to ensure that *inboundStream* and *outboundStream* are always set appropriately.

The first time *ChainStream* is called, it needs to return a readable stream that contains the SOAP message that will be deserialized by the runtime. Because SOAP extensions often modify the contents of the stream, they often return a new instance of the *MemoryStream* class. If *ChainStream* creates a new stream, it becomes the outbound stream.

The second time *ChainStream* is called, it needs to return a read/writable stream to the ASP.NET runtime. The ASP.NET runtime will use this stream to communicate the current contents of the message to the SOAP extension. Before the *BeforeSerialization* stage of *ProcessMessage* is called, the ASP.NET runtime will populate the stream with the contents of the SOAP message that was returned by the previously called SOAP extension. When *ProcessMessage* is finally called, the inbound stream can then be read by the SOAP extension, the message can be modified, and finally the new message can be written to the outbound stream. Therefore, the second time *ChainStream* is called, it needs to create a new stream for the inbound stream.

There is one more caveat. The *ChainStream* method cannot modify the stream it receives from the ASP.NET runtime. The received stream can be modified only by the *ProcessMessage* method. If *ChainStream* does access any properties or methods of the stream received from ASP.NET, a runtime exception will occur.

```
public override void ProcessMessage(SoapMessage message)
{
    switch (message.Stage)
    {
        case SoapMessageStage.BeforeDeserialize:
            CopyStream(inboundStream, outboundStream);
            break;

        case SoapMessageStage.AfterDeserialize:
            postSerializeHandlers = true;
            break;

        case SoapMessageStage.BeforeSerialize:
            break;

        case SoapMessageStage.AfterSerialize:
            WriteTraceLogEntry("Response");
            CopyStream(inboundStream, outboundStream);
            break;
```

(continued)

```
        default:
            throw new Exception("invalid stage");
    }
}
```

The *ProcessMessage* method is responsible for writing the contents of the inbound stream to the log file. This is accomplished by calling the *WriteTrace-LogEntry* helper function. It must also write the contents of the SOAP message to the outbound stream. This is accomplished by calling the *CopyStream* helper function. Finally *ProcessMessage* must set the *postSerializeHandlers* member variable used by the *ChainStream* method to *true* before exiting the *AfterDeserialize* stage.

```
private void WriteTraceLogEntry(string messageTitle)
{
    // Create a file stream for the log file.
    FileStream fs = new FileStream(fileName, FileMode.Append,
    FileAccess.Write);

    // Create a new stream writer and write the header of the trace.
    StreamWriter writer = new StreamWriter(fs);
    writer.WriteLine();
    writer.WriteLine("{0} Message Received at {1}:", messageTitle,
    DateTime.Now);
    writer.Flush();

    // Copy contents of the stream to the file.
    AppendStream(inboundStream, fs);
    fs.Close();
}
```

The *WriteTraceLogEntry* method writes an entry in the SOAP trace log. It first writes a header entry, and then it appends the log file with the contents of the inbound stream:

```
private void CopyStream(Stream sourceStream, Stream destinationStream)
{
    long sourcePosition = 0;
    long destinationPosition = 0;

    // If seekable, save starting positions of the streams
    // and set them both to the beginning.
    if(sourceStream.CanSeek)
    {
        sourcePosition = sourceStream.Position;
        sourceStream.Position = 0;
    }
```

```
    if(destinationStream.CanSeek)
    {
        destinationPosition = destinationStream.Position;
        destinationStream.Position = 0;
    }

    // Copy the contents of the "to" stream into the "from" stream.
    TextReader reader = new StreamReader(sourceStream);
    TextWriter writer = new StreamWriter(destinationStream);
    writer.WriteLine(reader.ReadToEnd());
    writer.Flush();

    // Set the streams back to their original position.
    if(sourceStream.CanSeek) sourceStream.Position = sourcePosition;
    if(destinationStream.CanSeek)
        destinationStream.Position = destinationPosition;
}
```

The *CopyStream* method writes the contents of the source stream to the destination stream. Because not all streams received by the ASP.NET runtime are seekable, a check is made before the position of a stream is modified:

```
private void AppendStream(Stream sourceStream, Stream destinationStream)
{
    long sourcePosition = 0;

    // If seekable, save starting positions of the streams
    // and set them both to the beginning.
    if(sourceStream.CanSeek)
    {
        sourcePosition = sourceStream.Position;
        sourceStream.Position = 0;
    }
    if(destinationStream.CanSeek)
    {
        destinationStream.Position = destinationStream.Length;
    }

    // Copy the contents of the "to" stream into the "from" stream.
    TextReader reader = new StreamReader(sourceStream);
    TextWriter writer = new StreamWriter(destinationStream);
    writer.WriteLine(reader.ReadToEnd());
    writer.Flush();

    // Set the streams back to their original positions.
    if(sourceStream.CanSeek) sourceStream.Position = sourcePosition;
}
```

The *AppendStream* method is used by *WriteTraceLogEntry* to append the contents of the inbound stream to the end of the log file stream.

Using the WSDL Utility to Generate Proxy Code

The ASP.NET page framework provides a set of classes and tools that greatly simplifies interacting with a Web service. The set of classes provides a base set of functionality for creating Web service proxies. One of the tools is a utility called WSDL.exe that consumes the WSDL for a Web service and then automatically generates proxy code for you.

WSDL.exe ships with the .NET Framework. You can use it to create a strongly typed proxy for accessing the targeted Web service. Just as ASP.NET will map a large number of .NET datatypes to their XML counterparts, WSDL.exe will map XML datatypes described within the Web service's WSDL document to their .NET equivalents.

The functionality of WSDL.exe is integrated within Visual Studio .NET. In Chapter 1, I used the Add Web Reference Wizard to create proxies to interact with the Payment Web service and the WebFileShare Web service. However, the wizard is not as configurable as WSDL.exe. Because some of the more-advanced configuration objects are usually desirable for production applications, the Add Web Reference Wizard is typically used for generating prototyping code.

Recall that the Securities Web service is located at *http://woodgrove-bank.com/Securities.asmx*. The following command will generate a proxy for interacting with the Securities Web service:

```
wsdl http://woodgrovebank.com/Securities.asmx?wsdl
```

The command will parse the WSDL document and generate Securities.cs, which contains C# code you can compile to form a strongly typed .NET *Securities* proxy class that exposes the functionality of the Securities Web service. By default, WSDL.exe will generate C# code that targets the SOAP implementation of the Web service interface.

Like ASP.NET Web services, WSDL.exe can create proxies only for the HTTP protocol. However, WSDL.exe-generated proxies can use one of three bindings: SOAP, HTTP GET, or HTTP POST. You can use optional command-line parameters to set the type of binding as well as other configurations such as the language in which the autogenerated code will be written. Table 6-10 lists the command-line switches that you can specify when you use WSDL.exe to generate a proxy for a Web service.

Table 6-10   Command-Line Switches for WSDL.exe

Switch	Description
/nologo	Suppresses the banner containing the version and copyright information.
/language:[CS | VB | JS] or /l:[CS | VB | JS]	Specifies the language in which the proxy code should be generated. The default is CS.
/server	Generates an abstract class definition for the Web service itself.
/namespace:[namespace] or /n:[namespace]	Specifies the .NET namespace in which the proxy code will reside.
/out:[filename] or /o:[filename]	Specifies the name of the file that will contain the generated code.
/protocol:[SOAP | HttpPost | HttpGet]	Specifies the binding the generated proxy code should target. The default is SOAP.
/username:[username] or /u:[username] /password:[password] or /p:[password] /domain:[domain] or /d:[domain]	Specifies the credentials that should be passed when connecting to a Web server that requires authentication. The supported authentication types include Basic Authentication and Windows NT Challenge/ Response.
/proxy:[url]	The URL of the proxy server. The default is to use the settings defined within the system's Internet Options.
/proxyusername:[username] or /pu:[username] /proxypassword:[password] or /pp:[password] /proxydomain:[domain] or /pd:[domain]	Specifies the credentials that should be used to log into the proxy server. The supported authentication types include Basic Authentication and Windows NT Challenge/ Response.
/appsettingurlkey:[key] or /urlkey:[key]	Generates code that sets the Url property of the proxy object to the value of the application setting with the specified key in the configuration file. If the application setting is not found, the value will be set to the URL that was originally targeted by WSDL.exe.
/appsettingbaseurl:[url] or /baseurl:[url]	Generates code that sets the Url property of the proxy object to the concatenation of the specified URL and the value of the application setting specified by the /appsettingurlkey switch.

The targeted URL can also point to a DISCO file instead of a WSDL file. A DISCO file provides a simple discovery mechanism and can reference zero or more Web services. I will discuss DISCO files in more detail in Chapter 10.

Targeting a DISCO file provides a convenient way to create proxies for multiple Web services. If WSDL.exe is pointed at a DISCO file, a proxy class will be generated for each Web service referenced by the DISCO file. You can also target multiple Web services by passing multiple URLs as arguments to WSDL.exe.

If multiple proxies are generated, the configuration parameters are applied to all generated proxy classes, which might not be ideal for some parameters. For example, */appsettingurlkey* will cause the *Url* property of every property to be set to the value of the application key. This outcome might not be desirable because in most cases each Web service will resolve to its own unique URL.

If multiple Web services are targeted, they must each reside within their own namespace. If the WSDL document references two schemas with the same namespace (two tempuri.org namespaces, for example), WSDL.exe will generate a warning and create a proxy for only one of the two schemas. To avoid this, you must change the name of one of the namespaces to ensure that they are both unique. The same holds true for duplicate XML Schema namespaces.

If you use WSDL.exe to generate proxy code that will be deployed to production, you should use the following command-line parameters:

- */language*   The proxy code should be created using the programming language standardized for the project.

- */namespace*   The proxy classes should reside within a namespace to prevent collisions with other datatype definitions.

- */appsettingurlkey*   The target URL for the Web service should be stored in the configuration file and not hard coded within the proxy. If the Web service is relocated, you do not need to recompile your code.

Proxy Class

I have discussed how to generate proxy code for accessing the Calculator Web service. Based on the suggestions I made, I will modify the command used to generate the proxy code:

```
wsdl /language:CS /namespace:BrokerageFirm
/appsettingurlkey:SecuritiesWebServiceUrl
http://woodgrovebank.com/Securities.asmx?wsdl
```

WSDL.exe will generate Securities.cs. The resulting proxy class, which will be used by a client to access the Securities Web service, is derived from the *SoapHttpClientProtocol* class. *SoapHttpClientProtocol* provides the implementation of the proxy. It exposes quite a few properties and methods that control its behavior.

Table 6-11 lists the properties, methods, and events for the *SoapHttpClientProto-col* class in addition to those exposed by the *Object* and *Component* classes.

Table 6-11   Selected Properties, Methods, and Events of the *SoapHttpClientProtocol* Class

Property	Description
AllowAutoRedirect	Specifies whether the proxy will automatically follow redirect requests sent by the server.
ClientCertificates	Specifies a collection of X.509 certificates that can be used to validate the client.
ConnectionGroupName	Specifies the name of the *HttpWebRequest* connection group to use when connecting to the Web service. A connection group provides a mechanism for allowing multiple clients within the same application to share connections open to a given Web server.
CookieContainer	Used to access the cookies maintained by the proxy. Also provides a mechanism for setting cookies for a particular domain.
Credentials	Specifies authentication credentials that can be used to log into the Web server. The supported methods of authentication include Basic Authentication, Windows NT Challenge/Response, Kerberos, and Digest.
PreAuthenticate	Specifies whether the authentication credentials should be sent immediately or as a result of receiving a 401 access denied error.
Proxy	Contains the information necessary to connect to the proxy server. This includes the URL, port, and user name/domain/password.
RequestEncoding	Specifies the type of encoding that will be used when serializing the request message. The default is UTF-8.
Timeout	Specifies the period of time, in milliseconds, that a synchronous Web request has to complete before the request is aborted. The default is infinity (−1).
Url	Specifies the address of the Web service endpoint.
UserAgent	Specifies the value of the user agent header in the HTTP request.

Method	Description
Abort	Used to abort any asynchronous method calls that are currently executing.
Discover	Used to dynamically discover the location of the Web service via the DISCO file referenced by the *Url* property.

Event	Description
Disposed	Used to provide notification when the proxy has been disposed.

Let's step through the code generated by WSDL.exe to see how the proxy class is implemented:

```
//-----------------------------------------------------------------------
// <autogenerated>
//     This code was generated by a tool.
//     Runtime Version: 1.0.xxxx.xx
//
//     Changes to this file may cause incorrect behavior and will be lost if
//     the code is regenerated.
// </autogenerated>
//-----------------------------------------------------------------------

//
// This source code was auto generated by WSDL, Version=1.0.xxxx.xx.
//
```

WSDL.exe first generates comments that document the version of the runtime as well as the version of WSDL.exe that was used to create the proxy. If the proxy will be included within a code base that is released to production, you might also want to record the date and time that the WSDL was generated along with a copy of the WSDL document itself.

The date and time can be recorded by promptly checking the file into a source code repository or by adding it as a comment to the generated file. The WSDL document can be obtained by WSDL.exe itself. You can accomplish this by using one of the optional command-line parameters I discuss later in this section.

```
namespace BrokerageFirm {
    using System.Diagnostics;
    using System.Xml.Serialization;
    using System;
    using System.Web.Services.Protocols;
    using System.Web.Services;

    /// <remarks/>
    [System.ComponentModel.DesignerCategoryAttribute("code")]

    [System.Web.Services.WebServiceBindingAttribute(Name="SecuritiesSoap",
    Namespace="http://woodgrovebank.com/Securities")]
    [System.Xml.Serialization.SoapIncludeAttribute(typeof(SoapReceiptHeader))]
    [System.Xml.Serialization.SoapIncludeAttribute(typeof(SoapPaymentHeader))]
    public class Securities : System.Web.Services.Protocols.
    SoapHttpClientProtocol {

        public SoapPaymentHeader SoapPaymentHeaderValue;

        public SoapReceiptHeader SoapReceiptHeaderValue;
```

The *Securities* class is defined within the *BrokerageFirm* namespace. It is derived from the *SoapHttpClientProtocol* class. *SoapHttpClientProtocol* serves as the base class for all ASP.NET proxies and contains the implementation necessary to communicate with most HTTP-based Web services.

The *Securities* class is also decorated with three attributes. The first is the *WebServiceBinding* attribute, which serves the exact same role on the client as it does on the Web service. This attribute allows you to formally reference a particular binding defined within another namespace. The two other attributes are *SoapInclude* attributes. They tell the XML Serializer to include the *SoapPaymentHeaderValue* and the *SoapReceiptHeaderValue* member variables within the SOAP message.

```
/// <remarks/>
public Securities() {
    string urlSetting =
    System.Configuration.ConfigurationSettings.AppSettings
    ["SecuritiesWebServiceUrl"];
    if ((urlSetting != null)) {
        this.Url = urlSetting;
    }
    else {
        this.Url =
        "http://localhost/BrokerageFirm/Securities.asmx";
    }
}
```

The constructor sets the object's *Url* property to the value of the *Securities-WebServiceUrl* application configuration parameter defined in the application's configuration file. If the value is not found, the *Url* property is set to the value contained within the HTTP extension element that defines the address of the endpoint within the WSDL document's service definition.

You should consider modifying the *else* logic to throw an exception instead of defaulting to a hard-coded value. This will make it easier to diagnose some problems within your application. For example, when you are trying to debug your application, it would be easy to overlook the fact that the *SecuritiesWebServiceUri* parameter is misspelled within your configuration file. (Did you catch the misspelling?)

You might need to dynamically modify the *Url* property at run time. For example, the application might want to reissue its request to another server in the event of failure. The *Url* property is a publicly exposed read/write property, so it can be modified by the client at run time.

You can also set the *Url* property to point to a DISCO file containing a reference to the targeted Web service. You can then call the *Discover* method to dynamically bind to the Web service contained within the DISCO file. I will cover DISCO files in more detail in Chapter 10.

Within the proxy class definition, methods are defined for each of the operations exposed by the Web service. For each operation, three methods are defined. The first method definition is for synchronously invoking the Web method, and the other two are used in combination to invoke the Web method asynchronously. Here is the synchronous definition for the *InstantQuote* method:

```
[System.Web.Services.Protocols.SoapHeaderAttribute
"SoapReceiptHeaderValue", Direction=System.Web.Services.
Protocols.SoapHeaderDirection.Out)]
[System.Web.Services.Protocols.SoapHeaderAttribute
("SoapPaymentHeaderValue")]
/// <remarks/>
[System.Web.Services.Protocols.SoapRpcMethodAttribute
("http://woodgrovebank.com/Securities/InstantQuote",
RequestNamespace="http://woodgrovebank.com/Securities",
ResponseNamespace="http://woodgrovebank.com/Securities")]
public System.Double InstantQuote(string symbol,
CurrencyType targetCurrency) {
    object[] results =
    this.Invoke("InstantQuote", new object[] {
            symbol, targetCurrency});
    return ((System.Double)(results[0]));
}
```

The *InstantQuote* method is decorated with the *SoapHeader*, *Debugger-StepThrough*, and *SoapRpcMethod* attributes. The *DebuggerStepThrough* attribute is used by the Visual Studio .NET debugger. The Visual Studio .NET debugger will not stop within the method marked with this attribute.

The *SoapHeader* and *SoapRpcMethod* attributes serve the same purpose as they do when applied to a Web method. The *SoapHeader* attribute indicates which member variable should be serialized into the header of the SOAP message. The *SoapRpcMethod* attribute indicates the encoding style and the format of the message as well as the value of the SOAP *HTTPAction* header.

The signature of the method itself is composed of .NET types that match their XML counterparts described within the *types* section of the WSDL document. This wrapper method definition allows code written against the proxy to take full advantage of the features provided by the .NET platform. For example, if a client attempts to pass invalid parameters, such as passing two strings to the *Add* method instead of two integers, the compiler will generate errors at compile time. Developers using Visual Studio .NET will also have full IntelliSense capabilities when they write code against the proxy.

The implementation of the *InstantQuote* method packages the parameters into an array of objects and calls the *Invoke* method. Because this method is publicly exposed, you can call it directly. However, using the method exposed by the WSDL.exe-generated proxy provides a more convenient and natural calling convention.

In many circumstances, making a synchronous call to a Web method is not ideal. This is especially true for Web services accessed via the Internet, where quality and speed of the connection might be uncertain. This might also be true for Web services hosted within the walls of a corporate data center. For example, a Web service might be used to expose data contained within a mainframe. A significant amount of initialization might need to be done to set up a connection to the mainframe, or the Web service might be accessed during times of peak load.

The next two methods defined for the *InstantQuote* operation are *Begin-InstantQuote* and *EndInstantQuote*. These methods are used to make an asynchronous call to the Securities Web service's *InstantQuote* Web method:

```
/// <remarks/>
public System.IAsyncResult BeginInstantQuote(string symbol,
CurrencyType targetCurrency, System.AsyncCallback callback,
object asyncState) {
    return this.BeginInvoke("InstantQuote",
    new object[] {symbol, targetCurrency},
    callback, asyncState);
}

/// <remarks/>
public System.Double EndInstantQuote(System.IAsyncResult
asyncResult) {
    object[] results = this.EndInvoke(asyncResult);
    return ((System.Double)(results[0]));
}
}
```

By convention, the method used to invoke the asynchronous call is prefixed with *Begin* and the method used to retrieve the parameters returned by the Web service is prefixed with *End*. The implementation invokes the *BeginInvoke* and *EndInvoke* methods, respectively.

The asynchronous methods are not decorated with attributes used to describe the formatting of the message. The *methodName* parameter contains the name of the method that the ASP.NET runtime will use to retrieve the formatting information. If the asynchronous message is decorated with any attributes such as *SoapDocumentMethod*, these attributes will be ignored.

```
[System.Xml.Serialization.SoapTypeAttribute("SoapReceiptHeader",
"http://woodgrovebank.com/Securities/encodedTypes")]
public class SoapReceiptHeader : SoapHeader {

    public System.Double Amount;
```

(continued)

```
        public int ReferenceNumber;
    }

[System.Xml.Serialization.SoapTypeAttribute("SoapPaymentHeader",
"http://woodgrovebank.com/Securities/encodedTypes")]
public class SoapPaymentHeader : SoapHeader {

    public string NameOnCard;

    public string CreditCardNumber;

    public CardType CreditCardType;

    public System.DateTime ExpirationDate;
    }

[System.Xml.Serialization.SoapTypeAttribute("CardType",
"http://woodgrovebank.com/Securities/encodedTypes")]
public enum CardType {

    VISA,

    MC,

    AMX,

    DISCOVER,
    }

[System.Xml.Serialization.SoapTypeAttribute("CurrencyType",
"http://woodgrovebank.com/Securities/encodedTypes")]
public enum CurrencyType {

    US_DOLLARS,

    UK_POUNDS,

    GE_DEUTSCHMARKS,
    }
}
```

Lastly WSDL.exe defines .NET counterparts to the *Payment* and *Receipt* SOAP headers as well as the *CurrencyType* and *CardType* enumerations. WSDL.exe uses the *SoapType* attribute to explicitly define type information used by the XML Serializer to map the .NET types to their XML Schema counterparts.

The use of the proxy to make a synchronous method call is fairly trivial. The following example writes the price of a security passed as a command-line argument out to the console:

```
using System;
using BrokerageFirm;

class Application
{
    public void Main(string[] args)
    {
        string symbol = args[0];
        Securities securities = new Securities();

        // Create and initialize the Payment header.
        SoapPaymentHeader paymentHeader = new SoapPaymentHeader();
        paymentHeader.CreditCardNumber = "12345";
        paymentHeader.ExpirationDate = DateTime.Today;
        paymentHeader.CreditCardType = CardType.VISA;
        securities.SoapPaymentHeaderValue = paymentHeader;

        Console.WriteLine("{0} = {1}", symbol,
            securities.InstantQuote(symbol, CurrencyType.US_DOLLARS));
    }
}
```

Because the *Payment* header is required to be passed to the *InstantQuote* method, I create a new *SoapPaymentHeader* object. Then I initialize it and set it to the *SoapPaymentHeaderValue* property on the *securities* object. The proxy is responsible for serializing the *SoapPaymentHeader* object within the header of the SOAP request message.

Invoking the *InstantQuote* Web method asynchronously involves a little more work. The following code is contained within a WinForm application. Let's walk through an example. I will write a console application that uses the Securities Web service proxy to make an asynchronous method call:

```
using System;
using System.Web.Services.Protocols;
using BrokerageFirm;

namespace SecuritiesClient
{
    class Application
    {
        static Securities securities = new Securities();
```

First I create a class that will contain the console application. Then I create a static instance of the Securities Web service proxy as a static member of the class. I do this because the static callback function that I will now define will need to access the proxy object:

```
static void Main(string[] args)
{
    string symbol = args[0];

    SoapPaymentHeader paymentHeader = new SoapPaymentHeader();
    paymentHeader.CreditCardNumber = "12345";
    paymentHeader.ExpirationDate = DateTime.Today;
    paymentHeader.CreditCardType = CardType.VISA;

    securities.SoapPaymentHeaderValue = paymentHeader;

    securities.BeginInstantQuote(symbol,
    CurrencyType.US_DOLLARS,
    new AsyncCallback(InstantQuoteCallback), symbol);

    System.Threading.Thread.Sleep(30000);
    Console.WriteLine("Terminating application.");
}
```

As you have learned, WSDL.exe will properly handle generating proxies for Web services that support headers. The generated proxy code will contain a class declaration for each header defined by the Web service. Depending on the direction of the header, instances of the header class can be either retrieved or set using an associated property defined by the proxy class for the Web service. By default, the property will have the same name as the class, with a prefix of *Value*. If the class declaration contains an *XmlType* attribute (discussed in Chapter 7), the property on the client will simply be the name given to the XML type.

The proxy class will also perform client-side validation of the SOAP headers before sending the message to the server. For example, the proxy will throw a *SoapException* if *SoapPaymentHeaderValue* was set to *null* when the Web method was invoked.

Within the *Main* function, a call is made to the *BeginInstantQuote* method. This method accepts two parameters in addition to the securities symbol and the target currency of the quote. I also pass an instance of the *Async-Callback* delegate that serves as a reference to the *InstantQuoteCallback* method I will define shortly. This tells the Web service proxy to execute the *InstantQuoteCallback* method once the Web service returns. If there is no callback method that should be invoked, you can pass *null* for the value of the parameter.

The fourth parameter is intended to pass state that should be associated with the method once the callback has been invoked. The parameter is of type *object* and therefore accepts an instance of any .NET type. In this case, I pass the symbol of the security for which I have requested the quote.

```
public static void InstantQuoteCallback(IAsyncResult result)
{
    // Obtain the results.
    double price = securities.EndInstantQuote(result);

    // Obtain the additional state that was sent by
    // the call to BeginCallback.
    WebClientAsyncResult webResult = (WebClientAsyncResult)result;
    string symbol = (string)webResult.AsyncState;

    // Display the results within a message box.
    Console.WriteLine("{0} = {1}", symbol, price);
}
}
}
```

The *InstantQuoteCallback* method receives a reference to the *IAsyncResult* interface of an object of type *WebClientAsyncResult*. This parameter is then passed to the *EndAdd* method to obtain the return value of the Web method call. Next I obtain the additional state information from the *AsyncState* property—in this case, the symbol passed to the *Add* method. Finally the price of the security is written to the console.

Cookies

Proxies derived from *SoapHttpClientProtocol* fully support HTTP cookies. However, the proxies have cookies disabled by default. To enable cookie support, you must set the *CookieContainer* property on the proxy object to reference an instance of a *CookieContainer* object.

Earlier in the chapter, I leveraged session state to configure the target currency. The client first sets the target currency by calling *SetCurrency*. Then the client calls *InstantQuote* to obtain the price of the security. Because the Web service relies on cookies to maintain session state, clients using this Web service need to explicitly enable cookies. The following code demonstrates how to enable session state:

```
using System;
using BrokerageFirm;
using System.Net;

class Application
{
    public void Main(string[] args)
    {
        string symbol = args[0];
```

(continued)

```
        Securities securities = new Securities();

        // Enable session state by creating a new cookie container.
        securities.CookieContainer = new CookieContainer();

        // Receive a quote on the requested security in UK pounds.
        securities.SetCurrency(CurrencyType.UK_POUNDS);
        Console.WriteLine("{0} = {1}", symbol,
            securities.InstantQuote(symbol));
    }
}
```

Once the proxy object has gone out of scope, all cookie information will be invalid. This is perfectly acceptable in the above console application. However, this might not be ideal if you need to maintain the cookie information across instances of the proxy. In such cases, it is necessary to persist the cookie collection and associate it to the new proxy object.

Summary

ASP.NET provides a robust, feature-rich platform for easily creating and consuming Web services. For a V1 product, it is remarkably feature complete.

An ASP.NET Web service is represented by an .asmx file hosted within an IIS Web application. The implementation of the Web service can be contained within the .asmx file or within a compiled DLL. If the code appears inline within the .asmx file, the ASP.NET runtime will automatically compile it the first time it is accessed.

A Web service is defined by a standard public class declaration. Public methods defined within the class can be exposed by the Web service if you decorate the method with the *WebMethod* attribute. This attribute exposes properties that can be optionally set to control the behavior of the ASP.NET runtime. The class can also be decorated with the *WebService* attribute.

All ASP.NET Web services expose a SOAP interface over HTTP. Depending on the complexity of the Web service's interface, an ASP.NET Web service might also support HTTP GET and HTTP POST. The ASP.NET runtime will automatically map data contained within requests from the client and their corresponding responses to their corresponding .NET datatypes.

The ASP.NET platform will automatically generate documentation for the Web service. A human-readable HTML version of the documentation can be obtained by calling the .asmx file with no parameters. A programmatic WSDL version of the documentation can be obtained by appending *&wsdl* to the URL that addresses the .asmx file.

ASP.NET supports two distinct encoding styles, Document and RPC. Document is the default and is used primarily for document-based message exchanges between the client and the server. RPC is used primarily for procedure-based communication between the client and the server. You can select RPC by using the *SoapRpcService* or *SoapRpcMethod* attribute.

You should be careful when you pass value types as parameters because the ASP.NET platform has some inconsistencies when identity is maintained. The identities of built-in value types such as *int* and *double* are never maintained, even when passed by reference. The identity of a custom value type when passed by reference is maintained when the encoding style is set to RPC. However, the identity of custom value types passed by value is improperly maintained when the encoding style is set to RPC.

Regardless of the style of encoding, SOAP formally defines how errors returned to the client should be encoded within a SOAP message. The ASP.NET runtime will automatically map .NET exceptions into a well-formed SOAP *Fault* element. You can also formally raise a fault by throwing an exception of type *SoapException*.

You can facilitate interface inheritance by referencing a port type or a binding definition from an external namespace. Of the two, ASP.NET supports referencing transport-specific binding definitions. You first reference the remote binding definition with the *WebServiceBinding* attribute, and then you associate the reference to the binding with a particular Web method via the *Binding* property of the *SoapRpcMethod* or *SoapDocumentMethod* attribute.

ASP.NET also provides a fairly robust state management system. It supports three configurations: In Process, Out of Process, and SQL Server. Of the three, In Process is the most performant configuration. You should consider Out of Process and SQL Server only if the Web service will be deployed on a Web farm. Regardless of which model you use, the programming model is exactly the same.

The ASP.NET platform also has good support for defining and consuming SOAP headers. A SOAP header is defined by deriving from the *SoapHeader* class. You then use the *SoapHeader* attribute to associate the header with a particular Web method. ASP.NET automatically deserializes any headers received from the client and serializes any headers sent from the Web server.

Finally, the ASP.NET framework provides an interception mechanism called SOAP extensions. The SOAP extensions framework lets you examine and, if necessary, modify the contents of the SOAP messages exchanged between the client and the server.

I didn't cover a couple of key topics related to ASP.NET Web services because they deserve chapters of their own. In Chapter 7, I will discuss how to control how individual parameters passed by a Web service or its client are encoded within a SOAP message. In Chapter 9, I will also cover the security services provided by ASP.NET.

7

XML Serialization

The ASP.NET runtime is built on top of a technology called XML serialization. XML serialization is responsible for serializing instances of .NET types to XML and deserializing XML to instances of .NET types. XML serialization is also responsible for serializing .NET type definitions to XML schemas and deserializing XML schemas to .NET type definitions.

Sometimes, this default behavior might not entirely meet your needs. For example, public properties and fields will be serialized into elements within the resulting XML document, but many existing and emerging Web services interfaces such as UDDI and .NET My Services expose interfaces that use attributes. Therefore, you need a means of controlling how .NET types and instances of .NET types are serialized into XML.

Consider the following SOAP message, which submits a purchase order:

```xml
<?xml version="1.0" encoding="utf-8"?>
<soap:Envelope xmlns:soap="http://schemas.xmlsoap.org/soap/envelope/"
xmlns:xsi="http://www.w3.org/2001/XMLSchema-instance"
xmlns:xsd="http://www.w3.org/2001/XMLSchema">
  <soap:Body>
    <PurchaseOrder xsi:type="CommentedPurchaseOrder"
    xmlns="http://tempuri.org/">
      <BillingAddress>
        <Name accountNumber="12345">ABC Company</Name>
        <Street>123 Some Street</Street>
        <City>Some Town</City>
        <State>CO</State>
        <ZipCode>80427</ZipCode>
      </BillingAddress>
      <ShippingAddress>
        <Name accountNumber="12345">ABC Company</Name>
        <Street>123 Some Street</Street>
        <City>Some Town</City>
```

(continued)

```
      <State>CO</State>
      <ZipCode>80427</ZipCode>
    </ShippingAddress>
    <Items>
      <Item partNumber="A1467">
        <Quantity>2</Quantity>
        <Price>23.5</Price>
        <Currency>US_DOLLAR</Currency>
      </Item>
      <Item partNumber="C2963">
        <Quantity>20</Quantity>
        <Price>10.95</Price>
        <Currency>US_DOLLAR</Currency>
      </Item>
      <Item partNumber="F4980">
        <Quantity>3</Quantity>
        <Price>82.65</Price>
        <Currency>US_DOLLAR</Currency>
      </Item>
    </Items>
    <Comments>Please do not ship a partial order.</Comments>
  </PurchaseOrder>
 </soap:Body>
</soap:Envelope>
```

The message contains a mixture of elements and attributes. For example, the part number for each item listed in the purchase order is serialized within the *partNumber* attribute of each *Item* element. The *Name* element within the billing and shipping addresses contains the name of the company as well as an attribute that contains the company's account number.

Controlling XML Serialization

For situations in which the default serialization support is not adequate, XML serialization provides mechanisms for altering the way .NET types are serialized to XML. You do this mostly by using the attributes defined in the *System.Xml.Serialization* namespace, which Table 7-1 describes.

You can use the XML serialization attributes only with literal, document-oriented SOAP messages. For example, the attributes will be ignored if the Web method is decorated with the *SoapRpcMethod* attribute or is decorated with the *SoapDocumentMethod* attribute and has the *Use* property set to *SoapBindingUse.Encoded*.

The attributes listed in the table control how XML serialization represents .NET types in XML. For Web services, the attributes control how instances of

.NET types are encoded into the body of a SOAP message. They also control how .NET types are represented as XML datatypes in the WSDL document that describes the Web service.

Table 7-1   XML Serialization Attributes

Attribute	Description
XmlAnyAttribute	Creates an "open" XML datatype in which any attribute can be added to its root node
XmlAnyElement	Creates an "open" XML datatype where any element can be included as a child element
XmlArray	Controls how the root node of an array is serialized
XmlArrayItem	Controls how an item of an array is serialized
XmlAttribute	Indicates that a public field, property, or parameter should be serialized as an attribute
XmlElement	Controls how a public field, property, or parameter is serialized as an element
XmlEnum	Controls how an enumeration is serialized
XmlIgnore	Indicates that XML serialization should not serialize the member
XmlInclude	Tells XML serialization to include a particular datatype definition of a class that derives from a base class exposed by a Web service's interface
XmlRoot	Identifies a type as the root of an XML document
XmlText	Specifies that the member variable be serialized as the content of the parent element
XmlType	Maps an XML type to a particular class, structure, enumeration, or interface declaration

In this chapter, I use the preceding attributes to create the *PurchaseOrder* .NET type, which can be used to define how a purchase order is serialized in the body of a SOAP message. I also create the *AcceptPO* Web method. This Web method is used to receive purchase orders similar to the one in the previous example.

Defining the Root *PurchaseOrder* Datatype

The first step is to define the *PurchaseOrder* class, which will represent the root element within the body of the SOAP message. Recall from Chapter 4 that you can set elements to *null* by setting the *xsi:nil* attribute to *true*. For the SOAP message to be valid, it must not contain a null reference to the purchase order.

The following code defines the *PurchaseOrder* class:

```
[XmlRoot(IsNullable=false)]
public class PurchaseOrder
{

    // Additional type definitions...

}
```

To define the *PurchaseOrder* XML datatype, I need to define a public class by the same name. I also need to ensure that the *PurchaseOrder* element cannot contain a *null* value. I can do this by decorating the class with the *XmlRoot* attribute.

One of the properties exposed by the *XmlRoot* attribute is *IsNullable*. This property indicates whether the schema generated by XML serialization will permit instance documents to contain a *PurchaseOrder* element with a *null* value.

You can also use the *XmlRoot* attribute to control the behavior of XML serialization. Table 7-2 describes the properties exposed by the *XmlRoot* attribute.

Table 7-2 *XmlRootAttribute* **Properties**

Property	Description
DataType	Specifies the XML datatype in which the class should be encoded.
ElementName	Specifies the name of the root XML element.
Form	Specifies whether the XML element must be namespace qualified. It is set to one of three values defined by the *XmlSchemaForm* enumeration: *None*, *Qualified*, or *Unqualified*.
IsNullable	Specifies whether the value of the XML element can be set to *xsd:nil*.
Namespace	Specifies the XML namespace in which the root element is qualified.

Most of the elements within the *PurchaseOrder* document contain attributes or child elements themselves. For example, the *BillingAddress* and *ShippingAddress* elements each contain *Name*, *Street*, *City*, *State*, and *ZipCode* child elements, as shown here:

```
<PurchaseOrder>
  <BillingAddress>
    <Name accountNumber="12345">ABC Company</Name>
    <Street>123 Some Street</Street>
    <City>Some Town</City>
    <State>CO</State>
    <ZipCode>80427</ZipCode>
  </BillingAddress>
  <ShippingAddress>
    <Name accountNumber="12345">ABC Company</Name>
    <Street>123 Some Street</Street>
    <City>Some Town</City>
    <State>CO</State>
    <ZipCode>80427</ZipCode>
  </ShippingAddress>

  <!-- Additional type definitions... -->

</PurchaseOrder>
```

You can model complex structures such as the preceding one using a class hierarchy. The following example defines an *Address* class and then defines two fields within the *PurchaseOrder* class, *BillingAddress* and *ShippingAddress*. Both fields are defined as type *Address*.

```
[XmlRoot(IsNullable=false)]
public class PurchaseOrder
{
    [XmlElement(IsNullable=true, DataType="normalizedString")]
    public string Comments;

    [XmlElement(IsNullable=false)]
    public Address BillingAddress;

    [XmlElement(IsNullable=false)]
    public Address ShippingAddress;
```

(continued)

```
    // Additional type definitions...

}

public class Address
{
    public CompanyName Name;
    public string Street;
    public string City;
    public string State;
    public string ZipCode;
}
```

The preceding code uses the *XmlElement* attribute to control how properties and fields are serialized as elements within the resulting XML document. For example, the *Comments* field can contain a *null* value, but neither the *ShippingAddress* field nor the *BillingAddress* field can be set to *null*. Like the *XmlRoot* attribute, the *XmlElement* attribute exposes an *IsNullable* property.

The *Comments* element can be set to *null* because XML serialization does not allow you to specify that a particular element or attribute be able to optionally occur within a document. This is because the *XmlElement* attribute does not provide a means of explicitly setting the *minOccurs* and *maxOccurs* constraints on an element. I discuss another potential workaround for this situation later in the chapter.

The *Comments* element contained within the *PurchaseOrder* document contains text related to the order. In addition to setting the *XmlElement* attribute's *IsNullable* property, the preceding code sets the *DataType* property for the *Comments* field.

XML serialization provides a default mapping between .NET types and the built-in datatypes defined by XML Schema. For example, the *Comments* property is defined as type *String*. By default, XML serialization will transform the *String* type to the XML built-in datatype *string*.

Suppose the back-end system that will record the receipt of the purchase order does not accept linefeeds or tabs. In order to communicate this to the client, I set the datatype of the *Comments* element to *normalizedString*. By definition, *normalizedString* cannot contain linefeeds or tabs.

XML serialization supports all XML built-in datatypes. Table 7-3 lists the supported mappings between XML datatypes and .NET types.

Table 7-3   Mapping Between XML Datatypes and .NET Types

XML Datatype	.NET Type	XML Datatype	.NET Type
anyUri	String	IDREFS	String
base64Binary	Byte (array)	Int	Int32
boolean	Boolean	language	String
byte	SByte	long	Int64
CDATA	String	Name	String
date	DateTime	NCName	String
dateTime	DateTime	negativeInteger	String
decimal	Decimal	NMTOKEN	String
double	Double	NMTOKENS	String
duration	String	nonNegativeInteger	String
ENTITY	String	nonPositiveInteger	String
ENTITIES	String	normalizedString	String
float	Single	NOTATION	String
gDay	String	positiveInteger	String
gMonth	String	QName	XmlQualifiedName
gMonthDay	String	string	String
gYear	String	short	Int16
gYearMonth	String	time	DateTime
hexBinary	Byte (array)	token	String
ID	String	unsignedByte	Byte
IDREF	String	unsignedInt	UInt32

Even though XML serialization will transform an XML datatype into its corresponding .NET type, it will not perform any validation on the data. For example, the XML datatype *integer* maps to the *String* .NET type, but the client can pass non-numeric data to the Web service. Therefore, it is up to the Web service to enforce additional constraints over and above what is provided by the .NET type.

The *XmlElement* attribute exposes additional properties that you can use to control how a .NET type is serialized to XML. Table 7-4 describes these properties.

Table 7-4   *XmlElementAttribute* **Properties**

Property	Description
DataType	Specifies the XML Schema built-in datatype in which the property or field should be encoded.
ElementName	Specifies the name of the XML element.
Form	Specifies whether the XML element must be namespace qualified. It is set to one of three values defined by the *XmlSchemaForm* enumeration: *None*, *Qualified*, or *Unqualified*.
IsNullable	Specifies whether the value of the XML element can have its *xsi:nil* attribute set to *true*.
Namespace	Specifies the XML namespace in which the element is defined.
Type	Specifies the .NET type that should be used to generate the schema that describes the element.

You can decorate a property or a field with more than one *XmlElement* attribute. Doing so specifies that an instance document must contain an element that complies with the criteria specified by one of the *XmlElement* attributes. Here is an example:

```
public class Person
{
    [XmlElement("SocialSecurityNumber")]
    [XmlElement("DriversLicenseNumber")]
    public string Identifier;

    public string Name;
}
```

The preceding .NET type definition creates the following XML datatype definition:

```
<s:complexType name="Person">
  <s:sequence>
    <s:choice minOccurs="1" maxOccurs="1">
      <s:element minOccurs="1" maxOccurs="1" name="DriversLicenseNumber"
      type="s:string" />
      <s:element minOccurs="1" maxOccurs="1" name="SocialSecurityNumber"
      type="s:string" />
    </s:choice>
    <s:element minOccurs="1" maxOccurs="1" name="Name" nillable="true"
    type="s:string" />
  </s:sequence>
</s:complexType>
```

An instance of the *Person* XML datatype must contain the person's name as well as the person's driver's license number or social security number.

You can use the *XmlType* attribute to control how .NET types are serialized to an XML datatype, and you can apply the attribute to a variety of .NET type definitions, including classes, structures, enumerations, and interface definitions. You can use the *XmlType* attribute to set the name of the resulting XML datatype and the namespace in which the datatype is defined. You can also use it to specify whether a datatype definition will be generated within the Web service's WSDL document.

Table 7-5 describes the properties exposed by the *XmlType* attribute to control how XML datatypes are generated.

Table 7-5 *XmlTypeAttribute* **Properties**

Property	Description
IncludeInSchema	Specifies whether the type will be included in the schema
Namespace	Specifies the XML namespace in which the XML schema datatype is qualified
TypeName	Specifies the name of the XML datatype that describes the targeted .NET type

You can also use the *XmlIgnore* attribute to exclude entities from type definitions. For example, suppose the internal implementation of the AcceptPO Web service needs to track a processing code. The following class definition adds a *ProcessingCode* public field to the class for maintaining the state of this information:

```
[XmlRoot(IsNullable=false)]
public class PurchaseOrder
{
    [XmlElement(IsNullable=true, DataType="normalizedString")]
    public string Comments;

    [XmlElement(IsNullable=false)]
    public Address BillingAddress;

    [XmlElement(IsNullable=false)]
    public Address ShippingAddress;

    [XmlIgnore]
    public int ProcessingCode;

    // Additional type definitions...

}
```

The *ProcessingCode* field is declared as public because it needs to be accessed by the internal implementation of the AcceptPO Web service. However, because the field should not be exposed to the client, it is decorated with the *XmlIgnore* attribute.

There is another use for the *XmlIgnore* attribute. Suppose it is important to know whether the *Comments* element is set to *null* or simply contains an empty string. Because the underlying .NET type is a value type, you will not be able to directly test for *null*.

To discover whether the element contains a null value, you can create a property that will be set by XML serialization. You can define a Boolean public field with the prefix *Specified*. This field will be set to *true* if the associated XML element contains a null value. The following code provides an example:

```
[XmlRoot(IsNullable=false)]
public class PurchaseOrder
{
    [XmlIgnore]
    public bool CommentsSpecified;
    [XmlElement(IsNullable=true, DataType="normalizedString")]
    public string Comments;

    // Additional type definitions...

}
```

This example extends the *PurchaseOrder* class definition by adding the *CommentsSpecified* public field. This field will be set by XML serialization and therefore should not be exposed within the *PurchaseOrder* type definition. Therefore, I decorated the *CommentsSpecified* field with the *XmlIgnore* attribute to ensure that the ASP.NET runtime will not include the field in the auto-generated WSDL document.

Defining the *Items* Array

The next step is to define the array of items contained within a purchase order. The following code defines the type that will represent an individual item within the purchase order. Recall that the individual *Item* elements within the *Items* array contain a combination of elements and attributes.

```
<Item partNumber="A1467">
  <Price>23.5</Price>
  <Quantity>2</Quantity>
</Item>
```

By default, public read/writable properties defined within a .NET type are serialized as XML elements. The *XmlAttribute* attribute is used to indicate that a property or a field should be serialized as an attribute instead of as an element. The following code defines the *partNumber* attribute for the *Item* element definition:

```
public class PurchaseOrderItem
{
    [XmlAttribute("partNumber")]
    public string      PartNumber;
    public int         Quantity;
    public double      Price;
    public CurrencyType Currency;
}
```

By convention, I use camel case when naming the *partNumber* attribute. In camel case, the first word that composes the entity name is all lowercase and the first letter of each subsequent word is capitalized. But the standard convention for public properties and fields exposed by a .NET type is Pascal case, in which the first letter of each word making up the entity name is uppercase.

By default, the name of the attribute in the serialized XML document is the name of the property or field. Because the name of the field does not match the name of the attribute, I pass the intended name of the attribute to the constructor for the *XmlAttribute* attribute. The value of the *Name* property is set to the string passed to the constructor.

The *XmlAttribute* attribute exposes additional properties that you can use to control how XML serialization serializes the associated property or field to an attribute. These properties are described in Table 7-6.

Table 7-6   *XmlAttributeAttribute* **Properties**

Property	Description
AttributeName	Specifies the name of the XML attribute.
DataType	Specifies the XML Schema built-in datatype in which the property or field should be encoded.
Form	Specifies whether the XML attribute must be namespace qualified. It is set to one of three values defined by the *XmlSchemaForm* enumeration: *None*, *Qualified*, or *Unqualified*.
Namespace	Specifies the XML namespace in which the attribute is defined.

The *Currency* element is of type *CurrencyType*. *CurrencyType* is an enumeration containing the valid currency types supported by the *AcceptPO* Web method. You can use the *XmlEnum* attribute to alter the name of an element typed to a particular enumeration. As an illustration, the following code uses the *XmlEnum* attribute to rename the public field for describing the currency that was used to price the item:

```
public class PurchaseOrderItem
{
    [XmlAttribute("partNumber")]
    public string    PartNumber;
    public int       Quantity;
    public double     Price;

    [XmlEnum("Currency")]
    public CurrencyType TypeOfCurrency;
}
```

The following code adds an array of *Item* elements to the *PurchaseOrder* class. Two attributes can be used to control how an array is serialized to XML: *XmlArray* and *XmlArrayItems*. Here is the *PurchaseOrder* class definition:

```
[XmlRoot(IsNullable=false)]
public class PurchaseOrder
{
    [XmlElement(IsNullable=false)]
    public Address BillingAddress;

    [XmlElement(IsNullable=false)]
    public Address ShippingAddress;

    [XmlArray("Items", IsNullable=false)]
    [XmlArrayItem("Item", IsNullable=false)]
    public PurchaseOrderItem [] Items;

    // Additional type definitions...

}
```

The *XmlArray* attribute is used to control how the root element of the array is serialized. Because the purchase order is valid only if the array of *Item* elements is not *null*, the *IsNullable* property is set to *false* in the preceding code.

The *XmlArrayItem* attribute is used to control how each item within the array is serialized. Because none of the items within the array can be set to *null*, the *IsNullable* property of the *XmlArrayItem* attribute is set to *false* in the preceding code.

In XML serialization, by default each element within the array has the same name as the type definition. In this example, the type definition name is *PurchaseOrderItem*. Because the name of the elements within the *Items* array should be named *Item*, I explicitly set the name of the element.

You can also use the *XmlArrayItem* attribute to define arrays containing instances of a mixture of datatypes. You can do this by decorating an array with multiple *XmlArrayItem* attributes. The following code defines an array that can contain items of type *string* and *int*:

```
[XmlArrayItem("MyInt", typeof(int))]
[XmlArrayItem("MyString", typeof(string))]
public object [] TestArray;
```

The preceding code will generate the following XML datatype definition:

```
<element minOccurs="1" maxOccurs="1" name="TestArray" nillable="true"
type="s0:ArrayOfChoice1" />

<complexType name="ArrayOfChoice1">
  <sequence>
    <choice minOccurs="0" maxOccurs="unbounded">
      <element minOccurs="1" maxOccurs="1" name="MyInt" type="int" />
      <element minOccurs="1" maxOccurs="1" name="MyString" type="string" />
    </choice>
  </sequence>
</complexType>
```

Notice that the *TestArray* element can contain any combination of child elements of type *string* and *int*. To accept data of different types from the client, the XML mixed array is mapped to a .NET array of type *Object*. The compiler will not throw an error if the .NET type is set to something other than *Object*—say, *Boolean*. However, the client will receive a run-time error if the client sends an instance of an XML datatype that cannot be transformed into the underlying .NET type.

The *XmlArray* and *XmlArrayItems* attributes expose additional properties that you can use to control how an array is serialized to XML. Tables 7-7 and 7-8 describe these properties.

Table 7-7   *XmlArrayAttribute* **Properties**

Property	Description
ElementName	Specifies the name of the XML element.
Form	Specifies whether the XML element must be namespace qualified. It is set to one of three values defined by the *XmlSchemaForm* enumeration: *None*, *Qualified*, or *Unqualified*.
IsNullable	Specifies whether the value of the XML element can have its *xsi:nil* attribute set to *true*.
Namespace	Specifies the XML namespace in which the element is defined.

Table 7-8   *XmlArrayItemAttribute* **Properties**

Property	Description
DataType	Specifies the XML Schema built-in datatype in which the property or field should be encoded.
ElementName	Specifies the name of the XML element.
Form	Specifies whether the XML element must be namespace qualified. It is set to one of three values defined by the *XmlSchemaForm* enumeration: *None*, *Qualified*, or *Unqualified*.
IsNullable	Specifies whether the value of the XML element can have its *xsi:nil* attribute set to *true*.
Namespace	Specifies the XML namespace in which the element is defined.
Type	Specifies the .NET type that should be used to generate the schema that describes the element.

As I mentioned earlier, the default behavior of XML serialization is to serialize an array as a root element, where each item is contained within a child element. However, sometimes it might be necessary to specify a collection of content that is not wrapped by a root element.

You can specify that each element of an array not be wrapped within a parent element by decorating the array with the *XmlElement* attribute. The following example creates the *BaseballTeam* type, which contains one *CoachName* child element and any number of *PlayerName* child elements:

```
public class BaseballTeam
{
    public string CoachName;

    [XmlElement("PlayerName")]
    public string [] Players;
}
```

The preceding .NET type definition creates the following XML datatype definition:

```
<complexType name="BaseballTeam">
  <sequence>
    <element minOccurs="1" maxOccurs="1" name="Coach" nillable="true"
    type="s:string" />
    <element minOccurs="0" maxOccurs="unbounded" name="PlayerName"
    type="s:string" />
  </sequence>
</complexType>
```

You can also decorate an array with multiple *XmlElement* attributes. Doing so specifies that an instance document can contain any combination and any number of elements defined by the *XmlElement* attributes. The following example defines a *BaseballTeam* XML datatype that contains one *CoachName* element and any combination of *PlayerName* and *PlayerNumber* elements:

```
public class BaseballTeam
{
    public string Coach;

    [XmlElement("PlayerName", typeof(string))]
    [XmlElement("PlayerNumber", typeof(int))]
    public string [] Players;
}
```

The preceding .NET type definition creates the following XML datatype definition:

```
<complexType name="BaseballTeam">
  <sequence>
    <element minOccurs="1" maxOccurs="1" name="Coach" nillable="true"
    type="s:string" />
    <choice minOccurs="0" maxOccurs="unbounded">
      <element minOccurs="1" maxOccurs="1" name="PlayerName" type="s:string" />
      <element minOccurs="1" maxOccurs="1" name="PlayerNumber" type="s:int" />
    </choice>
  </sequence>
</complexType>
```

Creating Derived Datatypes

XML serialization supports defining XML datatypes that are derived by extension from other XML datatypes. You can define a derived XML datatype by creating a derived .NET type and then decorating the base type with the *XmlInclude* attribute.

The following example defines a base type called *Tire* and creates two derived types called *AutoTire* and *MountainBikeTire*. The *XmlInclude* attribute is also used to notify XML serialization of these two derived types.

```
[XmlInclude(typeof(AutoTire))]
[XmlInclude(typeof(MountainBikeTire))]
public class Tire
{
    public int WheelDiameter;
    public int Width;
}

public class AutoTire : Tire
{
    public AspectRatio;
}

public class MountainBikeTire : Tire
{
    public TireLocationType Position;
}

public enum TireLocationType
{
    FRONT,
    REAR
}
```

The preceding code will generate an XML datatype called *Tire* and two datatypes that derive by extension from *Tire*: *AutoTire* and *MountainBikeTire*. Because *AutoTire* and *MountainBikeTire* are extended versions of the *Tire* datatype, Web service interfaces that accept the *Tire* datatype can also accept instances of *AutoTire* and *MountainBikeTire*.

Recall that I want to specify that the *Comments* element within the PurchaseOrder document be optional. Also recall that you cannot specify optional parameters for a Web service by explicitly setting the *minOccurs* restriction on the element declaration to 0. One potential workaround uses derived types and the *XmlInclude* attribute.

The following code creates a type that is derived from *PurchaseOrder*. The new type contains the optional *Comments* element.

```
[XmlRoot("PurchaseOrder", IsNullable=false)]
[XmlInclude(typeof(CommentedPurchaseOrder))]
public class PurchaseOrder
{
    [XmlElement(IsNullable=false)]
    public Address BillingAddress;

    [XmlElement(IsNullable=false)]
    public Address ShippingAddress;

    [XmlArray("Items", IsNullable=false)]
    [XmlArrayItem("Item", IsNullable=false)]
    public PurchaseOrderItem [] Items;

    // Additional type definitions...
}

public class CommentedPurchaseOrder : PurchaseOrder
{
    [XmlElement(IsNullable=true, DataType="normalizedString")]
    public string Comments;
}
```

The preceding example defines the *CommentedPurchaseOrder* XML datatype. It extends the *PurchaseOrder* datatype by allowing a *Comments* element to be included within a purchase order.

Creating an Open *PurchaseOrder* Schema

Sometimes it is necessary to allow data to be included within an instance of a particular XML datatype even if you did not anticipate this when you created the schema. For example, a company might submit a purchase order containing account information to be used to pay for shipping the requested items. Schemas that allow the inclusion of additional elements and attributes that are not formally defined within the schema itself are often referred to as *open schemas*.

You can create an open schema by decorating a public field or property with the *XmlAnyAttribute* and *XmlAnyElement* attributes. The *XmlAnyAttribute* attribute specifies that the parent element can contain any XML attribute in addition to the ones formally defined within the schema. The *XmlAnyElement* attribute specifies that the parent element can contain any XML element in addition to the ones formally defined within the schema.

The flexibility of open schemas can be very enticing. However, you should consider the consequences before you create an open schema because the code needed to handle and process the extended data can become very complex.

One popular method for allowing extended information to be included within an instance document in a semi-controlled fashion is to provide an area in the document definition for that information. The following example defines an element within the *PurchaseOrder* datatype that is designated for containing extended information about the purchase order:

```
[XmlRoot("PurchaseOrder", IsNullable=false)]
[XmlInclude(typeof(CommentedPurchaseOrder))]
public class PurchaseOrder
{
    [XmlElement(IsNullable=false)]
    public Address BillingAddress;

    [XmlElement(IsNullable=false)]
    public Address ShippingAddress;

    [XmlArray("Items", IsNullable=false)]
    [XmlArrayItem("Item", IsNullable=false)]
    public PurchaseOrderItem [] Items;

    [XmlElement("AdditionalInfo")]
    public AdditionalInfo Info;

    // Additional type definitions...
}


// Previously defined type definitions removed for clarity...

public class AdditionalInfo
{
    [XmlAnyAttribute]
    public XmlElement AdditionalAttributes;

    [XmlAnyElement]
    public XmlElement [] AdditionalElements;
}
```

The preceding code defines an additional element within the *PurchaseOrder* XML datatype called *AdditionalInfo*. This element can contain any attribute as well as any element. The above code generates the following schema containing the *AdditionalInfo* element definition:

```
<schema attributeFormDefault="qualified" elementFormDefault="qualified"
targetNamespace="http://tempuri.org/">
  <element name="PurchaseOrder" type="s0:PurchaseOrder" />
  <complexType name="PurchaseOrder">
    <sequence>
      <element minOccurs="1" maxOccurs="1" name="BillingAddress"
      type="s0:Address" />
      <element minOccurs="1" maxOccurs="1" name="ShippingAddress"
      type="s0:Address" />
```

```
        <element minOccurs="1" maxOccurs="1" name="Items"
        type="s0:ArrayOfPurchaseOrderItem" />
        <element minOccurs="1" maxOccurs="1" name="AdditionalInfo"
        type="s0:AdditionalInfo" />
      </sequence>
    </complexType>

    <!-- Additional definitions removed for clarity -->

    <complexType name="AdditionalInfo">
      <sequence>
        <any minOccurs="0" maxOccurs="unbounded" />
      <sequence>
      <anyAttribute />
    </complexType>
  </schema>
```

The public field or property decorated by the *XmlAnyAttribute* attribute can be of type *XmlElement* or *XmlNode*. Because the *XmlElement* and *XmlNode* types are part of the XML DOM that ships with .NET, you can use the methods and properties exposed by these types to navigate through the additional data that accompanied the purchase order.

Defining the *AcceptPO* Web Method

Now that I have defined the *PurchaseOrder* type, I need to define the Web method that will accept the purchase order. The body of the incoming SOAP message will contain an instance of the *PurchaseOrder* XML datatype. It needs to be decorated with the properly initialized *SoapDocumentMethod* attribute, as discussed in the previous chapter.

The root element of the body of the SOAP document must be named *PurchaseOrder*. By default, XML serialization will give the root element the same name as the input parameter of the Web method. Calling the parameter *PurchaseOrder* would create a name conflict with my class definition, so you must override how parameters are serialized using one of two approaches.

The first approach is to use the *XmlElement* attribute to decorate the parameters of a Web method to control how they will be serialized. The following code defines a Web method that accepts an instance of the *PurchaseOrder* XML datatype:

```
[WebMethod]
[SoapDocumentMethod(ParameterStyle=SoapParameterStyle.Bare)]
public void AcceptPO([XmlElement("PurchaseOrder", IsNullable=false)]
PurchaseOrder param1)
{
    // Implementation...
}
```

The *XmlAttribute* attribute can be applied to Web method parameters as well, but these parameters must be parameters of "wrapped" methods.

Because the *PurchaseOrder* class will be serialized as the root of the SOAP message body, I have a second option in addition to using the *XmlElement* attribute: I can decorate the class with the *XmlRoot* attribute. This attribute controls how a .NET type is serialized as the root of the document. Here is an example:

```
[XmlRoot("PurchaseOrder", IsNullable=false)]
[XmlInclude(typeof(CommentedPurchaseOrder))]
public class PurchaseOrder
{
    // Definitions...
}
```

Other attributes that you can apply to Web method parameters include *XmlAnyElement*, *XmlAnyAttribute*, and *XmlText*.

Server-Side Validation

Throughout this chapter, I create a definition for a strongly typed *PurchaseOrder* XML datatype. I also create a strongly typed interface for the *AcceptPO* Web method. You might be surprised by the fact that the ASP.NET runtime will not validate incoming requests against the schema I have so painstakingly created. For example, the following SOAP request message will be parsed by the ASP.NET runtime without throwing an exception.

```
<?xml version="1.0" encoding="utf-8"?>
<soap:Envelope xmlns:soap=http://schemas.xmlsoap.org/soap/envelope">
    <soap:Body>
    </soap:Body>
</soap:Envelope>
```

As you can see, the elements and attributes that are not allowed to be null are not contained within the preceding document. However, the document will be accepted and deserialized by the ASP.NET runtime. This is an obvious problem because you cannot count on the ASP.NET runtime to perform any validation on your behalf.

One way to overcome this problem is to validate each of the objects and their associated properties after the ASP.NET runtime deserializes the request message. This doesn't sound like much fun. Instead of writing my own validation code, I can leverage the XML DOM to do it for me.

I could write a SOAP Extension that would validate the XML request against the schema advertised in the Web service's WSDL document. Such an extension could intercept the stream before it is deserialized by the runtime. It could then initialize the DOM with the *schemas* section of the WSDL document and then attempt to load the document. If the DOM throws an exception, the exception could be packaged in an instance of a *SoapException* and then returned to the client.

Implementing Custom Serialization

XML serialization supports the ability to serialize instances of an ADO.NET *DataSet* as well as classes that derive from the *DataSet* class. It can do this because the *DataSet* class implements the *IXmlSerializable* interface.

A .NET type that needs more advanced control over the way it is serialized can implement the *IXmlSerializable* interface. As of this writing, the ADO.NET *DataSet* is the only .NET type that implements this interface. Unfortunately, this interface is intended to be used only internally within the .NET Framework. Hopefully, this interface will be available to developers in the future.

The signature of the *IXmlSerializable* interface is as follows:

```
public interface IXmlSerializable
{
    System.Xml.Schema.XmlSchema GetSchema();
    void ReadXml(System.Xml.XmlReader reader);
    void WriteXml(System.Xml.XmlWriter writer);
}
```

The *GetSchema* method is called when the ASP.NET runtime generates the WSDL document for the Web service. The *ReadXml* method is called when the SOAP message received from the client is being deserialized. The *WriteXml* method is called when the response SOAP message is being serialized.

When a strongly typed ADO.NET record set is exposed by the interface of a Web service, the schema for the strongly typed record set is resolvable using an external URL. For example, say I have a strongly typed record set called *MyRecordSet* that is exposed by a Web service addressable at *http://somedomain/MyWebService.asmx*. The schema for *MyRecordSet* would therefore be located at *http://somedomain/MyWebService.asmx?MyRecordSet*.

The URL that references the *MyRecordSet* schema is imported into the schema for the Web service itself. Calls to this URL will return the schema produced by calling the *WriteXmlSchema* method exposed by the *MyRecordSet* class.

Summary

XML serialization is responsible for serializing instances of .NET types to XML and deserializing XML to instances of .NET types. This includes support for instances of built-in .NET types, classes, and structures as well as composite types such as arrays, nested object hierarchies, and objects that support the *ICollection* and *IEnumerable* interfaces. It also supports serializing .NET type definitions into an XML schema.

XML serialization has default behaviors that might not be appropriate in all situations, so the .NET platform provides a collection of attributes that you can apply to .NET type definitions, variable declarations, and parameter declarations to control the behavior of .NET serialization.

If the collection of attributes is not sufficient, you can use the *IXmlSerializable* interface. This interface allows fine-grained control over how an instance of a .NET type is serialized to XML.

8

Using Remoting to Build and Consume Web Services

Practically every modern development platform provides a distributed object infrastructure that allows a client to communicate with a remote object. Prior to Microsoft .NET, this role was fulfilled by DCOM. The distributed object infrastructure for .NET is called Remoting. You can use it to build and consume Web services because one of the message formats it supports is SOAP.

In the previous chapter, I discussed how you can use ASP.NET to build and consume Web services. In some respects, ASP.NET provides a more complete platform for building Web services than Remoting does. For example, Remoting supports only RPC-style messages. Microsoft is also hyping ASP.NET as the preferred platform for building Web services. So when should you consider using Remoting instead of ASP.NET?

Remoting vs. ASP.NET

You should consider using Remoting over ASP.NET in at least three scenarios:

- **When you need to use a transport protocol other than HTTP** ASP.NET is tightly coupled to the HTTP transport protocol, but Remoting is transport protocol agnostic.

- **When you need to host a Web server in a process other than IIS** ASP.NET is tightly coupled to IIS, but Remoting can host a Web service in any .NET process.

- **When you need strong support for .NET types** The primary responsibility of the Remoting framework is to serve as the distributed object infrastructure for .NET, so Remoting provides the necessary extensions to facilitate this.

Let's discuss each of these scenarios in more detail.

HTTP is the most widely supported transport protocol used by Web services, but it might not be ideal in some situations. For example, a queuing application might find asynchronous protocols such as SMTP more appropriate. A Web service hosted by a satellite might not support the HTTP protocol at all.

Remoting allows a client to communicate with a remote object over a wide variety of transport protocols, including HTTP and raw TCP/IP. If a particular transport protocol is not supported out of the box, you can extend the Remoting framework to use the desired transport protocol.

Remoting also supports an extensible means of specifying the format of the message that is shipped between the client and the server. Remoting supports two message formats, binary and SOAP. Binary is more efficient and less verbose than SOAP. However, because it is not based on industry standards, it does not offer the same degree of interoperability that is provided by its SOAP counterpart. Therefore in this chapter, I limit my discussion to the SOAP message format.

I anticipate that Remoting will support the SOAP 1.2 specification as a new message format type. If this proves to be the case, the Remoting framework's support of pluggable message formats should dramatically simplify the task of maintaining SOAP 1.1 versions of Remoting Web services for backward compatibility.

You can alter which message format and transport an application uses by changing a configuration setting. This is ideal for distributed .NET applications that reside in a mixed environment. A .NET client residing on the same corporate network as a .NET server can use the more performant binary message format rather than TCP/IP. But the same .NET application can use the SOAP message format over HTTP if it needs to communicate through a firewall or an HTTP proxy server.

In Chapter 3, I described some of the limitations of the current SOAP specification relating to features typically supported by a distributed object infrastructure. For example, SOAP does not define a means of passing an object by reference between the client and the remote object. To fulfill its role, Remoting provides its own implementation to overcome these limitations.

Remoting provides a set of features for Web services in addition to the ones defined by industry-standard specifications. The value-added services Remoting provides include

- **Activation** Remoting provides the ability to remotely activate an object, including full support for parameterized constructors.

- **Lifetime support**   When a remote object is activated on behalf of a client, this mechanism ensures that the remote object is freed when it is no longer needed by the client.

- **Passing objects by reference**   Remoting provides the ability for a client to pass objects by reference. The SOAP specification defines only a means of passing objects by value between the client and a Web service.

- **Full fidelity for .NET types**   A Web service built on top of the Remoting framework exposes additional metadata about its types. This information is necessary to maintain full fidelity of the .NET types exposed by the Web service.

To support these features, the Remoting team had to define a proprietary set of extensions. If interoperability is a priority, be sure to not leverage these features within your Web service.

The Grabber.NET Application

Napster has heightened public awareness of peer-to-peer applications. A peer-to-peer application acts as both a client and a server. In the case of SOAP-based Web services, the application is capable of sending a SOAP request to a peer as well as accepting SOAP requests from a peer.

In this chapter, I build a .NET version of Napster called Grabber.NET. It is a WinForm application with a UI similar to Windows Explorer. The Grabber.NET client looks like this:

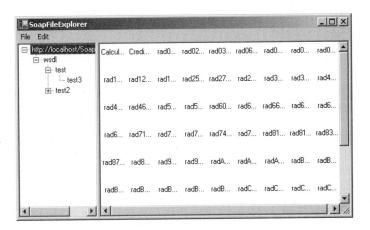

The user can connect to other Grabber.NET applications and browse the directory structure to locate files of interest. The user can also select specific files and copy them to a local directory.

Grabber.NET will communicate with other peers via SOAP over HTTP. Because the WinForm application will act as both a client and a server, Grabber.NET cannot be implemented using ASP.NET. In contrast, Remoting allows you to create a Web service that is hosted in any process, including a WinForm application.

Much of the implementation of Grabber.NET is UI related, so in this chapter I list only the code relevant to Remoting. The full source code for Grabber.NET is on the companion CD.

Remoting Architecture

Before I delve into the specifics of implementing and consuming Web services using Remoting, let's discuss the architecture for enabling a client to communicate with a remote object.

When a client creates an instance of a remote object, it receives a proxy instead of the object itself. The proxy exposes the same interfaces as the actual object. When a client invokes a method or accesses a field or property on the proxy, the proxy is responsible for forwarding the request to the remote object. The diagram on the next page shows the major components involved in facilitating communication between the client and the server.

The Remoting infrastructure is composed of four major components:

- **Remoting runtime** The Remoting runtime is responsible for dynamically creating proxies on behalf of the client. It is also responsible for invoking the appropriate channel on the server to listen for incoming requests.

- **Proxy** The proxy object is responsible for receiving the method calls from the user. Once a method call has been received, the proxy is responsible for eliciting the help of the appropriate formatter and transport to send the parameters to the remote object.

- **Formatter** The formatter is responsible for serializing the parameters into a format that can be shipped across the wire. Remoting ships with two formatters, binary and SOAP. In this chapter, I discuss the SOAP formatter.

- **Channel** The channel is responsible for sending formatted messages between the client and the server. The client-side channel is responsible for sending the message over the designated transport protocol. The server-side channel is responsible for monitoring incoming messages and passing those messages to the appropriate formatter. Remoting ships with two channels, TCP and HTTP.

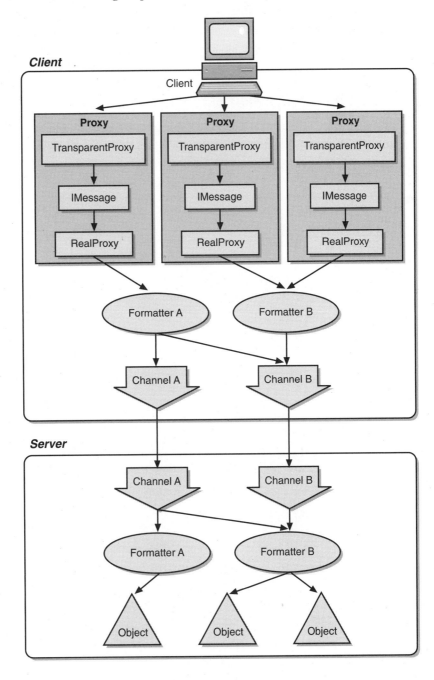

One important feature of the Remoting framework that I discussed earlier is support for pluggable formatters and channels. The preceding diagram highlights the ability to combine any formatter with any channel. As you will see in later sections, you can change which formatters and channels a Remoting application uses by modifying a configuration file. For example, by modifying the configuration file you can allow your SOAP-based Web service to switch from accepting requests over HTTP to accepting requests over raw TCP/IP.

Creating an IIS-Hosted Web Service

The illegal sharing of licensed content by peer-to-peer programs is a serious issue, so I will implement a Licensing Web service that Grabber.NET will use to verify that the client has a valid license to copy the requested content. All Grabber.NET peer applications will be responsible for validating the client's request for licensed content against the centrally hosted Licensing Web service, as shown here:

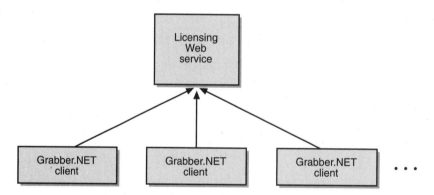

Creating the implementation of a Web service hosted by the Remoting runtime is trivial. The only requirement is that the object must derive from the *MarshalByRefObject* class. Deriving from *MarshalByRefObject* instructs the Remoting runtime to ensure that the object is confined to the application domain in which it was created.

When the client requests a new object derived from the *MarshalByRefObject* class, the remote object created on behalf of the client will not be passed by value to the client. Instead, the client will receive a proxy that will serve as a reference to the remote object.

The Licensing Web service will expose a *Validate* method that verifies whether the user is licensed to use the content. Here is the implementation:

```
using System;

namespace SomeRecordCompany
{
    class Licensing : MarshalByRefObject
    {
        public bool Validate(string resource, LicenseInfo licenseInfo)
        {
            bool isValid = true;

            // Implementation...

            return isValid;
        }
    }
}
```

The implementation of the Licensing Web service is contained within the *Licensing* class. The class contains the *Validate* method, which accepts two parameters: a string that identifies the resource and an object of type *LicenseInfo* that contains the client's license information. This class derives from *MarshalByRefObject*, so when the Web service is hosted by the Remoting runtime, the *Validate* method will be invoked on the record company's server.

Unlike the *Licensing* class, instances of the *LicenseInfo* object should be passed by value. This ensures that the Licensing Web service will maintain a high degree of compatibility with other SOAP implementations because SOAP 1.1 does not support passing objects by reference.

Even if the Licensing Web service were to be consumed only by Remoting clients, you would still want to pass the object by value. If the object were passed by reference, needless round-trips would occur between the client and the server as the properties exposed by the class are accessed.

For an object to be passed by value, it must be marked as serializable. You can mark an object as serializable by decorating the class with the *Serializable* attribute or having the class support the *ISerializable* interface.

Instances of a class that is decorated with the *Serializable* attribute are automatically serialized by the Remoting runtime. Unlike ASP.NET, Remoting is capable of serializing all properties and fields regardless of their visibility. Recall that ASP.NET can serialize only data exposed by public read/writable properties and fields.

Sometimes an object will want a degree of control over how it is serialized. For example, an object might contain state that is specific to the machine on which it is located, such as a handle to a system resource. In this case, the class can implement the *ISerializable* interface.

Instances of the *LicenseInfo* class can be serialized by the runtime, so I will decorate it with the *Serializable* attribute. Here is the rest of the Licensing Web service implementation, which defines the *LicenseInfo* class:

```
[Serializable]
public class LicenseInfo
{
    string license = "";
    DateTime expirationDate = new DateTime();

    public LicenseInfo(string license, DateTime expirationDate)
    {
        this.license = license;
        this.expirationDate = expirationDate;
    }

    public string License
    {
        get{ return this.license; }
    }

    public DateTime ExpirationDate
    {
        get{ return this.expirationDate; }
    }
}
```

Now that I have implemented the Licensing Web service, I need to configure it so that it is hosted by the Remoting runtime. The runtime provides two different activation models, well-known object and client-activated object.

Well-Known Object Activation Model

A well-known object accepts method requests without requiring the client to first formally instantiate the object. From the client's perspective, the object already exists and calls can be made to it without the need to create or initialize the object. This is the default behavior of SOAP-based Web services.

Remoting supports two configurations for well-known objects, single call and singleton. These configurations control when the well-known object that handles the client's requests is actually instantiated on the server.

The single call configuration is the most synonymous with ASP.NET. Each time a request is received, the Remoting service creates a new instance of the target object to process the request.

With the singleton configuration, the target object is instantiated when the first request is received. The object is kept alive by the Remoting runtime and is responsible for processing all subsequent requests by all clients. All requests received by the service from any client are handled by the same object.

You should consider the singleton configuration when the same expensive resources are leveraged across multiple method requests. An expensive resource can be initialized within the singleton object's constructor. It can then be used to process multiple method requests over the duration of the object's lifetime. Because the resource might be used to process multiple requests simultaneously, either the resource must be thread safe or you should use the appropriate synchronization primitives.

In general, remote objects that support the single call configuration are the easiest to develop. Because each request is processed by a separate instance of the remote object, the developer need not be concerned with coherency issues such as race conditions and deadlocks.

With either configuration, a client is never allocated its own object that spans across more than one method call. In the case of the single call configuration, the state is never maintained across method calls because each request is addressed by a new instance of the object. In the case of the singleton configuration, the state of the object is shared across all clients. Therefore, if a well-known object must manage state specific to a particular client, it must use an out-of-band mechanism.

Client-Activated Object Activation Model

In the client-activated scenario, a remote object is created on behalf of the client and is available to that client until it is garbage collected. Because SOAP does not define a protocol that supports activation, Remoting defines an extension mechanism for facilitating this behavior.

The Licensing Web service does not have to initialize expensive resources and does not require lifetime management services, so I will configure it as a well-known object that supports the single call mode.

You can configure the remote component by creating an XML file. The following XML file configures the Licensing Web service:

```
<?xml version="1.0" encoding="utf-8" ?>
<configuration>
  <system.runtime.remoting>
    <application>
      <service>
        <wellknown mode="SingleCall"
        type="SomeRecordCompany.Licensing, Licensing"
        objectUri="Licensing.soap"/>
      </service>
    </application>
  </system.runtime.remoting>
</configuration>
```

The *service* element contains the configuration for objects exposed to other applications. It can contain either a *wellknown* or *activated* element. (I cover configuring client-activated objects later in the chapter.)

You use the *wellknown* element to configure well-known objects. The element must contain three attributes: *mode, type,* and *objectUri.* The *mode* attribute indicates whether the well-known object should be hosted as a single call (*SingleCall*) or a singleton (*Singleton*). The *type* attribute contains the full type name and the assembly of the object that should be exposed by the Remoting runtime. The *objectUri* attribute specifies the URI where the object can be accessed. In the case of the Licensing Web service, the URI specified is Licensing.soap. Licensing.soap does not physically exist; requests sent to the URI are intercepted and processed by the Remoting runtime.

The Licensing Web service can be hosted within any process. Because many clients might access the Licensing Web service simultaneously, a good option is to host the Web service within Microsoft Internet Information Services (IIS). This allows the Web service to be hosted in a Web farm that takes advantage of applications that improve the manageability of the Web farm (such as Microsoft Application Center).

The Licensing Web service can be deployed within any IIS Web application. You can create a new Web application by opening the IIS MMC, right-clicking on the Web site, selecting New, and then choosing Virtual Directory. Once the Web application has been created, the contents of the configuration file I just created can be copied into the Web application's web.config file.

The Remoting runtime will expect the assemblies to be located within the Web application's *bin* directory. Therefore, you must create a *bin* subdirectory and copy the Licensing.dll assembly into the new directory.

You can access the Licensing Web service by addressing the Licensing.soap file within the Web application directory. For example, if the Licensing Web service is located in the SomeRecordCompany Web application on my local server, I can address it using the following URL:

```
http://localhost/SomeRecordCompany/Licensing.soap
```

If the Web service is hosted in IIS, the WSDL document will be automatically generated if *wsdl* is appended as a query string on the URL. The WSDL document for the Licensing Web service is available at the following URL:

```
http://localhost/SomeRecordCompany/Licensing.soap?wsdl
```

Creating a WinForm-Hosted Web Service

The primary purpose of Grabber.NET is to facilitate the exchange of files, so it needs a way to obtain a file from a remote computer. In this section, I create the

SoapFileShare Web service, which supports two endpoints, one for retrieving files and the other for navigating directories.

The *File* endpoint allows a client to obtain the contents of the requested file from a remote computer. Here is the implementation:

```
using System;
using IO = System.IO;

namespace SoapFileShare
{
    public class File : MarshalByRefObject
    {
        string rootDirectory = @"c:\temp\";

        public byte[] GetFile(string fileName, string license)
        {
            // Validate the license...

            // Obtain the contents of the requested file.
            IO.Stream    s = IO.File.Open(rootDirectory + fileName,
                                          IO.FileMode.Open);
            byte[]       fileContents = new byte[s.Length];
            s.Read(fileContents, 0, (int)s.Length);

            return fileContents;
        }
    }
}
```

The *File* endpoint exposes the *GetFile* method. The name of the targeted file and the necessary licensing information are passed to the *GetFile* method, which uses the information to determine whether the client is licensed to receive the file. If the client is licensed to receive the file, the *GetFile* method obtains a byte array for the requested file and returns it to the client. Later in the chapter, I discuss how to access the Licensing Web service, which validates the request.

Grabber.NET also needs to browse the remote computer to see what files are available, so I need to create the *Directory* endpoint. The *Directory* endpoint exposes methods that allow the client to navigate the directory hierarchy on the remote computer and obtain a list of files within a particular directory:

```
public class Directory : MarshalByRefObject
{
    string rootDirectory = @"c:\temp";

    // Get the list of files at the root directory.
    public string[] GetFiles(string path)
    {
```

(continued)

```
    // Obtain the list of files in the directory.
    string    [] fileNames =
            IO.Directory.GetFiles(rootDirectory + path);

    // Truncate the path information so that it is relative
    // to the root directory.
    for(int i = 0; i < fileNames.Length; i++)
    {
        char [] newFileName =
        new char[fileNames[i].Length - rootDirectory.Length];
        fileNames[i].CopyTo(rootDirectory.Length, newFileName, 0,
        fileNames[i].Length - rootDirectory.Length);
        fileNames[i] = new string(newFileName);
    }

    return fileNames;
}

// Get the list of files at the root directory.
public string[] GetDirectories(string path)
{
    string [] directories =
            IO.Directory.GetDirectories(rootDirectory + path);

    // Truncate the path information so that it is relative
    // to the root directory.
    for(int i = 0; i < directories.Length; i++)
    {
        char [] newDirectory =
        new char[directories[i].Length - rootDirectory.Length];
        directories[i].CopyTo(rootDirectory.Length, newDirectory, 0,
        directories[i].Length - rootDirectory.Length);
        directories[i] = new string(newDirectory);
    }

    return directories;
}
    }
}
```

The *Directory* endpoint exposes two methods, *GetFiles* and *GetDirectories*. *GetFiles* returns a list of files within a specified directory, and *GetDirectories* returns a list of subdirectories within a specified directory. You can use these two methods to navigate a directory hierarchy.

The primary purpose of Grabber.NET is to allow the exchange of files between peers. A peer-to-peer application has to act as both a client and a server. Therefore, the WebForms application itself must act as a Remoting server.

One major advantage of the Remoting framework over technologies such as ASP.NET is its ability to host a Web service in any process over any transport protocol. In this case, I want the Grabber.NET WinForm application to listen for SOAP requests over HTTP.

Any .NET application can listen for incoming requests by calling the *Configure* static method on the *RemotingConfiguration* object to initialize the appropriate listener. The method accepts the path to a configuration file as its only parameter. The configuration file is similar to the one I created for the Licensing Web service. However, unlike a Remoting Web service hosted in IIS, a Remoting Web service hosted within a process is not limited to HTTP. Therefore, the channel needs to be configured.

The following configuration file configures Remoting to listen on port 88 for HTTP requests for the *File* or *Directory* endpoint:

```xml
<?xml version="1.0" encoding="utf-8" ?>
<configuration>
  <system.runtime.remoting>
    <application name="SoapFileShare">
      <service>
        <wellknown mode="SingleCall" type="SoapFileShare.Directory,
        SoapFileShare" objectUri="Directory.soap"/>
        <wellknown mode="SingleCall" type="SoapFileShare.File, SoapFileShare"
        objectUri="File.soap"/>
      </service>
      <channels>
        <channel port="88" type="System.Runtime.Remoting.Channels.Http.
        HttpChannel, System.Runtime.Remoting" />
      </channels>
    </application>
  </system.runtime.remoting>
</configuration>
```

As with the Licensing Web service hosted in IIS, you must configure the Remoting runtime to host the Web service. Recall that a Remoting Web service can be hosted via any number of transport protocols. Because the Licensing Web service is hosted in IIS, the HTTP transport was assumed. Also, because the Licensing Web service is hosted in a particular Web application, I needed to specify only the filename of the endpoint. But the SoapFileShare Web service is not hosted within IIS, so I need to specify the channel as well as the full endpoint to the path.

As in Web services hosted in IIS, the *objectUri* property of the *wellknown* element specifies the filename that will serve as the address of the endpoint. But unlike in Web services hosted in IIS, you must specify the path to the file using the *name* attribute of the *application* element.

In the case of Grabber.NET, the directory is SoapFileShare, so the *Directory* endpoint is addressable at *http://localhost/SoapFileShare/Directory.soap*. You can also specify a subdirectory. For example, if the *name* attribute is set to *Grabber.NET/SoapFileShare*, the *Directory* endpoint is addressable at *http://localhost/Grabber.NET/SoapFileShare/Directory.soap*.

The transport protocols supported by Remoting are defined within the *channels* element. Each supported transport protocol is referenced within an individual *channel* element. The *channel* element contains two attributes, *port* and *type*. The *port* attribute specifies the port the transport protocol will use to communicate with the remote application, and the *type* attribute specifies the .NET type that implements the channel and the type's assembly.

By convention, the configuration file for the application has the same name as the assembly, with *.config* appended to it. In the case of Grabber.NET, the WinForm application is named SoapFileExplorer.exe, so I will name the configuration file SoapFileExplorer.exe.config.

Once the configuration file has been created, it must be explicitly loaded by the application. You do this by passing the path of the configuration file to the *Configure* static method exposed by the *RemotingConfiguration* object. In the case of Grabber.NET, the *Configure* method is called within the constructor for the main WinForm, as shown here:

```
public ExplorerForm()
{
    //
    // Required for Windows Form Designer support
    //
    InitializeComponent();

    // Load the Remoting configuration files.
    RemotingConfiguration.Configure("SoapFileExplorer.exe.config");
}
```

You can also configure a well-known object within the application code itself so that you can dynamically configure a well-known object at run time. The following code configures the *File* and *Directory* well-known objects:

```
RemotingConfiguration.ApplicationName = "SoapFileShare";
RemotingConfiguration.RegisterWellKnownServiceType(typeof(SoapFileShare.File),
"File.soap", WellKnownObjectMode.SingleCall);
RemotingConfiguration.RegisterWellKnownServiceType(typeof(SoapFileShare.
Directory), "Directory.soap", WellKnownObjectMode.SingleCall);
```

Regardless of how the well-known objects are configured, Remoting will spin up another thread to listen for and process incoming requests.

Accessing Web Services

Now that I have created the Licensing and SoapFileShare Web services for Grabber.NET, it is time to write the client portion of Grabber.NET to access these Web services. In this section, I discuss three ways to create a Remoting proxy that will be used to access a Web service.

Recall that the *GetFile* method of the *File* object is responsible for sending the requested file to the client. Before the file is sent, the licensing information received from the client must be verified against the Licensing Web service. For this example, I will use the *new* operator to create the proxy object.

new Keyword–Generated Proxy

You can configure the Remoting runtime to intercept calls to the *new* operator and return a dynamically generated proxy instead of the object itself. You do this by registering the well-known object within the Remoting configuration file. The following is the modified version of the SoapFileExplorer.exe.config file:

```
<?xml version="1.0" encoding="utf-8" ?>
<configuration>
  <system.runtime.remoting>
    <application name="SoapFileShare">
      <service>
        <wellknown mode="SingleCall" type="SoapFileShare.Directory,
        SoapFileShare" objectUri="Directory.soap" />
        <wellknown mode="SingleCall" type="SoapFileShare.File, SoapFileShare"
        objectUri="File.soap" />
      </service>
      <client>
        <wellknown type="SomeRecordCompany.Licensing, Licensing"
        url="http://localhost/SomeRecordCompay/Licensing.soap" />
      </client>
      <channels>
        <channel port="88" type="System.Runtime.Remoting.Channels.Http.
        HttpChannel, System.Runtime.Remoting" />
      </channels>
    </application>
  </system.runtime.remoting>
</configuration>
```

I added a *client* element that contains a list of Web service endpoints used by the client. Individual endpoints are referenced by adding a *wellknown* child element. Note that the *wellknown* element under the *client* element is different from the *wellknown* element under the *server* element.

The client *wellknown* element must contain two attributes, *type* and *url*. The *url* attribute contains the address of the targeted endpoint. The *type* attribute references the .NET type within a particular assembly that describes the remote object. The assembly can be the Licensing.dll that I previously deployed on IIS.

You can also register the well-known object reference using the *Register-WellKnownClientType* static method exposed by the *RemotingConfiguration* class. The following example registers the *Licensing* well-known object:

```
RemotingConfiguration.RegisterWellKnownClientType(typeof(SomeRecordCompany.
Licensing), "http://localhost/SomeRecordCompany/Licensing.soap");
```

Because the generated proxy is strongly typed, the same Licensing assembly that was referenced within the Remoting configuration file also needs to be referenced by the client application itself. In this case, the SoapFileShare Web service application must reference the Licensing.dll assembly.

In many cases, it is not practical to have clients reference the assembly that contains the implementation of the Web service. Later in this chapter, I discuss how to build a .NET assembly containing the necessary metadata from the Web service's WSDL file.

Once the configuration file has been modified and the License.dll assembly is referenced by the SoapFileShare project, the Remoting runtime will automatically create a proxy object on behalf of the client when the *new* operator is called. The *Validate* method can then be called on the resulting proxy object and the proxy will forward the call to the Licensing Web service. Here is the implementation:

```
// Validate the license info if it was sent by the client.
if(licenseInfo != null)
{
    SomeRecordCompany.Licensing licensing = new SomeRecordCompany.Licensing();
    licensing.Validate(fileName, licenseInfo);
}
```

Other than the fact that I load the Remoting configuration file when the WinForms application is initialized, the code for accessing the Licensing Web service is no different than if I were directly accessing the assembly.

GetObject-Generated Proxy

Next I need to create the client code to access the SoapFileShare Web service. Because the SoapFileShare Web service can be hosted by any number of Grabber.NET peers, using the *new* keyword to create the proxy raises a significant issue: once a well-known object has been configured by the Remoting runtime, the resulting proxy will always be associated with the same endpoint.

Another way to create a proxy for a well-known object is by calling the *GetObject* static method on the *Activator* class. When the *new* keyword is used to create a proxy object, the Remoting runtime actually calls the *GetObject* method to obtain the proxy. Because the *Activator* object is public, you can call it directly.

The *GetObject* method is overloaded and supports two method signatures. Both versions of the *GetObject* method accept two parameters, the type of object that should be created and the URL where the well-known object is located. The second *GetObject* method signature also accepts an object containing channel-specific data.

Recall that SoapFileExplorer has a look and feel similar to that of Windows Explorer. The right pane contains a TreeView control for navigating the directory structure, and the left pane has a ListView control. When a particular node in the TreeView control is selected, the ListView control is refreshed with all of the files contained within the particular directory. The following code updates the ListView control based on the list of files obtained from the SoapFileShare Web service:

```
private void directoryTree_AfterSelect(object sender,
System.Windows.Forms.TreeViewEventArgs e)
{
    // Create an instance of the SoapFileShare.Directory object.
    string url = ((DirectoryTreeNode)e.Node).Url + "Directory.soap";
    SoapFileShare.Directory directory = (SoapFileShare.Directory)Activator.
    GetObject(typeof(SoapFileShare.Directory), url);

    // Obtain the files within the selected directory.
    string [] filePaths = directory.GetFiles(((DirectoryTreeNode)e.Node).Path);

    // Display the files within the list view.
    this.fileList.Clear();
    foreach(string filePath in filePaths)
    {
        this.fileList.Items.Add(new FileListViewItem(url, filePath));
    }
}
```

First the URL of the targeted *Directory* endpoint of the SoapFileShare Web service is dynamically built. This URL is then passed to the *GetObject* method to obtain a proxy object for the *Directory* endpoint. A list of files is then obtained for the selected directory by calling the *GetFiles* method on the proxy.

By default, *GetObject* will create a proxy object that communicates with the well-known object via SOAP over HTTP. Therefore, you need not configure the Remoting runtime to execute the preceding code.

WSDL-Generated Proxy

To dynamically create a proxy, the Remoting runtime needs access to an assembly that contains type information that describes the targeted Web service. As I mentioned earlier, this can be the assembly that contains the implementation of the Web service.

Because Grabber.NET both hosts and consumes the SoapFileShare Web service, it is practical to have the Remoting runtime dynamically generate a proxy for the SoapFileShare Web service. However, it is not practical to have Grabber.NET reference the assembly that contains the implementation of the Licensing Web service. You need some way of creating an assembly that contains the type information used to describe the Web service without containing the implementation.

You can use one of the tools provided by the Remoting framework, SoapSuds, to convert the type information contained in a WSDL document into .NET type information. This type information can then be used by the Remoting runtime to create a proxy dynamically.

The following command creates an assembly containing metadata that describes the Licensing Web service:

```
soapsuds -url:http://localhost/SomeRecordLabel/Licensing.soap?wsdl
-oa:Licensing.dll -gc -nowp
```

This command creates an assembly called Licensing.dll as well as the source code for the assembly. Either the assembly can be referenced or the source code can be included by a client application such as Grabber.NET that creates proxies using the *new* keyword or the *GetObject* method.

Table 8-1 describes the command-line parameters supported by SoapSuds.

Table 8-1   Command-Line Parameters Supported by SoapSuds

Switch	Description
-domain:domainName or *-d:domainName*	The domain against which the passed credentials should be authenticated.
-generatecode or *–gc*	Tells SoapSuds to generate source code for the proxy.
-httpproxyname:proxy or *-hpn:proxy*	The name of the proxy server that should be used to connect to the Web server to obtain the WSDL.
-httpproxyport:port or *-hpp:port*	The port number for the proxy server that should be used to connect to the Web server to obtain the WSDL.
-inputassemblyfile:fileName or *-ia:fileName*	The name of the assembly file from which to obtain type information. Do not include the extension when specifying the filename.

Table 8-1   **Command-Line Parameters Supported by SoapSuds**   *(continued)*

Switch	Description
-inputdirectory:directory or *-id:directory*	The directory of the input assembly files.
-inputschemafile:fileName or *-is:fileName*	The name of the WSDL file from which to obtain type information.
-nowrappedproxy or *-nowp*	Specifies that the transparent proxy should not be wrapped within a derived version of the *RemotingClientProxy* class.
-outputassemblyfile:fileName or *-oa:fileName*	The name of the assembly file that will contain the generated proxy. Whenever an assembly is created, the associated source code will also be created.
-outputdirectory:directory or *-od:directory*	The directory where all output files will be saved.
-outputschemafile:fileName or *-os:fileName*	The filename of the generated WSDL or SDL document.
-password:password or *-p:password*	The password that should be used to authenticate against the server from which the WSDL or SDL document is obtained.
-proxynamespace:namespace or *-pn:namespace*	The namespace in which the resulting proxy class will reside.
-sdl	Specifies that SoapSuds should generate an SDL file that describes the types contained within a particular assembly.
-serviceendpoint:URL or *-se:URL*	The URL that should be placed within a generated WSDL or SDL file to describe the endpoint.
-strongnamefile:fileName or *-sn:fileName*	The file that contains the key pair that should be used to sign the generated assembly.
-types:type1,assembly[,endpointUrl] [type1,assembly[,endpointUrl]] [...]	The specific types that will serve as input.
-urltoschema:URL or *-url:URL*	The URL from which the WSDL or SDL file can be obtained.
-username:username or *-u:username*	The username that should be used to authenticate against the server from which the WSDL document is obtained.
-wrappedproxy or *-wp*	Specifies that the transparent proxy should be wrapped within a derived version of the *RemotingClientProxy* class.
-wsdl	Specifies that SoapSuds should generate a WSDL file that describes the types contained within a particular assembly.

One of the more interesting command-line parameters is the *-wp* switch. This parameter allows you to create a wrapped proxy. A wrapped proxy is a class that derives from the *RemotingClientProxy* class. Its primary purpose is to expose properties that allow you to more easily configure the HTTP channel. Table 8-2 describes the parameters exposed by the *RemotingClientProxy* class.

Table 8-2   Parameters of the *RemotingClientProxy* Class

Property	Description
AllowAutoRedirect	Determines whether the proxy will honor a redirect request sent by the server.
Cookies	Used to access the cookies that have been sent from the server.
Domain	The domain against which the passed credentials should be authenticated.
EnableCookies	Specifies whether cookies will be accepted by the proxy.
Password	The password that should be used to authenticate against the Web service.
Path	The URL of the Web service's endpoint.
PreAuthenticate	Determines whether the authentication credentials should be sent immediately or as a result of receiving a 401 (access denied) error.
ProxyName	The name of the proxy server that should be used to access the Web service.
ProxyPort	The port number of the proxy server that should be used to access the Web service.
Timeout	Determines the period of time, in milliseconds, that a synchronous Web request has to complete before the request is aborted. The default is infinite (-1).
Url	The URL of the Web service's endpoint.
UserAgent	The value of the user agent HTTP header sent to the Web service.
Username	The username that should be used to authenticate against the Web service.

By default, the HTTP channel uses the Internet settings configured on the client's machine using Control Panel, so in most cases it is not necessary to configure the proxy settings using the wrapped proxy. If the client's operating system is configured to route requests through an HTTP proxy server, these settings will be applied to the proxy as well.

Because SoapSuds will generate the source code for the wrapped proxy, you can extend its implementation. For example, you can add client-side logic to validate the parameters before a call is made to the remote server.

Adding SOAP Headers

The final piece of implementation I need to do is to integrate Grabber.NET with the Licensing Web service. Each time a client requests a file from another peer, the peer responding to the request must ensure that the client is licensed to receive the content.

The distribution of some files is limited by licensing agreements, and some of those files are in the public domain. Because license information is not part of the core functionality of the *GetFile* method of the File Web service, I will pass it within the SOAP header.

You can add headers to the message by using the *SetHeaders* static function exposed by the *CallContext* class. The *SetHeaders* method accepts an array of objects of type *Header*. Each instance of the *Header* class encapsulates data about a particular SOAP header. Table 8-3 describes the properties defined by the *Header* class.

Table 8-3   Properties of the *Header* Class

Property	Description
HeaderNamespace	The XML namespace of the header in which the element is defined. The default is *http://schemas.microsoft.com/clr/soap*.
MustUnderstand	Determines whether the header must be understood by the Web service. The default is *true*.
Name	The name of the header. Sets the name of the root element for the header within a SOAP message.
Value	The object that will be serialized within the header.

I will add the *License* header to calls made to the *GetFile* method of the *File* Web service. This header will contain the serialized contents of an object that holds the client's license information. First I need to declare a class that will be used to contain the license information. Here is the implementation:

```
[Serializable]
public class LicenseInfo
{
    string license = "";
    DateTime expirationDate = new DateTime();
```

(continued)

```
public LicenseInfo(string license, DateTime expirationDate)
{
    this.license = license;
    this.expirationDate = expirationDate;
}

public string License
{
    get{ return this.license; }
}

public DateTime ExpirationDate
{
    get{ return this.expirationDate; }
}
}
```

Because the contents of an instance of the *LicenseInfo* object will be serialized into the *License* header, I had to indicate that the object can be serialized. I did this by decorating the *LicenseInfo* class with the *Serializable* attribute.

Next I will add a call to the *SetHeaders* method of the *CallContext* object to add the header to the *GetFile* SOAP request. Grabber.NET calls the *GetFile* method as a result of handling the *click* event on the Copy menu item. Here is the implementation:

```
private void copyMenu_Click(object sender, System.EventArgs e)
{
    // Obtain the destination directory from the user.
    DirectoryForm directoryForm = new DirectoryForm();
    if(directoryForm.ShowDialog() == DialogResult.OK)
    {
        // Create an instance of the SoapFileShare.File object.
        string url = ((DirectoryTreeNode)directoryTree.SelectedNode).Url +
        "File.soap";
        SoapFileShare.File file = (SoapFileShare.File)Activator.GetObject
        (typeof(SoapFileShare.File), url);

        // Create the Licensing SOAP header.
        Header licenseHeader = new Header("Licensing", this.licenseInfo,
        false);

        string destinationDirectory = directoryForm.Path;

        // Copy the selected files into the destination directory.
        foreach(FileListViewItem fileNode in fileList.SelectedItems)
        {
            // Set the Licensing SOAP header.
            CallContext.SetHeaders(new Header [] {licenseHeader});
```

```
        // Obtain file contents.
        byte [] fileContents = file.GetFile(fileNode.Path);

        // Parse the filename from the file path.
        int index;
        for(index = fileNode.Path.Length - 1;
        index > 0 && fileNode.Path[index] != '\\'; index--);
        char [] text = new char[fileNode.Path.Length - index - 1];
        fileNode.Path.CopyTo(index + 1, text, 0,
        fileNode.Path.Length - index - 1);
        string fileName = new string(text);

        // Write file to the destination directory.
        Stream s;
        s = File.OpenWrite(destinationDirectory + fileName);
        s.Write(fileContents, 0, fileContents.Length);
        s.Close();
    }
  }
}
```

The preceding code displays the DirectoryForm dialog box to obtain from the user the directory to which the files should be copied. Then, for each file selected by the user, the file is copied into the destination directory. To place the *License* header in each *GetFile* SOAP request, I called the *SetHeaders* method each time just before I called the *GetFile* method.

The *GetFile* method can retrieve the SOAP header using the *CallContext* object's *GetHeaders* static method. Here is the implementation:

```
public byte[] GetFile(string fileName)
{
    LicenseInfo licenseInfo = null;

    // Make sure the client sent valid license information.
    Header [] headers = CallContext.GetHeaders();
    for(int i = 0; i < headers.Length || licenseInfo == null; i++)
    {
        licenseInfo = headers[i].Value as LicenseInfo;
    }

    if(licenseInfo != null)
    {
        // Validate the licensing information against
        // the Licensing Web service...
    }

    // The rest of the implementation...

}
```

First the *GetHeaders* method is called to obtain an array of *Header* objects. Then the array is iterated through until the *Licensing* header is found or the end of the array is reached. Finally, if the *Licensing* header is found, the information is passed to the Licensing Web service.

You should be aware of a couple of issues regarding the support for SOAP headers in Remoting. First, as you must with ASP.NET, you have to be careful about receiving a header containing the *mustUnderstand* attribute set to *true*. If a header that must be understood by the Web service was not processed after the method returns, the Remoting runtime will automatically generate an exception. So if the implementation of a method exposed by the Web service requires compensating logic in the event of an exception being thrown, you need to take appropriate action. Your choices would be to either verify that there are no unsupported required headers before you run your code or intercept the exception that results from an unhandled required header and then execute the necessary compensation logic.

The other issue is that supported headers will not be exposed within the WSDL that is dynamically generated by the Remoting runtime. If it is necessary to advertise the headers supported by the Web service, you will need to manually modify the WSDL. Two possible options would be either to create a static WSDL document or to intercept the dynamically generated WSDL and inject the header definitions.

Generating WSDL

One of the advantages of implementing Grabber.NET with SOAP over HTTP is that you are not limited only to sharing files with other Grabber.NET peers. You can create an application, potentially on other platforms, that can interact with Grabber.NET peers.

To implement a compatible Web service and proxy, you need access to the interface definition for the various Web services that are used by Grabber.NET. As you have seen, the WSDL describing a Remoting component hosted in IIS can be obtained by passing a query string containing *WSDL* to the Web service endpoint. However, this is not available to Remoting Web services that are hosted by processes other than IIS.

For these cases, you can use SoapSuds to generate a WSDL document to describe the interfaces supported by the Web service. The resulting WSDL document can then be sent directly to the developer or posted on a Web site. The following SoapSuds command generates a WSDL document that describes both the File and the Directory Web services:

```
soapsuds -wsdl -types:SoapFileShare.Directory,SoapFileShare,
http://localhost/SoapFileShare/Directory.soap;SoapFileShare.File,SoapFileShare,
http://localhost/SoapFileShare/File.soap;SomeRecordCompany.LicenseInfo,
SomeRecordCompany -os:SoapFileShare.wsdl
```

Unlike ASP.NET, the SoapSuds utility allows you to create WSDL documents that describe a Web service with multiple endpoints. The preceding command will generate a file named SoapFileShare.wsdl that contains one Web service definition with two endpoints, one for the *File* class and one for the *Directory* class.

One issue with the SoapSuds-generated WSDL documents is that there is no way of specifying the name of the Web service. The name of the Web service defaults to the name of the first endpoint specified by the *types* flag. Here is the service description within SoapFileShare.wsdl:

```
<service name='DirectoryService'>
    <port name='DirectoryPort' binding='ns0:DirectoryBinding'>
        <soap:address location=
        'http://localhost/SoapFileShare/Directory.soap'/>
    </port>
    <port name='FilePort' binding='ns0:FileBinding'>
        <soap:address location='http://localhost/SoapFileShare/File.soap'/>
    </port>
</service>
```

You can modify the name of the Web service within the generated WSDL document. If the endpoints within the document are not related, you can also wrap each endpoint within its own *service* element. In this case, because *File* and *Directory* are related, I could change the name of the service from DirectoryService to SoapFileShareService.

The *types* flag indicates which classes I want to have described within the WSDL document. The classes that I want exposed as Web services also include their respective endpoints. If the resulting WSDL document contained only one Web service definition, I could have specified the endpoint using the *se* flag. (See Table 8-1 earlier in the chapter for a list of command-line parameters for SoapSuds.)

You also need to list any additional types that must be represented within the schema. For example, the *LicenseInfo* type is used within the *License* SOAP header, so I included it within the *types* flag.

Suds WSDL Extension Elements

Remoting defines a set of WSDL extension elements called Suds. The Suds extension elements are used to contain additional metadata necessary to maintain full fidelity with the .NET platform.

The Suds extension elements appear in every Remoting-generated WSDL document. For example, every .NET type represented within a WSDL document will have a corresponding binding element that contains a *suds:class* element that describes additional information about the .NET type (such as its root type). The following is the binding definition for the *Directory* class:

```
<binding name='DirectoryBinding' type='ns0:DirectoryPortType'>
    <soap:binding style='rpc'
    transport='http://schemas.xmlsoap.org/soap/http'/>
    <suds:class type='ns0:Directory' rootType='MarshalByRefObject'>
    </suds:class>

    <!-- Additional definitions... -->

</binding>
```

The Suds extension elements are proprietary to the Remoting framework, but if your Web service does not leverage any services that extend the SOAP specification, the Suds extension elements can be safely ignored by other Web service implementations. A Web service developed on the Remoting framework can thus maintain a high degree of interoperability.

Summary

Remoting is the distributed object infrastructure for .NET. Because SOAP is one of the message formats it supports, you can use Remoting to create Web services. The primary purpose of the Remoting framework is to serve as a distributed object infrastructure, not a development platform for creating and consuming Web services.

In a number of scenarios, Remoting is a better choice than other technologies, such as ASP.NET, if not the only choice. It makes sense to build Remoting Web services applications when you need to use a transport protocol other than HTTP, when you need to host a Web server in a process besides IIS, and when you need strong support for .NET types.

In this chapter, you learn the difference between well-known objects and client-activated objects. You should use well-known objects when your Web service needs to interoperate with clients created on other Web service development platforms.

Remoting supports two configurations for well-known objects, singleton and single instance. If the well-known object is configured as a singleton, all requests will be processed by the same object. If the well-known object supports the single instance configuration, each request will be processed by a new instance of the object.

Remoting Web services can be hosted in any process. This is a significant advantage for creating Web services that are not practical to host in IIS, such as the peer-to-peer Grabber.NET application that I implemented in this chapter.

In this chapter, I show how to create a Web service hosted in IIS and another one hosted in a WinForms process. I then explain how to consume Web services using the Remoting platform. I show three ways to create a strongly typed proxy object: using the *new* operator, using the *Activator* class's static *GetObject* method to dynamically create a strongly typed proxy, and using the SoapSuds utility to create a proxy from a WSDL document or a .NET assembly.

The SoapSuds utility can create a wrapped proxy object, which provides convenient access to some of the properties of the underlying channel object. For example, a wrapped proxy object exposes properties that allow you to set the username and password that will be used to authenticate the client.

The Remoting framework provides a set of tools and services for generating WSDL documents for your Web services. A WSDL document is automatically generated for Remoting Web services hosted in IIS when you append a query string containing *wsdl* to the end of the port address. You can also use the SoapSuds utility to generate a WSDL document for a given set of .NET types. This allows a WSDL document to be produced for a Web service hosted within a process other than IIS.

Remoting provides support for setting and processing SOAP headers. It offers two mechanisms for setting SOAP headers through the *CallContext* object. You use the *GetHeaders* and *SetHeaders* static methods to set and retrieve the SOAP headers for a particular method call, and you use the *GetData* and *SetData* static methods to set and retrieve data that will be sent within the header of the SOAP request message sent to an object that resides within a particular context.

9

Discovery Mechanisms for Web Services

One of my main motivations for moving to Colorado several years ago was skiing, and because getting to the nearby ski areas often requires driving over snow-packed mountain passes, I bought an SUV.

It amazes me that the SUV that reliably gets me to my favorite ski areas all winter is assembled from parts mostly made by companies other than the automobile manufacturer. In fact, only about 30 percent of the parts that make up my SUV are manufactured by the automobile manufacturer. For the remaining 70 percent of parts, the automobile manufacturer has built up a vast network of second-tier and third-tier suppliers that feed its just-in-time inventory system.

Web services can provide considerable value to supply chain management (SCM) systems that coordinate transactions such as those between the automobile manufacturer and its suppliers. The automobile manufacturer can advertise via WSDL how it will electronically submit orders to its suppliers and how it expects to receive purchase orders for the goods received.

For example, let's say that a supplier called Fabrikam Wing Nuts needs to obtain the WSDL document from the automobile manufacturer called Contoso Motor Company in order to integrate with Contoso's SCM system. It could make a sales call to Contoso Motor Company and obtain the URI for the WSDL documents and give Contoso the URI where the orders should be sent. Or it could place a telephone call to Contoso to exchange the information.

But wouldn't it be nice if a vendor did not need to have explicit conversations with Contoso in order to learn about the Web services Contoso exposes? Wouldn't it be nice if Contoso could locate your business when it was in desperate need of wing nuts?

Companies need a way to advertise the Web services they support and for clients to discover those services. In this chapter, I discuss two types of discovery mechanisms for Web services: Universal Description, Discovery, and Integration (UDDI) and DISCO. UDDI is a central and hierarchical directory service; DISCO promotes a more free-form browsing model for locating Web services.

UDDI

To establish an electronic relationship with Contoso, Fabrikam Wing Nuts needs to obtain information about the Web services that Contoso Motor Company supports. It would be ideal if Contoso could publish the technical details in such a way that any supplier interested in doing business with Contoso could easily obtain them.

UDDI provides a central directory service for publishing technical information about Web services. UDDI is the result of an industry initiative backed by a significant number of technology companies, including Microsoft, IBM, and Ariba. (You can find a full list of participants in the UDDI initiative at *http://www.uddi.org/community.html*.)

UDDI is yet another example of the unprecedented level of industry cooperation around the adoption of Web services. Many companies believed that a directory service for advertising Web services would be crucial to Web services gaining critical mass, and they felt that the time needed to develop the UDDI specification through a standards body was unacceptable.

As a result, the UDDI specification and the infrastructure required to support it were developed cooperatively by a number of companies. Once UDDI has reached "a reasonable level of maturity," the project members have committed to submitting the UDDI specification to a standards body.

UDDI Architecture

The infrastructure that supports UDDI is composed of a set of registries and registrars. A registry contains a full copy of the UDDI directory; a registrar provides UDDI registration services on behalf of a customer.

A registrar can be an ISP, a host of a business-to-business (B2B) marketplace, an individual company, or the host of a registry itself. For example, Microsoft offers a registry and also provides an HTML UI for creating and maintaining records within the directory. Contoso could also serve as a registrar in an effort to encourage its suppliers to register their services within the UDDI directory.

As of this writing, Microsoft and IBM are the only two companies hosting registries. Both Hewlett-Packard and SAP have committed to hosting additional registries.

The registries are based on a single-master replication model. A business must choose a registry in which to maintain its information. All updates made to the directory will be replicated to all the other registries. Then the updated information can be queried from any registry.

The diagram below shows one user updating the UDDI business directory through a registrar and then another user accessing the updated information.

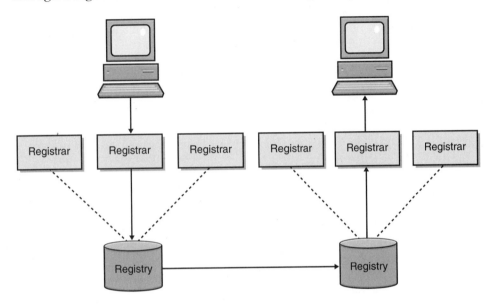

UDDI API

A UDDI registry is itself a Web service. It exposes a SOAP-based API for accessing and manipulating entries within the directory. Instead of maintaining data through a registrar, a developer can program directly against the API.

Version 1 of the UDDI API exposes about 30 methods for interacting with a registry, all of which behave synchronously. The following example shows how a UDDI request message is structured:

```
<?xml version="1.0" encoding="UTF-8" ?>
<Envelope xmlns="http://schemas.xmlsoap.org/soap/envelope/">
  <Body>
    <find_business generic="1.0" xmlns="urn:uddi-org:api">
      <name>MyTestBusiness</name>
    </find_business >
  </Body>
</Envelope>
```

A UDDI message must meet some minimal requirements in order to be valid. (Some of those required elements are shown in bold in the previous example.) They are as follows:

- The UDDI specification requires that the SOAP message be UTF-8 encoded.

- The elements within the body of the UDDI document must be scoped within the UDDI API namespace. The UDDI API namespace is identified by the *urn:uddi-org:api* URI.

- The request must contain a *SOAPAction* HTTP header whose value is an empty string. Any other value will be considered an error.

- The version of the targeted API must be stated within the body of the message using the *generic* attribute.

Let's examine the last bullet point in more detail. As with any system, UDDI will continue to evolve. As enhancements are made, the API will have to be modified to expose the new functionality. As of this writing, version 2 of the API has completed the review process, has been ratified by the UDDI.org members, and is currently being implemented. To avoid breaking existing clients, the UDDI organization devised a versioning system to maintain some degree of backward compatibility.

The version of the API is referred to as its *generic*. Every UDDI message, including request and response messages, must indicate which generic it targets. Its *generic* attribute indicates the version number of the targeted API within the root element of the SOAP body.

The registry is responsible for supporting the current as well as the previous generic. The registry must also support *generic* version 1.

The UDDI API methods can be divided into two categories: the inquiry methods and the publishing methods. The inquiry methods allow you to search and browse the directory, and the publishing methods allow you to modify the contents of the directory. The messages for the inquiry methods have a root element in the SOAP body prefixed by *find_* or *get_*. With a couple of exceptions, the messages for the publishing methods have a root element in the body of the SOAP message prefixed by *save_* or *delete_*.

The technical specification for the UDDI API is published as a WSDL document as well as an XML Schema document. The XML Schema version is located at *http://www.uddi.org/schema/2001/uddi_v1.xsd*. The WSDL document for the Inquiry API is located at *http://www.uddi.org/wsdl/inquire_v1.wsdl*, and the WSDL document for the Publish API is at *http://www.uddi.org/wsdl/publish_v1.wsdl*. Table 9-1 describes the inquiry methods.

Table 9-1   UDDI API Inquiry Methods

Message	Description
find_binding	Searches for *bindingTemplate* entities that match a specified set of criteria
find_business	Searches for *businessEntity* entities that match a specified set of criteria
find_service	Searches for *businessService* entities that match a specified set of criteria
find_tModel	Searches for *tModel* entities that match a specified set of criteria
get_bindingDetail	Obtains one or more specific *bindingTemplate* entities
get_businessDetail	Obtains one or more specific *businessEntity* entities
get_businessDetailExt	Obtains one or more specific *businessEntityExt* entities from a registry that may support additional attributes
get_serviceDetail	Obtains one or more specific *businessService* entities
get_tModelDetail	Obtains one or more specific *tModel* entities

The *find_* methods are for general searches, and the *get_* methods are for obtaining detailed information about a particular record. Table 9-2 describes the publishing methods.

Table 9-2   UDDI API Publishing Methods

Message	Description
delete_binding	Deletes one or more specified *bindingTemplate* entities
delete_business	Deletes one or more specified *businessEntity* entities
delete_service	Deletes one or more specified *businessService* entities
delete_tModel	Deletes one or more specified *tModel* entities
discard_authToken	Invalidates the previously obtained authentication token
get_authToken	Obtains an authentication token for the user
get_registeredInfo	Obtains a list of *businessInfo* and *tModelInfo* entities for a particular user
save_binding	Saves one or more *bindingTemplate* entities
save_business	Saves one or more *businessEntity* entities
save_service	Saves one or more *businessService* entities
save_tModel	Saves one or more *tModel* entities

As I said before, the publishing methods are responsible for manipulating data within the directory. Both creates and updates are handled by the *save_* messages. When a record is created using a *save_* method, the registry generates a unique identifier. The unique identifier is then passed to subsequent *save_* method calls to update the record. Each *save_* message has a corresponding *delete_* message for deletes.

The modifications made using the publishing methods must be done in a secure fashion. The UDDI specification states that all publishing messages must be exchanged between the client and the server over HTTPS. This prevents the contents of the message from being modified during transit.

A UDDI registry allows you to modify and delete only your own records, so you must include an authentication token with each request to prove your identity. This token is passed as part of the method signature of the *save_* and *delete_* methods.

You obtain an authentication token by passing your credentials to the *get_authToken* method. The implementation details of how a registry creates an authentication token are left up to the registry. The Microsoft registry uses Passport to authenticate its users. You pass a valid set of Passport credentials for a registered user, and the registry passes back a valid Passport token.

The methods defined by the UDDI API rely on a whole host of data structures. I discuss a number of them in the course of this chapter. You can find the entire list of data structures discussed in detail in the document titled "UDDI Programmer's API 1.0," which is posted in various formats at *www.uddi.org*.

UDDI SDK

Microsoft provides a UDDI SDK for developing UDDI-enabled applications. The UDDI SDK includes both a .NET and a COM-based object model for simplifying interaction with the registry. It also includes a standalone UDDI registry for development purposes.

As of this writing, the UDDI SDK is still in beta and is distributed as a separate download. Microsoft currently does not have plans to ship the release to manufacture (RTM) version of the SDK in conjunction with the .NET Framework. Instead, it plans to ship the RTM version of the UDDI .NET object model on a release schedule separate from that of the .NET Framework.

UDDI .NET Object Model

The UDDI .NET object model includes a set of types that encapsulate the various methods and data structures defined by the UDDI specification. Unlike in other object models, in UDDI every method is represented by a corresponding .NET type. The type's name corresponds to the name of the method. To conform to the *de facto* standard naming convention, the .NET types are Pascal cased with the underscores removed. For example, the *find_business* method has a corresponding *FindBusiness* .NET type.

The .NET type exposes properties for setting parameters to be sent to the UDDI registry. Each .NET type also exposes a *Send* method to invoke its corresponding UDDI method. This might sound confusing, but it is fairly straightforward once you get the hang of it.

Similar mapping is provided for the entity datatypes defined by the UDDI API. For example, one of the datatypes I will introduce shortly is *businessEntity*. The .NET object model contains a corresponding *BusinessEntity* .NET type.

UDDI Developer Edition

Another useful tool that ships with the UDDI SDK is the UDDI Developer Edition, a registry you can install on your local machine. It supports all version 1 interfaces and can be an invaluable resource for testing.

The sample code presented in this chapter targets the locally installed UDDI Developer Edition registry. Here is the necessary information for interfacing with the registry:

- **Publish URI**   *http://localhost/publish.asmx*
- **Inquiry URI**   *http://localhost/inquire.asmx*
- **User Name**   udditest
- **Password**   Blank password

The UDDI SDK ships with a couple of sample applications that you can use to administer the UDDI registry. Only the source code is provided, so you must compile the applications before you can use them. The applications are

- ***UDDIExplorer***   A simple UI for performing basic searches for *businessEntity* or *tModel* entries (described in the upcoming section)
- ***UDDIPublish***   Migrates your entries from one UDDI registry to another
- ***UDDIRegClean***   Removes all entries for a particular user

Because the UDDI Developer Edition supports only one user, *UDDIRegClean* is helpful for clearing all entries within the registry. *UDDIPublish* is useful when you want to copy the entries from a public registry and then perform testing against that data in a local environment.

UDDI Enterprise Server

Companies often need to discover services that are internal to the organization and not on the Internet. For example, a developer writing a reporting system for the sales department might be interested in learning what services the finance department exposes.

Practically every distributed object infrastructure provides a means of resolving the location of a particular component. The Service Control Manager provides this service for DCOM, and the Object Request Broker provides this service for CORBA. However, you can make a strong argument that UDDI is more robust and open than either the Service Control Manager or the Object Request Broker.

We need a corporate UDDI registry where internal services can be published. The UDDI Developer Edition was never intended to fill this role, so Windows .NET Server will feature native UDDI services that can be used to host a UDDI directory that is internal to a corporation.

UDDI services that ship with Windows .NET will have tight integration with the Active Directory as well as Windows security. When installed in an enterprise running Active Directory, the UDDI services will register themselves within Active Directory so that they can be easily discovered. The UDDI directory also supports integrated Windows security and can facilitate single sign-on via NT Challenge/Response. Finally, the UDDI services support role-based security and define three roles by default: Reader, Publisher, and Administrator. Check the MSDN UDDI Web site at *http://msdn.microsoft.com/uddi* for more information.

Registering the Purchaser

For Fabrikam to discover how to conduct electronic business with Contoso, Contoso must publish the necessary information to UDDI—including information about the Web services it exposes and the technical specifications they adhere to. In the process of registering Contoso, I will create and populate instances of six major UDDI datatypes:

- **businessEntity**   Defines the business itself

- **contact**   Contains information about a point of contact for the *businessEntity*

- **businessService**   Contains information about a collection of services

- **bindingTemplate**   Contains information about an entry point to a service

- **tModelInstanceInfo**   Serves as a cross-reference to a particular *tModel*

- **tModel**   Defines a particular specification for a service

Of the six types, the UDDI API provides methods for finding and creating four datatypes: *businessEntity*, *businessService*, *bindingTemplate*, and *tModel*. Instances of the other two datatypes are published using the *save_* method of its parent. The following diagram shows how the datatypes relate to each other.

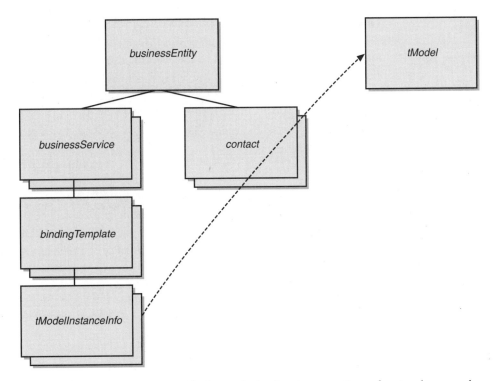

In the next section, I walk through the implementation of a simple console application that Contoso Motor Company can use to register itself in the UDDI directory.

Registering the Technical Specifications

First I need to register the technical specifications for the Invoice and the PurchaseOrder Web services. Note that UDDI is not responsible for holding the technical specification—it only provides a reference to the specification. You are responsible for making the specification available using some other means. This can be as simple as posting the specification on a Web site or publishing it within a repository such as BizTalk.org or RosettaNet.

The reference to the specification is contained within a *tModel*. A *tModel* is used to identify any unique abstract concept. For example, a *tModel* can serve as a reference pointer to a particular technical specification or it can be used to define a particular taxonomy. I will talk about how *tModel* entities are used to define taxonomies when I register the supplier.

Contoso needs to register two technical specifications, so it must define two *tModel* entities within the UDDI registry—one for how purchase orders will be issued to the supplier, and one for how the resulting invoice for goods shipped will be submitted back to Contoso.

How a specification is actually defined is irrelevant to UDDI because it is addressable via a URI. Because the *tModel* referencing the specification can be referenced by more than one service, the specification should not contain information specific to one instance of that service. Because both of Contoso's specifications define Web services, expressing the specifications in WSDL is a natural choice. In an effort to maximize reusability, you might want to ensure that the WSDL document does not contain information specific to a particular instance of the Web service.

Recall from Chapter 5 that a WSDL document contains one or more *service* sections. A *service* section contains port definitions that specify the endpoint of the Web service. Because a specification registered in UDDI should not contain information that is specific to one implementation, you should remove any *service* sections from the WSDL document before publishing it in UDDI.

Let's assume that both the Invoice and the PurchaseOrder WSDL documents were autogenerated by the ASP.NET runtime. In preparation for registering the Invoice and PurchaseOrder specifications with UDDI, I need to make a copy of the WSDL documents and remove the *service* sections from them. Then I need to publish them on Contoso's Web site so that they can be resolvable via a URI.

Here is the code to register *tModel* objects for the PurchaseOrder and Invoice Web services:

```
using System;
using Microsoft.Uddi.Api;
using Microsoft.Uddi;
using Microsoft.Uddi.Business;
using Microsoft.Uddi.ServiceType;
using Microsoft.Uddi.Service;
using Microsoft.Uddi.Binding;

class Application
{
    static void Main(string[] args)
    {
        // Initialize the publisher parameters.
        Publish.Url = "http://localhost/uddi/publish.asmx";
        Publish.User = "udditest";
        Publish.Password = "";
```

In the code, I reference various namespaces defined by the UDDI SDK. Note that you must add a reference to *Microsoft.Uddi.Sdk.dll* in order to reference the UDDI .NET types within your application.

Next I initialize the publisher parameters, including the URI, username, and password, by setting the associated static properties of the *Publisher* object.

The static properties are accessed by all of the UDDI .NET types that encapsulate UDDI method calls.

Because the static properties of the *Publish* class are shared, you must alter the properties before you publish to another registry. This requirement can be challenging, especially in a multithreaded environment. In addition, it prevents the system from caching multiple HTTP 1.1 connections on your behalf. (Future releases of the SDK will provide better support for publishing to multiple registries.)

```
// ******************************************************************
// * Register tModels for Invoice and PurchaseOrder Web services.
// ******************************************************************
SaveTModel saveTModel = new SaveTModel();
```

Next I create an instance of the *SaveTModel* class. This class lets you easily create a well-formed *save_tModel* message and submit it to the registry.

```
// Create tModel for the supplier invoice.
saveTModel.TModels.Add();
```

The *SaveTModel* type exposes a *TModels* property that contains a collection of *tModel* entities to be saved to the registry. In the preceding code, I call the *Add* method to create a new *tModel* for the Invoice Web service.

Next I set properties of the *tModel*, including its name, a description, the overview document, and category information. The *tModel* name can be any combination of up to 128 characters. In this case, I use a URI syntax to ensure that the name is unique.

```
saveTModel.TModels[0].Name = "www-contoso-com:Invoice";
```

Next I give the *tModel* a user-friendly description. The description is accompanied by code that specifies the targeted language, in this case *en* for English. You can find a full list of codes at *http://www.unicode.org/unicode /onlinedat/languages.html*.

```
saveTModel.TModels[0].Descriptions.Add("en",
"Defines the interface for accepting invoices from suppliers.");
```

Whenever a UDDI datatype allows you to set a description, the datatype can contain more than one description element. However, only one *description* element for a particular language code should appear within an instance of a UDDI datatype, as shown here:

```
saveTModel.TModels[0].OverviewDoc.OverviewURL =
"http://www.contoso.com/Invoice.wsdl";
saveTModel.TModels[0].OverviewDoc.Descriptions.Add("en",
"The WSDL document describing the Invoice Web service.");
```

Next I specify the overview document. In this case, it is the URI to the edited version of the WSDL document that is automatically generated by the .NET platform.

```
// Categorize the tModel.
saveTModel.TModels[0].CategoryBag.Add("uddi-
org:types", "wsdlSpec", "uuid:c1acf26d-9672-4404-9d70-39b756e62ab4");
```

Finally I add data to the *tModel* entity's category bag. The category bag is intended to contain metadata used to find specific *tModel* objects. For example, the Visual Studio .NET Add Web Reference Wizard will present only *tModel* entities that reference the *wsdlSpec* category.

A *tModel* can also contain an identifier bag. An identifier bag contains additional user-configurable identification numbers, which can be used as search parameters of the *find_tModel* method.

Three additional properties are exposed by the *tModel* object: *Operator*, *AuthorizedName*, and *TModelKey*. These properties are assigned by the registry when you publish a new *tModel* and therefore should be left blank when you create a new *tModel*.

The *Operator* property contains data indicating which registry holds the master copy of the *tModel*. The *AuthorizedName* property contains an identifier of the user that owns the record. The *TModelKey* property contains a unique identifier given to the record by the registry. Future versions of UDDI might allow you to provide your own more meaningful unique identifier.

Next I create a *tModel* for the PurchaseOrder Web service.

```
// Create tModel for the purchase order.
saveTModel.TModels.Add();
saveTModel.TModels[1].Name = "www-contoso-com:PurchaseOrder";
saveTModel.TModels[1].Descriptions.Add("en",
"Defines the interface for sending invoices to suppliers.");
saveTModel.TModels[1].OverviewDoc.OverviewURL =
"http://www.contoso.com/PurchaseOrder.wsdl";
saveTModel.TModels[1].OverviewDoc.Descriptions.Add("en", "The WSDL document des
cribing the PurchaseOrder Web service exposed by the supplier.");
saveTModel.TModels[1].CategoryBag.Add("uddi-
org:types", "wsdlSpec", "uuid:c1acf26d-9672-4404-9d70-39b756e62ab4");
```

Recall that I need to describe how a supplier interacts with Contoso. This interaction involves both the PurchaseOrder and the Invoice Web services. However, up to this point the Web services are described in isolation. I need to define the workflow that incorporates both of these Web services.

tModel entities are not limited to specifying a particular Web service. You can use them to represent other specifications, such as transport protocols and even workflows. However, UDDI has not standardized how a *tModel* referencing a workflow should be published. One limiting factor is the current lack of a standard for defining workflow.

Microsoft currently supports XLANG for expressing workflow. XLANG is an XML dialect generated by a technology called Orchestration. Orchestration currently ships only with Microsoft BizTalk Server. However, this technology has broader appeal, especially for Web services.

If your business partners can consume XLANG, it is a good way to represent workflow. However, if you need broader reach, you can opt for something as simple as an HTML document that describes the workflow in written form. For this example, the following code creates a *tModel* that references an HTML document:

```
// Create tModel for the supplier workflow.
saveTModel.TModels.Add();
saveTModel.TModels[2].Name = "www-contoso-com:PurchasingWorkflow";
saveTModel.TModels[2].Descriptions.Add("en", "Defines the workflow for
e-commerce transactions between the purchaser and its suppliers.");
saveTModel.TModels[2].OverviewDoc.OverviewURL =
"http://www.contoso.com/PurchasingWorkflow.html";
saveTModel.TModels[2].OverviewDoc.Descriptions.Add("en", "This document describ
es the workflow encompassing the PurchaseOrder and Invoice Web
service.");
```

The preceding code defines a *tModel* that references the workflow describing how Contoso conducts a transaction with one of its suppliers. The details of the transaction are outlined in the PurchasingWorkflow.html document.

Once I define the *tModel* objects, the final step is to save them to the UDDI registry.

```
// Save the newly defined tModel entities.
Console.WriteLine("The save_tModel message sent to the registry:");
Console.WriteLine(saveTModel.ToString());
TModelDetail savedTModelDetail = saveTModel.Send();
Console.WriteLine
("\nThe resulting tModelDetail message received from the registry:");
Console.WriteLine(savedTModelDetail.ToString());
```

Finally I use the *Send* method to submit the newly defined *tModel* entities to the registry and receive the resulting *tModelDetail*. The *tModelDetail* contains all the information about the *tModel*, including the properties populated by the UDDI registry. One of these properties, the unique identifier assigned to the Invoice *tModel*, will be referenced when I register Contoso's instance of this service.

The *ToString* method of the UDDI object model classes is overloaded to output the corresponding UDDI XML message. I use the *ToString* method to write both the *save_tModel* and the resulting *tModelDetail* messages to the console. The console output is shown here:

```
The save_tModel message sent to the registry:
<?xml version="1.0"?>
<save_tModel xmlns:xsi="http://www.w3.org/2001/XMLSchema-
instance" xmlns:xsd="http://www.w3.org/2001/XMLSchema" generic="1.0"
xmlns="urn:uddi-org:api">
  <tModel tModelKey="">
    <name>www-contoso-com:Invoice</name>
    <description xml:lang="en">Defines the interface for accepting invoices from
    suppliers.</description>
    <overviewDoc>
      <description xml:lang="en">The WSDL document describing the Invoice Web
      service.</description>
      <overviewURL>http://www.contoso.com/Invoice.wsdl</overviewURL>
    </overviewDoc>
    <categoryBag>
      <keyedReference tModelKey="uuid:c1acf26d-9672-4404-9d70-39b756e62ab4"
      keyName="uddi-org:types" keyValue="wsdlSpec" />
    </categoryBag>
  </tModel>
  <tModel tModelKey="">
    <name>www-contoso-com:PurchaseOrder</name>
    <description xml:lang="en">Defines the interface for sending a purchase
    order to a supplier.</description>
    <overviewDoc>
      <description xml:lang="en">The WSDL document describing the PurchaseOrder
      Web service exposed by the supplier.</description>
      <overviewURL>http://www.contoso.com/PurchaseOrder.wsdl</overviewURL>
    </overviewDoc>
    <categoryBag>
      <keyedReference tModelKey="uuid:c1acf26d-9672-4404-9d70-39b756e62ab4"
      keyName="uddi-org:types" keyValue="wsdlSpec" />
    </categoryBag>
  </tModel>
  <tModel tModelKey="">
    <name>www-contoso-com:PurchasingWorkflow</name>
    <description xml:lang="en">Defines the workflow for e-
commerce transactions
    between the purchaser and its suppliers.</description>
    <overviewDoc>
      <description xml:lang="en">This document describes the workflow
      encompassing the PurchaseOrder and Invoice Web service.</description>
      <overviewURL>http://www.contoso.com/PurchasingWorkflow.html</overviewURL>
    </overviewDoc>
  </tModel>
</save_tModel>
```

The resulting tModelDetail message received from the registry:

```xml
<?xml version="1.0"?>
<tModelDetail xmlns:xsi="http://www.w3.org/2001/XMLSchema-
instance" xmlns:xsd="http://www.w3.org/2001/XMLSchema" generic="1.0"
operator="Microsoft UDDI Developer Edition Test Operator" truncated="false" xml
ns="urn:uddi-org:api">
  <tModel tModelKey="uuid:a89493a6-d0d0-415b-8c41-a34caf8c6c43"
  operator="Microsoft UDDI Developer Edition Test Operator">
    <name>www-contoso-com:Invoice</name>
    <description xml:lang="en">Defines the interface for accepting invoices from
    suppliers.</description>
    <overviewDoc>
      <description xml:lang="en">The WSDL document describing the Invoice Web
      service.</description>
      <overviewURL>http://www.contoso.com/Invoice.wsdl</overviewURL>
    </overviewDoc>
    <categoryBag>
      <keyedReference tModelKey="uuid:c1acf26d-9672-4404-9d70-39b756e62ab4"
      keyName="uddi-org:types" keyValue="wsdlSpec" />
    </categoryBag>
  </tModel>
  <tModel tModelKey="uuid:2a1109ff-5d31-4df1-86f6-b8fcff797030"
  operator="Microsoft UDDI Developer Edition Test Operator">
    <name>www-contoso-com:PurchaseOrder</name>
    <description xml:lang="en">Defines the interface for sending a purchase
    order to a supplier.</description>
    <overviewDoc>
      <description xml:lang="en">The WSDL document describing the PurchaseOrder
      Web service exposed by the supplier.</description>
      <overviewURL>http://www.contoso.com/PurchaseOrder.wsdl</overviewURL>
    </overviewDoc>
    <categoryBag>
      <keyedReference tModelKey="uuid:c1acf26d-9672-4404-9d70-39b756e62ab4"
      keyName="uddi-org:types" keyValue="wsdlSpec" />
    </categoryBag>
  </tModel>
  <tModel tModelKey="uuid:b31cff85-8b1b-4502-bce1-92229f579238"
  operator="Microsoft UDDI Developer Edition Test Operator">
    <name>www-contoso-com:PurchasingWorkflow</name>
    <description xml:lang="en">Defines the workflow for e-
commerce transactions
    between the purchaser and its suppliers.</description>
    <overviewDoc>
      <description xml:lang="en">This document describes the workflow
      encompassing the PurchaseOrder and Invoice Web service.</description>
      <overviewURL>http://www.contoso.com/PurchasingWorkflow.html</overviewURL>
    </overviewDoc>
  </tModel>
</tModelDetail>
```

Registering Contoso Motor Company

Now that I have published the technical specifications necessary to facilitate communication between a purchaser and its suppliers, the next step is to register the purchaser. The UDDI entry for Contoso Motor Company will contain basic contact information as well as information about the Invoice Web service it exposes.

Information relating to a specific company is contained within a *businessEntity* datatype. This includes general information such as the company's address and phone number as well as technical information about the Web services it exposes.

The following code creates a *businessEntity* and publishes it to the registry using the *save_business* method:

```
// ****************************************************************
// * Register businessEntity for Contoso Motor Company.
// ****************************************************************
SaveBusiness saveBusiness = new SaveBusiness();

BusinessEntity contoso = new BusinessEntity();
saveBusiness.BusinessEntities.Add(contoso);
contoso.Name = "Contoso Motor Company";
contoso.Descriptions.Add("en",
"Striving to make the world a better place. (TM)");
```

I first create an object of type *BusinessEntity* and set its name and description. Unlike the previous code that created a *tModel*, I explicitly create an instance of the *BusinessEntity* class instead of implicitly creating one using the *SaveBusiness.Add* method. I did this to avoid requiring 24-inch-wide paper stock to print this section.

Because the *businessEntity* contains such a wide array of information, it defines a fairly deep hierarchy of nested datatypes. If I were to access the properties of the nested objects by navigating through an object of type *SaveBusiness*, my code would quickly become unwieldy.

Next I create a contact record and add it to the *businessEntity*. The *PersonName* property contains the contact's full name, and the *UseType* property contains an optional free-form text field that identifies the type of contact.

```
// Add primary contact information to the businessEntity.
Contact primaryContact = new Contact();
businessEntity.Contacts.Add(primaryContact);
primaryContact.PersonName = "James Smith";
primaryContact.UseType = "primary contact";
primaryContact.Descriptions.Add("en", "Primary Contact");
primaryContact.Phones.Add("800-555-0123", "main");
primaryContact.Emails.Add("james@contoso.com", "main");
primaryContact.Addresses.Add("1", "office");
```

```
primaryContact.Addresses[0].AddressLines.Add("P.O. Box 1234");
primaryContact.Addresses[0].AddressLines.Add("Dearborn, MI 56789");
businessEntity.Contacts.Add(primaryContact);
```

I set a similar *UseType* property for the phone number, e-mail address, and physical address. However, note that the *UseType* field of the phone number and e-mail address is not optional if more than one phone number or e-mail address is listed.

Note that the order of the address lines is significant. The registry will always return the address lines in the order in which they were originally saved.

Next I add a new *businessService* that describes a collection of Web services that enable Contoso's SCM process. A *businessService* describes a set of Web services used to solve a particular business problem. In this case, the *businessService* contains a single entry for the Invoice Web service.

```
// Add a businessService for the Web services related to SCM.
BusinessService scmService = new BusinessService();
contoso.BusinessServices.Add(scmService);
scmService.Name = "Supply Chain Management Web Services";
scmService.Descriptions.Add("en",
"Web services for conducting e-commerce with suppliers.");
```

The UDDI API also provides the *save_businessService* method for directly publishing a new *businessService*. This is encapsulated by the *SaveBusinessService* type in the .NET UDDI SDK.

If you use the *SaveBusinessService* type to create a new *businessService*, the *BusinessKey* property must point to a valid *businessEntity*. However, in this case the new *businessService* is nested within its parent *businessEntity* and can therefore have a blank *BusinessKey* property.

Finally, the *businessService* contains a category bag. Similar to the category bag exposed by the *businessEntity*, it categorizes a collection of services exposed by the *businessService*, as shown here:

```
// Add a bindingTemplate for the Invoice Web service.
BindingTemplate invoiceBinding = new BindingTemplate();
scmService.BindingTemplates.Add(invoiceBinding);
invoiceBinding.Descriptions.Add("en", "This template describes the technical
specifications you must comply with in order to submit invoices to Contoso.");
invoiceBinding.AccessPoint.Text = "http://contoso.com/Invoice.asmx";
invoiceBinding.AccessPoint.URLType = URLTypeEnum.Http;
```

Next I add a *bindingTemplate* for the Invoice Web service. The *bindingTemplate* defines a specific endpoint for a Web service. The URI of the endpoint is specified by the *AccessPoint* property.

Instead of specifying an endpoint, a *bindingTemplate* can reference another *bindingTemplate*. You can accomplish this by setting the *HostingRedirector* property equal to the UUID of another binding template. If the *HostingRedirec-tor* property is set, the client must obtain the URI of the endpoint from the referenced *bindingTemplate*.

As with the *businessService*, you can use an instance of the .NET UDDI SDK *SaveBindingTemplate* type to publish a new *bindingTemplate* to the registry. If you do this, the *ServiceKey* property must contain a valid reference to its parent *businessService*, as shown here:

```
// Add tModelInstanceInfo for Invoice.
TModelInstanceInfo invoice = new TModelInstanceInfo();
invoiceBinding.TModelInstanceDetail.TModelInstanceInfos.Add(invoice);
invoice.TModelKey = savedTModelDetail.TModels[0].TModelKey;
invoice.Descriptions.Add("en",
"The submitted invoice must be a result of receiving a PO from Contoso.");
invoice.InstanceDetail.Descriptions.Add("en",
"The WSDL document for this instance of the Invoice Web service.");
invoice.InstanceDetail.OverviewDoc.OverviewURL =
"http://contoso.com/Invoice.asmx?wsdl";
invoice.InstanceDetail.OverviewDoc.Descriptions.Add("en", "Some description.");
```

Next I add a *tModelInstanceInfo* to the *bindingTemplate*. The *tModelInstanceInfo* references a particular *tModel* in which the endpoint described by the parent *bindingTemplate* claims compliance.

Recall that the WSDL document referenced by the Invoice Web service *tModel* does not contain information specific to any one instance of a Web service. Many toolsets, including the ones provided by .NET, require a complete WSDL document in order to generate a fully functional proxy. Therefore, the *tModelInstanceInfo* datatype contains a reference to the WSDL document that imports the interface definitions and defines the implementation-specific *service* element.

In this case, I referenced the WSDL automatically generated by ASP.NET. The WSDL document imports the original interface definitions using the *Web-BindingService* attribute. (See Chapter 5 for more information.)

The *tModelInstanceInfo* contains a reference to a document that describes the specifics about the implementation of a particular *tModel*. The documentation might be for programmatic consumption—a WSDL document, for example. Or it might have a more user-friendly form, such as an HTML or a Word document. The document can be used to describe instance-specific details such as security and account registration.

The UDDI organization is currently defining best practices regarding the use of the *tModelInstanceInfo*. Check the UDDI Best Practices Web site at *http://www.uddi.org/bestpractices.html* for more information.

Next I add another *tModelInstance* that references the workflow.

```
// Add tModelInstanceInfo for SupplierWorkflow.
TModelInstanceInfo workflow = new TModelInstanceInfo();
invoiceBinding.TModelInstanceDetail.TModelInstanceInfos.Add(workflow);
workflow.TModelKey = savedTModelDetail.TModels[2].TModelKey;
workflow.Descriptions.Add("en", "This document describes the workflow
encompassing the PurchaseOrder and Invoice Web service.");
```

For this *tModelInstanceInfo*, I have decided to not publish information about the *tModel* that is specific to the implementation, so I don't include a *tModelInstanceInfo*.

```
Console.WriteLine("The save_Business message sent to the registry:");
Console.WriteLine(saveBusiness.ToString());
BusinessDetail businessDetail = saveBusiness.Send();
Console.WriteLine
("The resulting businessDetail message received from the registry:");
Console.WriteLine(businessDetail.ToString());
```

Finally I publish the *businessEntity* to the UDDI registry by calling the *Send* method of the *saveBusiness* object. As in the *tModel* example, I output the messages sent between the client and the registry to the console. Here is the resulting message sent to the UDDI registry and the response from the registry:

```
The save_Business message sent to the registry:
<?xml version="1.0"?>
<save_business xmlns:xsi="http://www.w3.org/2001/XMLSchema-
instance" xmlns:xsd="http://www.w3.org/2001/XMLSchema" generic="1.0"
xmlns="urn:uddi-org:api">
  <businessEntity businessKey="">
    <name>Contoso Motor Company</name>
    <description xml:lang="en">Striving to make the world a better place. (TM)
    </description>
    <contacts>
      <contact useType="primary contact">
        <description xml:lang="en">Primary Contact</description>
        <personName>James Smith</personName>
        <phone useType="main">800-555-0123</phone>
        <email useType="main">james@contoso.com</email>
        <address sortCode="1" useType="office">
          <addressLine>P.O. Box 1234</addressLine>
          <addressLine>Dearborn, MI 56789</addressLine>
        </address>
      </contact>
    </contacts>
    <businessServices>
      <businessService serviceKey="" businessKey="">
        <name>Purchasing Web Services</name>
```

(continued)

```
                    <description xml:lang="en">
            Web services for conducting purchasing related transactions.</description>
              <bindingTemplates>
                <bindingTemplate serviceKey="" bindingKey="">
                  <description xml:lang="en">
                  The Web service for submitting invoices to Contoso.</description>
                  <accessPoint URLType="http">
                  http://contoso.com/Invoice.asmx</accessPoint>
                  <tModelInstanceDetails>
                    <tModelInstanceInfo tModelKey=
                    "uuid:a89493a6-d0d0-415b-8c41-a34caf8c6c43">
                    <description xml:lang="en">The submitted invoice must be a result
                    of receiving a PO from Contoso
                    (www-contoso-com:SupplierInvoice).</description>
                      <instanceDetails>
                        <description xml:lang="en">The WSDL document for this
                        instance of the Invoice Web service.</description>
                        <overviewDoc>
                          <description xml:lang="en">Some description.</description>
                          <overviewURL>http://contoso.com/Invoice.asmx?wsdl
                          </overviewURL>
                        </overviewDoc>
                      </instanceDetails>
                    </tModelInstanceInfo>
                    <tModelInstanceInfo tModelKey=
                    "uuid:b31cff85-8b1b-4502-bce1-92229f579238">
                    <description xml:lang="en">This document describes the workflow
                    encompassing the PurchaseOrder and Invoice Web service.
                    </description>
                      <instanceDetails>
                        <overviewDoc />
                      </instanceDetails>
                    </tModelInstanceInfo>
                  </tModelInstanceDetails>
                </bindingTemplate>
              </bindingTemplates>
            </businessService>
          </businessServices>
        </businessEntity>
</save_business>

The resulting businessDetail message received from the registry:
<?xml version="1.0"?>
<businessDetail xmlns:xsi="http://www.w3.org/2001/XMLSchema-
instance" xmlns:xsd="http://www.w3.org/2001/XMLSchema" generic="1.0"
operator="Microsoft UDDI Developer Edition Test Operator" truncated="false"
xmlns="urn:uddi-org:api">
  <businessEntity businessKey="ac5782d8-d69b-4402-9262-caf189536c89"
  operator="Microsoft UDDI Developer Edition Test Operator">
    <discoveryURLs>
```

```
  <discoveryURL useType="businessEntity">
  http://localhost/uddi/discovery.ashx?businessKey=
  ac5782d8-d69b-4402-9262-caf189536c89</discoveryURL>
</discoveryURLs>
<name>Contoso Motor Company</name>
<description xml:lang="en">Striving to make the world a better place. (TM)
</description>
<contacts>
  <contact useType="primary contact">
    <description xml:lang="en">Primary Contact</description>
    <personName>James Smith</personName>
    <phone useType="main">800-555-0123</phone>
    <email useType="main">james@contoso.com</email>
    <address sortCode="1" useType="office">
      <addressLine>P.O. Box 1234</addressLine>
      <addressLine>Dearborn, MI 56789</addressLine>
    </address>
  </contact>
</contacts>
<businessServices>
  <businessService serviceKey="e5ae9f03-585b-4fee-8a89-5d29f0079b02"
  businessKey="ac5782d8-d69b-4402-9262-caf189536c89">
    <name>Purchasing Web Services</name>
    <description xml:lang="en">Web services for conducting purchasing
    related transactions.</description>
    <bindingTemplates>
      <bindingTemplate serviceKey="e5ae9f03-585b-4fee-8a89-5d29f0079b02"
      bindingKey="f9cfeb33-4b83-4cc5-9cd4-d332160530c0">
        <description xml:lang="en">
        The Web service for submitting invoices to Contoso.</description>
        <accessPoint URLType="http">
        http://contoso.com/Invoice.asmx</accessPoint>
        <tModelInstanceDetails>
          <tModelInstanceInfo tModelKey=
          "uuid:a89493a6-d0d0-415b-8c41-a34caf8c6c43">
          <description xml:lang="en">The submitted invoice must be a result
          of receiving a PO from Contoso
          (www-contoso-com:SupplierInvoice).</description>
            <instanceDetails>
              <description xml:lang="en">The WSDL document for this
              instance of the Invoice Web service.</description>
              <overviewDoc>
                <description xml:lang="en">Some description.</description>
                <overviewURL>http://contoso.com/Invoice.asmx?wsdl
                </overviewURL>
              </overviewDoc>
            </instanceDetails>
          </tModelInstanceInfo>
          <tModelInstanceInfo tModelKey=
          "uuid:b31cff85-8b1b-4502-bce1-92229f579238">
```

(continued)

```
        <description xml:lang="en">This document describes the workflow
        encompassing the PurchaseOrder and Invoice Web service.
        </description>
        <instanceDetails>
          <overviewDoc />
        </instanceDetails>
      </tModelInstanceInfo>
    </tModelInstanceDetails>
  </bindingTemplate>
  </bindingTemplates>
  </businessService>
  </businessServices>
  </businessEntity>
</businessDetail>
```

Searching for Contoso Motor Company

Now that Contoso Motor Company is registered, a supplier can obtain information about the registered services by querying the UDDI registry. To facilitate this, the UDDI API exposes a set of *get_* and *find_* methods. The *find_* methods are used to perform general queries. The information returned is typically enough to display a meaningful result set to the user. You can then use the *get_* methods to retrieve the full information about a particular entry.

The following example retrieves the *businessDetail* entry listed in the previous section:

```
// Search for all businesses that have the name Contoso Motor Company.
FindBusiness findBusiness  = new FindBusiness();
findBusiness.Name = "Contoso Motor Company ";
BusinessList businessList = findBusiness.Send();

// Get the businessDetail for the first entry in the result set.
GetBusinessDetail getBusinessDetail = new GetBusinessDetail();
getBusinessDetail.BusinessKeys.Add(businessList.BusinessInfos[0].BusinessKey);
BusinessDetail businessDetail = getBusinessDetail.Send();
Console.WriteLine
("The resulting businessDetail message received from the registry:");
Console.WriteLine(businessDetail.ToString());
```

I first search for all *businessEntity* entries with the name *Contoso Motor Company*. By default, UDDI performs leftmost name matching and is not case sensitive. For example, the search strings *CONTOSO, Contoso Motor,* and *Contoso Motor Co* will all locate the entry I published in the previous section.

You can modify the behavior of a query by specifying a qualifier within the *FindBusiness.FindQualifiers* property. Table 9-3 describes the find qualifiers that a UDDI registry must support. In addition, individual registries can support an extended set of qualifiers.

Table 9-3   UDDI Registry Find Qualifiers

Value	Description
exactNameMatch	Specifies that the entire string must match the name. By default, it is case insensitive.
caseSensitiveMatch	Specifies that case is relevant within the specified search string.
sortByNameAsc	Specifies that the result set should be sorted alphabetically in ascending order.
sortByNameDesc	Specifies that the result set should be sorted alphabetically in descending order.
sortByDateAsc	Specifies that the result set should be sorted by the date last updated in ascending order.
sortByDateDesc	Specifies that the result set should be sorted by the date last updated in descending order.

Obviously, *sortByNameAsc* and *sortByNameDesc* are mutually exclusive, as are *sortByDateAsc* and *sortByDateDesc*. However, any other combination of the find qualifiers is allowed. If more than one find qualifier is specified, the following order of precedence is applied:

1.   *exactNameMatch* and *caseSensitiveMatch*

2.   *sortByNameAsc* and *sortByNameDesc*

3.   *sortByDateAsc* and *sortByDateDesc*

Once I obtain my search results, I use the *getBusinessDetail* object to get the details of the first record returned in my search results. The *businessDetail* returned contains the information necessary for a supplier to establish an e-business relationship with Contoso. Items of importance include the *businessEntity* UUID, the *bindingTemplate* access point, and the UUIDs for the *tModel* objects.

Registering the Supplier

When a supplier registers itself in the UDDI directory, registering just the name, address, and phone number is not sufficient. It must register in such a way that Contoso and other potential customers can find it.

UDDI provides a way to categorize entries within the directory using well-known taxonomies. The supported taxonomies include the North American Industry Classification System (NAICS - 1997), the Universal Standard Products and Services Codes (UNSPSC - 3.01), the Standard Industrial Classification (SIC - 1987), and the GeoWeb geographic classification (August 2000).

I used a taxonomy earlier in this chapter when I specified the *www-contoso-com:Invoice* and *www-contoso-com:PurchaseOrder tModel* entities. Here is the portion of the code I used to register the *tModel* entities:

```
saveTModel.TModels[0].Name = "www-contoso-com:Invoice";

// Set additional properties...

saveTModel.TModels[0].CategoryBag.Add("uddi-org:types", "wsdlSpec",
"uuid:clacf26d-9672-4404-9d70-39b756e62ab4");
```

The preceding code uses the UDDI Type Taxonomy to categorize the *tModel* as one that references a WSDL document. A taxonomy is itself defined by a *tModel* definition. This is the other primary use of *tModel* entities besides representing a technical specification.

In the preceding example, the third parameter of the *CategoryBag.Add* method references the *tModel* that defines the UDDI Type Taxonomy. The UDDI Type Taxonomy is used to categorize the type of data a *tModel* references. The taxonomy is hierarchical in nature, as shown in the following figure. Table 9-4 lists the valid values defined by the taxonomy.

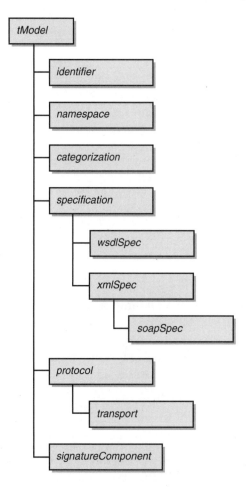

Table 9-4   UDDI Type Taxonomy Values

ID	Description
tModel	The root branch of the taxonomy hierarchy. End-user categorization on this value is not allowed.
identifier	Specifies that the *tModel* represents a taxonomy of unique identifiers. The DUNS number uniquely identifies a company and is an example of an identifier *tModel*.
namespace	Specifies that the *tModel* represents a scoping constraint. This value is synonymous with XML namespaces and is used to avoid naming collisions.
categorization	Specifies that the *tModel* represents a method of categorization. The NAICS and UNSPSC—and even the UDDI Type Taxonomy—are all examples of categorization *tModel* entities.
specification	Specifies that the *tModel* references a contract that defines the interaction with a particular service. COM and RPC services are examples of *specification tModel* entities.
xmlSpec	Specifies that the *tModel* references a contract that defines the interaction with a particular service using XML. Examples of *xmlSpec tModel* entities include a DTD and an XML Schema schema.
soapSpec	Specifies that the *tModel* references a contract that defines an interaction with a particular service using SOAP. The schema for the Inquire UDDI API is an example of a *soapSpec tModel*.
wsdlSpec	Specifies that the *tModel* references a WSDL document that defines an interaction with a particular service. The *www-contoso-com:Invoice tModel* is an example of a *wsdlSpec tModel*.
protocol	Specifies that the *tModel* references a particular protocol for interacting with a particular service.
transport	Specifies that the *tModel* references a particular transport protocol for interacting with a particular service. HTTP and FTP are examples of transport *tModel* entities.
signatureComponent	Specifies that the *tModel* does not represent the complete specification for a Web service. An example would be an individual step in a business process.

You can create your own taxonomies by creating a *tModel* that contains a *categorization* entry in its category property bag. However, to help ensure that potential purchasers can find Fabrikam when they are looking for a wing nuts manufacturer, I use a taxonomy that is core to UDDI. (The taxonomies that are essential to UDDI are listed at *http://www.uddi.org/taxonomies/Core_Taxonomy_OverviewDoc.htm*.)

Specifically, I categorize Fabrikam Wing Nuts using the UNSPSC. The UNSPSC is defined by the Electronic Commerce Code Management Association (ECCMA) and can be browsed at *http://eccma.org/unspsc/browse/*.

The following console application registers Fabrikam Wing Nuts in the UDDI directory:

```
using System;
using Microsoft.Uddi.Api;
using Microsoft.Uddi;
using Microsoft.Uddi.Business;
using Microsoft.Uddi.ServiceType;
using Microsoft.Uddi.Service;
using Microsoft.Uddi.Binding;

class Application
{
    static void Main(string[] args)
    {
        // Initialize the publisher parameters.
        Publish.Url = "http://localhost/uddi/publish.asmx";
        Publish.User = "udditest";
        Publish.Password = "";

        // Create a new businessEntity.
        SaveBusiness saveBusiness = new SaveBusiness();
        BusinessEntity fabrikam = new BusinessEntity();
        saveBusiness.BusinessEntities.Add(fabrikam);
        fabrikam.Name = "Fabrikam Wing Nuts";
        fabrikam.Descriptions.Add("", "Just a bunch of wing nuts.");

        // Add the UNSPSC code for wing nut manufacturer.
        fabrikam.CategoryBag.Add("unspsc-org:unspsc", "31.16.17.17.00",
            "uuid:CD153257-086A-4237-B336-6BDCBDCC6634");

        // Contact information...
```

The preceding code creates a *businessEntity* for Fabrikam Wing Nuts and categorizes it using the UNSPSC taxonomy. The code for wing nut manufacturers is 31.16.17.17.00. (Yes, there actually is a code defined for wing nut manufacturers.) If Fabrikam decides to diversify its product line, it can add more entries to the category property bag.

```
// Add a businessService for the Web services
// related to supply chain management.
BusinessService scmService = new BusinessService();
fabrikam.BusinessServices.Add(scmService);
scmService.Name = "Supply Chain Management Web Service";
scmService.Descriptions.Add("",
"Web services for conducting e-commerce with suppliers.");

// Add the binding template for the PurchaseOrder Web service.
BindingTemplate purchaseOrderBinding = new BindingTemplate();
scmService.BindingTemplates.Add(purchaseOrderBinding);
purchaseOrderBinding.Descriptions.Add("",
"The Web service for submitting purchase orders to Fabrikam Wing Nuts.");
purchaseOrderBinding.AccessPoint.Text =
"http://fabrikam.com/PurchaseOrder.asmx";
purchaseOrderBinding.AccessPoint.URLType = URLTypeEnum.Http;

// Add a reference to the www-contoso-com:PurchaseOrder tModel.
TModelInstanceInfo purchaseOrder = new TModelInstanceInfo();
purchaseOrderBinding.TModelInstanceDetail.TModelInstanceInfos.Add
(purchaseOrder);
purchaseOrder.TModelKey = "uuid:2a1109ff-5d31-4df1-86f6-b8fcff797030";

Console.WriteLine("The save_Business message sent to the registry:");
Console.WriteLine(saveBusiness.ToString());
BusinessDetail businessDetail = saveBusiness.Send();
Console.WriteLine
("The resulting businessDetail message received from the registry:");
Console.WriteLine(businessDetail.ToString());
    }
}
```

I register the Invoice Web services that are compliant with Contoso's *www-contoso-com:PurchaseOrder tModel*, and then I save the *businessEntity* to the registry.

Searching for the Supplier

When Contoso Motor Company needs to replenish its supply of wing nuts, it can search the UDDI directory for potential suppliers. The following code searches the UDDI directory for suppliers.

```
Inquire.Url = "http://test.uddi.microsoft.com/inquire";

FindBusiness findBusiness = new FindBusiness();
findBusiness.CategoryBag.Add("unspsc-
org:unspsc", "31.16.17.17.00", "uuid:CD153257-086A-4237-B336-6BDCBDCC6634");
findBusiness.TModelKeys.Add("uuid:2a1109ff-5d31-4df1-86f6-b8fcff797030");

BusinessList businessList = findBusiness.Send();
Console.WriteLine(businessList);
```

The preceding code searches for all *businessEntity* entries that are categorized as wing nut manufacturers and also expose the PurchaseOrder Web service. Because Fabrikam meets these criteria, it will be included in the resulting *businessList*.

The ability to search for potential suppliers in a centralized directory offers a couple of advantages. First, suppose Contoso already has an established relationship with another wing nut supplier. If, for some reason, this supplier cannot accommodate Contoso's orders, Contoso can search the directory for other potential suppliers.

Another advantage of a centralized directory is that companies other than Contoso can locate Fabrikam in the UDDI directory. For example, if Billy's Rocking Horse Manufacturing is putting together a new line that requires wing nuts, it can locate Fabrikam by performing a search of the UDDI directory.

Visual Studio .NET Integration

Visual Studio .NET supports UDDI. The two primary points of integration are the Visual Studio .NET Start page and the Add Web Reference Wizard.

The Visual Studio .NET Start page lets you register Web services as well as search for Web services registered in the UDDI directory. This functionality is available through the XML Web Services page, which serves as a portal to a registrar customized for Visual Studio .NET.

This Web page is hosted on the Internet, so it is subject to change. As of this writing, it has three tabs: Getting Started, Find A Service, and Register A Service. The latter two tabs are used to register and locate Web services in the Microsoft test and production UDDI registry.

The Find A Service tab presents a simple search screen for finding Web services that have been categorized using the VSCATEGORY taxonomy. You can easily add each resulting entry to the current project by clicking on the link provided.

The Register A Service tab provides a simple three-step UI for registering a Web service. On the first screen, you log in with your Passport credentials. The next screen gives you the option to publish against the Microsoft test or production registry. Here is the final screen, where you enter information about the Web service:

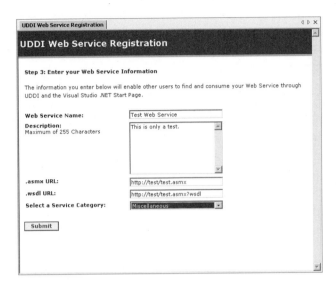

The information provided is used to create a *businessService* with an associated *bindingTemplate*. The Web Service Name and Description fields set the name and description of the *businessService*, respectively. The .asmx URL, .wsdl URL, and Service Category are used to set the appropriate properties on the *bindingTemplate*. The Visual Studio .NET registrar also registers a *tModel* on your behalf.

The following is the *businessService* entity that is created as a result of the above registration:

```
<businessService serviceKey="3a4d24a1-9722-4499-87bb-ed7cb39d01a5"
businessKey="c2a5e253-a10d-431c-a167-016d057f8890">
  <name>Test Web Service</name>
  <description xml:lang="en">This is only a test.</description>
  <bindingTemplates>
    <bindingTemplate serviceKey="3a4d24a1-9722-4499-87bb-ed7cb39d01a5"
    bindingKey="bcbdd1a4-3605-4950-bc83-46ddb17e51dc">
    <description xml:lang="en">This is only a test.</description>
    <accessPoint URLType="http">http://test/test.asmx</accessPoint>
    <tModelInstanceDetails>
      <tModelInstanceInfo tModelKey="uuid:e4fe05d6-2691-430a-bbfd-81d6e5491b91">
      <description xml:lang="en">WSDL Web Service Interface (Added by VS)
      </description>
      <instanceDetails>
        <description xml:lang="en">WSDL Web Service Interface (Added by VS)
        </description>
        <overviewDoc>
        <overviewURL>http://test/test.asmx?wsdl</overviewURL>
        </overviewDoc>
      </instanceDetails>
```

(continued)

```
        </tModelInstanceInfo>
      </tModelInstanceDetails>
      </bindingTemplate>
    </bindingTemplates>
    <categoryBag>
      <keyedReference tModelKey="uuid:4c1f2e1f-4b7c-44eb-9b87-6e7d80f82b3e"
      keyName="VSCATEGORY" keyValue="14" />
    </categoryBag>
</businessService>
```

In addition to using the Find A Service tab on the Visual Studio .NET Start page, you can also search for Web services registered in UDDI using the Add Web Reference Wizard. The wizard allows you to search for all Web services published by a particular *businessEntity*. The following is the result of a search for all Web services published by the GotDotNet *businessEntity*:

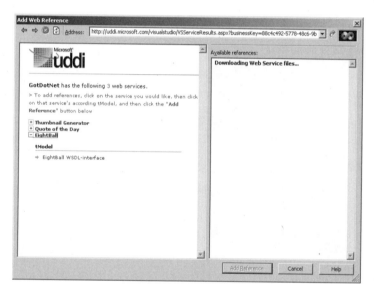

Only entries that reference *tModel* objects in the *wsdlSpec* category are listed. To add a reference to a Web service, click on the link to its WSDL interface and then click the Add Reference button.

DISCO

The mere name generates visions of John Travolta strutting his stuff in a polyester leisure suit. DISCO, which is short for Discovery, is yet another technology that you can use to advertise and discover Web services.

The DISCO protocol was developed by Microsoft, which currently has no formal plans for submitting the DISCO specification to a standards body. So, if we have UDDI, why DISCO?

Recall that UDDI is a structured, centrally managed directory service. Its ability to discover Web services is company-centric. It is difficult to query UDDI to determine what Web services are exposed by a particular server. For this type of query, you need a more decentralized mechanism for locating Web services.

DISCO allows you to discover the Web services running on a particular computer by providing a browse paradigm for locating a particular Web service. In some respects, DISCO is similar to the hyperlink navigation popularized by HTML. You can advertise a top-level index that contains references to specific Web services or to other DISCO files.

Because DISCO supports a browse paradigm, it is well suited to development environments. And because DISCO does not require you to formally register with UDDI, you can quickly expose your Web services to other developers. Developers can browse your development server to discover the URL of a particular Web service that they need to code against.

Visual Studio .NET and DISCO

By default, the Visual Studio .NET Add Web Reference Wizard uses DISCO files to locate Web services. However, you will probably want something other than a DISCO file to serve as the default page of your Web server.

Even if the Web site hosts only Web services, the default page will probably contain HTML documentation. Therefore, during the installation of Visual Studio .NET, a *link* HTML tag is placed within the default page of the Web server. Here is an example:

```
<HTML>
<HEAD>
<link type='text/xml' rel='alternate' href='Default.vsdisco'/>
</HEAD>
<BODY>
Welcome to my Web site!
</BODY>
</HTML>
```

If the default page of the Web site is an XML document, you can add an *xml-stylesheet* processing instruction. Here is an example:

```
<?xml version="1.0" ?>
<?xml-stylesheet type="text/xml" alternate="yes" href="Default.disco" ?>
<MyXmlDocument>Test</MyXmlDocument>
```

For the most part, Visual Studio .NET automatically creates the necessary DISCO files for you. During installation, Visual Studio .NET will automatically create a DISCO file for the default Web server.

Here is an example of the DISCO file created for a Web service project:

```
<?xml version="1.0" ?>
<dynamicDiscovery xmlns="urn:schemas-dynamicdiscovery:disco.2000-03-17">
<exclude path="_vti_cnf" />
<exclude path="_vti_pvt" />
<exclude path="_vti_log" />
<exclude path="_vti_script" />
<exclude path="_vti_txt" />
</dynamicDiscovery>
```

The DISCO file named Default.vsdisco is placed in the root directory of the Web server. All files hosted on Microsoft Internet Information Server (IIS) that contain the .vsdisco file extension will be handled by *DiscoveryRequestHandler* within ASP.NET. However, *DiscoveryRequestHandler* is disabled by default. To enable discovery support within your ASP.NET application, add an entry similar to the one below to the *httpHandlers* section of your web.config file. You can also apply the setting machine-wide by editing your machine.config file.

```
<httpHandlers>
  <add verb="*" path="*.vsdisco"
  type="System.Web.Services.Discovery.DiscoveryRequestHandler,
  System.Web.Services, Version=1.0.3300.0, Culture=neutral,
  PublicKeyToken=b03f5f7f11d50a3a" validate="false"/>
</httpHandlers>
```

DISCO files that contain the *dynamicDiscovery* element will prompt the ASP.NET ISAPI filter to search the immediate directory for all files containing an .asmx extension and to search all subdirectories for all files with a .vsdisco extension. Any path listed with an *exclude* element will be ignored.

For example, suppose the dynamic discovery file was generated on a server named DEVELOPMENT. The server will host the Invoice Web service in a subdirectory by the same name. In this case, the resulting DISCO file is as follows:

```
<?xml version="1.0" encoding="utf-8"?>
<discovery xmlns="http://schemas.xmlsoap.org/disco/">
  <discoveryRef ref="http://DEVELOPMENT/Invoice/Invoice.vsdisco" />
</discovery>
```

The DISCO document contains a *discoveryRef* element for each DISCO file it finds within its subdirectories. This element is similar in purpose to an HTML HREF. The client can follow the link to drill down further.

When Visual Studio .NET creates a Web services project, it creates a DISCO file. This file is given the same name as the project and a .vsdisco extension. The following are the contents of the Invoice.vsdisco file:

```
<?xml version="1.0" ?>
<dynamicDiscovery xmlns="urn:schemas-dynamicdiscovery:disco.2000-03-17">
<exclude path="_vti_cnf" />
<exclude path="_vti_pvt" />
<exclude path="_vti_log" />
<exclude path="_vti_script" />
<exclude path="_vti_txt" />
<exclude path="Web References" />
</dynamicDiscovery>
```

The contents of the Invoice.vsdisco file are similar to those of the Default.vsdisco file except that they exclude the Web References directory. When a client accesses the file, this DISCO file is dynamically generated:

```
<?xml version="1.0" encoding="utf-8"?>
<discovery xmlns="http://schemas.xmlsoap.org/disco/">
  <contractRef ref="http://DEVELOPMENT/Invoice/Invoice.asmx?wsdl"
  docRef="http://DEVELOPMENT/Invoice/Invoice.asmx"
  xmlns="http://schemas.xmlsoap.org/disco/scl/" />
</discovery>
```

The resulting DISCO document contains a single *contractRef* element that contains a reference to the WSDL document and the HTML documentation for the Web service.

Because it is expensive to perform a directory scan each time a dynamically generated DISCO file is accessed, you can opt to expose a static DISCO file instead. The easiest way to create a static DISCO file is to replace the file with the results of the dynamically generated DISCO file. For example, you might do this on heavily accessed development servers or before the Web service is deployed to production.

Summary

The two primary methods of publishing a Web service so that it can be discovered by others are UDDI and DISCO. UDDI is a central, highly structured directory service, and DISCO offers a free-form, browser-style discovery mechanism.

UDDI is a central repository for publishing technical specifications and company information, including services a company exposes over the Internet.

Data published to UDDI includes information about the company as well as references to technical specifications.

UDDI is composed of registries and registrars. A company publishes its information to a single public registry via a SOAP-based API. The registry is then responsible for replicating the information to its peer registries. A company can also use an HTML interface provided by a registrar to manage its information within the UDDI directory.

The four primary datatypes are *tModel, businessEntity, businessService,* and *bindingTemplate.* UDDI provides an API for publishing and locating instances of these datatypes.

A *tModel* serves a dual purpose. First, you can use it to reference a technical specification such as a WSDL document, a transport protocol, or a workflow specification. Second, a *tModel* can reference a particular taxonomy used to categorize the information published within the directory.

A *businessEntity* is usually a company or a division within a company. It contains information such as the company address and contact information. It also contains information that categorizes the company, such as the particular industry.

A *businessService* is a collection of related services that a company exposes. A *businessService* is composed of a collection of *bindingTemplate* objects. A *bindingTemplate* describes a particular service, including the service's endpoint and the technical specifications the service supports.

Microsoft provides the UDDI SDK to facilitate developing UDDI-aware applications. The SDK contains a .NET object model to simplify interacting with a UDDI registry. It also contains the UDDI Developer Edition, a standalone registry that is installed locally and that fully supports the UDDI API.

DISCO is a lightweight mechanism for discovering Web services. It is used primarily for development by the Visual Studio .NET IDE. Visual Studio .NET automatically creates the necessary DISCO files. The DISCO file for a particular server is created at installation time; the DISCO file for a particular Web service is created along with the Visual Studio .NET project in which it is contained.

10

Building Secure Web Services

By nature, many Web services reside in the most hostile of environments—the Internet. For this reason, your Web services must employ appropriate security technologies. You can use an approach known as *threat modeling* to determine which parts of your application are most at risk and what tools and techniques you should employ to mitigate the threats.

In this chapter, I explain threat modeling in detail and how it applies to building secure Web services. I then discuss security technologies provided by Microsoft Internet Information Services (IIS) 5 and 6, and I also discuss important XML-based security technologies such as XML Signatures and XML Encryption and how the Microsoft .NET Framework supports them. Finally I look at common security mistakes people make when building Web services and how you can avoid making errors that lead to insecure Web services.

An Introduction to Threat Modeling

You probably want to get right to the meat of how to build secure systems. But unfortunately, we need to first discuss the design phase because when software is designed in random fashion, security is often a victim of the chaos. One way to provide structure during the design phase is to create a *threat model*.

The principle behind threat modeling is that you cannot build secure systems unless you understand the threats to the application. The good news is that threat modeling is simple and enjoyable. As a bonus, it can form the basis of the security section of the design specifications! In my experience, services built with the aid of a threat model tend to have better-designed security features and thus more secure systems. So stick with me for a short while—it will be worth the effort.

It is important that you spend time doing threat modeling because it is cheaper to find a security design bug at the design stage and remedy it before coding starts. The threat modeling process has the following three main phases:

1. Brainstorming threats

2. Choosing techniques to mitigate the threats

3. Choosing appropriate technologies to apply the techniques

Let's look at each part of this process in turn.

Brainstorming Threats

A brainstorming meeting involves setting aside two or three hours for the development team to discuss areas of potential vulnerability. During the meeting, have someone draw up the proposed architecture on a whiteboard. Make sure the diagram covers all critical aspects of the Web service, including:

■   Data storage technologies (file storage, SQL databases, XML files, and registry)

■   Interprocess communication techniques (including RPC, .NET Remoting, and sockets)

■   User input techniques (SOAP arguments and HTTP messages)

■   Nonpersistent data (such as on-the-wire data)

Next you look at how each of the core components can be compromised. One method is to use the STRIDE threat modeling technique.

Employing the STRIDE Threat Model

Before you build your systems, it is often useful to ask questions such as the following:

■   How can an attacker hijack the online shopping cart?

■   What would be the impact of an attacker denying valid users access to the service?

■   How could an attacker view or change the data traveling from the service to the consumer?

One way to make sure you ask all the important questions is to use threat categories. In this case, we will use the STRIDE threat model. STRIDE is an acronym derived from the following six threat categories:

- **Spoofing identity**   Identity spoofing often means illegally accessing and then using another user's authentication information, such as username and password.

- **Tampering with data**   Data tampering involves malicious modification of data. Examples include making unauthorized changes to persistent data, such as that held in a database, and altering data as it flows between two computers over an open network such as the Internet.

- **Repudiation**   Repudiation occurs when users deny performing actions without other parties having any way to prove otherwise—for example, a user performing an illegal operation in a system that lacks the ability to trace the prohibited operation. Nonrepudiation is the ability of a system to counter repudiation threats. For example, if a user purchases an item, he might have to sign for the item upon receipt. The vendor can then use the signed receipt as evidence that the user received the package. As you can imagine, nonrepudiation is extremely important for e-commerce. The simplest way to think about repudiation is to utter the words "It wasn't me!"

- **Information disclosure**   Information disclosure threats involve exposure of information to individuals who are not supposed to have access to it—for example, a user being able to read a file for which she was not granted access or an intruder's ability to read data in transit between two computers.

- **Denial of service**   Denial of service (DoS) attacks deny service to valid users—for example, by making a Web server temporarily unavailable or unusable. You must protect against certain types of DoS threats simply to improve system availability and reliability.

- **Elevation of privilege**   In this type of threat, an unprivileged user gains privileged access and thereby has sufficient access to compromise or destroy the entire system. Elevation of privilege threats include situations in which an attacker has effectively penetrated all system defenses and has become part of the trusted system itself—a dangerous situation indeed.

If you look back at the three example questions noted earlier, you will notice that the first question concerns a data-tampering threat (T), the second one concerns a DoS threat (D), and the third concerns an information disclosure threat and a tampering threat (I and T).

The simplest way, by far, to apply the STRIDE model to your application is to consider how each type of threat will affect each solution component and each component's connections or relationships with other solution components. Essentially, you look at each part of the application and determine whether any S, T, R, I, D, or E threats exist for that component or process. Most parts will have numerous threats—be sure to record all of them.

Choosing Techniques to Mitigate the Threats

The next step is to determine appropriate mitigation techniques. Table 10-1 outlines some techniques and technologies for mitigating threats in the STRIDE categories.

Table 10-1 Threat Mitigation Techniques

Threat Type	Mitigation Technique
Spoofing identity	Authenticate principals using technologies such as basic authentication, digest authentication, NTLM authentication, Kerberos authentication, X.509 certificates, .NET Passport authentication, and forms-based authentication. Remember that sometimes you need to authenticate the client, and at other times you need to authenticate the server.
	You can also prove that data came from a principal by signing and verifying digital signatures, such as those employed by XMLDSIG and PKCS #7. These are both explained later in this chapter.
	Do not store secret data insecurely, especially authentication data such as passwords and PINs.
Tampering with data	Protect data with appropriate Access Control Lists (ACLs) or permissions. Determine whether data has been tampered with using hashes or message authentication codes. Protect on-the-wire data using SSL/TLS or IPSec.
Repudiation	Protection from repudiation often involves strong authentication and signed data, as well as extensive and secure logging or auditing.

Table 10-1   Threat Mitigation Techniques   *(continued)*

Threat Type	Mitigation Technique
Information disclosure	Data can be protected from prying eyes using appropriate ACLs and permissions. Also, consider that if you do not store the data in the first place, the data cannot be disclosed. Privacy techniques such as encryption can help if the keys used to encrypt and decrypt the data are also protected from disclosure threats. SSL/TLS and IPSec provide on-the-wire secrecy, and Encrypting File System (EFS) provides privacy for files and directories.
Denial of service	DoS threats are difficult to defend against because it is difficult to tell whether a busy server is simply busy or is under attack. If you throttle user requests, you might lock out access to valid users. Some simple defenses include limiting what nonauthenticated users can do. For example, you might allocate 10 percent of resources for anonymous users and 90 percent for validated users. (Resources include cache data, CPU time, disk space, network bandwidth, and connections to databases.)
	Some of these solutions are beyond your direct control in an application and might include firewalls and packet-filtering routers.
Elevation of privilege	Do not require privileges or permissions you do not need. That way, if your code has a security flaw and the attacker can execute malicious code or cause an insecure event to occur, he cannot cause much damage because the permissions are suppressed.

A Web Service Example

If all of this makes little sense to you so far, do not worry. An example will help. Let's look at a simple scenario in which a Web service client communicates with a Web service, which in turn communicates with a database and returns content to the client, as depicted in Figure 10-1. We will assume that the client is a user, not a peer process.

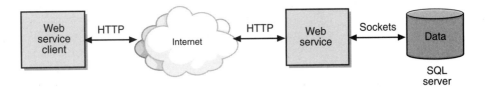

Figure 10-1   A sample Web service scenario.

This generic scenario applies to many Web services. Table 10-2 lists some of the threats to the system and how they can be mitigated.

Table 10-2   Threats to Web Services and Appropriate Mitigation Techniques

Target	ID	Threat Types	Description	Mitigation Techniques
Web service	1	S	Attacker knocks out Web service using distributed DoS attack and places his own rogue Web service on the Internet. The client application does not know that it is communicating with a rogue.	Use a client-initiated SSL/TLS connection to authenticate the server.
On-the-wire data from client to service	2	T and I	Attacker views or modifies data en route from the client to the server and vice versa.	Use SSL/TLS or IPSec to encrypt data as it travels to and from the Web service.
On-the-wire data from client to service	3	E	Attacker views password data en route from the client to the server; if the user is an administrator, the attacker can use the username and password.	Use an authentication mechanism that does not pass the password in the clear across the wire, or use SSL/TLS or IPSec to protect the channel.
Web Service	4	D	Attacker floods the Web service with thousands of bogus requests and slows down the Web service.	Use a firewall to restrict what data is allowable. Build logic that limits how much data can be sent by one user or IP address. Limiting by IP address can be problematic, however, because many legitimate users use ISPs that have a limited number of IP addresses, so numerous requests might appear to come from the same IP address when they are in fact coming from users behind a proxy server.

Table 10-2   Threats to Web Services and Appropriate Mitigation Techniques

Target	ID	Threat Types	Description	Mitigation Techniques
SQL Server data	5	T and I	Attacker accesses data in SQL Server directly rather than via the Web service.	Limit what is allowable in data used to construct SQL queries.
SQL Server	6	S, T, R, I, D, and E	Attacker uses the *xp_cmdshell* extended stored procedure built into SQL Server to call malicious code at the SQL database. This command can call any command at the server.	Limit what is allowable in data used to construct SQL queries. Remove unused extended stored procedures such as *xp_cmdshell*. Do not connect to SQL Server as the sysadmin account (sa) because this account can perform any SQL Server task, including calling *xm_cmdshell*.

This scenario should help you understand the process for determining what techniques and technologies to employ to build secure solutions. This approach is much better than simply sprinkling "magic security pixie dust" on an application and hoping that the application will be secure from attack.

Now let's turn our attention to the panoply of security technologies available to developers who build Web services on the Windows platform.

> **More Info**   You can learn more about threat analysis and building secure systems in *Writing Secure Code* by Michael Howard and David LeBlanc (Microsoft Press, 2001).

Web Service Security Technologies

The third phase of the threat modeling process involves choosing appropriate technologies to apply the threat mitigation techniques you have chosen. Before I describe specific technologies, let's take a look at what the current Web service infrastructure provides in the way of security features.

As of this writing, the primary communication protocol used by Web services, SOAP, does not define security protocols; it relies on the Web server, and potentially the client application, to provide those services. The main reason for this is that SOAP is transport independent; Web services use HTTP as a transport, but other SOAP-based services might use SMTP or other technologies as a transport. This can be problematic if your threat model determines that the data must be secure as it travels from the client to all back-end servers.

Let's look at an example, which is depicted in Figure 10-2. The client communicates with a Web service, and the service determines that it will protect the client data using SSL or TLS as the data moves between the client and the Web service. It will then send the client data to a back-end service that uses sockets as a transport.

Figure 10-2   A scenario using SSL or TLS to protect client and server data.

Can you see where the problem is? The protection provided by SSL/TLS applies only to the link between the client and the server, not to the link between the server and the back-end application server. In many instances, this might not be an issue. However, if you determine in your threat modeling that information disclosure threats exist as data leaves the Web service and the back-end server, SSL/TLS will not work. Even if the data is reprotected using SSL/TLS between the Web service and application server, it will remain in cleartext for a nonzero amount of time at the Web service and might be viewed by a user at the server. (Of course, you should trust the people administering the Web service!) Once again, this might be a risk you are willing to live with, but your decision should be based solely on your threat modeling.

Now that you have a basic understanding of the security features that the current Web service infrastructure provides, let's look at some ways to apply security technologies appropriately.

Web Services Authentication

Authentication is the ability to prove that an *entity*—for example, a user or a computer—is who it claims to be. You can verify this claim by having the entity, also called a *principal*, provide credentials. Credentials often take the form of a username and a password. Note that some authentication protocols are more secure than others—you can be more certain that the credential really came from the correct user and was not replayed by an attacker. A Web service running on top of IIS has a number of authentication protocols available to it, most notably

■   Anonymous authentication

■   Basic authentication

■   Digest authentication

■   Windows authentication

■   Certificate-based authentication

■   Forms-based authentication

■   .NET Passport authentication

Let's look at each in detail.

Anonymous Authentication

Anonymous authentication is just that—anonymous. No authentication takes place. This is the authentication mechanism you would use for public data. You do not need to update or add any code to your SOAP client because no authentication is taking place.

Basic Authentication

Basic authentication is probably the most common form of authentication on the Internet because of its simplicity. It is provided by every browser on every platform. It is also insecure because the username and password are sent on every request from the client to the server in the clear—the data is not encrypted. This means that you must use some form of channel encryption to protect the username and password from disclosure to malicious users. Of course, you technically do not have to encrypt the channel if you do not care whether the username and password are disclosed. And, frankly, this might be fine if your Web service serves nonconfidential data such as stock information or news headlines. There is a difference between using authentication as a means to protect access to data and using authentication as a means to identify users to give them the personalized content they require. Once again, you should use threat modeling to determine whether basic authentication is good enough for your application.

In IIS 5 and 6, accounts used for basic authentication must be valid Windows accounts. However, when basic authentication is used by ASP.NET or, by inference, is used by a Web service written using ASP.NET, you can use a database lookup to determine whether the credentials are correct. You can set basic authentication within the IIS administration tool.

If you use basic, digest, or Windows authentication, you can set the username and password in a SOAP client, as shown in the following VBScript code:

```
Set sc = CreateObject("MSSoap.SoapClient")
sc.mssoapinit("http://www.fabrikam.com/webservice/service.asmx?wsdl")
sc.ConnectorProperty("AuthName") = "username"
sc.ConnectorProperty("AuthPassword") = "password"
Status = sc.GetShippingStatus("10001")
```

If you wrote your client-side application using C++ and the ATL SOAP classes, you can set the username and password in the *CAtlHttpClient:: AddAuthObj* method. If your client code is written in C# or another managed language, such as Visual Basic .NET, you can use code such as the following to create an authenticated connection to the Web service. (This code will work for basic, digest, and Windows authentication.)

```
using System;
using System.Net;
using System.Web.Services.Protocols;

ClientApp.localhost.Service s = new ClientApp.localhost.Service();
s.Credentials = new NetworkCredential(username, password, domain);
string shipped = s.GetShippingStatus("10001");
```

In the overall scheme of things, basic authentication is incredibly weak, especially when SSL/TLS is not employed.

Digest Authentication

Like basic authentication, digest authentication is an Internet standard; both are described in RFC 2617 at *http://www.ietf.org/rfc/rfc2617.txt*. However, unlike basic authentication, digest authentication is not common because the only browsers that support digest authentication are Internet Explorer 5 and later. Digest authentication does not transfer the user's password in the clear; instead, a hash, or digest, of the password and data provided by the server is used to authenticate the user. Digest authentication is certainly a little more secure than basic authentication, and it has the added advantage that you do not need to use SSL to hide the user's password. But as I said, it is only a little more secure. Note also that digest authentication works in IIS 5 and 6 only if Active Directory is installed because Active Directory can be configured to store an encrypted plaintext copy of the user's password, which is required by digest authentication.

As with basic authentication, you can use the IIS administration tool to configure the Web server to require digest authentication.

Windows Authentication

As the name implies, Windows authentication uses authentication mechanisms built into Windows. From Windows 2000 on, this means NTLM and Kerberos. Kerberos authentication is applicable only when Active Directory is employed. The main downside to Windows authentication is that it does not work well across the Internet, but it is an exceptional intranet solution because it can use the user's logon information directly, without necessarily prompting the user to enter a username and password. Also, the password is never sent across the wire in plaintext.

Windows authentication can be configured like any other protocol, but in the case of ASP.NET Web services, you can opt for Windows authentication by adding the following code to the web.config file:

```
<authentication mode = "Windows">
</authentication>
```

You can also force ASP.NET to impersonate the calling user with the following web.config configuration entry:

```
<system.web>
  <identity impersonate="true" />
</system.web>
```

You can then get the name of the calling user by using the following code in your Web service:

```
using System.Security.Principal;
WindowsIdentity wi = WindowsIdentity.GetCurrent();
string name = wi.Name;
```

Certificate-Based Authentication

Certificates use large private keys rather than passwords to determine the principal's identity. Before I delve into how and why you would use certificates, let's take a quick detour through the technology behind certificates. Unlike symmetric key encryption, which uses a single key to encrypt and decrypt data, certificates use asymmetric encryption, also called public key encryption. When a certificate is created, two large keys are created, a private key and a public key. The former, as the name implies, is private and should be protected. The latter, the public key, can be made public and is embedded in the certificate, which contains information about the private key owner.

Public key cryptography also has the following important attributes:

- Data encrypted with the public key can be decrypted only using the private key.

- Data encrypted with the private key can be decrypted only using the public key.

If you have a private key, you can send authenticated messages to others. In other words, the recipient can prove that you sent the data. This is because you encrypt using the private key, which only you own; it is private, and only the public key can decrypt the message. The public key is in your certificate, which includes details about you, so you must have sent the data.

The process of encrypting using a private key is also called *signing*. If you have someone else's public key, you can send that person encrypted messages. Actually, the process of signing is a little more complex than that—the data itself is not signed, but a hash of the data is signed, for the sake of speed.

Most certificates today use a cryptographic algorithm called RSA, the U.S. patent for which expired in September 2000.

> **Note**   Some trivia: The RSA algorithm uses large prime numbers when creating its keys. The now-expired patent number for RSA is 4,405,829. It is a prime number!

When you use SSL/TLS, the session between the client and server is protected from prying eyes using symmetric encryption. However, the server is also authenticated. When you visit the Barnes & Noble bookstore on line at *http://www.bn.com* and you go to check out, an SSL/TLS session is established. During the handshake, the name of the Web site you are browsing is compared with the name in the certificate to determine whether the server can correctly decrypt random data provided by the client after it is encrypted with the site's public key from the certificate. If the site can decrypt the blob, the site must have the protected private key associated with the public key in the certificate. Also, the date validity is verified in the certificate. If all these steps succeed, the server is authenticated and the user knows she is communicating with the real Barnes & Noble Web site, not an imposter.

The good news about SSL/TLS is that it also supports an optional client authentication process. In this case, the server tells the client application to provide a certificate and to decrypt a blob that was encrypted using the public key in the certificate. After some other (we can hope successful) checks, the client is also authenticated. SSL/TLS client authentication is an optional step in the SSL/TLS connection process and is in fact rarely used except in very secure environments. In exceptionally secure environments, certificates and private keys can be stored on smart cards.

You can force the SOAP client to use a specific client certificate by using the following construct when you use the Microsoft SOAP Toolkit:

```
sc.ConnectorProperty("SSLClientCertificateName") = "mike@fabrikam.com"
```

You should specify the common name (CN) part of the certificate's subject name. Note that if you have more than one certificate with the same subject common name, the first will be chosen.

If your client code is written using the Visual Studio Web Reference Proxy code (which is generated after you make a Web reference), you can set the client certificate using the service's *ClientCertificate* collection. Note that you currently cannot access a certificate in a CryptoAPI (CAPI) store in the same fashion that the SOAP Toolkit code can; you must use a certificate file.

Forms-Based Authentication

Forms-based authentication is not an industry-standard way of authenticating users, but the method is very popular. Forms-based authentication generally refers to a system in which unauthenticated requests are redirected to an HTML form using HTTP redirection. The user provides credentials (username and password) and submits the form. If the application authenticates the request by performing a database or XML file lookup, the user is granted access.

Forms-based authentication uses HTML pages, so it is not supported by Web services because Web services have no UI. However, ASP.NET does support forms-based authentication.

.NET Passport Authentication

.NET Passport is a centralized authentication service provided by Microsoft that offers a single sign-on and profile services for member sites. This benefits the user because she no longer has to log on to access new protected resources or sites. If you want your site to be compatible with Passport authentication and authorization, this is the provider you should use. For more information, see the Passport documentation at *http://www.passport.com/business*.

Because Passport authentication uses cookies, it is not currently supported by Web services. However, this will change. ASP.NET does support Passport authentication, as does IIS 6.

A full explanation of the IIS 5 authentication techniques is available in *Designing Secure Web-Based Applications for Microsoft Windows 2000* by Michael Howard (Microsoft Press, 2000).

Web Services Authorization

Once your application identifies a principal by using an authentication mechanism, it needs to determine whether the user has access to the various resources your service protects and can call specific functions. Windows 2000 and later offer numerous ways to authorize access to resources, with the most prolific and important being ACLs.

Windows NT and later protect securable resources (such as files) from unauthorized access by employing discretionary access control, which is implemented through discretionary access control lists (usually abbreviated as ACLs rather than DACLs). An ACL is composed of a series of access control entries (ACEs). Each ACE lists a principal and contains information about the principal and the operations that the principal can perform on the resource. For example, some people might be granted read access and others might have full control.

ACLs are quite literally your application's last backstop against an attack, with the possible exception of good encryption and key management. If an attacker can access a resource, her job is done. Therefore, it is incredibly important that you have appropriate ACLs on the resources you protect. For example, should all users (also called Everyone) have full access to a sensitive file? Probably not, but certain users might.

The real beauty of ACLs is that they are always enforced the same way regardless of the access mechanism. So, if for some reason an attacker can bypass your service and hence circumvent application-level authorization logic and access a resource directly, the authorization policy in the resource's ACLs will still be enforced.

A little higher up the application layer is authorization in ASP.NET and within your application, or within the database permissions (assuming you are using a database).

ASP.NET offers a rich smorgasbord of authorization techniques; deploying such policies is as simple as setting an XML property. For example, you can restrict access to a portion of your Web service so that anonymous users are disallowed by adding the following to the web.config file:

```
<authorization>
  <deny users="?" />
</authorization>
```

In this case, *?* means anonymous users and *** means all users. You can also allow specific users using *<allow users="name" />*, where *name* is one or more names separated by commas.

Web Services Privacy and Integrity

When you think about privacy and the integrity of SOAP data, remember that there are two aspects to both technologies. The first aspect is securing the channel between the client and the Web service, and the second is securing the SOAP payload or data within the payload—not only as it travels from the client to the Web service and vice versa, but also when the data is persisted to some form of persistent data storage. The former scenario is well understood and is easily handled with no code modification by using SSL/TLS or IPSec. Because these protocols are below the application layer (the layer in which your service resides), they are completely transparent. A simple switch in the Web server, and *voila!*—you have a connection protected with SSL/TLS.

Presently, there is no standard way to encrypt SOAP messages or to provide for the integrity of the payload data. This is especially true if you want to allow any client to connect to your service, in which case you must support a standard way to achieve these goals. These standards are currently being designed. You can read more about future directions in the section titled "Future Web Service Security Technologies" later in this chapter.

So what happens if you want to roll your own encryption or integrity mechanism? You can do this if you have control over the client code and the server code because you can determine what the data formats will look like. You can find a very simple example of doing this with SOAP extensions at the MSDN site (*http://msdn.microsoft.com/library/en-us/dnaspnet/html/asp09272001.asp*). However, as of this writing, the code uses a hard-coded key to encrypt and decrypt the data using Data Encryption Standard (DES). If you plan to use the code in your SOAP application, you should store the key elsewhere on the computer, such as in the registry or in a protected XML configuration file (*protected* meaning that the file is not easily accessible through the Web server and is protected using good ACLs) and not in the source code itself. When you design systems using custom encryption, key management is a very hard problem to solve. One way around this is to use SSL/TLS to transfer the key from the server to the client. (Do not let the client determine the key—an attacker might choose a weak key!) Then perform communication in the open but encrypt the appropriate SOAP data.

You can determine whether a SOAP method is invoked over a channel secured using SSL/TLS by using the following code:

```
if (HttpContext.Current.Request.IsSecureConnection) {
    // Connection is using SSL/TLS.
} else {
    // Connection is not using SSL/TLS.
}
```

This code will not detect whether IPSec is used to protect the channel between the client and server. In fact, there is presently no way to determine this easily from the managed environment.

While we are on the subject of keys, if you need to generate good-quality random data, such as that used to create an encryption key, do not use the *Random* class—it is highly predictable. Instead, use code such as this, which creates 32 bytes of highly random data:

```
using System.Security.Cryptography;
byte[] b = new byte[32];
new RNGCryptoServiceProvider().GetBytes(b);
```

Security Technologies in the .NET Framework

The .NET Framework offers support for encrypting and signing data, most notably encrypting any data stream and signing any data stream, with special support for XML data. The latter is provided through support for the World Wide Web Consortium (W3C) standard XMLDSIG.

Once you have agreed on a key to use to encrypt and decrypt data between the two hosts, you can simply encrypt and decrypt using code such as the following, which uses the RC2 symmetric cipher:

```
static string Encrypt(string plaintext, byte [] key, byte [] IV) {
    try {
        MemoryStream ms = new MemoryStream();
        RC2 rc2 = new RC2CryptoServiceProvider();
        CryptoStream s = new CryptoStream(ms,
            rc2.CreateEncryptor(key, IV),
            CryptoStreamMode.Write);
        byte [] p = Encoding.UTF8.GetBytes(plaintext.ToCharArray());
        s.Write(p,0,p.Length);
        s.FlushFinalBlock();

        return Convert.ToBase64String(ms.ToArray());
    } catch(Exception) {
        return null;
    }
}

static string Decrypt(string ciphertext, byte [] key, byte [] IV) {
    try {
        MemoryStream ms = new MemoryStream();
        RC2 rc2 = new RC2CryptoServiceProvider();
        CryptoStream s = new CryptoStream(ms,
            rc2.CreateDecryptor(key, IV),
            CryptoStreamMode.Write);
        byte [] c = Convert.FromBase64String(ciphertext);
        s.Write(c, 0, c.Length);
        s.FlushFinalBlock();

        return Encoding.UTF8.GetString(ms.GetBuffer());
    } catch(Exception) {
        return null;
    }
}
```

So, rather than simply sending the Web method data across the wire as plaintext, you can encrypt the data and pass it as a Base64-encoded string or send sensitive data back from the server in the same way. Hence, what might be open to "inspection," such as the following SOAP:

```
<?xml version="1.0" encoding="utf-8"?>
<soap:Envelope xmlns:xsi="http://www.w3c.org/2001/XMLSchema-instance"
xmlns:xsd="http://www.w3c.org/2001/XMLSchema"
xmlns:soap="http://schemas.xmlsoap.org/soap/envelope/">
  <soap:Body>
    <GetMeetingResponse xmlns="http://www.fabrikam.com/soap">
      <GetMeetingResult>
        Meet at Midnight!
      </GetMeetingResult>
    </GetMeetingResponse>
  </soap:Body>
</soap:Envelope>
```

becomes this, which is more secure:

```
<?xml version="1.0" encoding="utf-8"?>
<soap:Envelope xmlns:xsi="http://www.w3.org/2001/XMLSchema-instance"
xmlns:xsd="http://www.w3.org/2001/XMLSchema"
xmlns:soap="http://schemas.xmlsoap.org/soap/envelope/">
  <soap:Body>
    <GetMeetingResponse xmlns="http://www.fabrikam.com/soap">
      <GetMeetingResult>
        Ls1O+R09UUMziJdQ1Q4P0POzaFxqGHS=
      </GetMeetingResult>
    </GetMeetingResponse>
  </soap:Body>
</soap:Envelope>
```

You achieve this result by simply calling the encryption functions on method exit. For example, this code snippet

```
[WebMethod]
Public string GetMeeting() {
    ...
    return meetingdata;
}
```

becomes

```
[WebMethod]
Public string GetMeeting() {
    ...
    return Encrypt(meetingdata, key, IV);
}
```

Notice that it is assumed that the key and initialization vector values have already been negotiated by the two parties.

What Is an IV?

An initialization vector (IV) is a random number, usually with the same number of bits as the encryption algorithm block size, that is used as a starting point to encrypt a set of data.

If IVs are not used, two identical ciphertext messages are generated when two identical plaintext messages are encrypted with the same key. However, if each plaintext message is encrypted with a different IV, the ciphertext messages generated are completely different.

For better security, you should encrypt each message with a different IV, particularly when the messages contain a large amount of duplication. Your application is responsible for transmitting the IV along with the encrypted message. There is no need to encrypt an IV.

The problem with this code is that it requires both ends to have custom code, which is fine if you control the client and the service but not if you want anyone to be able to connect to your service from any client. This brings us to what is on the horizon for Web service security.

Future Web Service Security Technologies

In October 2001, Microsoft announced the Global XML Web Services Architecture (GXA), which builds on current Web service protocols such as SOAP, WSDL, and UDDI and adds additional building blocks, including security called WS-Security.

WS-Security provides a security language for Web services. It describes enhancements to SOAP messaging to provide three capabilities: credential exchange, message integrity, and message confidentiality. You can use these three mechanisms independently or in combination to accommodate a wide variety of authentication and cryptographic technologies.

The full specification is available at *http://msdn.microsoft.com/ws/2001/10/Security*.

Common Security Mistakes

To build a Web service that can withstand attack, you cannot simply scatter security features here and there. As I stated earlier, you must design your application with security in mind.

Here are the three most serious security mistakes that developers (including Web service developers) make:

■   Storing secret data insecurely

■   Connecting to SQL Server incorrectly

■   Building insecure SQL strings

While the .NET common language runtime and the .NET Framework help mitigate many current security threats, such as buffer overruns, they cannot counter bad design decisions. (In fact, all three types of mistakes apply to all programming environments and operating systems.)

Let's look at each type of mistake in detail.

Mistake #1: Storing Secret Data Insecurely

Storing secret data securely is impossible in software—you can only make it more difficult for an attacker to get at your data. Secure data storage is somewhat easier at the server because the attacker does not have physical access to your software. However, storing secrets in client code is truly impossible. This makes things difficult if you think you can perform a secret handshake or perform a secret transaction based on a secret embedded in your client application. Attackers can easily reverse-engineer the client application to determine the secret.

Secret data includes private or personal data such as passwords, encryption keys, identification numbers, sales figures, and credit card numbers. When you store data, you should consider what the ramifications would be to you, your business, and your clients if the data were exposed to unscrupulous users (I in the STRIDE model) or tampered with by an attacker (T). (If you are having problems coming to grips with these issues, imagine that it is your personal data being stored!)

Information disclosure threats are easy to take care of—you simply do not store the data in the first place. I'm quite serious: in some situations, it is quite valid to give users the option of having you store the data for them, but let it be an opt-in situation. Users might get added ease of use when you store the data for them, but they might blame you if the data is not adequately protected against attackers.

In addition, some data does not require storage; it is simply used to validate that the user knows the data. One example is a password—you can determine whether a user knows a password without storing the password itself. You do this by hashing the data and storing only the hash, and then when the user provides the password, your code hashes the data and compares the hashes. If the two are the same, the user knows the password.

The following sample code shows how you can gather a password from a user and compare it to another hash:

```
public bool ComparePasswordHash(string password, byte[] hash) {
    SHA1Managed h = new SHA1Managed();
    UTF8Encoding e = new UTF8Encoding();
    byte[] p = e.GetBytes(password);

    h.ComputeHash(p);
    byte[] hr = h.Hash;

    bool same = true;
    for (int i =0; i < hr.Length; i++) {
        if (hr[i] != hash[i]) {
            same = false;
            break;
        }
    }

    return same;
}
```

But what if you have to use secret data such as a password? Where should you store it, and how can you secure it? One place you can store the data is in the web.config file; however, if an attacker can access the configuration file directly, he can read the data. The same applies to storing the data in an .aspx or .asmx file. Deployment issues aside, you should avoid storing sensitive data in any of these files; instead, store it outside the Web space. This might mean storing the data in the file system but outside the root of the Web file system space or storing it in a location not in the file system, such as the system registry.

Mistake #2: Connecting to SQL Server Incorrectly

Many developers incorrectly connect to SQL databases, including SQL Server, using the sysadmin account. They do this because testing is easier—everything works. Unfortunately, this might also mean that everything will work for attackers, too.

The SQL Server sysadmin account, sa, is the most capable and privileged account available to SQL Server. The account can do anything to a SQL Server database. If you must use SQL authentication (rather than Windows authentication), you should connect using an account that has only the permissions it requires in the SQL Server database and has no access to any other objects in the database.

Also, make sure the account has a very strong password.

Mistake #3: Building Insecure SQL Strings

Go on, admit it: you have constructed SQL strings like this:

```
string sql = "select * from table where name = '" + name + "'";
```

The variable name is provided by the user. The problem with this SQL string is that the attacker can piggyback SQL statements in the name variable.

Imagine the following input, where *name = "Blake"*, which builds this totally benign SQL statement:

```
select * from table
where name = 'Blake'
```

But what if an attacker enters *name = "Blake' delete from table where name = 'Lynne' --"*, which builds the following malicious statement?

```
select * from table
where name = 'Blake'
delete from table where name='Lynne' --'
```

This statement will return all the data in the table where the name is Blake, and then it will delete all the rows where the name is Lynne! Believe me, many attacks are more insidious than this. How can they happen? Because the SQL connection is made using the sysadmin account, which can do anything to the database, including delete any data. Note the use of the *' --'* sequence—it is a comment operator, which makes the attack much easier to pull off.

Now let's look at an example and some remedies.

An In-Depth Example

Now that we have looked at some best practices for building Web services and some common mistakes, let's look at an in-depth example. We will discuss a common insecure scenario, and then we will look at ways to secure the Web service.

The Insecure Version (Do Not Try This at Home!)

Look at the following C# code, and see if you can figure out the vulnerabilities:

```
[WebMethod(Description="Dangerous Shipping Status")]
public string GetShippingStatus(string Id) {
    string Status = "No";
    string sqlstring ="";
    try {
        SqlConnection sql= new SqlConnection(
            @"data source=localhost;" +
```

(continued)

```
                    "user id=sa;password=password;" +
                    "initial catalog=Shipping");
            sql.Open();

            sqlstring="SELECT HasShipped" +
                " FROM detail " +
                " WHERE ID='" + Id + "'";

            SqlCommand cmd = new SqlCommand(sqlstring,sql);
            if ((int)cmd.ExecuteScalar() != 0)
                Status = "Yes";

        } catch (SqlException se) {
            Status = sqlstring + " failed\n\r";
            foreach (SqlError e in se.Errors) {
                Status += e.Message + "\n\r";
            }
        } catch (Exception e) {
            Status = e.ToString();
        }

        return Status;
    }
```

Did you spot the bugs? OK, here they are. The first mistake is connecting to the SQL database as sa, the sysadmin account. You do not need such a high-powered account to simply query a table. A small slip-up, and sa can do anything it wants—it can delete or modify tables, even the master SQL Server table.

Next the sysadmin account has an easy-to-guess password. Third, the password is embedded in the Web service page. If an attacker accesses this page, she will know the connection details and know that SQL Server is on the Web service machine.

Perhaps the most dangerous issue is that the code is susceptible to SQL injection because the attacker can set the ID to a valid value followed by a series of dangerous SQL statements that are all executed. Also, if the SQL communication fails for some reason, such as an invalid SQL statement or a connection failure, the Web service will send a great deal of data back to the attacker, including the text that makes up the SQL statement. This is simply too much to tell an attacker. In fact, it is of little use to anyone other than a developer.

The code has one last bug—can you spot it? You probably will not because it is subtle. Imagine that the attacker sends a string to this code that causes an invalid SQL statement to be built. The SQL classes will throw an exception. However, the connection to SQL Server will not be closed. Eventually, it will be garbage-collected. But what if the attacker sends thousands of invalid requests? The connections to SQL Server will be exhausted, and valid connections will fail. Oops! This could be a wonderful DoS attack.

A Secure Solution

Now let's look at a version that has multiple layers of defense so that if one defensive mechanism fails, at least one other will protect the application and the data:

```
[SqlClientPermissionAttribute(SecurityAction.PermitOnly,
AllowBlankPassword=false)]
[RegistryPermissionAttribute(SecurityAction.PermitOnly,
Read=@"HKEY_LOCAL_MACHINE\SOFTWARE\Shipping")]

public string SafeGetShippingStatus(string Id) {

    SqlCommand cmd = null;

    string Status = "No";
    try {
        // Check for valid shipping ID.
        Regex r = new Regex(@"^\d{10}$");
        if (!r.Match(Id).Success)
            throw new Exception("Invalid ID");

        // Get connection string from registry.
        SqlConnection sqlConn= new SqlConnection(ConnectionString);

        // Add shipping ID parameter.
        string str="sp_HasShipped";
        cmd = new SqlCommand(str,sqlConn);
        cmd.CommandType = CommandType.StoredProcedure;
        cmd.Parameters.Add("@ID",Id);

        cmd.Connection.Open();

        if ((int)cmd.ExecuteScalar() != 0)
            Status = "Yes";

    } catch (Exception e) {
        if (HttpContext.Current.Request.UserHostAddress == "127.0.0.1")
            Status = e.ToString();
        else
            Status = "Error.";
    } finally {
        // Shut down connection--even on failure.
        if (cmd != null)
            cmd.Connection.Close();
    }

    return Status;
}
```

(continued)

```
// Get connection string.
internal string ConnectionString {
    get {
        return (string)Registry
                        .LocalMachine
                        .OpenSubKey(@"SOFTWARE\Shipping\")
                        .GetValue("ConnectionString");
    }
}
```

At first glance, the code looks more complex, but it really is not. Let me explain how this code is more secure than the first example. (I will hold off on explaining the attributes before the function call until the end of this section.)

First, this code mandates that a shipping identity number must be exactly 10 digits. This is indicated using the regular expression ^\d{10}$, which looks only for 10-digit numbers (\d{10}) from the start (^) to the end ($) of the input data. By declaring what is valid input and rejecting everything else, we have already made things safer—an attacker cannot simply append SQL statements to the shipping ID. (Regular expressions are exposed through *System.Text. RegularExpressions.*)

The code includes even more defenses. Notice that the *SqlConnection* object is built from a connection string from the registry. Also, take a look at the accessor function *ConnectionString*. In order to determine this string, an attacker would have to not only access the source code to the Web Service but also access the appropriate registry key.

The data in the registry key is the connection string:

```
data source=db007a;
user id=shipuser;
password=&ugv4!26dfA-+8;
initial catalog=Shipping
```

Notice that the SQL database is now on another computer. An attacker who compromises the Web service will not gain automatic access to the SQL data. Also, the code does not connect as sa; instead, it uses a specific account, shipuser, with a strong password. And this special account has only read and execute access to the appropriate SQL objects. If the connection from the Web service to the database is compromised, the attacker can run only a handful of stored procedures and query the appropriate tables; she cannot destroy the master database.

The SQL statement is not constructed using the insecure string concatenation technique; rather, the code uses parameterized queries to call a stored procedure. Calling the stored procedure is faster and more secure than using string concatenation because the database and table names are not exposed and stored procedures are optimized by the database engine.

Note that when an error does occur, the user (or attacker) is told nothing unless the request is local or on the same machine where the Web service resides. If you have physical access to the Web service computer, you "own" the computer anyway!

Next, the SQL connection is always closed down in the *finally* handler so that if an exception is raised in the *try/catch* body, the connection is gracefully cleaned up, thereby mitigating the DoS threat.

As promised, I will explain the two security attributes at the start of the function call. The first, *SQLClientPermissionAttribute*, allows the SQL Server .NET Data Provider to ensure that a user has a security level adequate to access a data source—in this case, the use of blank passwords is forbidden. If you inadvertently attempt to connect to SQL Server using this code and using a blank password, it will raise an exception. The second attribute, *RegistryPermissionAttribute*, limits which registry key or keys can be accessed and to what degree (read, write, and so on). In this case, only one specific key, which holds the connection string, can be read. If an attacker tries to make this code access other parts of the registry, it will fail.

All these mechanisms together lead to a very secure Web service. You should always use such mechanisms and layer them in such a way that your code is safe from attack.

Summary

In this chapter, I described some of the security features available to you as a Web service developer. The security features are not defined in the SOAP protocol itself because SOAP is not restricted to using HTTP; hence your application must leverage existing Web server security features. It is important that any features you choose are based on data gathered from a threat modeling exercise. For example, you can use basic, digest, or .NET Passport authentication to help mitigate client spoofing threats. SSL/TLS can mitigate server spoofing threats as well as data tampering and information disclosure threats by employing encryption and message authentication codes. SSL/TLS can also provide support for client authentication by using optional client authentication certificates. Work is in progress to provide security features for SOAP messages. This technology is called the Global XML Web Services Architecture.

Finally I outlined some very common mistakes made by Web application and Web service developers, most notably those which focus on trusting that user input is well-formed and benign. If you use input without first validating it for cleanliness, you have a serious security disaster waiting to happen. Ignore this advice at your peril!

11

Debugging Web Services

It is human nature to make mistakes. Each time I attempt to build a newly written block of code, the compiler reminds me just how frequently I make mistakes. Unfortunately, some mistakes will not be caught by the compiler and will surface as run-time bugs.

Many of these bugs will be caught by testers during the QA process. But testers are human as well, so every now and then a bug will find its way into the released application.

As long as programs are written and tested by humans, there will always be the need to locate and fix bugs throughout the project lifecycle. Fortunately, numerous resources are at the developer's disposal to help with the process of locating bugs.

In this chapter, I talk about many of the debugging tools provided by Microsoft Visual Studio .NET and the Microsoft .NET platform. If you take the time to learn how to use these tools, I guarantee that you will find plenty of opportunities to leverage your newfound skills.

Interactive Debugging

One of the most powerful tools in a developer's arsenal is the debugger. A debugger allows you to attach to a process, peer into its state, and, depending on the debugger, even control the flow of the application. If the debugger supports remote debugging, the target process can be located on another machine.

You have many choices of debuggers for your .NET Web services. The .NET Framework ships with two debuggers, the CLR Debugger (DbgCLR.exe), which is Microsoft Windows based, and the Runtime Debugger (CorDbg.exe), which is command-line based. Visual Studio .NET also has its own debugger. In addition, you can choose from a number of third-party debuggers.

In this section, I discuss functionality supported by most debuggers. However, my examples will be based on the Visual Studio .NET debugger.

I assume that you have basic knowledge of how to debug applications. For example, I do not cover topics such as stepping through code and setting breakpoints. If you are unfamiliar with these concepts, I suggest you learn about them before proceeding further.

The Basics of Debugging

One of the strengths of Visual Studio .NET is its tight integration with the runtime environment. For example, when you build an ASP.NET Web service project, Visual Studio .NET will automatically deploy the application to the Web server.

This integration extends to support for debugging Web services. As you know by now, you can start debugging a Web service by pressing F5. A reasonable amount of work will be done for you. Visual Studio .NET will automatically perform the following tasks:

1. **Compile the Web service.** This will help ensure that the compiled application matches the underlying source code.

2. **Deploy the Web service.** Visual Studio .NET will deploy to the Web server the newly compiled DLL and any other files that have changed. You can deploy the Web service by using Microsoft FrontPage Server Extensions or by using a file share that is mapped to the underlying file system hosting the Web service.

3. **Launch the .asmx page within the browser.** This will cause the ASP.NET worker process to load the Web service application.

4. **Attach to the ASP.NET worker process.** To do this, the Visual Studio .NET debugger locates the correct ASP.NET worker process running the Web service, even if it is running on a different machine.

The technology that enables Visual Studio .NET to automatically locate and attach to the remote ASP.NET process that is hosting a Web service has a powerful derivative: While you are debugging a Web service client, when you get to the line that calls to the Web service via a proxy, you can press F11 to step into the implementation of the Web service method. Visual Studio .NET will intercept the call to the Web service, attach to the process, and then set a breakpoint at the beginning of the method.

This feature is referred to as *causality*. To facilitate causality, the Web service client must have appropriate security rights. If the Web service client is an ASP.NET application, the default account under which the application runs does not have sufficient permissions to facilitate causality. Therefore, to enable this feature, you must modify the *userName* and *password* attributes of the *processModel* element in the machine.config file so that the ASP.NET application calling the Web service runs under an account with administrative privileges. See Chapter 10 for more information.

After you are finished debugging your managed code application, you can detach from the process and it will continue to execute. However, if your application also invokes unmanaged code and you want to debug it as well, you will not be able to detach from the process without terminating it.

One way to overcome this limitation is to install the dbgproxy service. After you are finished debugging unmanaged code, dbgproxy will keep the debug handles open for you. You can then detach from the process without terminating it.

You can install dbgproxy by executing the following commands:

```
dbgproxy -install
net start dbgproxy
```

The first command installs the dbgproxy service, and the second command starts it.

Remote Debugging

To facilitate some of the remote debugging features described in the previous section, you must make sure that your environment is properly configured. If you have had, shall we say, a less than optimal experience configuring remote debugging in previous versions of Visual Studio, you will be pleasantly surprised by how simple and straightforward this task is in Visual Studio .NET.

The machine that hosts the remote process must have a collection of COM components installed. The easiest way to install these components is to install Visual Studio .NET on that machine. In most cases, especially if the machine is in the production environment, this solution would be suboptimal, so Visual Studio .NET setup gives you the option of installing only the remote debugging components.

To install the remote debugging components, insert the Visual Studio .NET setup disk into the target computer and select the Remote Components Setup link at the bottom of the opening screen, as shown in the following graphic.

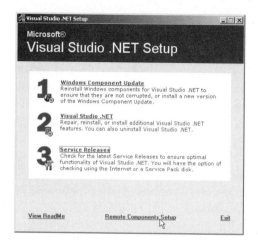

Remote debugging is facilitated through DCOM. Therefore, once you have installed the remote debugging components, you must make sure that you have sufficient permissions to attach to and debug the target process on the remote machine. In order to simplify this process, Setup creates a local group on the target machine called Debugger Users.

Users added to the Debugger Users group will have sufficient permissions to conduct a remote interactive debugging session. However, they also need permissions to attach to the process itself.

By default, the ASP.NET worker process hosting the Web service will run under the System user account. Adding yourself to the local Administrators group will give you sufficient permissions to attach to the worker process. However, if doing so is unacceptable with your system administrator, work with her to configure the machine to achieve the desired security exposure.

Web Services–Friendly Call Stack

A *call stack* is a data structure that is used to keep track of information about nested calls made by a particular thread within an application. For each nested call, a stack frame is created and added to the call stack. For example, if the *Main* method within an application calls method X on object A and method X in turn calls method Y on object B, you will have a call stack containing three stack frames, as shown here:

The stack frame tells the computer how to return control to the caller once a method has finished executing. Once the method returns, its stack frame is popped off of the call stack.

The stack frame also contains the parameters that were passed to the method, plus other housekeeping data. Visual Studio .NET can interpret the individual stack frames on the stack to obtain information about the current state of a particular thread. When execution of an application domain is suspended, you can view the following information from within the Call Stack window:

- The name of the module that contains the implementation of the method
- The names, types, and current value of the method's parameters
- The line number currently being executed within the method
- The language in which the method was implemented

Knowing the sequence of calls that were made and the value of each parameter that was passed can be invaluable when you are trying to debug your application. However, if one of the methods calls into a Web service, the continuity of the call stack will be broken. Because the Web service will be executed on a different thread, and more than likely on a different machine, it will have its own call stack.

Visual Studio .NET simplifies debugging applications that span multiple processes and multiple machines by providing a consolidated view of the call stacks that compose a single logical thread of execution. You can see the entire call chain by right-clicking in the Call Stack Window and choosing Include Calls To/From Other Threads.

To ensure that you have a complete call stack, you must rethrow exceptions correctly within your application. To rethrow an exception, you call *throw* without any parameters. If you pass the exception as a parameter to *throw*, the stack will unwind to the stack frame to the method throwing the exception and the final recipient of the exception will not have a complete stack trace.

Here is an example of two different ways to rethrow an exception:

```
try
{
    // Implementation...
}
catch(SystemException se)
{
    // Causes the stack to unwind to this method call
    throw se;
}
catch(ApplicationException ae)
{
    // The recipient of the exception will have a full stack trace.
    throw;
}
```

Your application might use code to which you do not have the source that improperly throws an exception. To facilitate obtaining a full stack trace, you can configure Visual Studio .NET to catch first-chance exceptions. Choose Debug, Exceptions to open the Exceptions dialog box. Click Common Language Runtime Exceptions, and then select the Break Into The Debugger option in the When The Exception Is Thrown section, as shown here:

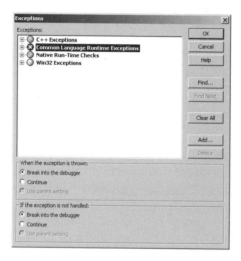

Information the Debugger Needs

The debugger needs certain information in order to perform tasks such as setting breakpoints and displaying the call stack. This information comes from three primary sources: the metadata contained within the assembly, the program database, and the JIT compiler tracking information.

In this section, I explain what types of information the debugger needs and how it uses the information. I also explain how to ensure that the information is available for debugging a Web service. Finally I offer recommendations for creating release and debug builds for Web service projects. The goal for release builds is to create the information that the debugger needs in order to effectively diagnose problems that might emerge in the production environment.

Assembly Metadata

From the .NET assembly's metadata, the debugger needs information about the types defined within the assembly. The debugger uses this information to display the friendly name of types, the methods they expose, and the names of instances of types and to populate the call stack, local watch windows, and so on. This metadata is always contained within a .NET assembly, so the debugger will always have enough information to display a call stack composed of friendly names.

Program Database

Some debugging features require more information than what is provided by the metadata contained within an assembly. For example, the assembly's metadata does not contain enough information to allow you to interactively step through the source code that implements the Web service.

To facilitate source code–level debugging, the debugger needs information about how to map the program image to its original source code. The program database, which can be optionally generated by the compiler, contains a mapping between the Microsoft intermediate language (MSIL) instructions within the assembly and the lines in the source code to which they relate.

The program database is in a separate file with a .pdb file extension and typically has the same name as the executable (.dll or .exe) with which it is associated. The .pdb file often resides in the same directory as its associated .dll or .exe.

The executable and the associated .pdb file generated by the compiler are considered a matched pair. The debugger will not let you use a .pdb file that is either newer or older than the executable running in the targeted process. When the compiler generates the executable and its associated .pdb file, it stamps both of them with a GUID, which the debugger uses to make sure that the correct .pdb file is loaded.

There is no equivalent mechanism for associating the .pdb file with the version of the source code from which it was created, so it is possible to interactively debug your application using an incorrect version of the source code. To avoid this situation, you should maintain tight version control over the executable, the .pdb file, and source control. At the very least, you should check all three into your source control database before deploying the database on an external machine.

The Visual C# compiler (csc.exe) generates a .pdb file if you specify the */debug* switch. Table 11-1 describes all the variations of the Visual C# compiler */debug* switch.

The first two items in the table are pretty straightforward. The third item requires further explanation. In the next section, I discuss why the .pdb file generated by the */debug:pdbonly* switch cannot be used for source-level debugging by default.

Table 11-1   Visual C# Compiler Debugging Switches

Switch	Description
/debug, /debug+, or */debug:full*	Specifies that the compiler will generate a .pdb file.
/debug-	Specifies that the compiler will not generate a .pdb file. This is the default setting.
/debug:pdbonly	Specifies that the compiler will generate a .pdb file. However, source-level debugging will be disabled by default.

You can also use the */optimize* switch to specify whether your code will be optimized before being executed. By default, optimization is disabled—the same as specifying the */optimize-* switch. However, this results in significant performance penalties.

You can enable optimization by specifying the */optimize+* switch. Doing so reduces the fidelity of source-code debugging, however. For example, code might appear to execute out of order or not at all. As a result, optimization is often disabled during development and then enabled before the application ships.

You can specify whether optimization is enabled or whether a .pdb file will be created for a Visual Studio .NET project by modifying the Generate Debugging Information and Optimize Code project settings in the Project Settings dialog box. To open this dialog box, select a project in the Solution Explorer and then choose Project, Properties, or right-click on the project and choose Properties.

Visual Studio .NET will automatically create two configurations for your project, Debug and Release. For the Debug configuration, Generate Debugging Information is set to *true* and Optimize Code is set to *false*. For the Release configuration, Generate Debugging Information is set to *false* and Optimize Code is set to *true*.

You will find that .pdb files can be invaluable for diagnosing problems, especially those that appear only in production. I strongly encourage you to generate .pdb files for every assembly you release to production. However, before I make recommendations about specific build settings, I need to paint a more complete picture.

Tracking Information

So far, I have told you only half the story. In the previous section, I discussed the behavior of the Visual C# complier as it relates to debugging. However, the Visual C# compiler does not generate the code that is ultimately executed and therefore debugged. It generates MSIL, and the resulting MSIL is compiled by the JIT compiler to native code before being executed by the processor.

When you debug a Web service, you attach your debugger to the process that is executing the output of the JIT compiler. The JIT compiler thus has just as much influence as the Visual C# compiler does over your ability to interactively debug the code for a Web service.

Recall that the program database generated by the Visual C# compiler maps the generated MSIL to the original source code. But because the MSIL is compiled by the JIT compiler before it is executed, the program database does not contain enough information to facilitate interactive debugging.

To facilitate interactive debugging, the debugger must be able to map the native code executing within the process to the MSIL and then to the source code. Half of the mapping, from the MSIL to the source code, is provided by the .pdb file. The other half, from the native machine code instructions to the MSIL, must be created by the JIT compiler at run time.

The mapping created by the JIT compiler is referred to as *tracking information*. Tracking information is generated whenever MSIL is compiled to native code by the JIT compiler. The debugger uses the combination of the information in the .pdb file and the tracking information generated by the JIT compiler to facilitate interactive source-code debugging.

With tracking disabled, you cannot perform source-level debugging on the targeted executable. When source code is compiled using the */debug* switch, the resulting assembly will be marked to enable tracking. The JIT compiler learns of this because the assembly is decorated with the *Debuggable* attribute, whose *IsJITTrackingEnabled* property is set to *true*. When the JIT compiler loads the assembly, it looks for this attribute; the value of *true* for its *IsJITTrackingEnabled* property overrides the default behavior.

So why should you care whether tracking is enabled? Because when tracking is enabled, it imposes a slight performance penalty when your application is executed. Specifically, application warm-up is slightly slower because the JIT compiler has to generate the tracking information in addition to compiling the MSIL the first time a method is called.

Once a method has been JIT compiled, no additional costs are associated with tracking. Therefore, in most cases the benefits of improved debugging support for the Web service will outweigh the costs associated with tracking, especially for Web services. An instance of a Web service usually supports multiple requests from multiple clients, so the costs associated with generating the tracking information are quickly amortized away.

In some situations, however, you might not want to incur the costs associated with tracking unless the application is experiencing a problem. You can compile your application using the */debug:pdbonly* switch so that the resulting assembly will have an associated .pdb file generated for it but will not have the *Debuggable* attribute's *IsJITTrackingEnabled* property set to *true*.

Note that you cannot configure the Visual Studio .NET build properties to invoke the same behavior that the */debug:pdbonly* switch does. If you want to generate a .pdb file and not set the *IsJITTrackingEnabled* property within the assembly, you must use some other means of building the application.

If you suspect a problem with an application that was compiled using the */debug:pdbonly* switch, you must enable tracking at run time. The two primary ways to enable tracking at run time are by using the debugger and by configuring an .ini file. Note that with the current version of .NET, modifications to the *IsJITTrackingEnabled* property take effect only when the application is reloaded by the common language runtime. Both methods of configuring tracking at run time require you to restart your application.

The first method of enabling tracking at run time is by creating an .ini file that is used to set the JIT compiler debugging options. The .ini file should have the same name as the application and should reside in the same directory. For example, the .ini file for MyRemotingWebService.exe would be named MyRemotingWebService.ini. The contents of the .ini file would look something like this:

```
[.NET Framework Debugging Control]
GenerateTrackingInfo=1
AllowOptimize=0
```

This example configures the JIT compiler to generate tracking information for the application. As you can see, you can use the .ini file to control whether the JIT compiler generates optimized code. This example does not allow the JIT compiler to generate optimized native code.

The second method of enabling tracking at run time is by using a debugger. If the executable is launched within a debugger such as Visual Studio .NET, the debugger will ensure that tracking is enabled and optimization is disabled.

You can launch an executable in Visual Studio .NET by opening an existing project of type Executable Files (*.exe). Select the executable you want to launch within the debugger. When you start debugging, you will be required to save the newly created Visual Studio .NET solutions file. Then Visual Studio .NET will launch the application with tracking enabled.

The two methods of enabling tracking at run time are effective for .NET .exe applications such as those that host Remoting Web services and clients that interact with Web services. However, they do not work for applications hosted by ASP.NET, primarily because ASP.NET applications are hosted within a worker process (aspnet_wp.exe). This worker process is unmanaged and hosts the common language runtime.

The common language runtime host processes, such as ASP.NET, can programmatically set the debugging options for the JIT compiler. But the current version of ASP.NET does not provide a means of setting the debugging options at run time, so if you want to interactively debug your ASP.NET-hosted Web service, you must build the component using the */debug* option.

The good news is that the performance costs associated with generating the tracking information are much less relevant with respect to ASP.NET-hosted Web services. Methods exposed by the Web service tend to be JIT compiled once and then executed many times. The amortized cost of generating the tracking information becomes insignificant.

I encourage you to compile the release version of your Web services using the */debug* switch. You will not incur a performance penalty once your code has been JIT compiled. And, in most cases, the ability to perform interactive source-level debugging will far outweigh the slight performance penalty that tracking incurs during warm-up.

If the overhead related to tracking is a concern for your ASP.NET-hosted Web services, consider building two release versions of your DLL, one using */debug:pdbonly* and one using */debug*. The reason to build a .pdb file for both DLLs is in case future versions of the ASP.NET runtime allow you to enable tracking at run time.

In general, you should compile the release version of your application using the */optimize+* switch. The optimizations performed by the JIT compiler will reduce the fidelity of interactive source-level debugging. However, the performance costs associated with disabling optimization are significant and span the entire lifetime of your application.

Debugging Dynamically Compiled Source Code

Recall that the implementation of a Web service can also be contained in the .asmx file itself. In this case, the ASP.NET runtime generates the MSIL; you must tell the ASP.NET runtime to generate the information needed to facilitate interactive source-code debugging.

You can enable support for debugging for a particular .asmx page, an entire directory, or an entire application. Doing so will cause a program database and tracking information to be generated at run time. In addition, optimization will be disabled.

You can enable debugging at the page level by setting the *Debug* attribute in the @ *WebService* directive. Here is an example:

```
<@ WebService Debug="true" Language="C#" Class="MyWebService" >
using System;
using System.Web.Service;

public class MyWebService
{
    [WebMethod]
    public string Hello()
    {
        return "Hello world.";
    }
}
```

You can also enable debugging using the web.config file. Depending on where it is located, you can use the web.config file to configure files either within a specific directory or within the entire application, as shown here:

```
<configuration>
  <system.web>
    <compilation debug="true"/>
  </system.web>
</configuration>
```

Enabling debugging also disables optimization, so the Web service will incur a performance penalty. You should therefore disable debugging in production whenever possible.

Instrumenting Web Services

Although source-level debugging is very powerful for debugging applications, in plenty of situations it is not practical. For example, if you interactively debug an ASP.NET Web service, you effectively block all threads from servicing other requests. This is not very practical if the Web service is being hosted in a production environment and you have no ability to isolate it.

In such situations, instrumentation can be invaluable. Instrumentation is the process of generating output directed at the developer or administrator that provides information about the running state of your Web service.

The .NET Framework offers developers many options for instrumenting Web services and the applications that consume them. In this section, I cover three techniques that you can use to instrument your Web service: tracing, the Event Log, and performance counters.

Tracing

Tracing is the process of recording key events during the execution of an application over a discrete period of time. This information can help you understand the code path taken within the application. Tracing information can also contain information about the changes made to the state of the application.

Different levels of tracing are often needed during different phases of a product's lifecycle. For example, during development, the information might be quite verbose. But when the application ships, only a subset of that information might be useful.

The *System.Diagnostics* namespace contains the *Debug* and *Trace* classes, which provide a straightforward means of outputting tracing information from your application. These two classes exhibit similar behavior. In fact, internally they both forward their calls to corresponding static methods exposed by the private *TraceInternal* class. The primary difference between them is that the *Debug* class is intended for use during development and the *Trace* class is intended for use throughout the lifecycle of the application.

Table 11-2 describes the properties and methods exposed by the *Debug* and *Trace* classes. I discuss most of the properties and methods in greater detail later in this section.

Table 11-2   Properties and Methods of the *Debug* and *Trace* Classes

Property	Description
AutoFlush	Specifies whether the *Flush* method should be called after every write
IndentLevel	Specifies the level of indentation for writes
IndentSize	Specifies the number of spaces of a single indent
Listeners	Specifies the collection of listeners that monitor the debug output

Method	Description
Assert	Evaluates an expression and then displays the call stack and an optional user-defined message in a message box if the expression is false
Close	Flushes the output buffer and then closes the listener
Fail	Displays the call stack and a user-defined message in a message box
Flush	Flushes the output buffer to the collection of listeners
Indent	Increases the value of the *IndentLevel* property by one
Unindent	Decreases the value of the *IndentLevel* property by one
Write	Writes information to the collection of listeners
WriteLine	Writes information and a linefeed to the collection of listeners
WriteLineIf	Writes information and a linefeed to the collection of listeners if an expression evaluates to *true*

Each of the static methods exposed by the *Debug* and *Trace* classes is decorated with the *Conditional* attribute. This attribute controls whether a call made to a particular method is executed based on the presence of a particular preprocessing symbol.

The methods exposed by the *Debug* class are executed only if the DEBUG symbol is defined. The methods exposed by the *Trace* class are executed only if the TRACE symbol is defined.

You define symbols at compile time; you can define them within the source code or using a compiler switch. The compiler will generate MSIL to call a method decorated with the *Conditional* attribute only if the required symbol is defined. For example, a call to *Debug.WriteLine* will not be compiled into MSIL unless the DEBUG symbol is defined.

With Visual C#, you can use the *#define* directive to define a symbol scoped to a particular file. For example, the following code defines both the DEBUG and TRACE symbols:

```
#define DEBUG
#define TRACE
```

You can also define a symbol using the Visual C# compiler */define* switch. Symbols defined in this manner are scoped to all the source code files compiled into the executable. The following command defines the DEBUG and TRACE symbols at compile time:

```
csc /define:DEBUG;TRACE /target:library MyWebServiceImpl.cs
```

In general, the DEBUG and TRACE symbols are defined when you compile debug builds, and only the TRACE symbol is defined when you compile release builds. This is the default in Visual Studio .NET. You can change which symbols are defined at compile time by configuring the project settings under Configuration Properties, Build, and then Conditional Compilation Constants.

Now that you know how to set the appropriate symbols, let's look at how to use of some of the key methods exposed by the *Debug* and *Trace* classes.

Asserting Errors

Developers often have to strike a balance between writing robust code and maximizing an application's performance. In an effort to write robust code, they often find themselves writing a considerable amount of code that evaluates the state of the application.

Rich validation code can be invaluable for tracking down issues quickly during development, but an overabundance of validation code can affect the application's performance. In general, publicly exposed Web services should validate the input parameters received from the client. But in certain situations it is not necessary to validate member variables that are considered implementation details of the Web service.

In cases where it makes sense to perform validation only during development, you can use the *Assert* method exposed by the *Debug* and *Trace* classes. This method evaluates an expression, and if the expression evaluates to *false*, it returns information about the assertion. The error information includes text defined by the application as well as a dump of the call stack.

The ability to programmatically generate error information that includes a dump of the call stack is quite handy. There might be certain places in your code where you always want to do this. For these situations, you can call the

Fail method of the *Debug* and *Trace* classes. Calling *Fail* is the equivalent of calling *Assert* where the expression always evaluates to *false*.

Let's take a look at an example. The following code demonstrates the use of the *Assert* and *Fail* methods:

```
#define DEBUG
using System.Web.Services;
using System.Diagnostics;

public class Insurance
{
    [WebMethod]
    public double CalculateRate(int age, bool smoker)
    {
        StreamReader stream = File.OpenText("RateTable.txt");
        Debug.Assert((stream.Peak() == -1),
        "Error reading the rate table.",
        "The rate table appears to be empty.");

        try
        {
            // Implementation...
        }
        catch(Exception e)
        {
            Debug.Fail("Unhandled exception.");
            throw;
        }
    }
}
```

The code generates an assertion if the RateTable.txt file is empty or if an unhandled exception is caught.

Because the *Assert* and *Fail* methods are called within a Web service, there is an issue with the default behavior of these methods. By default, the *Assert* and *Fail* methods display dialog boxes if the expression evaluates to *false*. But this is obviously not practical for server-side code. You can alter the web.config file to redirect the output to a log file, as shown here:

```
<configuration>
  <system.diagnostics>
    <assert assertuienabled="false"
    logfilename="c:\Logs\Assert.log"/>
  </system.diagnostics>

  <!-- The rest of the configuration information... -->

</configuration>
```

This portion of the web.config file specifies an *assert* element to alter the default behavior of the *Assert* and *Fail* methods. First I set the *assertuienabled* attribute to *false* to specify that an assertion should not result in the display of a modal dialog box. I then specify the file where the asserts will be written using the *logfilename* attribute. I also need to create the Logs directory and give the ASPNET user sufficient permissions to create and write to the Assert.log file because, by default, the ASPNET user does not have permissions to write to the file system.

Finally, note that the default behavior of the *Assert* and *Trace* methods is to ignore the error and continue. For this reason, do not use the *Assert* and *Fail* methods as a substitute for throwing an exception.

Conditional Preprocessor Directives

Recall that the *Conditional* attribute provides a means of defining methods that should be called only if a particular preprocessing symbol is defined. However, at times you might want to have finer-grained control over implementation that is compiled into an application when a particular preprocessing symbol is defined. For example, you might want to have extended test routines embedded within your code during development. You can gain this finer-grained control by specifying conditional preprocessor directives within your application.

Conditional preprocessor directives mark blocks of code that will be compiled into MSIL only if a particular symbol is defined. Table 11-3 describes the key conditional preprocessor directives used to do this.

Table 11-3   Conditional Preprocessor Directives

Directive	Description
#if	Begins a conditional compilation block. Code following the *#if* directive will be compiled only if the condition evaluates to *true*.
#else	Specifies statements that should be compiled only if the condition specified by the *#if* directive evaluates to *false*.
#endif	Terminates a conditional compilation block.
#define	Defines a preprocessing symbol.
#undef	Negates the definition of a preprocessing symbol.

For public Web services, there is rarely a good reason to return a stack trace to the user in the event of an exception. A stack trace offers minimal benefit to an external user of your Web service, plus the information provided by the stack trace can be used against you to probe for security vulnerabilities within your Web service. During development, however, this additional information can be helpful for debugging.

The following example uses conditional preprocessor directives to return stack trace information only if the application was compiled with the DEBUG symbol defined:

```
#define DEBUG
using System.Web.Services;
using System.Web.Services.Protocols;

public class Insurance
{
    [WebMethod]
    public double CalculateRate(int age, bool smoker)
    {
        try
        {
            // Implementation...
        }
        catch(Exception e)
        {
#if DEBUG
            throw new SoapException
            ("An unhandled exception was encountered.",
            SoapException.ServerFaultCode, e);
#else
            throw new SoapException
            ("An unhandled exception was encountered.",
            SoapException.ServerFaultCode);
#endif
        }

        // Implementation...

    }
}
```

The example throws a *SoapException* if an unhandled exception is caught. The data returned within the *SoapException* depends on whether the DEBUG symbol is defined. If the DEBUG symbol is defined, a new instance of the *SoapException* class is initialized with the caught exception. If the DEBUG symbol is not defined, a new instance of the class is initialized with only a generic error message.

Trace Log

So far, I have focused mostly on error conditions. However, instrumenting normal operations of an application can be equally valuable. The *Debug* and *Trace* classes provide a set of methods and properties for logging tracing information within your application.

Output is written to the log using the *Write*, *WriteLine*, and *WriteLineIf* methods. The *Write* method outputs text to the trace log, and *WriteLine* outputs text followed by a linefeed. If text should be written to the trace log only if a certain condition is met, you can use the *WriteLineIf* method.

The *Debug* and *Trace* classes also expose properties and methods to control the format of the output. You can use the *IndentLevel* property to set the number of times a new line of text is indented. The *Indent* and *Unindent* methods increment and decrement the *IndentLevel* property, respectively. The *IndentSize* property specifies the number of spaces in an indent.

You can specify when the output buffer will be flushed to the trace log by calling the *Flush* method. You can also set the *AutoFlush* property to *true* to cause the output buffer to be flushed after every write to the trace log.

Recall that the *Debug* and *Trace* classes defer their implementation to the *TraceInternal* class. Therefore, modifying the static variables using one class affects the other. For example, setting *Debug.IndentSize* to *4* also affects the indent size of the *Trace* class.

The following example shows the use of the trace methods within the context of a Web service:

```
#define TRACE
using System.Diagnostics;
using System.Web.Services;

public class WebService
{
    public WebService()
    {
        Trace.IndentSize = 4;
        Trace.AutoFlush = true;
    }

    [WebMethod]
    public void MyWebMethod(string param)
    {
        Trace.WriteLine("MyWebMethod");
        Trace.Indent();
        Trace.WriteLine("Start: " + DateTime.Now);

        // Implementation...

        Trace.WriteLine("End: " + DateTime.Now);
        Trace.Unindent();
    }
}
```

Both the *IndentSize* and *AutoFlush* properties are set within the constructor of the method. You can also set them at run time within the web.config file, as shown here:

```
<configuration>
  <system.diagnostics>
    <trace autoflush="true" indentsize="0"/>
  </system.diagnostics>
</configuration>
```

You can use the *trace* element to set the initial value of the *AutoFlush* and *IndentSize* properties. Any changes made to these properties by the application will override these default settings.

You should be aware of one issue when you call the *WriteLineIf* method. Consider the following code fragment:

```
Trace.WriteLineIf(someCondition, "Some error message.",
someLargeObject.ToString());
```

Because the text that will be written to the logs is passed to the *WriteLineIf* method, the *someLargeObject* object must be serialized to a string even if the condition evaluates to *false*. To avoid unnecessary processing, we can rewrite the code as follows:

```
#if TRACE
if(someCondition)
{
    Trace.WriteLine("Some error message.",
    someLargeObject.ToString());
}
#endif
```

The *someLargeObject* object will be serialized to a string only if the *someCondition* variable is equal to *true*. This ensures that the costs associated with serializing *someLargeObject* are incurred only if the resulting text will be written to the trace log.

Trace Listeners

The *Debug* and *Trace* classes support outputting the tracing log to multiple listeners. A listener must inherit from the *TraceListener* class. The .NET Framework provides three listeners: *DefaultTraceListener*, *EventLogTraceListener*, and *TextWriterTraceListener*.

The *DefaultTraceListener* is added to the collection of listeners by default. It generates output that can be captured by debuggers for managed and unmanaged code. The tracing information is sent to managed code debuggers via the *Debugger.Log* method and to unmanaged code debuggers by means of the *OutputDebugString* Win32 API. In the case of Visual Studio .NET, the output is displayed in the Output window.

You can add or remove listeners using the *Listeners* property of the *Debug* and *Trace* classes. The following example removes the instance of the *Default-TraceListener* and adds an instance of the *TextWriterTraceListener* to the collection of listeners:

```
// Remove instance of the DefaultTraceListener.
Debug.Listeners.Remove(Debug.Listeners[0]);

// Add instance of the TextWriterTraceListener.
System.IO.FileStream fs =
System.IO.File.OpenWrite(@"c:\Logs\Tracing.log");
Debug.Listeners.Add(new TextWriterTraceListener(fs));
```

You can also add or remove listeners at run time. The following example performs the same task as the previous code, but by modifying the web.config file, as you see here:

```
<configuration>
  <system.diagnostics>
    <trace>
      <listeners>
        <add name="Text"
        type="System.Diagnostics.TextWriterTraceListener,System"
        initializeData="c:\Logs\Tracing.log"/>
        <remove type="System.Diagnostics.DefaultTraceListener,System"/>
      </listeners>
    </trace>
  </system.diagnostics>
</configuration>
```

In either case, you will need to create the Logs directory and give the ASP-NET user sufficient permissions to create and write to the Tracing.log file because, by default, the ASPNET user does not have permissions to write to the file system.

Trace Switches

The DEBUG and TRACE preprocessing symbols allow you to configure the level of tracing generated by an application at compile time. However, sometimes you might need finer-grained levels of tracing or you might need to change the level of tracing at run time. For example, you might want to record errors and warnings only under normal operating conditions, but when an issue arises, you might want to enable more verbose tracing without having to recompile the code.

You can achieve this functionality by leveraging classes that inherit from the *Switch* class within your code. The .NET Framework includes two such classes, *BooleanSwitch* and *TraceSwitch*. Much like the preprocessing symbols, the *BooleanSwitch* class provides a mechanism to indicate whether tracing should be enabled. However, you can indicate this at run time by modifying the application configuration file.

For example, suppose I want to create an instance of the *BooleanSwitch* class that allows me to control whether trace information is displayed about when the beginning and ending of a method is reached.

```
using System;
using System.Diagnostics;

public class Application
{
    private static BooleanSwitch profileMethodsSwitch =
    new BooleanSwitch("ProfileMethods", "Controls whether
    start and end times are displayed for each method.");

    static public void Main(string[] args)
    {
        Application.DoSomething("test", 3);
    }

    private void DoSomething(string param1, int param2)
    {
        Trace.WriteLineIf(profileMethodsSwitch.Enabled,
        "Start DoSomething:  "  +  DateTime.Now);

        // Implementation...

        Trace.WriteLineIf(profileMethodsSwitch.Enabled,
        "End DoSomething:  "  +  DateTime.Now);
    }
}
```

I define a *BooleanSwitch* to determine whether method-profiling information should be written to the tracing log. First I create a static variable of type *BooleanSwitch* and define the name and description of the switch within the constructor. When the switch's constructor is called, it will read the application configuration file to determine its value (*true* or *false*).

Next I use *profileMethodsSwitch* as the condition of the calls to *WriteLineIf* that display method profile information. Notice that this switch can be used by the *WriteLineIf* method of both the *Trace* and *Debug* classes. For that matter, the switch can be specified by any conditional statement within the application.

Once the switch has been defined, you can configure it within the application's configuration file. The configuration file shown on the next page enables the *ProfileMethods* switch.

```
<configuration>
  <system.diagnostics>
    <switches>
      <add name="TraceMethods" value="1" />
    </switches>
  </system.diagnostics>
</configuration>
```

I enable the *TraceMethods* switch by specifying an *add* element with its *name* attribute set to the same string used to initialize the constructor of the switch. If the *TraceMethods* switch is not listed in the configuration file, the default value will be 0 or *false*.

If you want to achieve more granularity when you configure which tracing information to display, you can use the *TraceSwitch* class. You can set an instance of a *TraceSwitch* class to a numeric value to indicate the level of tracing information that should be displayed.

The *TraceSwitch* class supports five levels of tracing, from 0 through 4. Table 11-4 describes these tracing levels.

Table 11-4   Properties and Their Associated Tracing Levels

Property	Tracing Level	Description
N/A	0	Tracing is turned off.
TraceError	1	Error messages only.
TraceWarning	2	Warning and error messages.
TraceInfo	3	Informational, warning, and error messages.
TraceVerbose	4	Verbose.

Setting an instance of the *TraceSwitch* class to a particular value is cumulative. For example, if the value is set to 3, not only is *TraceInfo* enabled, but *TraceWarning* and *TraceError* are enabled as well.

Event Log

Some tracing information should be recorded regardless of switch settings or what preprocessing symbols are defined. You should trace, for example, a critical error encountered by a Web service that needs the immediate attention of a system administrator.

Critical information about the execution of an application should be written to the Event Log. The Event Log provides a common repository for storing events from multiple sources. By default, the system has three logs: the Application Log, the Security Log, and the System Log. Events raised by your application should typically be posted to the Application Log.

Because the Event Log is an infrastructure component provided by the operating system, it comes with supporting infrastructure that you would otherwise have to create yourself. For example, an Event Log Service will automatically control the size of individual logs so that you never have to truncate the log yourself. You can use the Event Log Viewer to view and sort the entries in the log. You can also obtain additional tools that operate on the Event Log and perform such tasks as notifying the system administrator in the event of an application failure.

You can use the *EventLog* class to post messages to the Event Log. But before you write to the Event Log, you must first register an event source. The event source is usually associated with your application. The following code shows how to register an event source:

```
if(! EventLog.SourceExists("My Web Service"))
{
    EventLog.CreateEventSource("My Web Service", "Application");
}
```

The preceding code first determines whether a particular event source is already registered. If it is not, the code will register it. You can then write entries to the Event Log, as shown in this code:

```
EventLog.WriteEntry("My Web Service",
"Unable to connect to the database", EventLogEntryType.Error);
```

This code writes a warning event to the Application Log. The three categories of events are errors, warnings, and informational events. You can also include additional information with the event, including an application-defined event ID and category ID as well as raw binary data that can be helpful when you try to diagnose the problem.

By default, the ASPNET user does not have permissions to write to the event log. To provide these permissions, set the \\HKEY_LOCAL_MACHINE\SYSTEM\CurrentControlSet\Services\Eventlog\Application\RestrictGuestAccess registry key to 0 and reboot the machine.

By default, the ASPNET user also does not have permissions to create event sources. You can overcome this limitation by registering the event source as part of the installation procedure of your Web service. If you want to register event sources at run time, you need to grant the ASPNET user read/write permissions to the \\HKEY_LOCAL_MACHINE\SYSTEM\CurrentControlSet\Services\Eventlog registry key as well as all of its subkeys.

The *EventLog* class also supports additional functionality such as receiving notification when a new entry is created. Table 11-5 describes the properties, methods, and event exposed by the *EventLog* class.

Table 11-5   Class Properties, Methods, and Event

Property	Description
EnableRaisingEvents	Specifies whether the instance of the *EventLog* class will receive *EntryWritten* event notifications
Entries	Retrieves a collection of instances of the *EventLog-Entry* class
Log	Specifies the name of the event log that will be accessed
LogDisplayName	Retrieves the friendly name of the event log
MachineName	Specifies the name of the machine where the targeted event log resides
Source	Specifies the name of the source of the events written to the event log

Method	Description
Clear	Removes all entries from the targeted event log
Close	Closes the handle to the event log
CreateEventSource	Registers a new event source within the system registry
Delete	Deletes the specified event log
DeleteEventSource	Unregisters a new event source
Exists	Indicates whether the specified event log exists
GetEventLogs	Retrieves an array of *EventLog* objects from the targeted machine
LogNameFromSourceName	Retrieves the name of the Event Log associated with a particular event source
SourceExists	Indicates whether the specified event source is registered
WriteEntry	Writes an entry to the event log

Event	Description
EntryWritten	Fires when an event is written to the Event Log on the local machine

Performance Counters

So far, I have limited my discussion of the methods of instrumentation to asynchronous forms of communication. The application writes data to a text file or the Event Log, and then the client opens the information source and reads the data. However, at times the client might need to monitor the state of the application in real time.

For example, suppose I develop a Web service that accepts purchase orders from my customers. I might be interested in knowing the number of requests per second that my Web service receives. Information such as this can be communicated using performance counters.

As you probably know, many applications publish a lot of data using performance counters. ASP.NET is no exception. It publishes numerous counters about its run-time state, including the number of applications currently running and the number of worker processes running.

ASP.NET also publishes numerous counters about the run-time state of individual applications that it is hosting. These counters include the number of requests per second, the number of requests queued, and the average request execution time.

If the Web service I just described accepts only purchase orders, I can monitor the number of requests received per second without writing a single line of code. I can simply use an application that ships with Windows called Performance Monitor. (The steps required to launch Performance Monitor vary depending on your operating system, so consult online help.)

With Performance Monitor running, you can add counters that you want to have charted. First click the button with the plus sign to open the Add Counters dialog box. Select ASP.NET Applications in the Performance Object drop-down list, and then select the Requests/Sec counter. Then select the instance that corresponds to the application you want to monitor. The name of the application will be associated with the name of the directory in which the application lives.

The Add Counters dialog box should look similar to this:

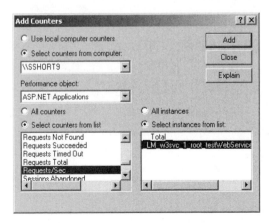

You can also create your own performance counters by using the *PerformanceCounterCategory* and the *PerformanceCounter* classes. The following example shows how to use the *PerformanceCounterCategory* class to register a new performance counter:

```
if(! PerformanceCounterCategory.Exists("My Web Service"))
{
    PerformanceCounterCategory.Create("My Web Service",
    "Performance counters published by My Web Service.",
    "Total Purchase Orders Processed",
    "The total number of purchase orders processed.");
}
```

The preceding code registers a category called My Web Service and a counter called Total Purchase Orders Processed if the category does not already exist.

After the counter is registered, you can publish to it using an instance of the *PerformanceCounter* class. The following code creates a performance counter object and increments the counter by one:

```
PerformanceCounter processedPOs =
new PerformanceCounter("My Web Service",
"Total Purchase Orders Processed", false);
processedPOs.Increment();
```

I create an instance of the *PerformanceCounter* class and initialize it to enable writes to the Total Purchase Orders Processed counter. I then increment the counter by 1 by invoking the object's *Increment* method.

This is fine, but my goal is to publish the average number of purchase orders processed per second. If my Web service exposes more than one Web method, I will not be able to leverage the Requests/Sec counter exposed by ASP.NET to achieve my purpose. I need to create another custom counter.

To create this new custom counter, I must leverage the *CounterCreationData* class to register the counter. This class allows me to set the type of counter I need. The following example registers counters to monitor total purchase orders processed as well as the amount processed per second:

```
if(! PerformanceCounterCategory.Exists("My Web Service"))
{
    CounterCreationDataCollection counterCDC =
    new CounterCreationDataCollection();
    counterCDC.Add(new CounterCreationData
    ("Purchase Orders Processed/sec",
```

```
" The number of purchase orders processed per second.",
PerformanceCounterType.RateOfCountsPerSecond32));
counterCDC.Add(new CounterCreationData
("Total Purchase Orders Processed",
" The total number of purchase orders processed.",
PerformanceCounterType.NumberOfItems32));
PerformanceCounterCategory.Create("My Web Service",
" Performance counters published by My Web Service.",
counterCDC);
}
```

First I create an instance of the *CounterCreationDataCollection* class that will be used to pass the counters I want to register. I then create two instances of the *CounterCreationData* class to register the counters. Notice that I do not have to write any code to calculate the average number of purchase order requests per second. This is handled for me by the Performance Monitor.

By default, the ASPNET user has permissions to write to a particular performance counter but not to create performance counters and categories. You can overcome this limitation by registering the performance counters as part of the installation procedure of your Web service.

Sometimes you might want to create performance counters at run time. For example, you might want to associate an instance of a performance counter with a particular instance of your Web service or possibly with a particular user. In order to register a performance counter at run time, you need to grant the ASPNET user read/write permissions to the \\HKEY_LOCAL_MACHINE\SOFTWARE\ Microsoft\Windows NT\CurrentVersion\Perflib registry key as well as all of its subkeys.

Tables 11-6, 11-7, and 11-8 describe the properties and methods exposed by the *CounterCreationData*, *PerformanceCounter*, and *PerformanceCounter-Category* classes, respectively.

Table 11-6   *CounterCreationData* Class Properties

Property	Description
CounterHelp	Specifies the help string that describes the counter
CounterName	Specifies the name of the counter
CounterType	Specifies the type of counter

Table 11-7 *PerformanceCounter* **Class Properties and Methods**

Property	Description
CategoryName	Specifies the name of the category in which the counter is registered
CounterHelp	Retrieves the counter help text
CounterName	Specifies the name of the counter
CounterType	Retrieves the type of the counter
InstanceName	Specifies the name of the instance with which the counter is associated
MachineName	Specifies the name of the machine with which the counter is associated
RawValue	Specifies the uncalculated value of this counter
ReadOnly	Specifies whether the counter is read-only

Method	Description
BeginInit	Used by Visual Studio .NET to start the initialization of a counter
Close	Closes the counters and releases any acquired resources
Decrement	Decrements the counter by one within an atomic operation
EndInit	Used by Visual Studio .NET to end the initialization of a counter
Increment	Increments the counter by one within an atomic operation
IncrementBy	Increments the counter by the specified value within an atomic operation
NextSample	Retrieves the uncalculated value of a counter sample
NextValue	Retrieves the calculated value of a counter sample
RemoveInstance	Removes the category instance associated with the counter

Table 11-8 *PerformanceCounterCategory* **Class Properties and Methods**

Property	Description
CategoryHelp	Retrieves the category help text
CategoryName	Specifies the name of the category
MachineName	Specifies the machine on which the category exists

Table 11-8   *PerformanceCounterCategory* **Class Properties and Methods**

Method	Description
CounterExists	Indicates whether a specific counter is registered under a particular category
Create	Registers a category and one or more counters
Delete	Deletes the category and its registered counters
Exists	Indicates whether a particular category is registered
GetCategories	Retrieves the list of registered categories
GetCounters	Retrieves the list of registered counters for the particular category
GetInstanceNames	Retrieves the list of instances for a particular category
InstanceExists	Indicates whether a particular instance of the category is registered
ReadCategory	Gets the instance data associated with each counter registered under the category

Tips and Tricks for Debugging

Some of the information that can aid in your efforts to debug Web services does not clearly belong in any of the previous sections, so I present it in the following list:

- When you use Microsoft Internet Explorer to view documents that are automatically generated by the runtime (such as WSDL and results returned from the ASP.NET test harness), you should disable the display of friendly error messages, WSDL, and the results of any display-friendly error messages. Doing so will allow you to see the actual error message returned. Simply take the following steps:

  - In Internet Explorer, choose Tools, Internet Options.

  - On the Advanced tab of the Internet Options dialog box, deselect Show Friendly HTTP Error Messages.

- If Internet Explorer serves you a blank page, view the source. Sometimes an error message returned by the runtime will not display in the browser. To see these error messages, view the underlying source directly by clicking the View menu item and then selecting View Source.

- When you debug a Web service that is accessed through a proxy, you should increase the timeout value of the proxy to a large value. For ASP.NET proxies that derive from the *SoapHttpClientProtocol* class or for Remoting wrapped proxies that derive from the *RemotingClientProxy* class, set the Timeout property to –1 (infinity). Before you release the client application to production, be sure to set the timeout value back to a reasonable value.

- Visual Studio .NET allows you to debug multiple types of code within an application, including ASP, ASP.NET, unmanaged code, and SQL Server stored procedures. Make sure that the appropriate debugging options are selected within your project settings. For example, if you have an ASP.NET Web service that calls unmanaged code and you want to debug the entire implementation of the Web service, be sure to enable debugging support for both ASP.NET and unmanaged code.

Summary

This chapter covers interactive source-code debugging, the information needed by the debugger, and how to instrument your applications.

First I describe some core features of the Visual Studio .NET debugger that help simplify the task of developing Web services. One of the unique requirements for debugging Web services is strong support for remote debugging. The key features that Visual Studio .NET provides for supporting remote debugging include these:

- Visual Studio .NET automatically attaches to the remote ASP.NET process hosting the Web service.

- It allows you to configure the target server to allow remote debugging.

- It can display a logical call stack that spans multiple threads.

- It ensures that you get a complete call stack when an unhandled exception occurs within your application.

Next I explain what information the debugger needs in order to perform essential tasks. Specifically, it needs information for creating a readable call stack; that information is contained within the metadata in the module that contains the types that compose the call stack.

Interactive source-code debugging requires mapping between the original source code and the machine code generated by the JIT compiler. One half of the mapping, between the source code and the MSIL, is provided by the program database (.pdb) file. The other half of the mapping, between the MSIL and the native machine code, is provided by the tracking information generated by the JIT compiler.

The tracking information is generated when the MSIL is JIT compiled into native code. Because the compiled native code is unaffected by the generation of the tracking information, the slight performance penalty associated with tracking occurs only during application warm-up.

You can also specify whether the JIT compiler generates optimized code. If optimization is turned on, you might experience a loss of fidelity between the compiled machine code and the original source code. Because you incur a significant performance hit as a result of generating machine code that is not optimized, I suggest that you enable optimization for release builds.

Finally I explain the various technologies provided by .NET for instrumenting your Web services and the client applications that interact with them. I explain the similarities and differences between the *Debug* and *Trace* classes and show you how to add and remove listeners at compile time as well as at run time.

I also explain how to leverage the Event Log for communicating important information to the system administrator, and I demonstrate how to use performance counters to publish real-time information about the current state of the application.

12

Scalability and Availability

The primary reason for developing Web services is so that developers will use them to build solutions for their customers. No matter how cool or useful your Web service is, it can't provide any value if it is down. For a Web service to be adopted by developers, it must be reliable.

As your Web service becomes more popular, it must scale to meet the increasing demands of its clients, particularly if your Web service either indirectly or directly generates revenue for your company.

For example, suppose Woodgrove Bank allows its customers to transfer funds electronically from one account to another. And suppose the bank develops a Web service, called Banking, that allows its customers to request that funds be transferred. If the Banking Web service is consumed by personal financial management software packages such as Microsoft Money, it might need to support hundreds of thousands or possibly millions of clients.

The overall scalability and availability of a Web service is determined by its weakest link. Nontrivial Web services often leverage multiple resources such as databases and directory services. If a particular resource does not scale to meet the needs of the Web service, the Web service itself will not scale to meet the needs of its clients.

The Banking Web service relies on multiple resources to process a customer's request. These resources include a SQL Server database that holds customer account information as well as a legacy line-of-business (LOB) application that is used to coordinate the transfer of funds with other banks.

In this chapter, I present techniques for increasing the scalability and availability of your Web services as well as the resources they use. I also examine scalability and availability from the perspective of the client and explore ways to minimize the risks associated with using a Web service that is not under your direct control.

Scaling Your Web Service

To be successful, your Web service must scale to handle an increasing number of client requests. If your Web service is hosted on the Internet, you might eventually have enormous numbers of requests from clients from all over the world.

You should establish scalability goals early in the project. One classic mistake is setting scalability goals based on the average number of requests over a period of time. You should instead establish goals based on the total number of peak requests.

For example, let's say the Securities Web service has an expected usage of 300,000 requests per month. Assuming a 30-day month, that equates to 10,000 requests per day. However, 40 percent of the transfers occur on the 1st and 15th days of the month, when customers typically get paid. This means that the Web service should actually be capable of handling 60,000 requests per day.

In the following sections, I examine two strategies for scaling a Web service and the resources it uses: *scaling up* and *scaling out*.

Scaling Up

Scaling up a Web service involves moving it to a bigger, faster, more powerful machine to accommodate increased workloads. One main advantage of this strategy is that it makes the infrastructure easier to manage: it does not increase the number of servers the system administrator has to maintain.

One of the main disadvantages of the scale-up strategy is cost. You typically pay premium prices for higher-end computers, so the cost per transaction for high-end servers is often higher than for their commodity counterparts. This is further compounded when redundant servers are required to meet availability requirements.

Another disadvantage of the scale-up strategy is that you can scale only as much as the fastest machine will allow. Also, high-end servers are often multiprocessor boxes, so resources must be designed to take advantage of multiprocessors to fully utilize the box.

In general, you should consider a scale-up strategy for resources that are difficult to scale out. (I address the scale-out strategy in the next section.) For example, stateful resources such as relational databases are often difficult to scale out, especially if the data is dynamic, highly relational, and shared across multiple clients.

Recall that the Banking Web service stores all user state within a SQL Server database. You can often scale up the machine hosting SQL Server and still keep hardware expenditures within reasonable levels. If so, the scale-up strategy is probably your ideal course of action.

For resources that are difficult to scale up, look for opportunities to minimize the work they execute. For example, avoid implementing business logic within database stored procedures or performing data transformations within the database engine itself. Instead, move these activities out of the database and into a business logic layer that can be more easily scaled out.

Scaling Out

When scaling up is not feasible, you can scale out a resource by hosting it on a cluster of machines and then distributing the requests made to that resource across multiple machines in the cluster. As the load on the resource increases, you can add more computers to the cluster to accommodate the increase. (I realize that you might be accustomed to a more specific definition of *cluster*, but here I use the word in a broader sense, to refer to a group of computers that are used to host a particular resource.)

One advantage of the scale-out strategy is that you can often achieve near-linear scalability as you add more computers. The cost per transaction remains relatively constant as the infrastructure is scaled.

One disadvantage of scaling out is increased complexity. Instead of maintaining a single box, you must maintain multiple machines in the cluster. For example, you must install and maintain each Web server in the Web farm.

You can use products such as Microsoft Application Center to help reduce the costs associated with maintaining multiple machines in a cluster. The primary goal of Application Center is to allow an administrator to maintain a clustered resource as if it were installed on a single system. Application Center provides out-of-the-box support for Web-based applications, so it is well suited for deploying and managing HTTP-based Web services.

Network Load Balancing

A clustering technology known as network load balancing (NLB) involves distributing requests across the nodes in the cluster at the network protocol level. The client sends a request to a particular IP address, and the NLB system intercepts the request and ensures that only one node in the cluster processes it.

Because the requests are handled at the network protocol level, the client sees the resource as a single system image. The client is oblivious to which node is actually handling the request, so in most cases it is not required to make any changes in the way the resource is accessed.

One common use of NLB is in the creation of a Web farm. A Web farm is a cluster of Web servers that are front-ended by a hardware- or software-based NLB system. Because a Web farm is designed to handle HTTP requests, you can use it to host an HTTP-based Web service.

NLB is not limited to distributing HTTP requests; you can use it to distribute network requests for a variety of protocols, including such non-HTTP resources as an FTP server or even a Common Internet File System (CIFS) file share.

To ensure that your network load–balanced resource offers the highest degree of availability, make sure it has the characteristics described in the following three sections.

The Nodes in the Cluster Should Be Independent of One Another

Each node needs to be capable of handling the client's request independently of the other nodes in the cluster because any node could fail at any time. Such a failure should not hinder any other nodes from processing requests.

For example, a node is not independent if it has data stored locally that is required for completion of the client's request. If the node fails, no other node in the cluster can complete the request.

Any Node Should Be Able to Handle Any Request

If a request can be handled by any node in the cluster, the load balancing system can more evenly distribute the requests across the nodes in the cluster. This characteristic also ensures that nodes can be easily added or removed, allowing the cluster to be expanded or contracted to meet changes in demand.

For any node to be able to handle any request, a resource cannot rely on state stored locally between requests. If the resource is stateful, all requests from a given client must be routed to the same node in the cluster. The following code shows an example of a stateful Web service:

```
using System;
using System.Web.Services;

class Banking : WebService
{
    [WebMethod(EnableSession=true)]
    public void Initialize(int accountNumber)
    {
        this.Session["AccountNumber"] = accountNumber;
    }

    [WebMethod(EnableSession=true)]
    public void RequestWireTransfer(bool destinationAccount,
                                    double amount)
    {
        string accountNumber = this.Session["AccountNumber"];

        // Set up bill to be paid via funds
        // in the designated account....
    }
}
```

This implementation of the Banking Web service relies on session state between the call to *Initialize* and the call to *RequestWireTransfer*. By default, session state is saved locally on the server, so the call to *RequestWireTransfer* must be routed to the same node from which *Initialize* was called.

You can maintain server affinity based on the client's IP address, but this approach is problematic because many clients access the Internet through a cluster of proxy servers, and it is possible for two requests from the same client to go through two different proxy servers with two different IP addresses.

In most cases, you can solve the problem by routing all requests from a class C address space to a particular node in the cluster. However, large ISPs such as AOL might have a cluster of proxy servers that span multiple class C address spaces. In such cases, a more sophisticated server affinity strategy is needed, such as the cookie-based system provided by Microsoft Application Center.

It is best to completely avoid imposing server affinity. In the previous scenario, you can take two approaches to avoiding server affinity. The first way is to configure ASP.NET session state so that it is stored on a central server that is accessible to all Web servers in the Web farm. The second way is to look for opportunities to remove the dependency on session state altogether. For example, you can require the client to pass the account number with every call to *PayBill*, thereby avoiding the need to implement the *Initialize* method.

There are a few reasons why you should look for opportunities to avoid using session state. First, the Web service client must support cookies. As you recall from Chapter 6, ASP.NET proxies do not support cookies by default. Also, the implementation of *PayBill* incurs the cost of a network round-trip to obtain the account number. Finally, the central session state server introduces a single point of failure to the system.

Requests Should Be Distributed Evenly Across All Nodes in the Cluster   How you distribute requests evenly across all nodes in the cluster is often determined by how resource intensive it is to process an individual request. If a request is not very CPU or memory intensive, you can employ a load-balancing mechanism that uses a hash algorithm or a round-robin algorithm and achieve fairly uniform distribution across all nodes in the cluster.

NLB is one technology that you can use to distribute lightweight requests across nodes in a cluster. NLB ships with Windows 2000 Advanced Server and uses a hash algorithm based on the client's IP address and port number to determine which node will process the client's request.

If requests are CPU or memory intensive, you might want to use a load-balancing system that routes requests based on utilization of the nodes in a cluster. Such a system monitors the state of each node and then routes requests to the least-utilized nodes.

Partitioning the Resource

You can use partitioning to provide a scale-out strategy for resources that cannot effectively be network load balanced. *Partitioning* means dividing a particular resource across multiple servers. For example, say I have one database server that handles all client requests for the Banking Web service. As the load increases, I can split the data contained in the database across two or more servers based on ranges of account numbers.

Devising a way to partition a resource so that requests are evenly distributed across all the servers can be a tough challenge. In general, it is easier to partition a resource when you have a small number of clients that need access to a particular subset of the data that must be partitioned. Partitioning becomes more challenging when you have a large number of clients that need access to the same set of data.

For example, a client of the Banking Web service has access only to data associated with its account number. Therefore, it is relatively easy to partition the data across multiple servers in the cluster based on ranges of account numbers. However, it is relatively difficult to partition data in a reporting system that supports ad hoc queries.

In general, it is costly to create and maintain a partitioned resource. Without support from the application, partitioning usually requires a lot of manual and time-intensive work. Not only do you have to design and implement a partitioning scheme, but you also have to maintain it.

You also have to constantly monitor the workload of each node in the cluster to ensure that no nodes are overloaded. When a particular node becomes overloaded, you must repartition the data. For example, a number of highly active accounts might happen to reside within the same database partition used by the Banking Web service. In that case, you would need to adjust the ranges of accounts hosted on each partition in the cluster.

SQL Server supports a feature called *updateable distributed partitioned views* that simplifies partitioning data contained in one or more tables across multiple servers. However, this approach makes performing backups and disaster recovery operations more difficult. You must synchronize backups across each partition to ensure that referential integrity is maintained. Due to this increased complexity, you should consider partitioning only when scaling up is not feasible.

Replicating the Resource

The final scale-out strategy I will examine is replication. Replication involves duplicating the data hosted by a resource across all nodes in the cluster. This is an especially effective strategy for scaling out resources that provide access to read-only or mostly read-only data.

For example, suppose the Banking Web service has a database table that contains the fees charged to a client for using its service. Because the fees are relatively static, they can be replicated on multiple database servers. The implementation of the Web service can then obtain the fees from any database server in the cluster.

If the data is writable, implementing a replication strategy becomes more complicated. One issue with replicating writable data is maintaining the coherence of the data across the nodes in the cluster. Because multiple copies of the data reside within the cluster, you must ensure that updates made to one node are reflected across the other nodes in the cluster.

You also need to resolve merge conflicts. A merge conflict occurs when the same data is updated with two different values on two different nodes at the same time. One way to resolve a merge conflict is to allow the last write to win. This technique is used by Active Directory. For this strategy to be effective, the nodes in the cluster must have synchronized clocks.

Another way to resolve merge conflicts is to avoid them altogether. For example, you can allow writes to occur on only one node in the cluster. However, this scenario is practical only if the data is read more often than it is written because all writes are performed on one server.

Another design issue is how replication should be handled by the cluster. Replication takes a certain amount of time to perform. While replication is occurring, a node in the cluster might be queried and retrieve the original value. This can cause problems for your application.

For example, suppose a client modifies some data and then views the data to verify the results. If the data is written to one node in the cluster and then viewed from another node before the changes have had time to replicate, it will look like the data was not modified.

Some resources, such as SQL Server, support transactional replication order to solve this problem. When a client adds, modifies, or deletes data on one node in the cluster, the data can be accessed only after it has been successfully replicated to all other nodes in the cluster. The downside to transactional replication is that modifications made to replicated data will take longer to complete as more servers are added to the cluster.

Overcoming Scalability Bottlenecks

Sometimes your Web service will need to access resources that do not scale well. For example, the Banking Web service needs to coordinate fund transfer requests with other banks. This task is accomplished via a legacy LOB application.

The LOB application can handle 15,000 requests per day, but our peak load is around 60,000 requests per day. Unfortunately, it is not practical to scale the LOB application to meet the needs of the Banking Web service. However, recall that if the requests are averaged across the month, it comes out to only 10,000 requests per day, which is well under the 15,000-requests-per-day maximum load.

What we need is a way to buffer the LOB application from the peak load on the 1st and the 15th of every month. We can accomplish this by placing a queue between the Banking Web service and the LOB application. Instead of issuing the requests to transfer funds synchronously, the system queues the requests and the LOB application processes the requests at a steady pace.

One downside to this technique is that a request received from the Web service to transfer funds might not be processed promptly by the LOB application. In the case of the Banking Web service, the 60,000th request received on either the 1st or the 15th will not be processed until 24 hours later. If you leverage queuing to address scalability issues, you must manage your clients' expectations about the time it might take to process their requests.

Maintaining High Availability

A Web service might be able to scale to handle the volume of requests received from clients, but it will be useful only if it is up and running. Ensuring that a Web service provides the necessary level of availability is just as important as ensuring that it can scale to meet the needs of its clients.

Availability is often defined as the percentage of time the system is up during its scheduled hours of operation. For example, if a Web service has 99.9 percent availability, that means the system experiences one or more outages 0.1 percent of the total time the system is scheduled to be operational.

The percentage of uptime is meaningful only if you know the Web service's scheduled hours of operation. For example, a Web service that must be operational 24×7 and requires 99.999 percent uptime can have only 5.3 minutes of downtime per year, including downtime for maintenance. Compare that to a Web service that needs to be available only between 9 A.M. and 5 P.M. on weekdays. If the Web service requires 99.999 percent uptime, it can experience only about one minute of unscheduled downtime a year but can have a total of 6656 hours of maintenance per year.

One key factor in creating a highly available Web service is to ensure that there are no single points of failure. This encompasses every resource used by the Web service—including the server that hosts the Web service, the network elements responsible for routing the requests to the Web service, and the power for the network elements and servers.

Once you have determined that there are no single points of failure, you need to ensure that if one of the components should fail, the infrastructure supporting the Web service is still capable of carrying the entire load. For example, if the cluster hosting your Web service is front-ended by two network routers, you should ensure that a single router is capable of handling the network traffic.

When you are planning the maximum capacity that any one element within the system should carry, take into consideration the total cumulative effect of that one element. For example, suppose during normal operations you have two servers within the cluster that are actively servicing client requests. When determining the amount of memory that should be installed in each system, take into account issues such as memory fragmentation. If each node is running at 50 percent memory usage and one node fails, the other node might not be able to handle the additional requests due to memory fragmentation. (Note that this is less of an issue with managed applications since the Garbage Collector is capable of compacting the heap.)

More important, you must ensure that the necessary procedures are in place for administering and maintaining a highly available Web service. These include a solid disaster recovery plan, documentation of the server configuration, and a solid change management strategy.

In short, you should make sure that your Web service is managed by qualified administrators. You can find many excellent resources for administrators that examine best practices for managing highly available applications. One of them is the Microsoft Operations Framework (MOF); you can find information about it at *http://www.microsoft.com/mof.*

Next I provide a high-level overview of the software and hardware required to create a highly available Web service. Then I explain some of the paradigm shifts you should make when you program against a highly available resource.

Highly Available Scale-Up Resources

By definition, a resource that relies on the scale-up strategy is a single point of failure. If the server hosting the resource goes down, the resource is no longer available. To achieve high scalability for a resource hosted on a single server, you can use a failover cluster.

A failover cluster is composed of multiple machines; one machine is active, and one or more machines serve as backups. If the active machine is unable to service requests, a backup machine is brought on line and client requests are automatically directed to it.

For Windows, the predominant failover cluster platform is Microsoft Clustering Service (MSCS). MSCS ships with both Windows 2000 Advanced Server and Windows 2000 Datacenter Server. The former supports two-node clusters, and the latter supports four-node clusters.

Any resource can be hosted on an MSCS cluster, but only MSCS-aware resources can take full advantage of the functionality provided by an MSCS cluster. A number of resources are cluster aware, including SQL Server, MSMQ, and NTFS file shares.

MSCS supports the "shared nothing" model in which each node in the cluster has its own system bus and access to disk subsystems and the network. In general, the active node in the cluster is given exclusive access to a particular disk subsystem. You can access specific data on a particular resource only through one node of the cluster at any given time.

If a disk subsystem contains data used by the resource to process client requests, it must be accessible by every node in the cluster. If the active node fails, MSCS will designate another node in the cluster to serve as the active node. As part of the failover process, the new active node will gain exclusive access to the disk subsystem.

The disk subsystem containing the data necessary to process client requests is a single point of failure. If the disk subsystem fails, none of the nodes in the cluster will be able to process client requests. Therefore, the disk subsystem is usually hosted on a RAID 5 disk array.

MSCS Components

MSCS has three primary components: the Cluster service, the Resource Monitor, and the Resource DLL.

The Cluster service is a Windows NT service that is responsible for the overall control of the cluster. It has the following responsibilities:

- Monitoring the status of the nodes in the cluster

- Coordinating the initialization and cleanup process when nodes are added and removed from the cluster

- Maintaining a database that contains information about the cluster, including the cluster's name and resource types installed on the cluster

The Resource Monitor enables communication between the Cluster service and one or more resources hosted on a node in the cluster. If the Cluster service fails, the Resource Monitor is responsible for taking the resources on a particular node off line.

The Resource Monitor is hosted within its own process. This prevents a misbehaving resource from taking down the cluster. In addition, multiple Resource Monitors can be hosted on a particular node. If you have a resource hosted on the MSCS cluster that is particularly unstable, you can configure it within its own Resource Monitor.

Cluster-aware resources have their own Resource DLL that is installed on each node in the cluster. The Resource DLL is loaded by the Resource Monitor and is accessed via a well-known set of interfaces defined by the Cluster API.

These interfaces enable the Cluster service to obtain information about the resource and also allow the Resource Monitor to tell the Resource DLL to take the resource on line or off line.

If your Web service will leverage a clustered resource in production, it is often helpful to develop against a clustered resource within the development environment. However, installing production-quality clustering hardware in a development environment is often prohibitively expensive. An alternative is to install SCSI adapters in two servers and connect them to an external SCSI disk drive. After you get MSCS installed and running, you can install any number of MSCS resources on the cluster.

Highly Available Scale-Out Resources

Although scale-out resources are hosted on multiple servers, basic scale-out strategies do not inherently provide high availability. Ensuring that a resource deployed using the scale-out strategy is fault tolerant takes deliberate planning.

Partitioned resources are not fault tolerant. A node hosts a portion of the resource, and if the node is no longer available, the portion of the resource hosted by the node is no longer available. Each node within a partitioned resource is a single point of failure.

To ensure that a partitioned resource is fault tolerant, you must create a failover cluster for each node. For example, if the resource is partitioned across five servers, you must create and maintain five failover clusters. This bolsters the argument for avoiding partitioned resources whenever possible.

What might be less obvious is that a network load–balanced cluster is not inherently fault tolerant. The NLB system must know whether the resource itself is on line. For example, if a node hosting the Banking Web service loses its connection to the database, it returns a SOAP exception to the user. Because IP traffic can still be routed to the node, the NLB system continues to route requests to the instance of the Web service that is unable to connect to the database.

NLB algorithms that route requests based on server utilization can worsen the problem by actually increasing the number of requests routed to the troubled node. For example, suppose the NLB system used to route requests to the Banking Web service routes requests to the node with the lowest CPU utilization. And suppose the HTTP service stops on one of the nodes in the cluster and therefore can no longer process requests. Its CPU utilization will drop significantly because the server is no longer processing requests. As a result, the NLB system will route even more requests to the disabled Web server because it has very low CPU utilization compared to the other nodes in the cluster.

The algorithm used to detect when a node is no longer able to process requests is usually specific to the resource that is being load balanced. You can use products such as Microsoft Application Center to monitor nodes in a cluster to ensure that they are capable of processing requests.

You can configure Microsoft Application Center to periodically send each node in the cluster an HTTP request and parse the response to ensure that a success message is returned. If a success message is not returned, Microsoft Application Center will communicate with the NLB system to remove the node from the cluster.

If you are on a budget, you can use the HTTPMon utility that ships with the Windows 2000 Resource Kit to monitor nodes in a cluster. HTTPMon is not as feature rich or as easy to use as Microsoft Application Center, but it monitors Web servers within an NLB cluster by posting HTTP requests and parsing the results. If an unexpected result is received, the node is removed from the cluster.

Programming Against a Highly Available Resource

One common characteristic shared by load-balanced clusters and failover clusters is that they are generally invisible to the client. The client should not be able to tell the difference between a clustered resource and a stand-alone server. The client should use the same API regardless of whether the resource is clustered.

Even though the method of accessing a clustered resource does not change, you take special measures to make sure that you maximize the benefits of programming against a highly available clustered resource. Here are some of these measures:

- **When a request made to the resource fails, retry the request.** Most high-availability technologies are reactive and will remove a machine from the cluster only when a request made to that machine fails, so be sure you have the appropriate retry logic within your application.

- **Take into account the time it takes for the clustered resource to recover from a failure.** When you retry the request, be aware of the time it takes for the cluster to recover from a server failure. For example, if a server fails in an NLB cluster, by default it will take at least five seconds for the other servers in the cluster to start the convergence process to recover from the failure. Depending on the resource, an MSCS cluster can take considerably longer to recover from a failure. If the application performs a single retry without regard to time, the application will fail and therefore not exploit the availability the cluster offers.

■   **Take into account state that might not be automatically rehy-
     drated on the new server.** You must take into account any state
     that cannot be failed over to another node in the cluster if a server in
     the cluster fails while the client is in the middle of a session with a
     resource that maintains state. Any resource that requires server affin-
     ity falls into this category. If the resource is a Web service, it is an
     excellent candidate to be refactored so that requests made to it are
     atomic and any state persisted between requests is saved to a data
     store that is accessible by other nodes in the cluster.

Third-Party Web Services and Availability

Web services enable you to leverage functionality exposed by third-party Web
services via the Internet. However, the overall availability of your application
will be affected by the availability of the third-party Web services. In this section, I offer some techniques you can use to help ensure that a third-party Web
service does not adversely affect your application's uptime.

One option is to eliminate dependence on a third-party Web service altogether by reproducing its functionality in house. However, you should weigh
the potential benefits of increased control against the time and cost this
approach will require. For example, the Microsoft TerraServer .NET Web service
provides access to terabytes of satellite images. Reproducing this functionality
would be very expensive and time intensive.

In addition, the third-party Web service might actually provide higher
availability than the client application that uses it. High availability requires a
discipline that few IT organizations have mastered. In other words, I anticipate
a strong market for reliable third-party Web services that meet a business need.

If you have decided to leverage a third-party Web service, consider estab-
lishing a service-level agreement (SLA) with the provider. An SLA is a contract
between you and the Web service provider that defines the service level you
expect (uptime, response time, and so forth). If the service level is not met,
penalties are often imposed on the Web service provider. Penalties can range
from waiving the fees for accessing the Web service based on the amount of
time the Web service is down to compensation based on the financial impact on
your business.

Even if you choose a reliable provider and draft a strong SLA, outages can
still occur. You might consider implementing a strategy so that if the third-party
Web service becomes unavailable, the outage will not adversely affect your clients. In the next sections, I examine two such strategies: failing over to an alternative Web service and implementing an offline mode.

Failing Over to an Alternative Web Service

When practical, you can consider forwarding failed requests to an alternative Web service. For example, say that Woodgrove Bank also hosts a Stock Quote Web service that you use within your application. If the Web service goes down and is no longer returning stock quotes, you can obtain the stock price from another Web service rather than return an error to the client. The following code shows a relatively simple failover technique:

```
using System;
using System.Threading;

public class StockQuoteProxy
{
    bool useBackup = false;
    WoodgroveProxy primary = new WoodgroveProxy();
    ProsewareProxy backup = new ProsewareProxy();
```

I declare two proxy objects for accessing the Stock Quote Web service, one exposed by Woodgrove Bank and one exposed by Proseware Bank. I also declare a Boolean field to indicate whether the proxy should fail over and use the backup proxy object.

```
    public double GetQuote(string symbol)
    {
        if(! useBackup)
        {
            try
            {
                // Obtain quote from primary proxy.
                return primary.GetQuote(symbol);
            }
```

Next I define the *GetQuote* method. By default, it will attempt to obtain a quote for the specified stock symbol via the primary proxy object.

```
            catch(Exception e)
            {
                // Fail over to the backup proxy.
                useBackup = true;

                // Configure object to revert to the primary proxy
                // in 15 minutes.
                Thread thread = new Thread(new ThreadStart(this.Reset));
                thread.Start();

                // Obtain quote from backup proxy.
                return backup.GetQuote(symbol);
            }
        }
```

If the primary proxy object throws an exception, I set the *useBackup* property to *true* so that the instance of *StockQuoteProxy* will fail over to the backup proxy object. A new thread will also be spawned, with the responsibility of reverting to the primary proxy object in 15 minutes. Finally the backup proxy will be used to try to obtain the quote.

```
    else
    {
        // Obtain quote from backup proxy.
        return backup.GetQuote(symbol);
    }
}
```

If the *GetQuote* method is called when *useBackup* is set to *false*, the backup proxy is immediately called.

```
private void Reset()
{
    Thread.Sleep(15000);
    useBackup = false;
}
}
```

Finally I implement the *Reset* method. This method is invoked within its own thread, where it waits for 15 minutes and then sets the *useBackup* field back to *false*. The next time the *GetQuote* method on the instance of the *StockQuoteProxy* class is called, the object will attempt to obtain the quote from the primary proxy.

Another alternative is to leverage UDDI. If the Web service supports a standard interface that is published in UDDI, you can query the UDDI directory to locate alternatives if your primary Web service becomes unavailable. The following code demonstrates this technique:

```
using System;
using System.Threading;
using Microsoft.Uddi;
using Microsoft.Uddi.Binding;

public class StockQuoteProxy2
{
    primaryUrl = "http://www.woodgrove.com/StockQuote.asmx";
    string [] backupUrls;
    int backupUrlIndex = 0;
    WoodgroveProxy proxy = new WoodgroveProxy();

    public StockQuoteProxy2()
    {
        Inquire.Url = "http://uddi.microsoft.com";
```

(continued)

```
        // Find all bindingTemplate entities that expose
        // the StockQuote interface.
        FindBinding findBinding = new FindBinding();
        findBinding.TModelKeys.Add("uuid:272208dd-4f22-4df1-83a6-b8fcff936523");
        BindingDetail bindingDetail = findBinding.Send();

        // Populate the array of backup URLs.
        int count = bindingDetail.BindingTemplates.Count;
        proxyUrls = new int[count];
        for(int i = 1; i < count; i++)
        {
            proxyUrls[i] = bindingTemplate.AccessPoint.Text;
        }
    }

    public double GetQuote(string symbol)
    {
        if(! useBackup)
        {
            try
            {
                // Obtain quote from primary proxy.
                proxy.Url = primaryUrl;
                return proxy.GetQuote(symbol);
            }
            catch(Exception e)
            {
                // Fail over to the backup proxy.
                useBackup = true;

                // Configure object to revert to the primary proxy
                // in 15 minutes.
                Thread thread = new Thread(new ThreadStart(this.Reset));
                thread.Start();

                // Obtain quote from backup proxy.
                return this.GetQuote(symbol);
            }
        }
```

If the primary proxy object throws an exception, the *useBackup* property is set to *true* so that the instance of *StockQuoteProxy* will fail over to the backup proxy object. A new thread will also be spawned, with the responsibility to revert back to the primary proxy object in 15 minutes. Finally the backup proxy is used to try to obtain the quote.

```
        else
        {
            // Obtain quote from backup proxy.
```

```
proxy.Url = backupUrls[backupUrlIndex];
try
{
    return this.GetQuote(symbol);
}
catch(Exception e)
{
    // If there is another backup proxy, call it.
    // Otherwise, rethrow the exception.
    if(backupUrls.NextUrl)
    {

    lock(backupUrls)
    {
        if(backupUrls.Position < (backupUrls.Count - 1))
        {
            backupUrls
    backupUrlIndex ++;
    if(backupUrlIndex < (backupUrls.Count-1))
    {
        throw;
    }
    return this.GetQuote(symbol);
        }
    }
}
```

If the *GetQuote* method is called when *useBackup* is set to *false*, the backup proxy will immediately be called.

```
private void Reset()
{
    Thread.Sleep(15000);
    useBackup = false;
}
}
```

Finally I implement the *Reset* method. As in the previous example, the *Reset* method causes the instance of the *StockQuote2Proxy* class to retry the primary proxy after 15 minutes. Notice that the *Reset* method does not reset the index for the backup proxy. If the primary proxy fails again, the current backup proxy will once again be called.

Creating an Offline Mode of Operation

In some cases, using an alternative Web service is not practical. For example, I cannot use another bank's Web service to modify the banking services I set up with Woodgrove Bank. In these situations, you should determine whether you can provide an offline mode for interacting with the Web service.

When you consider your offline strategy, take a hard look at the synchronous interactions with the Web service and determine whether they can be performed asynchronously. For example, the client application for the Banking Web service might allow users to request fund transfers. If the request is not honored within a specified period of time, the client can be notified.

When the client issues a request to transfer funds, the request will be queued on the client. If the Banking Web service is on line, the request will immediately be taken off the queue and processed. If the Web service is off line, the request will stay queued until the Web service comes on line or the request has expired. If the request expires, the client will be notified.

Let's say the Banking Web service also allows users to modify their account information, such as their mailing address. And suppose that the application used to modify the information presents the customer with a form prepopulated with the current information. The customer can make the necessary modifications and then submit the updated information.

The client application must first obtain the current state of the customer's account information to display it to the user. If the Web service is unavailable, there is no way to obtain that information.

But obtaining the most current information from a Web service is often not absolutely necessary. For example, the customer's account information is relatively static. When the Web service is on line, the client application can cache the state of the user's account information. If the Web service becomes unavailable, the client application can display the cached data to the user.

After the customer has modified the account information, the client application can submit the updated information back to the Banking Web service via the queuing method I described earlier.

Optimizing Performance

The performance of your Web service can significantly affect how well it scales. If your Web service can host only a handful of clients, scaling out to handle a large number of clients can quickly turn into an exercise in futility.

When you leverage a resource within your Web service, there is usually a right and a wrong way to program against it. You should follow recommended best practices for leveraging the particular resource. Here are a number of best practices for programming against a database using ADO.NET:

- If a managed provider is available for your database, use it instead of its OLEDB and ODBC counterparts.

- Use stored procedures instead of dynamically generated SQL statements whenever possible.

■   When you iterate through a large result set, use *DataReader* instead of *DataSet*.

You should also design the interface of your Web service with scalability in mind. For example, try to reduce the number of network round-trips. An interface that supports a small number of large requests is usually better than one that supports a large number of small requests.

Also, look for opportunities to reduce the amount of data that is sent across the wire. Avoid passing parameters by reference because doing so involves sending the parameter to the server and then back to the client. If the parameters do not need to be returned back to the client, consider passing instances of value types such as *Int32*, *Boolean*, and structures. Finally, if a value is only returned from the Web service, decorate the parameter with the *out* keyword.

Also consider stripping out formatting characters such as tabs, linefeeds, and spaces from the SOAP messages sent between the client and the server. ASP.NET does this for all SOAP messages generated by an .asmx file.

Caching

If used properly, caching can significantly increase the performance of your Web services. You can use caching to reduce the amount of work a Web service needs to perform to process a request. For example, you might cache a data structure that is expensive to initialize, such as a large hash table. You might also cache a set of previously calculated results.

You can also use caching to improve the locality of data used by your Web service. Whenever you access data over a network, the latency associated with the network can significantly affect the performance of your Web service. You can greatly reduce the cost of retrieving that data if you can retrieve it from an in-memory cache instead of going across the network.

Static read-only data is the best candidate for caching. If the data being cached is not read-only, you should implement a cache coherency strategy to ensure that the data in the cache does not become stale.

ASP.NET provides an easy-to-use mechanism for caching the response from a Web service for a period of time. If the Web service receives a similar request, it will return the cached response to the user instead of executing the particular Web method. This can significantly improve the performance of some Web services.

You can configure the cache using the *CacheDuration* property exposed by the *WebMethod* attribute. For example, recall that the Banking Web service exposes the *GetStockQuote* Web method. Suppose the quote received from the

Web service can be delayed up to 20 minutes. The following example illustrates the use of the *CacheDuration* property:

```
using System;
using System.Web.Services;

public class Banking
{
    [WebMethod(CacheDuration=1200)]
    public double GetStockQuote(string symbol)
    {
        double price = 0;

        // Obtain the current price for the security....

        return price;
    }
}
```

When a request for a particular security is received, the Web method returns the price of the security. Because the *CacheDuration* property is set, if a request for the same security is received in the next 20 minutes (1200 seconds), the ASP.NET runtime will not invoke the *GetStockQuote* Web method. Instead, it will return the cached response to the client.

Sometimes it is not practical to cache the entire SOAP response returned from a Web method. However, you might have opportunities to cache discrete pieces of data used within the implementation of a Web method. For these situations, the ASP.NET runtime provides a more generic caching mechanism.

Recall that the Banking Web service charges a fee based on the amount transferred. Suppose the fee charged to the customer for performing the wire transfer is maintained in an XML document similar to the one shown here:

```
<?xml version="1.0"?>
<Fees>
  <Fee minExclusive="0" maxInclusive="100">.50</Fee>
  <Fee minExclusive="100" maxInclusive="250">1.00</Fee>
  <Fee minExclusive="250" maxInclusive="500">1.50</Fee>
  <Fee minExclusive="500" maxInclusive="1000">2.00</Fee>
  <Fee minExclusive="1000" maxInclusive="999999">3.00</Fee>
</Fees>
```

The document contains a list of fees based on the amount transferred. The implementation of the *RequestWireTransfer* method uses the data in the XML document to determine the fee that should be charged to the client.

```
using System;
using System.Web.Services;
using System.Xml;
using System.Configuration;
```

```
public class Banking
{
    [WebMethod]
    public void RequestWireTransfer(int sourceAccount,
        int destinationAccount, double amount)
    {
        // Obtain the Fees.xml document.
        XmlDocument feesDocument= new XmlDocument();
        string filePath =
            (string)HttpContext.GetAppConfig("FeesXmlDocument");
        feesDocument.Load(filePath);

        // Obtain the fee that should be charged.
        string xpathQuery = string.Format("//Fee[@minExclusive < {0}
            and @maxInclusive >= {0}]", amount);
        XmlNode result = feesDocument.SelectSingleNode(xpathQuery);
        double fee = double.Parse(result.InnerText);

        // The rest of the implementation....

    }
}
```

The *RequestWireTransfer* Web method first obtains the path for the XML document containing the fees from the web.config file. After the document is loaded, I issue an XPath query to retrieve the fee based on the amount to be transferred.

You can add application-specific configuration parameters to the web.config file by adding *add* child elements to the *appSettings* element. The following is a portion of the web.config file that contains the *FeesXmlDocument* configuration parameter:

```
<?xml version="1.0" encoding="utf-8" ?>
<configuration>
  <appSettings>
    <add key="FeesXmlDocument" value="c:\Fees.xml"/>
  </appSettings>

  <!-- The rest of the configuration file... -->

</configuration>
```

The problem with this implementation is that the Fees.xml document will be loaded every time the method is called. Because the XML document is relatively static, this is horribly inefficient.

One way to improve performance is to scope the instance of the *XmlDocument* class containing the Fees.xml document to the application. The Fees.xml document can be loaded into memory once and then used multiple times. The following code illustrates this technique:

```
using System;
using System.Web.Services;
using System.Xml;
using System.Configuration;

public class Banking
{
    private static feesDocument;

    static Banking()
    {
        // Obtain the Fees.xml document.
        feesDocument = new XmlDocument();
        string filePath =
            (string)HttpContext.GetAppConfig("FeesXmlDocument");
        feesDocument.Load(filePath);
    }

    [WebMethod]
    public void RequestWireTransfer(int sourceAccount,
        int destinationAccount, double amount)
    {
        // Obtain the fee that should be charged.
        string xpathQuery = string.Format("//Fee[@minExclusive < {0}
            and @maxInclusive >= {0}]", amount);
        XmlNode result = feesDocument.SelectSingleNode(xpathQuery);
        double fee = double.Parse(result.InnerText);

        // The rest of the implementation...

    }
}
```

I loaded the XML document within the class's constructor and set the instance of the *XmlDocument* class to a static variable. The .NET runtime will ensure that the class constructor is called prior to the creation of an instance of the *Banking* class. Once initialized, the *feesDocument* static variable can be referenced by all subsequent invocations of the *RequestWireTransfer* Web method.

The primary issue with this code is that if the rates are updated in the underlying XML document, they will not be reflected in the cache. What we need is a cache coherence strategy so that when the underlying data source changes, the entry in the cache will be updated.

ASP.NET provides a caching mechanism for caching data used by your Web service. Central to the caching mechanism is the *Cache* class. An instance of the *Cache* class is created within each application domain hosted by the ASP.NET runtime and is accessible via the *HttpContext* class.

The following example loads the XML document within the ASP.NET cache and then reloads the XML document each time it is modified:

```
using System;
using System.Web.Caching;
using System.Xml;
using System.Configuration;

class Banking
{
    [WebMethod]
    public void RequestWireTransfer(int sourceAccount,
        int destinationAccount, double amount)
    {
        double fee = Fees.GetFee(amount);

        // The rest of the implementation...

    }
}
```

The *RequestWireTransfer* method calls the static *GetFee* method on the *Fees* class to obtain the fee for the amount. The *Fees* class encapsulates all interactions with the ASP.NET cache as well as the business logic used to determine the fee that should be charged to the client.

```
class Fees
{
    static Fees()
    {
        Fees.LoadFeesIntoCache();
    }

    private static void LoadFeesIntoCache()
    {
        // Obtain the Fees XML document.
        string filePath =
            (string)HttpContext.GetAppConfig("FeesXmlDocument");
        filePath =
            (string)ConfigurationSettings.AppSettings["FeesXmlDocument"];
        XmlDocument feesDocument = new XmlDocument();
        feesDocument.Load(filePath);

        // Create a new cache dependency on the underlying XML file.
        CacheDependency cacheDependency = new CacheDependency(filePath);
```

(continued)

```
    // Create a new callback object used to invoke the
    // Fees_OnRemove method when the cache entry is invalidated.
    CacheItemRemovedCallback callback =
        new CacheItemRemovedCallback(Fees_OnRemoved);

    // Load the Fees XML document into the cache.
    HttpContext.Current.Cache.Insert("Fees", feesDocument,
        cacheDependency, Cache.NoAbsoluteExpiration,
        Cache.NoSlidingExpiration, CacheItemPriority.NotRemovable,
        cache);
}
```

The static constructor is responsible for initializing the cache. This is accomplished by calling the *LoadFeesIntoCache* static method.

The *LoadFeesIntoCache* static method obtains the Fees XML document and loads it into the ASP.NET cache. In doing so, it creates a dependency on the underlying XML file. If the Fees XML file is changed, the ASP.NET runtime can invoke a callback.

The *CacheDependency* class provides multiple overloaded constructors for creating dependencies on a number of different types of entities. You can create a dependency on a file or a directory. You can also create a dependency on a collection of files or directories. If any file or directory within the collection changes, the entry will be invalidated. Finally, you can create a dependency on other instances of the *CacheDependency* class as well as other cache entries.

In the preceding example, the *Fees_OnRemoved* method will be invoked when the Fees XML document is modified. This is accomplished by registering the *Fees_OnRemoved* method as a callback.

Finally I create a new entry in the cache by calling the *Insert* method. The *Insert* method has overloads that allow you to set either an exact time or a time window when the entry should expire.

You can also pass the priority of the cache entry as a parameter to the *Insert* method. If the server runs low on memory, the runtime will use the priority to determine which entries to delete from the cache first. Because I don't want the Fees XML document to be removed from memory, I set the priority to the *NonRemovable* static property exposed by the object.

```
public static double GetFee(double amount)
{
    // Obtain the Fees.xml document from the cache.
    XmlDocument feesDocument = null;
    while(feesDocument == null)
    {
        (XmlDocument)HttpContext.Current.Cache["Fees"];
    }
```

```
// Obtain the fee that should be charged.
string xpathQuery = string.Format("//Fee[@minExclusive < {0}
    and @maxInclusive >= {0}]", amount);
XmlNode result = feesDocument.SelectSingleNode(xpathQuery);

return double.Parse(result.InnerText);
}
```

The *GetFee* method obtains the Fees XML document from the ASP.NET cache and then executes an XPath query to determine the fee based on the amount transferred. Notice that I implemented a spin lock to ensure that I received the Fees XML document instead of a null reference. This is necessary to avoid a race condition with the code responsible for reloading the Fees XML document in the event it is changed.

```
public static void Fees_OnRemoved(String k, Object v,
    CacheItemRemovedReason r)
{
    Fees.LoadFeesIntoCache();
}
}
```

Finally I implement the *Fees_OnRemoved* event handler. If the Fees XML document is removed from the cache, the *LoadFeesIntoCache* method will be called to reload the updated document.

The *Cache* class exposes properties and methods that you can use to maintain the items within the cache. Table 12-1 lists the fields, properties, and methods that the *Cache* class supports.

Table 12-1   Fields, Properties, and Methods of the *Cache* Class

Field	Description
NoAbsoluteExpiration	A static field intended to be passed to the *Insert* method. Indicates that the item in the cache should not expire by a particular date and time.
NoSlidingExpiration	A static field intended to be passed to the *Insert* method. Indicates that the item in the cache should not expire within a particular interval of time.

Property	Description
Count	Retrieves the number of items in the cache.
Item	Accesses an item in the cache at a specified index.

Table 12-1   Fields, Properties, and Methods of the *Cache* Class   *(continued)*

Method	Description
Add	Adds an item to the cache.
Get	Retrieves an item in the cache at a specified index.
GetEnumerator	Retrieves an enumerator used to iterate through the keys of the items in the cache.
Insert	Adds an item to the cache.
Remove	Removes a specified item from the cache.

Summary

The scalability and availability of a Web service can be critical to its success. Not only does the Web service need to scale and provide high availability, but also, the resources it uses to process a client's request cannot hinder its scalability and availability. This chapter introduces techniques and technologies that you can use to achieve your scalability and availability goals.

The two primary types of scalability strategies are scale up and scale out. Scale up involves hosting the resource on a more powerful computer. Scale out involves dividing the work performed by the resource across multiple computers. I explain how to divide work across the nodes in a cluster by employing NLB partitioning and replication. Each strategy has its weaknesses and strengths.

The strategy used to scale a resource will often dictate the strategy used to ensure that a resource is highly available. Resources that are scaled up are often hosted on a failover cluster. Resources that are scaled out using load balancing often require a mechanism to detect when a node is no longer capable of processing a client's request. Resources that are scaled out using partitioning often require that every node that hosts a portion of the resource reside in a failover cluster.

I also introduce techniques for programming against a highly available resource. Finally I explain the importance of performance in ensuring that your Web service scales in an effective and manageable way.

13

The Future of Web Services

The technologies used to build Web services and the ways developers leverage these technologies are in their infancy. At the time of this writing, standards bodies are well underway drafting the next version for a number of existing specifications such as SOAP and UDDI. In addition, companies are developing new and creative uses for Web services.

In this chapter, I first examine a set of Web services currently in development within Microsoft that is receiving a considerable amount of attention—Microsoft .NET My Services. Microsoft .NET My Services exposes a number of Web services that allow users to control their personal data. Among these are a set of user-focused Web services that allows users to store their personal information securely in remote locations and then access it from any device in any location and even allows others to access it (but strictly on terms the user defines). I explain how you can leverage .NET My Services from within your own applications.

The existing suite of industry-standard specifications that define Web services has some significant omissions. In many cases, developers are stifled with respect to the type of services that they can provide their customers. In the case of .NET My Services, I point out areas that are not covered by the current set of Web service specifications.

In an effort to fill in gaps not covered by the current set of Web service specifications, Microsoft introduced the Global XML Web Services Architecture (GXA). At the time of this writing, the GXA consists of five specifications that address key areas not covered by current industry standards. Once the specifications mature, Microsoft intends to turn over the specifications to recognised standards bodies so that they can be ratified and released as recommendations. In this chapter, I provide a brief overview of all five specifications.

Finally I examine some of the emerging infrastructural components for developing and deploying Web services. Specifically, I provide a brief explanation of Microsoft's plans to provide dynamic application topologies, the ability to host a Web service across a number of geographically distributed servers. I also review the BizTalk Orchestration for Web Services technical preview.

Note   The material in this chapter is based on beta software and specifications, so changes are likely prior to final release.

Introducing .NET My Services

Consider the personal information you have stored electronically: multiple user-names and passwords to access an array of Web sites; bookmarks stored on your home PC, which you cannot access from the office; calendars that you must synchronize on PCs in different locations and on your PDA; and separate contact lists held by your cell phone, PDA, and home and office PCs. And this is merely a fraction of the information the average user must manage. Users will soon have a solution to this problem with .NET My Services, a set of XML Web services that gives a user control over his personal data.

.NET My Services allows a user to store personal information remotely in a secure "digital deposit box." The user can then permit individuals or organizations to access parts of this information on the user's terms. For example, a user might allow an airline access to her schedule for a single operation so that the airline can enter flight departure and arrival times. Not only can the user control her information, but she can also access that information at any time from any device. For example, a user might access her information using PCs at various locations, a cell phone such as the Stinger smart phone, or even an Xbox. This is possible because .NET My Services is like any other Web service—it communicates over existing transport protocols using XML and it returns XML to a client, which must then interpret and render the information in an appropriate fashion.

The beta release of .NET My Services will consist of a set of core services. Later, Microsoft and approved third parties will develop and release additional .NET My Services services. The initial core services are as follows:

- **.NET My Services service**   Records the services to which a user subscribes.

- **.NET Alerts**   Allows a user to manage subscriptions to alerts or notifications and allows Web sites and Web services to send a user alerts. For example, a Web service might send an alert to a user if a particular stock drops in price.

- **.NET ApplicationSettings**   Stores a user's application settings. For example, an application that accesses the service can adjust itself to the stored settings for toolbars in order to match the user's preferences.

- **.NET Calendar**   Stores a user's calendar information, such as time and task management information.

- **.NET Categories**   A list of categories that allows a user to group data documents together. For example, a user can group contacts (from .NET Contacts) together to form a contact list.

- **.NET Contacts**   Stores a user's contact information, such as colleagues' e-mail addresses and phone numbers. For example, a user can store a colleague's contact details while at the office and then look up these details using his cellular phone while out of the office.

- **.NET Devices**   Stores information about the devices a user plans to use to access .NET My Services. For example, a user can store the display attributes of her PDA. Incidentally, you can deliver information from services to mobile devices using the Mobile Internet Toolkit, which allows you to write ASP.NET pages that the runtime formats to match the display attributes and markup language that the client's device supports.

- **.NET Documents**   Stores a user's documents both securely and remotely.

- **.NET FavoriteWebsites**   Stores a list of the user's favorite Web sites.

- **.NET Inbox**   A centralized access point for users to access their e-mail. For example, a user can access her Hotmail account from a PDA while away from a PC.

- **.NET Lists**   Stores user-defined free-format lists. For example, a user can store a list of all the countries he wants to visit on an around-the-world tour.

- **.NET Locations**   Stores the location of the actual user at a given time. For example, a user might set her location to The Office or At Home.

- **.NET Presence**   Stores information about a user's availability for receiving alerts. For example, a user can set his presence status to indicate that he is currently off line and thus cannot receive an alert.

- **.NET Profile**   Stores a user's personal information. For example, a user can store her name, family birthdays, and personal photographs.

■ **.NET Wallet** Stores information the user needs to make payments, as well as items such as receipts and coupons that relate to payments. For example, the user can securely store his credit card details so that he does not have to enter card information each time he wants to make an online payment.

.NET My Services will offer exciting opportunities not only to users but also to businesses and developers. Businesses will be able to offer levels of service that the Web simply cannot deliver today. For example, with the aid of .NET My Services, an e-commerce business will be able to interact with a new customer as if she were an existing customer. All the user has to do is log in using .NET Passport, and the business will be able to access her personal details, delivery information, and payment information. The business can even send alerts to her cell phone when a new product arrives in stock or update her schedule so that she knows when the product will be delivered.

From a developer's perspective, .NET My Services eliminates many of the problems of securing data, providing encrypted transport channels, and reconciling disparate data sources. And all of this is achievable using XML Web services, so businesses are spared the drastic learning curve associated with new technologies and the need to make any radical changes to their development and production environments.

The following graphic shows a simplified view of the .NET My Services architecture. It shows that a client can consume a .NET My Services service in the same way that it consumes a regular Web service (at least at a high level), with the exception of the authentication service that .NET Passport provides. A client can make requests to .NET My Services services using XML using a protocol such as HTTP or Direct Internet Message Encapsulation (DIME) as a transport mechanism. Authentication is necessary in this architecture to ensure that only individuals or organizations that a user wants to grant access to can access that user's information.

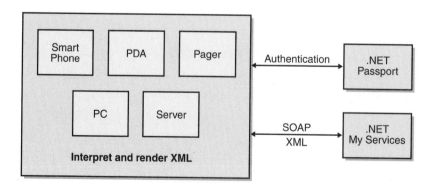

Securing .NET My Services

.NET Passport is at the heart of the .NET My Services security architecture and provides authentication services through the use of Kerberos. The .NET Passport service authenticates users and provides access to a .NET My Services service through the issuing of tickets, which are in effect temporary encryption keys. The following graphic shows the process of authenticating a user and allowing that user access to a .NET My Services service.

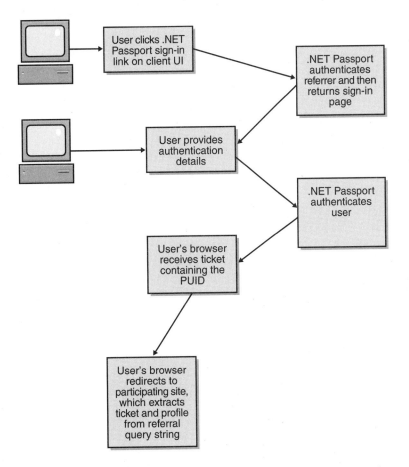

> **Note**   Kerberos is an industry-standard protocol created at the Massachusetts Institute of Technology (MIT) that provides strong authentication over a network. Several operating systems implement this protocol, including Microsoft Windows 2000 and Windows XP.

As you can see, once the user clicks on a .NET Passport link, he is redirected to the .NET Passport server. When this redirection occurs, the referring site passes an ID unique to that site and a return URL. .NET Passport uses these to verify that the referring site is indeed the site it claims to be. If verification is successful, .NET Passport presents the user with a log-in screen, where the user enters a username and password. If .NET Passport can authenticate the user's credentials, it extracts a Passport Unique Identifier (PUID) and a Passport Profile from a database. .NET Passport then uses these to create three encrypted .NET Passport cookies (a ticket, a profile, and a visited-sites cookie), which it returns to the user's browser. .NET Passport then redirects the user to the referring Web site, where the site extracts the ticket and profile information and sends them to a Passport Manager object. This object decrypts the information and authenticates the user.

Under the .NET My Services model, the user no longer stores her own personal information but instead allows Microsoft or a trusted third party to store that information on her behalf. This paradigm shift requires the user to establish a trust relationship with the holder of her information—the user must be confident that her information will be made available only to appropriate parties. Authentication partially addresses this issue, but the issues of the security of the data store and the availability of information to third parties still remain.

In terms of data-store security, Microsoft ensures that database servers are not accessible over the Internet and that only Microsoft-certified personnel can access these databases. In addition, Microsoft can rotate encryption algorithms to further enhance the integrity of the data stores. Privacy of information is a different matter because it relies on the integrity or philosophy of an organization rather than on a physical means of protection.

Microsoft states that it will not allow secondary use of data and supports this with the following two measures:

- Microsoft will be audited by Safe Harbor, a controlling body of the European Union (EU).

- Microsoft states that it will adhere to its own Fair Information Practices.

Working with .NET My Services

When you work with .NET My Services, you can think of it as an XML database—a database of user information that, for example, you can execute queries against and that will return the results of those queries as XML fragments. It is then up to you to interpret that data and render it appropriately for your client. In reality, .NET My Services stores all data as XML service documents, and you access this data using XML messages rather than using a query language such as SQL.

HSDL, the .NET My Services data manipulation language, defines the following six XML messages, which are common to all .NET My Services services:

- **queryRequest**   Allows you to issue a query against a document, which will return an XML node set.

- **deleteRequest**   Deletes a specified node set from a specified document.

- **updateRequest**   Allows you to define a composite message, which can consist of a series of insert, delete, and replace requests.

- **replaceRequest**   Replaces a specified node set with another node set.

- **insertRequest**   Inserts XML in a document at a specified location.

- **subscriptionResponse**   Requests a subscription to specified data; when data changes, you receive a notification.

As you can see, each of these messages allows you to either insert data into or extract data from a service document. You can also see that most of the messages manipulate node sets rather than individual elements within an XML document. These node sets are demarcated by specially designated elements that allow HSDL messages to use XPath-style node selection. At the highest level within a document is a root element whose name matches that of the corresponding service. This element is known as the *root*, and HSDL labels this as a blue element. HSDL also labels the children of this element (that is, top-level elements) as blue elements.

The following example shows sample XML with the blue elements shown in bold:

```
<myAddress changeNumber="..." instanceId="...">
  <address changeNumber="..." id="...">
    <cat ref="..."></cat>
    <officialAddressLine xml:lang="..."></officialAddressLine>
    <internalAddressLine xml:lang="..."></internalAddressLine>
    <primaryCity xml:lang="..."></primaryCity>
    <secondaryCity xml:lang="..."></secondaryCity>
    <subdivision xml:lang="..."></subdivision>
    <postalCode></postalCode>
    <countryOrRegion xml:lang="..."></countryOrRegion>
    ...
    <!-- Further Elements -->
    ...
  </address>

  <webSite changeNumber="..." id="...">
```

(continued)

```
    <cat ref="..." id="..."></cat>
    <url></url>
    ...
    <!-- Further Elements -->
    ...
  </webSite>


  ...
  <!-- Further Blue Elements -->
  ...
</myAddress>
```

The listing shows that the following elements are blue:

- *<myAddress/>*

- *<address/>*

- *<webSite/>*

These elements demarcate the node sets, which you can manipulate using the previously described HSDL messages. Each blue element contains one or more red elements or attributes, which the previous example shows as underlined. You can use the red elements to assist in the selection of a blue element when you use HSDL messages. The remaining elements—those that are neither red nor blue—you cannot address directly, but you can include them within a reference to a red item.

You can use both red and blue items in XPath predicates within HDSL messages, but be careful that you understand how the following commands work:

- **insertRequest** Inserts a blue item into a document or a red item into a selected blue item

- **deleteRequest** Deletes a blue item from a document or a red item from within a blue item

- **replaceRequest** Replaces a blue item or a red item

- **queryRequest** Returns a blue item (or items) or a set of instructions that tell you whether cached information is valid

A Sample .NET My Services Request

As a developer, you are probably eager to see how HSDL works in practice. Although you cannot write real code against .NET My Services today, we can still walk through a short example of using HSDL against a .NET My Services service. This example creates a SOAP message that inserts an entry containing a user's name and e-mail address into the .NET Profile service document.

Here is the complete example, with the HSDL operation shown in bold:

```
<?xml version='1.0'?>
<s:Envelope
s:encodingStyle="http://schemas.xmlsoap.org/soap/envelope/"
xmlns:s="http://schemas.xmlsoap.org/soap/envelope/">

<s:Header>
  <x:path xmlns:x="http://schemas.xmlsoap.org/rp/">
    <x:action>
    http://schemas.microsoft.com/hs/2001/10/core#request
    </x:action>
    <x:rev><x:via /></x:rev>
    <x:to>http://species8472</x:to>
    <x:id>35b4474a-a7d9-11d5-bf0e-00b0d0ccc121</x:id>
  </x:path>
  <ss:licenses
  xmlns:ss="http://schemas.xmlsoap.org/soap/security/2000-12">
    <h:identity mustUnderstand="1">
      <h:kerberos>1</h:kerberos>
    </h:identity>
  </ss:licenses>
  <h:request
  xmlns:h="http://schemas.microsoft.com/hs/2001/10/core"
  service="myProfile"
  document="content"
  method="insert"
  genResponse="always">
    <h:key instance="0" cluster="0" puid="3066" />
  </h:request>
</s:Header>

<s:Body>
  <hs:insertRequest
  xmlns:hs="http://schemas.microsoft.com/hs/2001/10/core"
  xmlns:m="http://schemas.microsoft.com/hs/2001/10/myProfile"
  hs:select="/m:myProfile">
    <m:name
    xmlns:m="http://schemas.microsoft.com/hs/2001/10/myProfile">
      <m:givenName xml:lang="en-us">John</m:givenName>
      <m:surName xml:lang="en-us">Chen</m:surName>
    </m:name>
    <m:emailAddress
    xmlns:m="http://schemas.microsoft.com/hs/2001/10/myProfile">
      <m:e-mail>john@fabrikam.com</m:e-mail>
      <m:name xml:lang="en-us">John Chen</m:name>
    </m:e-mailAddress>
  </hs:insertRequest>
</s:Body>

</s:Envelope>
```

As you can see, most of the XML isn't the HSDL command, but the remainder of the SOAP envelope. When Microsoft makes .NET My Services publicly available, you can use the .NET My Services SDK to generate the SOAP message for you, so I will not provide a detailed explanation of the entire SOAP envelope here. However, you should note a few points.

- The *path* element contains information about the forward path of the SOAP message; it can optionally contain additional information that specifies the return path. (I discuss the future of Web services routing later, in the section titled "WS-Routing.")

- The child elements of the *licenses* element are shown without any content in the previous example, but in the future you will be able to define information pertaining to authentication using Kerberos and .NET Passport. (I discuss this later, in the section titled "WS-Security and WS-License.")

- The *request* element does contain information that relates to the HSDL command the SOAP message issues. The *service* attribute defines the target service, which in this instance is *myProfile*. The *document* attribute can have two possible values: *content* if the request is for data-related purposes, and *admin* if the request is for administrative purposes. Finally, the *method* attribute defines the type of request the client wants to have performed on his behalf, which in this case is an insert.

As shown in the preceding listing, the SOAP body element contains the actual HSDL message. As you can see, the message itself is quite simple. The *name* and *emailAddress* elements are blue elements, which (as I mentioned previously) means you can insert, modify, or delete the node sets that these elements demarcate. In the preceding example, you insert data into the *name* node set and the *emailAddress* node set. You can do this because these node sets are blue elements, but what you cannot do is directly address one of their children. To insert only a user's e-mail address, you must insert an *emailAddress* node set that contains an *e-mail* element rather than insert just an *e-mail* element.

The Global XML Web Services Architecture (GXA)

Today, Web services are built on a set of baseline specifications, which include SOAP, Web Services Description Language (WSDL), and Universal Description, Discovery, and Integration (UDDI). Together, these specifications allow you to write Web services, which are not constrained by programming languages or platforms. The true value of Web services lies in their ability to operate in these heterogeneous environments, but these environments also pose challenges that Web services do not currently address.

- ■   **Security**   Web services must operate within the context of an end-to-end security architecture that allows for authentication and authorization across a heterogeneous, distributed environment.

- ■   **Routable Messages**   In some cases, a message might need to be routed through multiple intermediaries across multiple transports. In these cases, you need the ability to define the route a message must take to reach its intended recipient.

- ■   **Referral Service**   Often the route to an intended recipient must be dynamically configured. For example, many computers, especially those owned by corporations, are located behind a network address translation (NAT) server. A computer located behind a NAT server can open a connection to another server. However, the first computer is not addressable by computers located on the opposite side of the NAT server. In this case, the message needs to be dynamically routed to its intended recipient.

- ■   **Browsable Discovery**   Sometimes it is necessary to advertise your Web service so that it can be discovered using a browse paradigm. For example, a developer might want to browse a peer's server to determine which Web services are exposed.

Unfortunately, the current Web services architecture does not provide specifications that define how these types of operations can occur. This means that an organization implementing Web services today will choose either to ignore these issues or to develop its own proprietary solutions to these problems.

For example, an organization that wants to ensure message integrity might implement a technique based on a proprietary security mechanism. Anyone who interacts with this organization must adhere to this technique. Obviously, this approach requires that the consumer and the producer of the Web service agree on how this solution is implemented. However, the Web service consumer might discover that another Web service producer she deals with implements a different solution, and thus the consumer must modify her applications to interact using another proprietary solution. As you can see, this breaks the fundamental ethos of Web services—that of interoperability.

To respond to the need for universal specifications that ensure interoperability, routable messages, referral service, and browsable discovery support, Microsoft and its partners are defining a set of new specifications. Once these specifications mature, Microsoft will propose them to the appropriate entities for consideration as universal standards, in much the same way that it did with SOAP. Together, these specifications will form the GXA.

So far, the GXA consists of the following five specifications:

- Web Services Inspection Language (WS-Inspection)

- Web Services Security Language (WS-Security)

- Web Services License Language (WS-License)

- Web Services Routing Protocol (WS-Routing)

- Web Services Referral Protocol (WS-Referral)

These specifications leverage the extensible nature of SOAP to provide SOAP modules that build on the baseline specifications of today's Web services. The modular nature of the architecture allows you to select which of the modules you want to use. For example, if you have an application for which security is of no concern, you will not need to use the modules pertaining to security (WS-Security and WS-License). In addition, each module is expressed in the same terms regardless of whether it is used individually or with other modules. Finally, modules are independent of the platforms or programming languages at the message endpoints, thus allowing Web services to use the architecture in heterogeneous environments.

WS-Inspection

Recall that in Chapter 9 I explained two methods of locating a Web service, UDDI and DISCO. UDDI provides a centralized directory that can be searched to locate published Web services. UDDI does provide the ability to browse for the Web services exposed by a particular business entity. However, it does not provide a means of discovering the Web services exposed by a particular server.

Today this role is filled by DISCO. DISCO provides a browse paradigm similar to hypertext links in HTML documents. However, DISCO has its drawbacks. DISCO is not an industry standard, is not extensible, and is currently supported only by the .NET platform.

WS-Inspection is intended to offer an industry-standard mechanism for discovering Web services via a browse paradigm while overcoming the known issues with DISCO. Similar to DISCO, a WS-Inspection document can contain a list of pointers to WSDL documents as well as to other WS-Inspection documents. Unlike DISCO, WS-Inspection is extensible and allows you to reference any number of resources, including UDDI directory entries.

WS-Inspection Document Syntax

The grammar of a WS-Inspection document is quite simple, as the following example shows:

```
<wsil:inspection>
  <wsil:abstract xml:lang=""? ... /> *
  <wsil:service> *
    <wsil:abstract xml:lang=""? ... /> *
    <wsil:name xml:lang=""? ... /> *
    <wsil:description referencedNamespace="uri" location="uri"?> *
      <wsil:abstract xml:lang=""? ... /> *
      <-- extensibility element --> ?
    </wsil:description>
  </wsil:service>

  <wsil:link referencedNamespace="uri" location="uri"?/>  *
    <wsil:abstract xml:lang=""? ... /> *
    <-- extensibility element --> ?
  </wsil:link>
</wsil:inspection>
```

Each WS-Inspection document has an *inspection* root element. This element must contain at least one *service* element or *link* element. The *service* element must have one or more *description* elements, which act as pointers to other service description documents. The *description* element's *referencedNamespace* attribute identifies the namespace that the referenced document belongs to, and the *location* attribute references the actual service description document.

For example, the following XML fragment shows a reference to a WDSL document accessible via HTTP:

```
<description referencedNamespace=http://schemas.xmlsoap.org/wsdl/
location=http://example.com/weatherreport.wsdl/>
```

The *service* element has two other child elements: *abstract* and *name*. The *abstract* element allows you to add a text description within the element. This description is intended for human eyes rather than for consumption by an application. Likewise, the *name* element allows you to associate a human-readable name with a service.

In contrast to the *service* element, the *link* element references another aggregation of service documents, such as another WS-Inspection document. Similar to the *service* element's attributes, the *link* element's *referencedNamespace* points to the namespace of the linked aggregation, and you can use the *link* element's *location* attribute to provide a link to the actual linked aggregation source.

For example, the following XML links a WS-Inspection document to two other WS-Inspection documents, which other directories on a Web server contain:

```
<inspection xmlns=
  "http://schemas.xmlsoap.org/ws/2001/10/inspection/">
  <link referencedNamespace=
  "http://schemas.xmlsoap.org/ws/2001/10/inspection/"
  location="http://example.com/weather/inspection.wsil"/>
  <link referencedNamespace=
  "http://schemas.xmlsoap.org/ws/2001/10/inspection/"
  location="http://example.com/events/inspection.wsil"/>
</inspection>
```

Notice that the actual WS-Inspection document and the two links all reference the schema because they all belong to the same namespace. When a user accesses this document, she can obtain the aggregated list of services that the two linked documents advertise. As you can see, this type of chaining allows multiple common entry points to a site to advertise the services on offer throughout the site without having to repeat lists of references.

Publishing WS-Inspection Documents

To allow users to look up the services referenced by a WS-Inspection document, you must place the document where users can locate and access it. WS-Inspection provides two methods for doing this. The first, Fixed Name, requires you to place WS-Inspection documents at the common entry points to your Web site or application. You should save the WS-Inspection document with the name *inspection.wsil* so that users know to request a document with a standard name. If you provide services from more than one location on your server, you must provide a separate WS-Inspection document at each of these locations. Of course, you can chain these documents—as shown previously—to avoid duplicating service information.

The second method, Linked, allows you to advertise services through other types of content. For example, you can link to multiple WS-Inspection documents through an ordinary HTML Web page. To do this, you simply reference the WS-Inspection documents from the *content* attribute of the HTML *META* tag, as shown here:

```
<HTML>
    <HEAD>
        <META name="serviceInspection"
            content="http://example.com/weather/inspection.wsil">
        <META name="serviceInspection"
            content="http://example.com/events/inspection.wsil">
    </HEAD>
    <BODY>
        <!-- Other HTML tags -->
    </BODY>
</HTML>
```

As you can see, the HTML links to the two WS-Inspection documents that I previously defined. Note that when you link to documents in HTML, you must link only to WS-Inspection documents and not to other HTML documents.

WS-Security and WS-License

One challenge that developers of Web services face is securing messages to and from Web services. In Chapter 10, we looked at how developers can address those issues today. Specifically, you learned about ways to provide authentication, authorization, data integrity, and nonrepudiation for data exchanged between a client and a Web service. The solutions I examined relied on technologies outside of the actual SOAP messages themselves, such as the following:

- IIS authentication mechanisms such as Basic authentication and Digest authentication

- SSL/TLS or IPSpec for securing transport channels

- Cryptography algorithms for encrypting and signing data

The problem with leveraging these technologies is that they are not integrated with SOAP. For example, the IIS authentication mechanisms are tightly coupled to the HTTP protocol and provide no benefit if the message is sent over another transport protocol. SSL/TLS and IPSec are connection-oriented protocols and do not provide an end-to-end solution if the message needs to be routed through multiple intermediaries. If the message is signed or encrypted using a standard cryptography algorithm, there is no standard way of presenting the recipient with the information to validate the signature or decrypt the message. What is needed is a solution that is SOAP-oriented, one that is standards based and transport-protocol agnostic.

The GXA defines WS-Security and WS-License, which together define a standard way to build secure solutions for SOAP messages. These specifications provide support for the following:

- Multiple security authentication credentials

- Multiple trust domains

- Multiple encryption technologies

Because the specifications do not dictate a particular implementation, they allow you to securely exchange SOAP messages in a platform-independent and technology-independent way. As long as a client application can build and understand SOAP messages and has access to appropriate libraries—for example, a Kerberos library—it can interact securely with a Web service.

Specifically, the modules provide support for multiple security authentication credentials, multiple trust domains, and multiple encryption technologies through the following three main mechanisms:

- Credential passing
- Message integrity
- Message confidentiality

The modular nature of the architecture allows you to use these mechanisms together for an integrated security solution or to use them individually to address specific scenarios. For example, if you run a weather report Web service in which authentication is the only requirement, you can simply use credential passing as a means of authenticating users. If you run a Web service that supplies sensitive sales data to remote offices, requires you to authenticate and authorize users, and requires you to ensure the integrity and privacy of the data exchanged between the client and the server, your security solution will require using all three security mechanisms.

Let's explore each of these mechanisms in more detail.

Credential Passing

When two parties want to communicate securely or one party wants to authenticate the identity of another party, they typically exchange security credentials. The WS-Security specification allows parties to exchange a wide variety of credentials regardless of the underlying transport protocol or delivery mechanism. It does this by inserting an additional header into a SOAP message known as the *credentials* header. The *credentials* header contains credential and license information that parties can use to authenticate each other.

In terms of WS-Security, *credentials* refer to licenses and supporting information together. The specification is independent of any specific license or credential format, but it does provide explicit support for X.509 certificates and Kerberos tickets. The WS-License specification defines the XML elements that describe these licenses. Thus, to pass credentials, you use WS-Security and WS-License together. Specifically, WS-License defines the following four subtypes of the WS-Security *credentials* type:

- **abstractLicense** The abstract class for all licenses, from which all WS-License licenses derive. You can extend the specification by creating your own subtype of this type.

- **binaryLicense** Represents an instance of a license that is binary encoded. The two possible values for this type are X.509 certificate and Kerberos ticket.

■   **abstractCredential**   The abstract class for all credentials, from which all WS-License credentials derive. You can extend the specification by creating your own subtype of this type.

■   **binaryCredentials**   Used to pass a security credential, which is not a license but is binary encoded. The specification does not define specific values for this type; instead, it accepts user-defined values.

The following example shows a SOAP message that contains an X.509 certificate. It also shows the relationship between the WS-Security and WS-License specifications.

```
<?xml version="1.0" encoding="utf-8"?>

<S:Envelope xmlns:S=http://schemas.xmlsoap.org/soap/envelope/
xmlns:xsd=http://www.w3.org/2001/XMLSchema
xmlns:xsi=http://www.w3.org/2001/XMLSchema-instance>
<S:Header>
  <m:path xmlns:m="http://schemas.xmlsoap.org/rp">
    <m:action>http://tickers-r-us.org/getQuote</m:action>
    <m:to>soap://tickers-r-us.org/stocks</m:to>
    <m:from>mailto:johnsmith@isps-r-us.com</m:from>
    <m:id>uuid:84b9f5d0-33fb-4a81-b02b-5b760641c1d6</m:id>
  </m:path>

  <wssec:credentials xsi:type="wslic:CREDENTIALS"
  xmlns:wssec=http://schemas.xmlsoap.org/ws/2001/10/security
  xmlns:wslic="http://schemas.xmlsoap.org/ws/2001/10/license">
    <wslic:binaryLicense wslic:valueType="wslic:x509v3"
    xsi:type="xsd:base64Binary">
      MIIEZzCCA9CgAwIBAgIQEmtJZc0rqrKh5i...RnSNBe8DQve
      qD6a3gUACyZ6XVe3u
    </wslic:binaryLicense>
  </wssec:credentials>
</S:Header>
...
<!-- Body here-->
...
</Envelope>
```

As you see, the message contains a *credentials* element (as defined by the WS-Security specification). This element has a child element of *binaryLicense* (as defined by the WS-License specification), which contains the X.509 certificate. If you want to pass an alternative form of license or alternative credentials, you can replace *binaryLicense* with the appropriate option from those previously listed.

Message Integrity

In Chapter 10, you learned that you must have control of both the client and the Web service in order to ensure the integrity of data, and that no current SOAP standard provides for integrity. This situation will change because the integrity mechanism of the WS-Security specification provides privacy through the use of signatures that are compliant with the XML-Signature specification. You insert these signatures into an *integrity* SOAP header.

Signatures provide two benefits: integrity (the message has not been altered in transit) and nonrepudiation (you must have sent it because you signed it). The specification allows you to include one signature for an entire message or multiple signatures, each relating to a different portion of the message. For example, this is particularly useful when a message is forwarded from one department to another and each department adds to the message; the signatures can provide a history of integrity for the document.

Another important issue that the specification addresses is that of SOAP headers, which are volatile and often in flux. For example, the WS-Routing specification (more on this a little later) allows SOAP headers to change legitimately; thus, a message receiver might not be able to verify a signature based on the entire SOAP envelope, including these headers, even though the message body has not changed. The use of multiple signatures can negate these effects, but the specification recommends the use of a Routing Signature transform. A Routing Signature transform bases its signature digest computation on the SOAP envelope but excludes the WS-Routing headers, which are liable to change legitimately. A message recipient can thus verify the signature even though some of the WS-Routing SOAP headers might have changed. In addition to the Routing Signature transform, the specification supports all the algorithms and transforms defined by the XML-Signature specification.

The following example shows a SOAP message that contains a single XML-Signature. The *integrity* node set, which contains all the signature information, is shown in bold.

```
<?xml version="1.0" encoding="utf-8"?>

<S:Envelope xmlns:S=http://schemas.xmlsoap.org/soap/envelope/
xmlns:xsd=http://www.w3.org/2001/XMLSchema
xmlns:xsi=http://www.w3.org/2001/XMLSchema-instance>
<S:Header>
  <m:path xmlns:m="http://schemas.xmlsoap.org/rp">
    ...
        <!-- Standard path headers here -->
    ...
    </m:path>

  <wssec:credentials
```

```
  xmlns:wssec="http://schemas.xmlsoap.org/ws/2001/10/security">
    <wslic:binaryLicense
    xmlns:wslic=http://schemas.xmlsoap.org/ws/2001/10/licenses
    wslic:valueType="wslic:x509v3" xsi:type="xsd:base64Binary"
    id="X509License">

      ...
      <!-- The very long encrypted certificate here -->
      ...
    </wslic:binaryLicense>
  </wssec:credentials>

  <wssec:integrity
  xmlns:wssec="http://schemas.xmlsoap.org/ws/2001/10/security">
    <ds:Signature xmlns:ds="http://www.w3.org/2000/09/xmldsig#">
      <ds:SignedInfo>
      <ds:CanonicalizationMethod
      Algorithm="http://www.w3.org/Signature/Drafts/xml-exc-c14n"/>
      <ds:SignatureMethod
      Algorithm="http://www.w3.org/2000/09/xmldsig#rsa-sha1"/>
      <ds:Reference>
        <ds:Transforms>
          <ds:Transform Algorithm=
          "http://schemas.xmlsoap.org/2001/10/security
          #RoutingSignatureTransform"/>
          <ds:Transform Algorithm=
          "http://www.w3.org/TR/2001/REC-xml-c14n-20010315"/>
        </ds:Transforms>
        <ds:DigestMethod
        Algorithm="http://www.w3.org/2000/09/xmldsig#sha1"/>
        <ds:DigestValue>
          EULddytSo1zHgU1jA31HABwSv7A=
        </ds:DigestValue>
      </ds:Reference>
      </ds:SignedInfo>
      <ds:SignatureValue>
BL8jdfToEb1l/vXcMZNNjPOVt8Wqc72Ht7GEHtpJj3n33WjNEYpU5ZYv/5aXeU5eFSJP3UM
0suDTORH8s8PsnS218aoyRvA3jJYnxEkPKVTDAXq7LK3zZ28iWpOhN98nwSnZ4L4Hqe3G40
gUv3jOhLZRkx6czpJux1cD1hibbmY=
      </ds:SignatureValue>
      <ds:KeyInfo>
        <wssec:licenseLocation="#X509License"/>
      </ds:KeyInfo>
    </ds:Signature>
  </wssec:integrity>

</S:Header>

...
<!-- Body here-->
...
</S:Envelope>
```

The *integrity* element can contain multiple *Signature* elements, but in this instance it contains just one. The *Signature* element has three children. The first is the *SignedInfo* element, which you use to pass information about the encryption algorithms used to create the signature and the digest on which it is based, as well as the URI of any transforms you have applied. The second element is the *SignatureValue* element, which contains the actual XML signature. The final child element is the optional *KeyInfo* element, which references a license with which the user can determine the trust level of the signed data. In this example, the license is an X.509 certificate, which is also included within the SOAP header.

Message Confidentiality

You have seen how WS-Security can help you ensure the integrity of data, but in some instances simply checking whether a malicious party has modified data in transit is not enough—you need to ensure that the data remains confidential so that even if someone gains access to it, it is of no use to them. For example, when users pass credit card details to a Web service, it is imperative that no one be able to see the credit card numbers while the data is in transit. In these instances, you must encrypt the data—that is, the SOAP envelope's actual payload. The WS-Security confidentiality mechanism provides a way to do this using XML Encryption.

In terms of algorithms, the specification has the same requirements as the XML Encryption specification and, unlike the integrity mechanism, it does not recommend any additional algorithms. To send a message whose body or a portion of whose body is encrypted, you encode the SOAP message based on the XML Encryption specification. However, if you want to send encrypted attachments, you do not use the functionality XML Encryption offers but instead use the WS-Security *confidentiality* SOAP header. This header acts as a container for references to encrypted parts and attachments, each of which you reference using an *EncryptedData* element.

The following example shows the use of the *confidentiality* header to reference an encrypted attachment:

```
<?xml version="1.0" encoding="utf-8"?>
<S:Envelope xmlns:S="http://schemas.xmlsoap.org/soap/envelope/"
xmlns:"xsd=http://www.w3.org/2001/XMLSchema"
xmlns:xsi="http://www.w3.org/2001/XMLSchema-instance">
  <S:Header>
    <m:path xmlns:m="http://schemas.xmlsoap.org/rp">
      <m:action>http://tickers-r-us.org/getQuote</m:action>
      <m:to>soap://tickers-r-us.org/stocks</m:to>
      <m:from>mailto:johnsmith@isps-r-us.com</m:from>
      <m:id>uuid:84b9f5d0-33fb-4a81-b02b-5b760641c1d6</m:id>
```

```
    </m:path>
    <wssec:confidentiality
    xmlns:wssec="http://schemas.xmlsoap.org/ws/2001/12/security">
      <enc:EncryptedData xmlns:enc="'http://www.w3.org/2001/04/xmlenc#">
        <enc:EncryptionMethod
        Algorithm="http://www.w3.org/2001/04/xmlenc#3des-cbc"/>
        <ds:KeyInfo xmlns:ds="http://www.w3.org/2000/09/xmldsig#">
          <enc:EncryptedKey>
            <enc:EncryptionMethod
            Algorithm="http://www.w3.org/2001/04/xmlenc#rsa-1_5"/>
            <enc:CipherData>
              <enc:CipherValue>
                AQIAAANmAAAApAAAX2mbWyA...
                1Y0TwnDRoTIc0Bke5jPEKszdWwV66DGxjmCjQHo=
              </enc:CipherValue>
            </enc:CipherData>
          </enc:EncryptedKey>
        </ds:KeyInfo>
        <enc:CipherData>
          <enc:CipherReference URI="cid:122326"/>
        </enc:CipherData>
      </enc:EncryptedData>
    </wssec:confidentiality>
  </S:Header>
  <S:Body>
    <tru:AttachedList xmlns:tru="http://tickers-r-us.org/payloads"/>
  </S:Body>
</S:Envelope>
```

WS-Routing

Developers currently face the challenge of having to figure out how to configure routing of messages that must pass through intermediaries before they
reach their final destinations. Even though SOAP allows you to specify multiple
intermediaries that a message must pass through en route to its final destination, it does not provide a mechanism for specifying the order in which the
message passes through those intermediaries.

WS-Routing provides a solution to this problem by allowing you to specify
message routes—that is, it allows you to specify the order that a message travels
through intermediaries on the way to its final recipient. WS-Routing also allows
you to define return, or reverse, paths for messages so that you can create applications that use various messaging paradigms, such as one-way messaging,
two-way messaging, and long-running dialogs. As with the other components
of the GXA, WS-Routing is independent of underlying protocols—it can operate
over a wide array of transport protocols, including TCP, UDP, DIME, SMTP,
HTTP, and TLS.

When you use WS-Routing, a *path* SOAP header contains the routing information for the message. This header contains child elements that specify the message path. For example, the following SOAP message demonstrates the use of the *path* header:

```
<S:Envelope xmlns:S="http://www.w3.org/2001/06/soap-envelope">
<S:Header>
  <w:path xmlns:w="http://schemas.xmlsoap.org/rp/">
    <w:action>http://www.microsoft.com/weather</w:action>
    <w:to>soap://D.com/some/destination</w:to>
    <w:fwd>
      <w:via>soap://B.com</w:via>
      <w:via>soap://C.com</w:via>
    </w:fwd>
    <w:from>soap://A.com/some/origin</w:from>
    <w:id>uuid:82e9a994-d345-ace1-b2ba-09a2c5d466</w:id>
  </w:path>
</S:Header>
<S:Body>
  ...
  <!-- Message body here -->
  ...
</S:Body>
</S:Envelope>
```

The code provides a message path that originates from a sender (A) who sends to an intermediary (B), who forwards the message to C, who forwards the message to D, the message recipient. The code references these four parties through child elements of the *path* header, namely these:

- **from**   The message sender (A)

- **fwd**   The intermediaries (B and C), each of which is declared in a *via* element

- **to**   The message recipient (D)

In addition to these elements, the *path* header contains an *action* element and an *id* element. The *action* element contains a URI identifying the action the message points toward—that is, its intent. The *id* element contains an ID for the message. When you specify this ID, be sure it is unique—for example, by using a hash of the message's content.

WS-Routing also allows you to specify a reverse path for a message. This can be useful in a number of situations, such as peer-to-peer messaging or returning error messages. To set a reverse path, you use the *path* header's child element, *rev*. Note that only the message sender can insert a *rev* element into a message; intermediaries cannot. If you do not stipulate a reverse path, one will be built dynamically as the message moves along the forward path. However, you can specify a reverse path if you want, by using *via* child elements in the same way that I did for the forward path in the previous example.

When you define reverse paths, you might want to associate one message with another. For example, in a peer-to-peer message exchange, it is important to know which message response relates to which original message. Likewise, it is important to identify which message an error message relates to. WS-Routing allows you to perform this form of correlation using the *relatesTo* element. This element simply takes a value, which is the ID of the message to which it must correlate.

The following example shows a simple SOAP message that uses the *rev* element and the *relatesTo* element:

```
<S:Envelope xmlns:S="http://schemas.xmlsoap.org/soap/envelope/">
<S:Header>
  <w:path xmlns:w="http://schemas.xmlsoap.org/rp/">
    <w:action>http://www.microsoft.com/weather</w:action>
    <w:to>soap://D.com/some/destination</w:to>
    <w:fwd>
      <w:via>soap://B.com</w:via>
      <w:via>mailto:C@cpandl.com</w:via>
    </w:fwd>
    <w:rev>
      <w:via/>
    </w:rev>
    <w:from>soap://A.com/some/origin</w:from>
    <w:id>uuid:82e9a994-d345-ace1-b2ba-09a2c5d466</w:id>
    <w:relatesTo>
      uuid:dd089c-c569-987a-bc23-6532c24da2
    </w:relatesTo>
  </w:path>
</S:Header>

<S:Body>
...
<!-- Message body here -->
...
</S:Body>
</S:Envelope>
```

The example highlights two further points of interest. First, it specifies the reverse path as an empty *via* element. This indicates that the underlying transport protocol handles the reverse path. For example, TCP can handle the reverse path, but UDP cannot because it does not operate on a request-response model. The second point of interest is that intermediary B acts as a transport protocol bridge because the example references C through the *mailto* scheme.

WS-Referral

As you have seen, WS-Routing allows you to stipulate both forward and backward message routes. What it does not do is dynamically alter these routes—more specifically, it does not allow one WS-Routing node (a SOAP router) to dynamically insert, delete, or query routing information in another SOAP router. For example, A might want to pass a message to B, but if B now requires the message to pass through an additional intermediary, C, WS-Routing is not appropriate because it does not provide a mechanism for B to inform A of this change of policy. Fortunately, WS-Referral does provide a mechanism to allow B to pass a message to A that indicates that all future messages must pass through C.

Specifically, WS-Referral provides the following four mechanisms that allow you to insert, delete, and query routing entries in a SOAP router:

- **WS-Referral statement** Describes referral information (such as that just described)

- **WS-Referral query message exchange** Allows a SOAP router to request referral statements from another SOAP router

- **WS-Referral registration message exchange** Allows a SOAP router to request that another SOAP router explicitly accept or reject a referral statement

- **WS-Referral header** Allows a SOAP router to send referral statements to another SOAP router without using WS-Referral query message exchange or WS-Referral registration message exchange

As this list shows, all operations involving WS-Referral revolve around WS-Referral statements.

The following example shows a statement that asks A to route all messages through C if the referral takes less than 21,600,000 milliseconds (6 hours):

```
<r:ref xmlns:r="http://schemas.xmlsoap.org/ws/2001/10/referral">
  <r:for>
    <r:exact>soap://A.com/weather</r:exact>
  </r:for>
  <r:if>
    <r:ttl>21600000</r:ttl>
  </r:if>
  <r:go>
    <r:via>soap://C.com</r:via>
  </r:go>
  <r:refId>uuid:82e9a994-d345-ace1-b2ba-09a2c5d466</r:refId>
  <r:desc>
```

```
  <r:refAddr>
    http://B.com/referralDocs/09a2c5d466.xml
  </r:refAddr>
 </r:desc>
</r:ref>
```

The main part of the WS-Referral statement that the example shows is the *for-if-go* construct. The *for* element contains a list of targets, which the statement is intended for. You list each potential recipient using either the *exact* element (as shown in the example) or the *prefix* element, which matches any URI that starts with the value defined within the element. The *if* element places a condition on the statement. If the *if* condition returns true, the contents of the *go* element are acted on. In this instance, the *go* element provides the redirect URI.

In addition to the *for-if-go* construct, the example shows the *refId* element, which allows the SOAP router to uniquely identify the statement, and the *desc* element. The *desc* element allows you to provide a description of the statement, which in this case is a URI that points to the physical location of a document containing the statement. The *desc* element is optional.

WS-Referral Query Message Exchange

The WS-Referral query message exchange provides a mechanism by which one SOAP router can request WS-Referral statements from another SOAP router. For example, a SOAP router might want to obtain an update for a WS-Referral statement that has exceeded its time to live. To send a query message exchange, you simply construct a SOAP message that contains a *query* element within its body. The *query* element contains a list of intended recipients of the statement.

The following example shows a query in which A requests a WS-Referral statement from B. B responds with a WS-Referral response, which is a simple SOAP message that contains a list of WS-Referral statements within its body.

```
<S:Envelope xmlns:S="http://www.w3.org/2001/09/soap-envelope">
<S:Header>
  <rp:path xmlns:rp="http://schemas.xmlsoap.org/rp/">
    <rp:action>
      http://schemas.xmlsoap.org/ws/2001/10/referral#query
    </rp:action>
    <rp:to>soap://B.com</rp:to>
    <rp:rev>
      <rp:via/>
    </rp:rev>
    <rp:id>uuid:82e9a994-d345-ace1-b2ba-09a2c5d466</rp:id>
  </rp:path>
</S:Header>
```

(continued)

```
<S:Body>
  <r:query xmlns:r="http://schemas.xmlsoap.org/ws/2001/10/referral">
    <r:for>
      <r:exact>soap://A.com</r:exact>
    </r:for>
  </r:query>
</S:Body>
</S:Envelope>
```

WS-Referral Registration Message Exchange

WS-Referral registration message exchange is a mechanism that allows a SOAP router to explicitly request that another SOAP router accepts or rejects a WS-Referral statement. For example, B might want to route all requests to itself to SOAP router C, perhaps because B wants to reduce the load on itself. B can send A a WS-Referral registration message that asks A to reroute all messages to C. A can then choose to accept or reject the request and send a WS-Referral registration response confirming its intent.

To issue a WS-Referral registration message, you must construct a SOAP message whose body contains a *register* element, which contains a *ref* element, which in turn contains the WS-Referral statement to accept or reject. Here is a registration message in which B sends a request to A:

```
<S:Envelope xmlns:S="http://www.w3.org/2001/09/soap-envelope">
<S:Header>
  <rp:path xmlns:rp="http://schemas.xmlsoap.org/rp/">
    <rp:action>
      http://schemas.xmlsoap.org/ws/2001/10/referral#register
    </rp:action>
    <rp:to>soap://A.com</rp:to>
    <rp:rev>
      <rp:via/>
    </rp:rev>
    <rp:id>uuid:82e9a994-d345-ace1-b2ba-09a2c5d466</rp:id>
  </rp:path>
</S:Header>

<S:Body>
  <r:register
  xmlns:r="http://schemas.xmlsoap.org/ws/2001/10/referral">
    <r:ref>
      <!-- WS-Referral statement here -->
    </r:ref>
  </r:register>
</S:Body>
</S:Envelope>
```

WS-Referral Header

The two previous mechanisms allow a SOAP router to either request a WS-Referral statement or issue a statement, which the receiver must accept or reject. However, in some instances, you might simply want to forward referral statements to a SOAP router, which can then do with them what it wants. The WS-Referral header provides a mechanism that allows you to do this. The header is simply a SOAP header that contains a *referrals* element, which contains the statements to forward.

Here is an example of a SOAP header that contains a WS-Referral header:

```
<S:Envelope xmlns:S="http://www.w3.org/2001/09/soap-envelope">
<S:Header>
  <r:referrals
  xmlns:r="http://schemas.xmlsoap.org/ws/2001/10/referral">
    <r:ref>
      <!-- WS-Referral statement here -->
    </r:ref>
    <r:ref>
      <!-- WS-Referral statement here -->
    </r:ref>
  </r:referrals>
</S:Header>
</S:Envelope>
```

Dynamic Application Topologies

One of the technologies the GXA is enabling is dynamic application topologies. Even though the Internet facilitates ubiquitous communication between the client and the server, the locality of a Web service and its client play a factor in the overall performance. The same problem exists today with HTML-based applications. Companies such as Akamai and Inktomi are providing solutions by caching static Web page content on servers geographically distributed around the world.

Content is hosted on what are termed *edge servers*. Edge servers are often strategically placed inside ISP networks in effort to reduce the latency of requests made by the ISP's customers. Client requests for the content are then dynamically routed to an edge server that is deemed to provide the lowest network latency for the client.

In addition to performance, another advantage of this infrastructure is that it has the potential to offer excellent availability and scalability. If an edge server becomes unavailable or heavily burdened with requests, the delivery service is responsible for routing the client's request to another server that is better capable of handling the request.

One of the efforts underway is to take these same concepts and apply them to Web services. A variety of companies, including Microsoft, are developing infrastructures that will allow you to host stateless Web services on edge servers.

At the time of this writing, very little information has been publicly released regarding Microsoft's plans to support dynamic application topologies. However, one of the goals that have been announced is the ability to allow developers to decorate which portions of their Web applications can be fanned out geographically. Since the application is self-describing, the supporting infrastructure can make intelligent decisions such as distributing certain portions of the application to a new datacenter recently brought on line.

One of the issues with creating an infrastructure to support dynamic application topologies is abstracting the physical location of a requested resource. Resources such as Web services are often identified by a URL. The URL contains either an IP address or a domain name. An IP address is very tightly coupled with the physical location of the resource. The default behavior of DNS is to associate a particular domain name with a particular IP address, making it tightly coupled to the resource as well.

Services such as Akamai leverage the fact that a domain name provides a level of abstraction from the IP address. These services ensure that their own DNS servers handle name resolution to a particular domain. This allows the service's DNS server to apply an algorithm for determining which IP address will be returned to the client.

There are a few potential issues with this technique. First, you cannot rely on the federated nature of DNS. All name resolutions need to be performed by the service's DNS infrastructure. Second, the URL for a particular resource is often scoped to the domain name of the service provider. If you switch service providers, you need to ensure that all your clients reference the new URL. Finally, the resource is often an obscure series of characters embedded in the URL, further tying you to your service provider. In the future, you will see the evolution of a virtual topology that is more capable of abstracting the physical structure of the Internet.

Orchestrating Web Services

Almost all non-trivial applications have a logical path of execution as well as implementation details. The logical path of execution, or the workflow of the application, often has a clear start point and a clear endpoint. Throughout the course of execution, work is performed on behalf of the client. With applications written in languages such as C#, the logical path of execution and the implementation details are intertwined within the same code base. However, there are advantages to separating the flow of an application and its implementation details.

By separating an application's workflow from the implementation details, a runtime environment is able to provide a set of services specific to an application's workflow. One such runtime environment is BizTalk Orchestration. Orchestration provides a framework for defining the flow of an application and the interaction with business components that provide the implementation details. Orchestration also provides a set of services that can be leveraged by your application's workflow.

One of the services provided by Orchestration is inherent support for multithreading. Orchestration allows you to define a fork and a matching join within your workflow. For example, suppose in order to process a purchase order, you need to get approval from three different departments. Instead of processing those three activities serially, Orchestration allows you to define a fork with three branches. Each of the three activities will be located on an individual branch of the fork. The Orchestration runtime will execute the three activities in parallel without the developer directly manipulating threads.

You can alter the behavior of the runtime by modifying the metadata associated with the join. The join can be defined as an *AND* or an *OR*. An *AND* will instruct the runtime not to proceed past the join until all branches complete, whereas an *OR* will continue past the join as soon as one of the branches completes.

Orchestration also provides a set of services for supporting long-running transactions. An instance of an Orchestration workflow is known as a *schedule*. A schedule might leverage Web services that have a high latency between the time that a request is made and the time the response is received. The degree of latency can adversely affect the number of schedules that can be running at any one point in time.

To help resolve this issue, BizTalk Orchestration provides a service known as *hydration*. If the server running the application becomes resource constrained, the Orchestration runtime has the ability to dehydrate some of the running schedules and then rehydrate them when server resources become less constrained. The runtime uses hints regarding the degree of latency provided from the developer to determine which schedules are the best candidates for dehydration.

Everything I have explained up to this point is available today. You can leverage Orchestration today to coordinate the workflow within your Web services as well as the applications that leverage your Web services by using BizTalk 2002 and the BizTalk .NET Framework Resource Kit. So why am I covering it in a chapter dedicated to future technologies? The reason is that BizTalk Orchestration is currently being overhauled to provide even tighter integration with ASP.NET-hosted Web services.

Developers caught a glimpse of the direction Microsoft is heading at the 2001 Professional Developers Conference with the release of the technical preview titled BizTalk Orchestration for Web Services. The future version of Orchestration will provide tight integration with the .NET framework and the ASP.NET runtime. In order to leverage BizTalk Orchestration today within a Web service, the Web service itself must explicitly communicate with the Orchestration runtime via well-known APIs. If a schedule invokes a Web service via a proxy generated by WSDL.exe, it must do so via a shim .NET component or via the COM interop layer.

In the technology preview, a workflow is able to expose itself as a Web service. In fact, the workflow itself is compiled into a .NET assembly and is executed by the CLR. If a schedule needs to be dehydrated, the Orchestration runtime will leverage the ASP.NET Session Store. If a schedule needs to invoke a method exposed by a Web service, the WSDL.exe-generated proxy can be directly called from within the schedule.

The technical preview also introduced XLANG/s, a scriptable version of XLANG. Today schedules are created using Microsoft Visio and are persisted using an XML syntax called XLANG. In the future, you will be able to write schedules using the XLANG/s scripting language. In order to demonstrate the XLANG/s syntax, I will create a simple Web service that is similar to the Hello World application generated by Visual Studio .NET.

Recall that BizTalk Orchestration allows you to separate the Web service's workflow from the implementation details. In order to demonstrate this, I will separate the implementation of the Web service into three parts: one that defines the interface, one that defines the workflow, and one that defines the implementation details. First I will cover the code that defines the interface.

The following C# code contains the interface definition for the Web service:

```
using System;
using System.Web.Services;

namespace Interface
{
    public interface ISimpleWebService
    {
        [WebMethod]
        string Hello(string name);
    }
}
```

The Web service exposes one Web method, *Hello*. The *Hello* Web method accepts a string containing the individual's name and returns a string containing the greeting.

Next I define the workflow using XLANG/s.

```
module SimpleExample
{
    // Import the namespace in which the Web service interface
    // is defined.
    using namespace Interface;

    public service MyWebService
    {
        // Declare the messages that will be used by the Web service.
        message ISimpleWebService.Hello<request> requestMessage;
        message ISimpleWebService.Hello<response> responseMessage;

        // Declare the ports that will be exported or imported
        // by the Web service.
        port export ISimpleWebService simpleWebService;

        // Define the implementation of the Web service.
        body
        {
            // Listen for a request.
            activate simpleWebService >> requestMessage;

            // Construct the response message.
            construct responseMessage
            {
                responseMessage.RetResult =
                Implementation.Hello(requestMessage.name);
            };

            // Send the response message.
            simpleWebService << responseMessage;
        }
    }
}
```

As you can see, the XLANG/s syntax is rather explicit. I declare the request and response messages and also define when the request is received and when the response is sent. One of the benefits this model provides is that the workflow can extend beyond the scope of the Web method. With a traditional ASP.NET Web service, the execution of the Web method stops as soon as the response is sent to the client.

The XLANG/s document is compiled at run time. Therefore, I need to register the XLANG/s compiler within the Web service's web.config file.

```xml
<?xml version="1.0" encoding="utf-8" ?>
<configuration>
  <system.web>
    <compilation defaultLanguage="c#" debug="true">
      <compilers>
        <compiler language="xs;xlangs" extension=".xs"
        type="Microsoft.XLANGs.XLANGsCodeProvider, XLANGsCompiler,
        Version=1.0.702.0, Culture=neutral,
        PublicKeyToken=6464f78e20e2eac9" />
      </compilers>
    </compilation>
  </system.web>
</configuration>
```

The preceding web.config file registers the XLANG/s compiler with the ASP.NET runtime. When a document whose filename ends with an .xs extension is referenced or a code section with its language attribute set to either "xs" or "xlangs" is defined, the ASP.NET runtime will invoke the XLANG/s compiler.

The XLANG/s syntax defined previously was saved within a file named SimpleWebService.xs. Therefore, the following .asmx file is used to serve as the endpoint of the Web service:

```
<%@ WebService Class="SimpleExample.MyWebService.simpleWebService" %>
<%@ Assembly Src="SimpleWebService.xs"%>
```

Finally I define the implementation. Recall that during the construction of the response message, I called the *Hello* static method exposed by the *Implementation* class. The following code defines the *Implementation* class:

```csharp
using System;

namespace SimpleExample
{
    public class Implementation
    {
        private Implementation()
        {
        }

        static public string Hello(string name)
        {
            return "Hello " + name;
        }
    }
}
```

The preceding example took considerably more code to implement the Web service without much perceived benefit. However, the benefit of the XLANG/s syntax would have been realized if the implementation required a more complex workflow and would be especially true if the Web service leveraged the services of the BizTalk Orchestration runtime, such as its native support for parallel execution of tasks.

In conclusion, you can leverage BizTalk Orchestration within your Web services today using BizTalk 2002 and the BizTalk .NET Framework Resource Kit. However, future versions will offer even tighter integration with .NET and the ASP.NET runtime. XLANG/s will provide an alternative for expressing the workflow of your Web service in addition to the Visio interface provided today.

Summary

In this chapter, I examine some of the technologies that will help define the future of Web services. Specifically, I covered .NET My Services, the GXA, and BizTalk Orchestration for Web Services.

.NET My Services provides a set of Web services that allow access and management of personal data associated with a user. You can programmatically query and manipulate the data stored within .NET My Services using the five messages defined by HSDL: *queryRequest*, *deleteRequest*, *updateRequest*, *insertRequest*, and *subscriptionResponse*. However, you can access only your own data or the data of other users as long as those users have given you the appropriate permissions. Identity of a user is determined by authenticating against the Passport Kerberos domain authority.

In addition to authentication credentials, HSDL messages need to include routing information as well. In an effort not to create a proprietary solution, Microsoft released the GXA. The GXA is currently composed of a set of five specifications: WS-Security, WS-Licensing, WS-Referral, WS-Routing, and WS-Inspection. Each specification is layered on top of SOAP in a modular fashion. Therefore, any GXA specification can be used in combination with any other GXA specification.

Microsoft released the specifications for comment by other leading technology companies as well as customers. Once the specifications have matured, Microsoft intends to hand off the specifications to a standards body. Once the standards body ratifies the specifications, Microsoft has committed to ensure that its product offerings will comply with the specifications.

Finally I examined two infrastructural components for building and deploying Web services. The first was dynamic application topologies, which enable you to deploy your Web service across a geographically distributed network of computers. Requests are routed by the delivery service to the computer most capable of handling the request, which in turn improves both the scalability and the availability of the Web service.

The second infrastructural component I explored was BizTalk Orchestration for Web Services. Orchestration allows the developer to separate the application's workflow from the implementation details. Doing so enables the Orchestration runtime to provide advanced services for the workflow such as hydration and management of long-running transactions.

Appendix

XML Schema Built-In Types

Type	Example	Description
string	This is a string.	A sequence of legal XML 1 characters.
normalizedString	This is a normalized string.	A sequence of legal XML 1 characters that does not contain carriage returns, line feeds, or tabs.
token	Token1 Token2 Token3	A tokenized string of legal XML 1 characters that does not contain carriage returns, line feeds, or tabs.
byte	−128	A numeric value from −128 through 127.
unsignedByte	255	A numeric value from 0 through 255.
base64Binary	6e7P	Base64-encoded binary data. Base64 encoding is described in RFC 2045.
hexBinary	B2AF	Hex-encoded binary data. Each binary octet is encoded into its two-character hexadecimal equivalent. The example has a binary representation of 1011001010101111.
integer	123456789	A numeric value meeting the mathematical definition of an integer. Basically, an infinitely bounded number that can be positive or negative.
positiveInteger	123456789	A numeric value that meets the mathematical definition of a positive integer. Basically, an infinitely bounded positive number, not including zero.
negativeInteger	−123456789	A numeric value that meets the mathematical definition of a negative integer. Basically, an infinitely bounded negative number, not including zero.

(continued)

(continued)

Type	Example	Description
nonNegativeInteger	123456789	A numeric value that meets the mathematical definition of a non-negative integer. Basically, an infinitely bounded positive number, including zero.
nonPositiveInteger	−123456789	A numeric value that meets the mathematical definition of a nonpositive integer. Basically, an infinitely bounded negative number, including zero.
int	−2147483648	A numeric value from −2147483648 through 2147483647.
unsignedInt	4294967295	A numeric value from 0 through 4294967295.
long	−9223372036854775808	A numeric value from −9223372036854775808 through 9223372036854775807.
unsignedLong	18446744073709551615	A numeric value from 0 through 18446744073709551615.
short	−32768	A numeric value from −32768 through 32767.
unsignedShort	65535	A numeric value from 0 through 65535.
decimal	1234.56789	A finite sequence of decimal digits that must contain a single period as a decimal indicator.
float	−123.456789E2, −123.456789e2, or −12345.6789	A numeric value that meets the requirements of the IEEE single-precision 32-bit floating-point type. The legal special values include positive and negative zero (0,−0), positive and negative infinity (*INF*, −*INF*), and not a number (*NaN*).
double	−123.456789E2, −123.456789e2, or −12345.6789	A numeric value that meets the requirements of the IEEE single-precision 64-bit floating-point type. The legal special values include positive and negative zero (0,−0), positive and negative infinity (*INF*, −*INF*), and not a number (*NaN*).
boolean	1 or true	A value containing *true* or *false*.

(continued)

Type	Example	Description
time	01:22:15-07:00	A value containing a specific time of day in the format *HH:MM:SS*. Midnight is represented as 00:00:00. Time is represented using 24-hour notation. The time zone is indicated by the number of hours after Coordinated Universal Time. (Mountain Standard Time in the U.S. is represented as −07:00.)
date	2001-05-21	A value containing a calendar day in the format *YYYY-MM-DD*.
dateTime	2001-05-21T01:22:15-07:00	A value containing a specific instance of time in the format *YYYY-MM-DDTHH:MM:SS*.
duration	P3Y1M24DT11H22M10.4S	A value containing a duration of time in the format P#Y#M#DT#H#M#S or any subset, such as P#M#S.
gMonth	--05--	A value containing a Gregorian month in the format *--MM--*.
gYear	2001	A value containing a Gregorian year in the format *YYYY*.
gYearMonth	2001-05	A value containing a Gregorian month in a particular year in the format *YYYY-MM*.
gDay	---21	A value containing a recurring Gregorian day of the month in the format *---DD*.
gMonthDay	--05-21	A value containing a recurring Gregorian day of the month in the format *--MM-DD*.
Name	Address	A value containing an XML 1 name.
QName	po:Address	A value containing a qualified XML 1 name.
NCName	Address	A value containing a "noncolonized" XML 1 name (a *QName* without the prefix).
anyURI	http://www.microsoft.com	A value containing a URI. The URI can be relative or absolute.
language	en-US	A value containing a natural language identifier as defined by RFC 1766.

(continued)

(continued)

Type	Example	Description
ID		A value containing an XML 1 *ID* attribute type.
IDREF		A value containing an XML 1 *IDREF* attribute type.
IDREFS		A value containing an XML 1 *IDREFS* attribute type.
ENTITY		A value containing an XML 1 *ENTITY* attribute type.
ENTITIES		A value containing an XML 1 *ENTITIES* attribute type.
NOTATION		A value containing an XML 1 *NOTATION* attribute type.
NMTOKEN		A value containing an XML 1 *NMTOKEN* attribute type.
NMTOKENS		A value containing an XML 1 *NMTOKENS* attribute type.

Index

Send feedback about this index to *mspindex@microsoft.com*

A

Abort method (SoapHttpClientProtocol class), 193
abstract attribute (service element, WS-Inspection), 385
abstract interface for Web services, 151–54
abstract keyword (ASP.NET), 151
abstract property (XML type declarations), 90
abstractCredential class (WS-License specification), 389
abstractLicense class (WS-License specification), 388
AcceptPO Web method (example), 223
access control lists (ACLs), 301–2
action element (path SOAP header), 394
Action property
  SoapDocumentMethod, SoapRpcMethod attributes
    (ASP.NET), 145
  SoapMessage class (ASP.NET), 183
activated element (service element, WSDL), 236
Activator class, GetObject method, 242–43
Active Server Pages. *See* ASP.NET
actor attribute (SOAP), 34–36
Actor property
  SoapException class, 142
  SoapHeader class, 165
actors, SOAP, 32, 34–36
  faultactor element (SOAP), 38
  Kevin Bacon (example), 52–54
add element (protocols element, ASP.NET), 135
Add method (Cache class), 372
Add Web Reference Wizard, WSDL.exe vs., 190
AddArray method (SOAP), 43
address element
  http namespace, 119
  soap namespace, 113
ADO.NET DataSet, serializing instances of, 225
affinity, server, 351
AfterSerialize stage (ProcessMessage method), 178,
  180–83
all element (XML Schema), 84
AllowAutoRedirect property
  RemotingClientProxy class, 246
  SoapHttpClientProtocol class, 193
ampersand, encoding in XML Schema, 64
anonymous authentication, 297
anonymous type definitions (XML Schema), 78
any element (XML Schema), 84
anyAttribute element (XML Schema), 84
anyType type (XML Schema example), 84
anyUrl datatype (XML), 211
API for Web services, 9

apostrophe, encoding in XML Schema, 64
Application Log, 336–38
Application property (WebService class, ASP.NET), 160
application state, maintaining in ASP.NET, 160–65
/appsettingbaseurl switch (WSDL.exe), 191–92
/appsettingurlkey switch (WSDL.exe), 191
arrays, encoding in SOAP, 42–46
  optimizing as partial or sparse, 47–49
  WSDL descriptions, 102
arrayType attribute (SOAP), 43
.asmx files, debugging support for, 325–26
ASP.NET, 127–204
  caching data, 365–66
  compiling code, 129–30
  documenting Web services, 136–40
  encoding SOAP styles, 143–50
    encoding references, 146–50
  error raising, 140–42
  interface inheritance, 150–54
  performance counters, 338–43
  proxy code, generating
    cookies, 201–2
    datetime information, 194
    Soapsuds utility, 244–47
    WSDL.exe, 190–202
  Remoting vs., 227–29
  server-side validation, 224
  SOAP extensions, 173–90
    attributes of, 174–76
    initialization, 178–80
    message processing, 180–90
  SOAP headers, defining and processing, 165–73
    unknown headers, 172–73
  state management, 155–65
    application state, 160–65
    session state, 155–59
  transport protocols and bindings, 134–36
  Web service for (example), 128–34
.aspx (Web Form) files, 12–14
  credit card service with, 17–18
  Web service implementation, 128–31
assembly files
  metadata, debugging and, 320–21
  Web service implementation in, 130–31
Assert method (Debug, Trace classes), 327–30
asserting errors, 328–30
asymmetric encryption, 299

411

Scott Short

Scott Short is currently a Senior Consultant with Microsoft Consulting Services. He works with a number of high-tech companies, helping them develop scalable, available, and maintainable e-business applications. He is always interested in working with companies to solve challenging problems, so feel free to contact him at *sshort@microsoft.com*.

Scott has also contributed to a number of books about developing .NET applications and is a frequent speaker at professional developer conferences.

Scott's primary motivation for moving to Colorado was to be closer to the Rocky Mountains. When not glued to his computer, Scott enjoys spending time with his family and friends skiing, backpacking, hiking, and rock climbing. He also loves spending evenings with his wife Suzanne and his son Colin.

Combination Square

A **combination square** is shaped so that it can check both inside and outside 90° and 45° angles; it usually includes a small bubble level for quickly checking level and plumb positions as well. Some combination squares are also fitted with an extra centering head, which you can use to find the center of round stock such as dowels. You can remove both heads, leaving the blade free as a handy straightedge.

At Microsoft Press, we use tools to illustrate our books for software developers and IT professionals. Tools are an elegant symbol of human inventiveness and a powerful metaphor for how people can extend their capabilities, precision, and reach. From basic calipers and pliers to digital micrometers and lasers, our stylized illustrations of tools give each book a visual identity and each book series a personality. With tools and knowledge, there are no limits to creativity and innovation. Our tag line says it all: *The tools you need to put technology to work.*

The manuscript for this book was prepared and galleyed using Microsoft Word. Pages were composed by Microsoft Press using Adobe FrameMaker+SGML for Windows, with text in Garamond and display type in Helvetica Condensed. Composed pages were delivered to the printer as electronic prepress files.

Cover Designer:	Methodologie, Inc.
Interior Graphic Designer:	James D. Kramer
Principal Compositor:	Dan Latimer
Interior Artists:	Rob Nance and Joel Panchot
Principal Copy Editor:	Holly M. Viola
Indexer:	Seth Maislin

Learn XML fundamentals

with this step-by-step guide!

U.S.A. **$39.99**
Canada $57.99
ISBN: 0-7356-1465-2

Teach yourself how to put the latest XML technology and standards to work—one step at a time! This thoroughly updated and expanded book expertly guides you through the process of creating XML documents and displaying them on the Web. Use the easy-to-follow lessons and hands-on exercises to learn essential techniques—and stay ahead of the curve by working with real-world examples in the Microsoft® Internet Explorer 6.0 browser and the Microsoft XML Parser (MSXML) 4.0. No matter what kind of content you want to get on line, this practical, proven tutorial shows how you can quickly and easily apply XML to the task.

microsoft.com/mspress

Learn how to use XML

and the Microsoft .NET Framework
to **build extensible, end-to-end applications**

U.S.A. **$59.99**
Canada $86.99
ISBN: 0-7356-1185-8

XML Web services will play a central role in the next era of computing by initiating a new cycle of opportunities for developers and customers. Get detailed instructions and insights about how to take advantage of XML and Microsoft® development tools in this comprehensive reference. Taking an architectural approach, it describes the XML functionality in Microsoft Visual Studio® .NET, Microsoft SQL Server™ 2000, and Microsoft BizTalk™ Server 2000. It also demonstrates step-by-step how to convert a traditional client/server application to an XML-based application. This book is the ideal resource for anyone who wants to make maximum use of Visual Studio .NET, other XML-enabled Microsoft development tools, and the Microsoft .NET Framework to create extensible, end-to-end applications that work across multiple devices and platforms.

microsoft.com/mspress

The definitive
one-stop resource
for developing on the revolutionary
.NET platform

U.S.A. **$59.99**
Canada $86.99
ISBN: 0-7356-1376-1

This core reference for Microsoft® .NET provides everything you need to know to build robust, Web-extensible applications for the revolutionary Microsoft development platform. Leading Windows® programming authority Jeff Prosise masterfully distills this new Web-enabled programming paradigm and its Framework Class Library—easily one of the most complex collections ever assembled—into a conversational, easy-to-follow programming reference you can repeatedly visit to resolve specific .NET development questions. Prosise clearly explains all the critical elements of application development in the .NET environment, including Windows Forms, Web Forms, and XML Web services—illustrating key concepts with inline code examples and many complete sample programs. All the book's sample code and programs—most of them written in C#—appear on the companion CD-ROM so you can study and adapt them for your own Web-based business applications.

Microsoft®
microsoft.com/mspress

Get a **Free**
e-mail newsletter, updates,
special offers, links to related books,
and more when you

register on line!

Register your Microsoft Press® title on our Web site and you'll get
a FREE subscription to our e-mail newsletter, *Microsoft Press
Book Connections.* You'll find out about newly released and upcoming
books and learning tools, online events, software downloads, special
offers and coupons for Microsoft Press customers, and information
about major Microsoft® product releases. You can also read useful
additional information about all the titles we publish, such as detailed book descriptions, tables of contents and indexes, sample
chapters, links to related books and book series, author biographies,
and reviews by other customers.

Registration is easy. Just visit this Web page and fill in your information:

http://www.microsoft.com/mspress/register

Microsoft®

Proof of Purchase

Use this page as proof of purchase if participating in a promotion or rebate offer on
this title. Proof of purchase must be used in conjunction with other proof(s) of
payment such as your dated sales receipt—see offer details.

Building XML Web Services for the Microsoft® .NET Platform
0-7356-1406-7

CUSTOMER NAME

Microsoft Press, PO Box 97017, Redmond, WA 98073-9830

MICROSOFT LICENSE AGREEMENT

Book Companion CD

IMPORTANT—READ CAREFULLY: This Microsoft End-User License Agreement ("EULA") is a legal agreement between you (either an individual or an entity) and Microsoft Corporation for the Microsoft product identified above, which includes computer software and may include associated media, printed materials, and "online" or electronic documentation ("SOFTWARE PRODUCT"). Any component included within the SOFTWARE PRODUCT that is accompanied by a separate End-User License Agreement shall be governed by such agreement and not the terms set forth below. By installing, copying, or otherwise using the SOFTWARE PRODUCT, you agree to be bound by the terms of this EULA. If you do not agree to the terms of this EULA, you are not authorized to install, copy, or otherwise use the SOFTWARE PRODUCT; you may, however, return the SOFTWARE PRODUCT, along with all printed materials and other items that form a part of the Microsoft product that includes the SOFTWARE PRODUCT, to the place you obtained them for a full refund.

SOFTWARE PRODUCT LICENSE

The SOFTWARE PRODUCT is protected by United States copyright laws and international copyright treaties, as well as other intellectual property laws and treaties. The SOFTWARE PRODUCT is licensed, not sold.

1. **GRANT OF LICENSE.** This EULA grants you the following rights:

   a. **Software Product.** You may install and use one copy of the SOFTWARE PRODUCT on a single computer. The primary user of the computer on which the SOFTWARE PRODUCT is installed may make a second copy for his or her exclusive use on a portable computer.

   b. **Storage/Network Use.** You may also store or install a copy of the SOFTWARE PRODUCT on a storage device, such as a network server, used only to install or run the SOFTWARE PRODUCT on your other computers over an internal network; however, you must acquire and dedicate a license for each separate computer on which the SOFTWARE PRODUCT is installed or run from the storage device. A license for the SOFTWARE PRODUCT may not be shared or used concurrently on different computers.

   c. **License Pak.** If you have acquired this EULA in a Microsoft License Pak, you may make the number of additional copies of the computer software portion of the SOFTWARE PRODUCT authorized on the printed copy of this EULA, and you may use each copy in the manner specified above. You are also entitled to make a corresponding number of secondary copies for portable computer use as specified above.

   d. **Sample Code.** Solely with respect to portions, if any, of the SOFTWARE PRODUCT that are identified within the SOFTWARE PRODUCT as sample code (the "SAMPLE CODE"):

      i. **Use and Modification.** Microsoft grants you the right to use and modify the source code version of the SAMPLE CODE, *provided* you comply with subsection (d)(iii) below. You may not distribute the SAMPLE CODE, or any modified version of the SAMPLE CODE, in source code form.

      ii. **Redistributable Files.** Provided you comply with subsection (d)(iii) below, Microsoft grants you a nonexclusive, royalty-free right to reproduce and distribute the object code version of the SAMPLE CODE and of any modified SAMPLE CODE, other than SAMPLE CODE, or any modified version thereof, designated as not redistributable in the Readme file that forms a part of the SOFTWARE PRODUCT (the "Non-Redistributable Sample Code"). All SAMPLE CODE other than the Non-Redistributable Sample Code is collectively referred to as the "REDISTRIBUTABLES."

      iii. **Redistribution Requirements.** If you redistribute the REDISTRIBUTABLES, you agree to: (i) distribute the REDISTRIBUTABLES in object code form only in conjunction with and as a part of your software application product; (ii) not use Microsoft's name, logo, or trademarks to market your software application product; (iii) include a valid copyright notice on your software application product; (iv) indemnify, hold harmless, and defend Microsoft from and against any claims or lawsuits, including attorney's fees, that arise or result from the use or distribution of your software application product; and (v) not permit further distribution of the REDISTRIBUTABLES by your end user. Contact Microsoft for the applicable royalties due and other licensing terms for all other uses and/or distribution of the REDISTRIBUTABLES.

2. **DESCRIPTION OF OTHER RIGHTS AND LIMITATIONS.**

   - **Limitations on Reverse Engineering, Decompilation, and Disassembly.** You may not reverse engineer, decompile, or disassemble the SOFTWARE PRODUCT, except and only to the extent that such activity is expressly permitted by applicable law notwithstanding this limitation.

   - **Separation of Components.** The SOFTWARE PRODUCT is licensed as a single product. Its component parts may not be separated for use on more than one computer.

   - **Rental.** You may not rent, lease, or lend the SOFTWARE PRODUCT.

   - **Support Services.** Microsoft may, but is not obligated to, provide you with support services related to the SOFTWARE PRODUCT ("Support Services"). Use of Support Services is governed by the Microsoft policies and programs described in the user manual, in "online" documentation, and/or in other Microsoft-provided materials. Any supplemental software code provided to you as part of the Support Services shall be considered part of the SOFTWARE PRODUCT and subject to the terms and conditions of this EULA. With respect to technical information you provide to Microsoft as part of the Support Services, Microsoft may use such information for its business purposes, including for product support and development. Microsoft will not utilize such technical information in a form that personally identifies you.

- **Software Transfer.** You may permanently transfer all of your rights under this EULA, provided you retain no copies, you transfer all of the SOFTWARE PRODUCT (including all component parts, the media and printed materials, any upgrades, this EULA, and, if applicable, the Certificate of Authenticity), **and** the recipient agrees to the terms of this EULA.

- **Termination.** Without prejudice to any other rights, Microsoft may terminate this EULA if you fail to comply with the terms and conditions of this EULA. In such event, you must destroy all copies of the SOFTWARE PRODUCT and all of its component parts.

3. **COPYRIGHT.** All title and copyrights in and to the SOFTWARE PRODUCT (including but not limited to any images, photographs, animations, video, audio, music, text, SAMPLE CODE, REDISTRIBUTABLES, and "applets" incorporated into the SOFTWARE PRODUCT) and any copies of the SOFTWARE PRODUCT are owned by Microsoft or its suppliers. The SOFTWARE PRODUCT is protected by copyright laws and international treaty provisions. Therefore, you must treat the SOFTWARE PRODUCT like any other copyrighted material **except** that you may install the SOFTWARE PRODUCT on a single computer provided you keep the original solely for backup or archival purposes. You may not copy the printed materials accompanying the SOFTWARE PRODUCT.

4. **U.S. GOVERNMENT RESTRICTED RIGHTS.** The SOFTWARE PRODUCT and documentation are provided with RESTRICTED RIGHTS. Use, duplication, or disclosure by the Government is subject to restrictions as set forth in subparagraph (c)(1)(ii) of the Rights in Technical Data and Computer Software clause at DFARS 252.227-7013 or subparagraphs (c)(1) and (2) of the Commercial Computer Software—Restricted Rights at 48 CFR 52.227-19, as applicable. Manufacturer is Microsoft Corporation/One Microsoft Way/Redmond, WA 98052-6399.

5. **EXPORT RESTRICTIONS.** You agree that you will not export or re-export the SOFTWARE PRODUCT, any part thereof, or any process or service that is the direct product of the SOFTWARE PRODUCT (the foregoing collectively referred to as the "Restricted Components"), to any country, person, entity, or end user subject to U.S. export restrictions. You specifically agree not to export or re-export any of the Restricted Components (i) to any country to which the U.S. has embargoed or restricted the export of goods or services, which currently include, but are not necessarily limited to, Cuba, Iran, Iraq, Libya, North Korea, Sudan, and Syria, or to any national of any such country, wherever located, who intends to transmit or transport the Restricted Components back to such country; (ii) to any end user who you know or have reason to know will utilize the Restricted Components in the design, development, or production of nuclear, chemical, or biological weapons; or (iii) to any end user who has been prohibited from participating in U.S. export transactions by any federal agency of the U.S. government. You warrant and represent that neither the BXA nor any other U.S. federal agency has suspended, revoked, or denied your export privileges.

DISCLAIMER OF WARRANTY

NO WARRANTIES OR CONDITIONS. MICROSOFT EXPRESSLY DISCLAIMS ANY WARRANTY OR CONDITION FOR THE SOFTWARE PRODUCT. THE SOFTWARE PRODUCT AND ANY RELATED DOCUMENTATION ARE PROVIDED "AS IS" WITHOUT WARRANTY OR CONDITION OF ANY KIND, EITHER EXPRESS OR IMPLIED, INCLUDING, WITHOUT LIMITATION, THE IMPLIED WARRANTIES OF MERCHANTABILITY, FITNESS FOR A PARTICULAR PURPOSE, OR NONINFRINGEMENT. THE ENTIRE RISK ARISING OUT OF USE OR PERFORMANCE OF THE SOFTWARE PRODUCT REMAINS WITH YOU.

LIMITATION OF LIABILITY. TO THE MAXIMUM EXTENT PERMITTED BY APPLICABLE LAW, IN NO EVENT SHALL MICROSOFT OR ITS SUPPLIERS BE LIABLE FOR ANY SPECIAL, INCIDENTAL, INDIRECT, OR CONSEQUENTIAL DAMAGES WHATSOEVER (INCLUDING, WITHOUT LIMITATION, DAMAGES FOR LOSS OF BUSINESS PROFITS, BUSINESS INTERRUPTION, LOSS OF BUSINESS INFORMATION, OR ANY OTHER PECUNIARY LOSS) ARISING OUT OF THE USE OF OR INABILITY TO USE THE SOFTWARE PRODUCT OR THE PROVISION OF OR FAILURE TO PROVIDE SUPPORT SERVICES, EVEN IF MICROSOFT HAS BEEN ADVISED OF THE POSSIBILITY OF SUCH DAMAGES. IN ANY CASE, MICROSOFT'S ENTIRE LIABILITY UNDER ANY PROVISION OF THIS EULA SHALL BE LIMITED TO THE GREATER OF THE AMOUNT ACTUALLY PAID BY YOU FOR THE SOFTWARE PRODUCT OR US$5.00; PROVIDED, HOWEVER, IF YOU HAVE ENTERED INTO A MICROSOFT SUPPORT SERVICES AGREEMENT, MICROSOFT'S ENTIRE LIABILITY REGARDING SUPPORT SERVICES SHALL BE GOVERNED BY THE TERMS OF THAT AGREEMENT. BECAUSE SOME STATES AND JURISDICTIONS DO NOT ALLOW THE EXCLUSION OR LIMITATION OF LIABILITY, THE ABOVE LIMITATION MAY NOT APPLY TO YOU.

MISCELLANEOUS

This EULA is governed by the laws of the State of Washington USA, except and only to the extent that applicable law mandates governing law of a different jurisdiction.

Should you have any questions concerning this EULA, or if you desire to contact Microsoft for any reason, please contact the Microsoft subsidiary serving your country, or write: Microsoft Sales Information Center/One Microsoft Way/Redmond, WA 98052-6399.